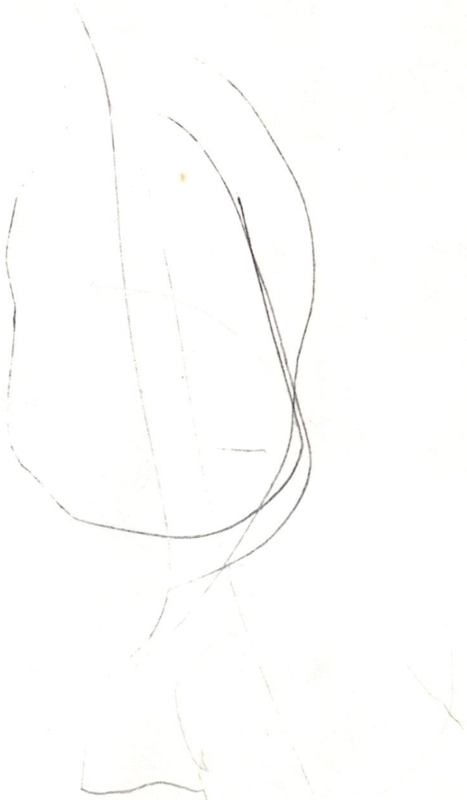

Introduction to Data Processing

Beryl Robichaud, Ph.D.

Consultant and Former Senior Vice President
McGraw-Hill, Inc.
New York, New York

Associate Research Professor
Center for Coastal and Environmental Studies
Rutgers University
New Brunswick, New Jersey

Eugene Muscat, Ed.D.

Associate Professor
McLaren College of Business
University of San Francisco
San Francisco, California

Cofounder
Center for Business Education and Research
University of San Francisco
San Francisco, California

Alix-Marie Hall, M.B.A. Candidate

Vice President
Administration/Planning and Development
Information Systems Company
McGraw-Hill, Inc.
New York, New York

Business Planning Consultant
National Training and Evaluation Center, Inc.
New York, New York

Introduction to Data Processing

THIRD EDITION

GREGG DIVISION

MCGRAW-HILL BOOK COMPANY

New York Atlanta Dallas St. Louis
San Francisco Auckland Bogotá Guatemala
Hamburg Johannesburg Lisbon London
Madrid Mexico Montreal New Delhi Panama
Paris San Juan São Paulo Singapore
Sydney Tokyo Toronto

Sponsoring Editor: Susan Muller
Editing Supervisor: Gary Schwartz
Design Supervisor: Patricia Lowy
Production Supervisor: Kathleen Morrissey
Photo Editor: Mary Ann Drury

Cover Artist: Jack Weaver
Cover Photographer: Karen Leeds
Technical Studio: VIP Graphics

Library of Congress Cataloging in Publication Data

Robichaud, Beryl., date.
Introduction to data processing.

Includes index.
1. Electronic data processing. I. Muscat, Eugene, date. II. Hall, Alix-Marie, date. III. Title.
HF5548.2R6 1982 651.8 82-61
ISBN 0-07-053194-3 AACR2

2 3 4 5 6 7 8 9 0 DODO 8 0 9 8 7 6 5 4 3

ISBN 0-07-053194-3

CONTENTS

PREFACE

Virtually all workers today process data in some form in their jobs. Office workers may spend their entire day doing a variety of data processing tasks. Even salespersons, factory workers, or farmers must spend part of their time doing *paperwork*, another name for data processing.

Young people ready to enter the job market, as well as those already in it who would like to advance their careers, find that knowledge of data processing and computers is a skill in great demand. Because of this phenomenon, there is a widespread interest in computerized and other data processing methods used in business.

Introduction to Data Processing, Third Edition, explores the field of data processing: its meaning, its methods, its careers, and its equipment. The textbook presents the basics of modern methods of processing data, while assuming no familiarity with data processing on the part of the instructor or the student. This new edition also provides an understanding of such key topics as the concepts of computers, the use of computers and various types of data processing equipment, and the application of different data processing methods to typical business situations. Computer data processing is emphasized because of its ever-increasing importance to modern business. The textbook traces the development of computer technology and examines computer hardware, programming, and systems. The use of computers for problem solving in business is also examined. The use of personal computers to satisfy individual data needs is explored.

Introduction to Data Processing, Third Edition, is designed to meet the needs of two types of students: those students who should be computer literate as they affect careers in general and those students who will pursue a business data processing career.

The discussions and illustrations of various jobs throughout the textbook enable students to picture a variety of business workers interacting on the job, to understand the flow of data from one worker to the next, and to appreciate the need for careful planning, accuracy, and good communication. The career information that is interspersed throughout the textbook encourages all business students to look ahead and to decide if any additional education and training will be necessary in order to realize their career potential.

Components of the Program

The third edition of *Introduction to Data Processing* includes a textbook, a *Data Processing Work Kit* with actual business forms, microcomputer applications on diskette for popular microcomputer models, and a *Source Book and Key* that includes tests and transparency masters for duplication.

Textbook. The textbook is divided into four parts that cover the following areas: concepts of data processing, computers and business, systems and procedures, and preparing for a career in data processing. These parts are divided into chapters that begin with performance goals. The chapters are subdivided into short, readable topics. Each topic contains exercises that reinforce the concepts that have been presented. There are review questions, discussion questions, and a section entitled "Data Processing Activities," which summarizes the work assignments the students will find in the work kit at the conclusion of each chapter.

A glossary appears at the back of the book to aid students in the development of data processing vocabulary. The glossary is drawn from key data processing terms and concepts introduced in the textbook.

A short lesson in the BASIC programming language follows each chapter for those teachers who wish to include an introduction to programming languages in the course. The BASIC projects will be explained in greater detail later.

Part 1, *Concepts of Data Processing,* introduces students to the concept of processing data, to the operations that make up a data processing cycle, and to the development of modern business data processing. Students are exposed to the wide array of business equipment now used in modern offices for data input, processing, and output. A separate chapter deals with punched-card equipment still in use and the fast growing field of word-processing equipment.

Part 2, *Computers and Business,* examines computer hardware and software. This section builds student understanding of computers: how computers operate and in what ways they differ from other machines. The functions performed by different units of hardware are described and the major types of computer systems are differentiated. Throughout, the role of people in operating and programming computers is emphasized. Programming assignments are described and examples of programming languages are explained.

Part 3, *Systems and Procedures,* describes how the work of people and machines is organized into systems and procedures so as to produce the information a business needs. The role of data bases, records, and file maintenance in business data processing is explained and illustrated. The steps involved in systems design are defined and successively applied in a typical billing and inventory system and in a payroll data processing system.

Part 4, *Preparing for a Career in Data Processing,* discusses some of the personal characteristics and general aptitudes that lead to success in a data processing career. The characteristics of 30 important data processing jobs are described, and students are told of opportunities that exist in larger and smaller companies, in government, and in the major industries for data processing careers. A separate chapter on Personal Computing advises students how to select hardware and software to meet rapidly growing personal computing needs. In the final chapter, changes in technology are predicted and their potential impact on data processing careers described. A list of sources where additional career information can be obtained is also included. This part encourages students to assess their interests and abilities in terms of the requirements of typical data processing jobs.

Data Processing Work Kit. This self-contained packet of activities consists of an instruction manual, a booklet of business forms and working papers, a flowcharting template, and an assortment of punched cards. Although the kit may be used independently of the textbook, the 14 sets of activities correlate with the 14 chapters of the textbook.

The purpose of the *Work Kit* is to teach students data processing job skills. Each section of the instruction manual contains a statement of skills-directed performance goals. The activities that the manual directs students to perform are set in realistically described job environments. The students thus become familiar with the types of assignments they will face in employer-sponsored training programs and on the job. All the procedures and definitions students will need in completing the activities are detailed, and no equipment beyond that provided in the kit is necessary. Working tips appear throughout the kit to provide students with valuable hints for completing the work assignments.

Source Book and Key. The source book and key contains teaching suggestions for both the textbook and the *Work Kit.* Included are sample answers for the end-of-chapter discussion questions and suggested classroom activities, scheduling options for courses of varying length, and suggested methods to evaluate students' work. Also included are references to a variety of transparencies, films, books, and magazines that are useful in expanding discussions of textbook topics in ways relevant to local business needs. There is a section containing microcomputer applications that introduce the assignments that the student will find on the optional program diskette.

Tests. The *Source Book and Key* contains a test for each chapter of the textbook and a midterm and a final. The tests are easily duplicated. These tests, which are keyed to the performance goals that introduce each chapter, assess students' acquisition of vocabulary and concepts. The *Work Kit* test in the *Instructor's Manual and Key* evaluates students' grasp of concepts learned by performing the activities.

Features

Introduction to Data Processing, Third Edition, contains many special features.

Content. The textbook has been thoroughly updated to include data processing equipment and methods found in modern offices at the beginning of the 1980s. A wide array of equipment, ranging from simple devices to complex computers, is used for input, processing, and output operations. Although the emphasis in the text is on computers, new developments in basic machines, including word-processing equipment, are covered. Programming concepts have been expanded, and projects that follow each chapter offer an introduction to the programming language BASIC. The importance of the rapidly growing field of personal computing is acknowledged by the inclusion of a separate chapter on this subject.

Career Information. Career information is abundant in both the textbook and the *Work Kit.* The textbook not only familiarizes the students with data processing jobs but also encourages them to think about the type of industry and employer for whom they would like to work. It introduces students to organization charts and to a typical hierarchy of data processing employees in a business organization. Both the textbook and the *Work Kit* encourage students to develop tentative career ladders. In the *Work Kit,* students are also given an opportunity to try out exercises that they may later find on aptitude tests for business data processing careers.

Performance Goals. Both the textbook and the *Work Kit* set forth performance goals. In the textbook, the goals appear at the beginning of each chapter and are concept-oriented. In the *Work Kit,* the performance goals appear in each of the activities and are skills-directed.

Constant Reinforcement. At the start of each textbook chapter, there is a vocabulary list as well as a set of performance goals. Chapters are divided into small units of instruction, and each of these units is followed by a set of exercises. Each chapter concludes with a series of review questions, discussion questions, and a description of work settings for the activities in the *Work Kit.* Marginal notes appear throughout the textbook and serve both to highlight important concepts and to remind the students of key definitions introduced in earlier chapters. The testing program described previously enables both the student and the instructor to evaluate student learning throughout the course.

Activities. The third edition of the *Introduction to Data Processing* program introduces students to activities that are typical of a variety of job situations in both merchandising and service businesses. Throughout the *Work Kit,* students sample activities that are common to such major areas of employment as banking and insurance. Procedures and forms relating to government agencies and payroll operations are also introduced. These activities help students apply their textbook learning to prepare for entry-level positions in business.

Microcomputer Applications. An optional, diskette-based set of interactive exercises is available. These projects allow students to develop keyboarding, problem solving, and word-processing skills.

BASIC Projects. Each chapter offers students the opportunity to develop a conceptual, or *hands on,* awareness of computer programming in the language BASIC. These activities, called BASIC Projects, are designed to introduce students to the fundamentals of a computer language. If the proper equipment is available, sample programs can be keyboarded, and modified to enhance student understanding. A review test is included in the *Source Book and Key* to certify student competency.

Acknowledgments

The authors would like to thank the many instructors and business persons who have helped make the third edition of *Introduction to Data Processing* both relevant to today's student and useful to tomorrow's business worker. The authors are especially grateful to the following educators for their thoughtful review and helpful suggestions: Michael Tempel (Associate Director, LOGO: The

Computer Learning Center, New York, New York); Herman Heacker (Teacher, Sequoyah Vocational-Technical Center, Daisy, Tennessee); R. Conway Spitler (Chairman, Business Department, William S. Hart Union School District, Canyon County, California); Kathleen Drabant (Teacher, Glenbrook North High School, Northbrook, Illinois); Aileen Warner (Teacher, Severna Park Senior High School, Severna Park, Maryland); Bette Shapiro (Teacher, Bayonne High School, Bayonne, New Jersey); Marian Rosenberry (Teacher, Robert E. Lee High School, Jacksonville, Florida); Vincent Rauzino (Former Director, Market Studies and Consulting, Datapro Research Corporation, 1805 Underwood Boulevard, Delran, New Jersey); Anthony Olinzock (Instructor, Ohio State University, 1945 North High Street, Columbus, Ohio).

Beryl Robichaud
Eugene Muscat
Alix-Marie Hall

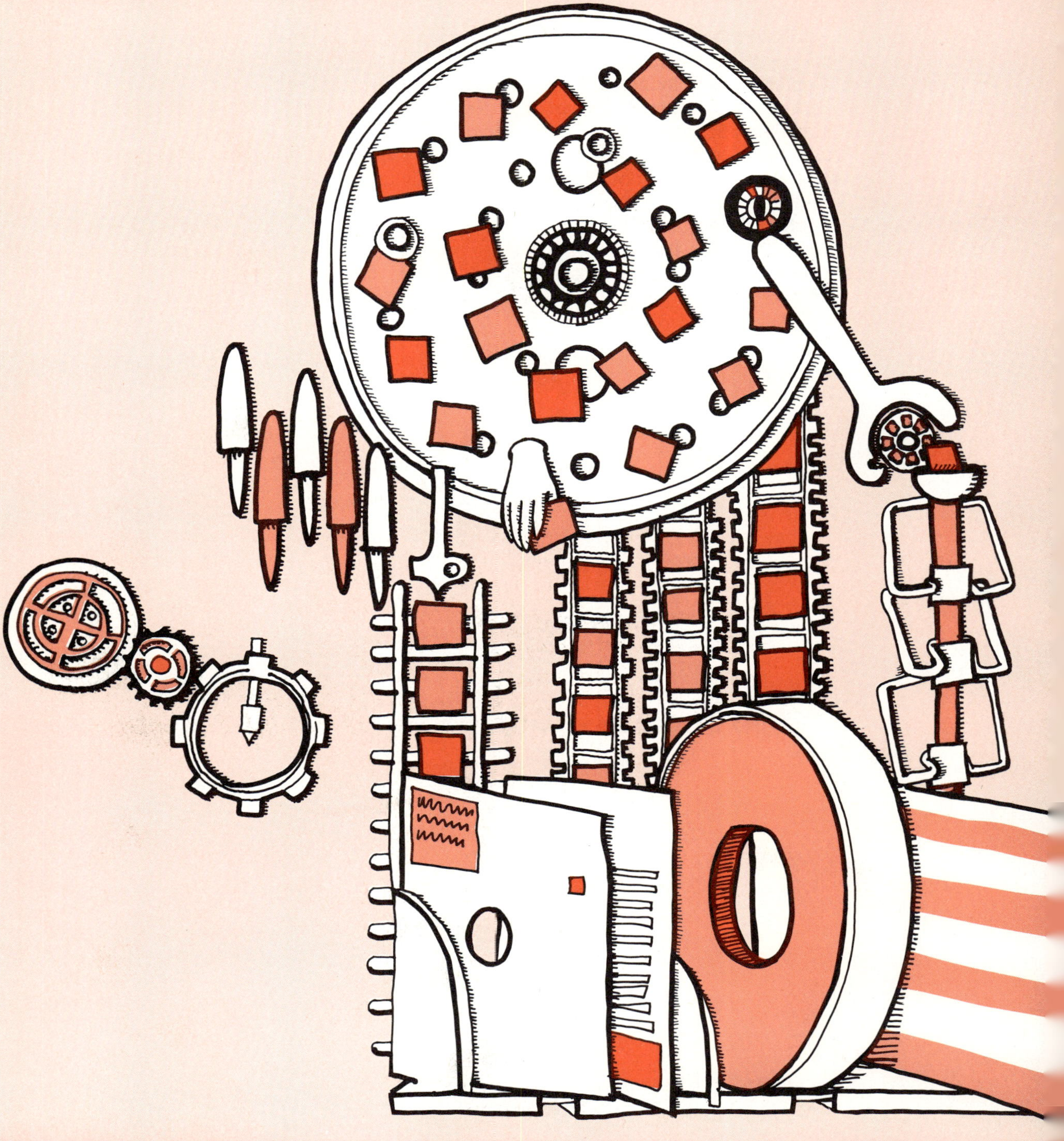

PART 1

Concepts of Data Processing

CHAPTER

1

Business Data Processing in the 1980s

DATA PROCESSING TERMINOLOGY

Data
Data processing
Business data processing
Input data
Output data
Data processing cycle
Recording data
Classifying data
Sorting data
Calculating data
Storing data
Summarizing data
Retrieving data
Reporting data
Copying data
Communicating data
Inputting
Hard copy
Source documents
Manual data processing
Mechanical data processing
Punched-card data processing
Computer data processing
Electronic data processing
Automation
Data bank
Office of the future

PERFORMANCE GOALS

- Define the terms *data*, *data processing*, and *business data processing.*
- State three needs for business data processing within every business.

- **Name the three stages of a business data processing cycle.**
- **Define *input data* and *output data.***
- **State ten types of data processing operations.**
- **Name four periods of development in business data processing prior to the 1980s.**
- **List five characteristics of business data processing in the 1980s.**

Data processing is the handling of facts.

Data processing is a modern term for an activity that is as old as recorded history. **Data** means facts, and **data processing** just means the handling of facts. Ancient peoples all handled facts about their business, government, and consumer affairs. Just as people do today, they made sales records, recorded inventories, found the costs of buying goods, and computed profits. Whether done with the help of clay tablets, paper, punched cards, or computers, data processing has always had this purpose: to produce useful information from unorganized facts.

Business data processing refers to the activities used to produce useful information about a business.

Business data processing refers to the activities performed to produce useful information about a business. In the 1980s millions of people are using computers with simpler office equipment to process business data. Business data processing is different from scientific data processing, which refers to the operations performed to produce mathematical information in a scientific laboratory. The subject of this book is business data processing.

Why Business Needs Data Processing

Businesses ask themselves many questions. How much money did we earn this year? How much money did we spend each month? What is the average pay of our computer programmers? These are the types of questions answered by business data processing activities today. No matter how large or small a business is, it needs data processing to produce information that will satisfy three basic needs.

THREE NEEDS FOR DATA WITHIN EVERY BUSINESS

1. **To operate a business.**
2. **To control a business.**
3. **To satisfy outside needs for data.**

1. **To operate a business.** To keep itself running, a business must process data. For example, data about customers' orders must be processed so that the shipping department can fill the orders and the billing department can prepare customers' bills.
2. **To control a business.** To make future plans about a business, managers need specific information about performance and results. Managers must know, for example, both the volume and the cost of goods sold. By studying this information, managers can make plans for the future manufacture of products.

3. **To satisfy outside needs for data.** Businesses must satisfy outside demands for information. The Treasury Department of the federal government requires every corporation to file quarterly reports on taxes withheld from employees' pay. The Equal Employment Opportunity Commission reviews employment data of businesses to ensure that minorities and women are given equal opportunities. Stockholders want detailed information about earnings from companies whose stock they own.

These three needs for data vary with each business. Banks must record the amounts deposited and withdrawn by each customer. Airlines must process data to handle passenger reservations on thousands of flights daily. Manufacturing plants and research laboratories must handle data about production, research, and operating costs. Department stores must keep track of merchandise and sales, while schools must keep records of students' courses and grades. Schools also collect career information and make it available to students.

In business, data initially appears as unorganized facts recorded in the form of numeric (digit) and alphabetic (letter) characters on business forms. When this data is processed or organized, it becomes useful information. This is the purpose of business data processing—to produce useful information.

CHECK YOURSELF

Supply the missing words.

1. The purpose of business data processing is to produce __?__ __?__ .
2. __?__ data processing is different from business data processing.
3. The amounts of bank deposits and withdrawals are examples of business __?__ .
4. Business data is recorded in __?__ and __?__ characters.
5. __?__ __?__ is the handling of facts.
6. Three needs for data within every business are: (a) to operate a __?__ , (b) to __?__ a business, and (c) to satisfy __?__ needs for data.

Operations in a Business Data Processing Cycle

The purpose of business data processing is to produce useful information.

The steps in business data processing can be viewed as a cycle. The starting point of the cycle is a collection of unorganized data, called **input data**. At the end of the cycle is useful information,

THREE STAGES OF THE DATA PROCESSING CYCLE

1. **Input data**
2. **Ten processing operations**
3. **Output data**

called **output data.** The term **data processing cycle** refers to all the processing operations that occur in changing unorganized input data into useful output data.

From start to finish, a processing cycle may have a few or a large number of processing steps depending on the complexity of the output data to be produced. There are ten different processing operations that form the core of business data processing. Sometimes an operation may be repeated one or more times. Also, not all ten operations are performed in every data processing cycle. The operations may be performed in the order listed below, or they may be performed in a different order. What is important is that all data processing includes at least one of these operations.

Business data processing involves ten different operations.

1. Recording data
2. Classifying data
3. Sorting data
4. Calculating data
5. Summarizing data
6. Storing data
7. Retrieving data
8. Copying data
9. Communicating data
10. Reporting data

Recording Data

To start a data processing cycle, input data must be collected and recorded in a form that can be processed. Recording is usually the first operation in a business data processing cycle. **Recording** simply means the writing of data by hand or the keying of data on a machine. This operation has often been called *posting*. In modern data processing the starting recording operation is usually called **inputting.**

DATA PROCESSING CYCLE

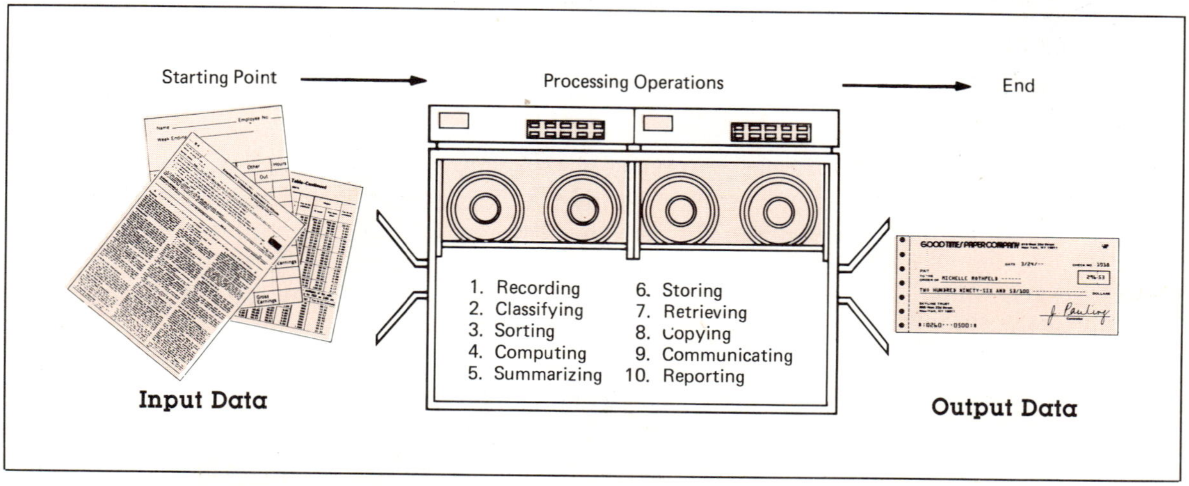

Recording is the writing of data by hand or the keying of data by machine.

The recording operation may take place when a salesclerk prepares a sales slip or when a bank teller records the amount deposited by a depositor. Factory machinists record the quantities of parts produced. Filling station attendants use a credit card to imprint a customer's name and address on a charge ticket for gasoline and oil. To reserve space for a passenger, airline reservations clerks enter input data on a keyboard with a TV-like screen called a *cathode ray tube* (CRT). All these actions are examples of recording business data.

If data is recorded in a form readable by humans, the recording operation is said to produce **hard copy.** Hard copy can be prepared in several ways. A document such as a customer bill can be prepared by hand or by typewriter. Data is not always recorded in a form readable by people. Data is often recorded in the form of punched holes in cards or magnetized spots on magnetic disks. These holes and spots are meant to be read by machine.

RECORDING. An airline reservations clerk records data on a cathode ray tube (CRT) terminal. Jill Mariani

Recording, as the first operation in the data processing cycle, is of special importance. An error in recording will result in errors in other operations. An error in recording one amount on a sales slip will mean the summarizing and reporting of wrong totals on the final sales report. Business forms on which data is recorded as the starting operation in a data processing cycle are sometimes called **source documents.** Obviously, it is essential that all data recorded on source documents be accurate.

Classifying Data

Recording is often followed by classifying. **Classifying** is identifying data and distinguishing one kind of data from another. Classifying is done in two ways: particular and group.

NONREADABLE FORM. Magnetic disks contain data in a form meant to be read only by machine. Courtesy Radio Shack, A Division of Tandy Corporation

1. **Particular.** Data may be classified so that it identifies a particular person or item, such as a customer, an employee, or a product. For example, a purchase order comes from a particular customer who must be identified. Often the purchase order names the salesperson who is to receive credit for the sale, and it must always identify the product ordered.
2. **Group.** Data may be classified so that it identifies a group of similar items. For example, all customers of a company may be classified in one of a number of geographic groups: those in the Northwest, the Southwest, the Midwest, the Northeast, or the Southeast.

Classifying usually means assigning code numbers or code letters. These codes distinguish different things from one another and group similar things together. Our own names are an example of classification. A last name identifies a family group, and a first name identifies a particular person in that family group.

Your home telephone number is a code number. A telephone number usually consists of ten numbers. The first three numbers stand for all telephones within a specific geographic area, such as a state or a section of a state. The next three digits (three numbers or two letters and a number) stand for all telephones within a specific city or part of a city or town. The last four numbers distinguish a particular telephone.

TWO WAYS OF CLASSIFYING

1. Particular
2. Group

A good example of classifying business data by code numbers is the use of social security numbers. The federal government gives each person covered by social security a unique nine-digit code number for identification purposes because it is easier to identify people by number than by name. Not only is the social security number shorter than a person's name, but it also provides more precise identification of the person. No two people have the same social security number, but many people have the same name. For instance, in just one city, there are over 3,500 Smiths; 2,500 Cohens; and 1,800 Rodriguezes—a number of whom may have the same first names.

EXAMPLES OF CODES

1. Names
2. Phone numbers
3. Social security numbers
4. ZIP Codes
5. Account numbers

A coding system may consist of numeric characters (numbers), alphabetic characters (letters), or both. A coding system that is made up of both numeric and alphabetic characters is called an **alphanumeric code system.** Of the three types of codes, numeric codes are the most common because they are the simplest to use in machine data processing.

A good example of a completely numeric code system is the post office ZIP Code that should appear as part of the address on all mail. The ZIP Code is a five-digit number identifying the particular post office responsible for delivering the mail to the correct address. New Jersey, for example, is divided into many postal areas, each of which has a different ZIP Code number. The ZIP Code for Hightstown, New Jersey, is 08520; the city of Freehold, which is 20 miles (approximately 32 kilometers) away, has the ZIP Code 07728.

CA	CALIFORNIA
CO	COLORADO
FL	FLORIDA
IL	ILLINOIS
MA	MASSACHUSETTS
NY	NEW YORK
OK	OKLAHOMA
TX	TEXAS

The post office has established another code that is alphabetic; it is used to identify the name of each state. Examples of this code are shown in the margin.

An alphanumeric code system is used by some state motor vehicle bureaus for the identification of automobiles owned by residents of the state. These codes are recorded in the motor vehicle files and appear on automobile license plates.

The classifying operation is time consuming if not done by machine. That is why every effort is made to classify data before it is used—that is, to classify data even before it is recorded. Banks

CLASSIFYING. Codes on credit cards permit easy identification of customers. Courtesy Mobil Oil Courtesy Interbank Card Association Courtesy VISA U.S.A. Inc.

TWO TYPES OF SORTING SEQUENCES

1. **Numeric**
2. **Alphabetic**

identify customers by printing the customer account number on each customer's blank checks. Gasoline companies and airlines identify customers by issuing them credit cards showing customer numbers. Supermarkets identify different items of merchandise by labeling them with identifying symbols for categories such as meat, produce, and dairy.

Sorting Data

Arranging related information in a desired sequence (order) is called **sorting.** For example, classifying is when various business forms such as rental agreements or sales checks are assigned code numbers. Sorting is when these documents are physically arranged in the sequence of their code numbers. The sorting required in the delivery of mail is the largest data processing sorting activity in the United States. The next largest is that of sorting billions of bank checks a year by customer account number.

There are two types of sorting sequences: numeric and alphabetic.

1. A **numeric sequence** is the arrangement of items of data by numbers. The numbers are arranged in *ascending* (from the lowest to the highest) or *descending* (from the highest to the lowest) order. Look at the illustration in the margin on the next page showing data listed in ascending order by year.

   Arrangement in numeric sequence also includes sorting data by groups of numbers. For example, accounts receivable (cus-

SORTING. Sorting the mail is the largest job of its kind in the United States. Courtesy U.S. Postal Service

NUMERIC SEQUENCE (ASCENDING ORDER)	
1945	WITT, JAMES B.
1948	PEREZ, CARMEN
1950	YANG, PETER J.
1951	KENT, JOHN B.
1953	BURNS, JUDY E.
1954	MILL, JACK I.

ALPHABETIC SEQUENCE	
BURNS, JUDY E.	1953
KENT, JOHN B.	1951
MILL, JACK I.	1954
PEREZ, CARMEN	1948
WITT, JAMES B.	1945
YANG, PETER J.	1950

tomers who owe money to a business) are often grouped by the number of days the account balance is overdue—1 to 30 days, 31 to 60 days, 61 to 90 days.

2. An **alphabetic sequence** is the arrangement of items of data by alphabetic characters from A to Z. The data in the margin, which before was listed in numeric sequence (by year), is now listed in alphabetic sequence (by name).

Numeric sorting, whether it is done by hand or by machine, can be done faster than alphabetic sorting. Imagine the task of sorting thousands of bank checks alphabetically! Code numbers not only provide an abbreviated identification of a particular customer, but they can also specify the particular branch at which a customer's account is located, the type of account the customer has, and the amount of credit the bank is prepared to allow that customer. The fewer the numbers or letters in the code, the faster the sorting operation.

Calculating Data

Calculating is adding, subtracting, multiplying, or dividing.

Calculating is performing one or more of the arithmetic operations of addition, subtraction, multiplication, and division. All four operations are used frequently in scientific work, although much business data processing can be done with just addition and subtraction. Multiplication is also used, but not as frequently. Division is infrequently used.

CALCULATING. In business arithmetic, operations are usually done on an electronic machine. Courtesy Victor Business Products

Summarizing Data

Summarizing means reducing a large volume of data into a smaller volume of information. There are several reasons for summarizing business data. The first is to make information more usable. Factory managers, for example, must keep informed about the total number of overtime hours worked in their plant so that they can decide whether additional staffing is needed. A long list of the daily overtime hours worked by each employee would be confusing to the plant manager. Instead, the daily employee overtime hours can be summarized into weekly totals by factory departments to make the information more concise and usable for decision making.

Summarizing is reducing a large volume of data into a more compact form.

A second reason for a summarizing operation is to simplify further processing of data. Often daily sales data is summarized each week into weekly totals so that there is a smaller volume of data to be processed for monthly totals of sales. By summarizing data throughout the month, information about results for the total month can be made available sooner.

DAN.OP.DP8200

FRIDAY, JULY 25, 19--, 1:15 P.M. PAGE 1

* * * * S-T-A-T-U-S O-F C-U-R-R-E-N-T C-L-A-I-M-S * * * *					0000100
POLICY	CLAIM	TYPE	AMOUNT OF	AMOUNT	0000200
HOLDER	NUMBER	CLAIM	CLAIM	PAID	0000300
					0000400
SCHULTZ, M.J.	372386	MEDICAL	46.50	10.00	0000500
	432232	MEDICAL	199.95	100.95	0000600
	015595	SURGICAL	1,240.00	1,240.00	0000700
					0000800
TYLER, L.L.	648981	ACCIDENT	104,735.17	84,735.10	0000900
	536704	MATERNITY	22.50	0.00	0001000
	476858	MATERNITY	1,211.00	1,211.00	0001100
	893595	HOSPITAL	127.00	127.00	0001200
					0001300
SHOPPEE, C.W.	442927	HOSPITAL	36.00	30.00	0001400

SUMMARIZING. An insurance manager summarizes data on current claims. Sepp Seitz/ Woodfin Camp & Associates

Storing Data

Saving data for future use is called **storing.** The period of time that the data remains in storage may vary from seconds to years. For example, a bill is usually kept until the date on which its payment must be prepared. After it has been paid, records of proof of payment may be kept for weeks or even years. Other items of data must be kept in storage for reference or audit. They must be available when needed any time during the working day. This is usually true of inventory data, which may have to be checked whenever a customer order is received.

Until recently, storing data usually meant manually filing documents in a file drawer. However, it is now possible for machines to store large volumes of data in nonreadable form automatically and very quickly.

Retrieving Data

Storing is saving data for future use.

Data placed in storage, whether for a short period or for a long period, is often needed later. **Retrieving data** from storage, by hand or by machine, is searching for and locating the data required. Then the required data is selected or removed from the file.

Retrieving data is searching for and locating data.

Recent developments have made it possible to retrieve data from storage by machine. Machine retrieval from storage is extremely important in modern business data processing. In almost all types of business data processing, data is worked on, held, or stored only to be used or reprocessed at a later date. Data retrieval may require a good deal of time if it is done manually. On the other hand, data retrieval may take less than seconds if it is done electronically.

STORING. One way of storing data for a long period of time is putting it on microfilm.
Photo Courtesy of Eastman Kodak Company

Copying Data

As the size of a business increases, more and more data must be *copied,* or reproduced. Sometimes only selected items of data may need to be reproduced. For instance, just the account number and the amount from a check may need to be copied. In other cases, entire documents may need to be copied. Whatever the degree of reproduction, the operation is referred to as **copying data.** Such an operation does not always produce a readable (hard-copy) document. Data can also be copied into a machine-readable form such as punched cards or magnetic disks. The data that is to be copied does not always have to be in hard-copy form, either. Data recorded on magnetic media can be copied onto new magnetic media.

RETRIEVING. Data stored in small form on film can be retrieved using a machine called a reader. Courtesy A.T.&T. Company

Communicating Data

Copying is reproducing data. A copying machine is one means of reproduction.

Communicating is sending data from one place to another.

Communicating is sending data from one place to another. Information about customer orders must often be communicated within a business from the sales department to the order fulfillment department and from the order fulfillment department to the warehouse.

One type of data communication is the physical transportation of documents from one place to another. Documents can be transported by messenger, by mechanical equipment such as conveyors or pneumatic tubes, and by the United States Postal Service. Before the 1950s, selected items of data could be communicated by wire transmission but at relatively slow speeds. In modern data processing, there are many devices for high-speed data communication. Data can be transferred quickly from desk to desk, from office to warehouse, from production line to office, or from an airline ticket office to a computer thousands of miles away. With modern communication methods, reproductions of whole documents can be transmitted across the country in just a few minutes.

Reporting Data

The results of data processing are made available by the operation known as **reporting.** Because the purpose of business data processing is to produce information, most data processing cycles end with the reporting of data.

The processed data may be reported in different forms, depending upon how the results are to be used. Some types of results

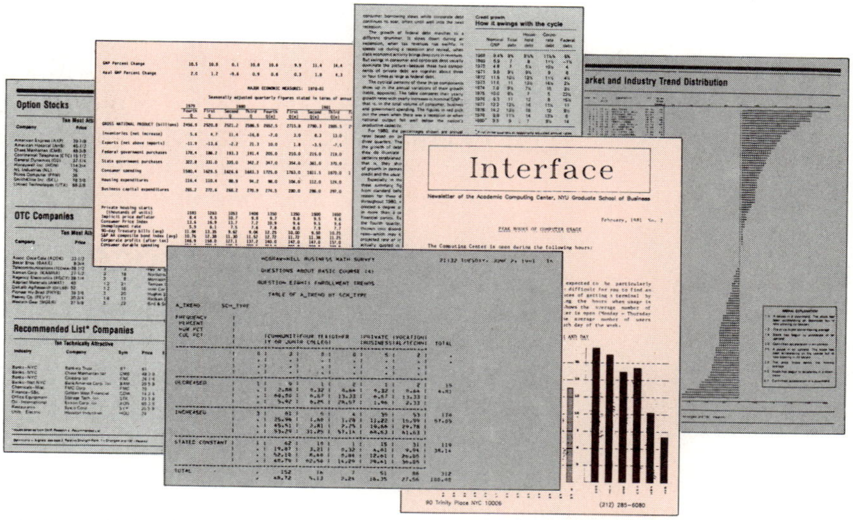

REPORTING. Showing the results of data processing is reporting.

are printed out on report forms with column headings. Other results may be reported on specially designed forms such as customer invoices or checks. In modern business data processing, output data is often not reported in hard-copy form. Rather, it might be stored in reduced size, for example, on microfilm.

CHECK YOURSELF

Match each term with the word or phrase that best defines it.

1. Classifying
2. Sorting
3. Recording
4. Inputting
5. Communicating
6. Reporting
7. Retrieving
8. Hard copy
9. Calculating
10. Numeric
11. Storing
12. Summarizing

a. Adding, subtracting, multiplying, or dividing.
b. A recording operation that starts a data processing cycle.
c. Sending data from one place to another.
d. Data readable by people.
e. Arranging data in sequence.
f. Posting.
g. Identifying and distinguishing.
h. Referring to numbers.
i. Reducing a large volume of data into a more compact form.
j. Listing the results of data processing.
k. A way of classifying data.
l. Saving data.
m. Searching for, locating, and selecting data.

How Modern Business Data Processing Developed

FOUR METHODS OF PROCESSING BUSINESS DATA

1. Manual
2. Mechanical
3. Punched-card/tape
4. Computer

Today's computers and other modern office equipment used for business data processing have evolved from simpler devices designed to do the same operations but at much slower speeds.

Manual Data Processing, Prior to 1900

Manual data processing is data processing done by hand.

For thousands of years, all data processing was done by hand. Think of how much work it must have been to keep records on stone tablets, the first known method of keeping records. The invention of paper was a great advance for recordkeeping. Workers called scribes were employed by owners of businesses to write letters, to make entries of transactions in daybooks and ledgers, to send notices to customers of amounts owed, and to prepare contracts. Data processing done by hand is called **manual data processing.**

From the beginning of time, people have searched for ways to replace manual effort. The abacus was the earliest calculator. It was invented over 2,000 years ago to speed up computation, and it is still used today. Various machines for office use appeared in the 1600s, 1700s, and 1800s, but none had much widespread use.

The Industrial Revolution, which began in England in the 1800s, started a chain of inventions that improved the manufacture and production of goods. In this period, however, mechanization in office operations did not keep pace with factory methods.

Mechanical Data Processing, 1900 to 1925

By the early 1900s, extensive use of machinery led to mass production in factories in the United States. This meant that many more products could be made at a much lower cost. It was Henry

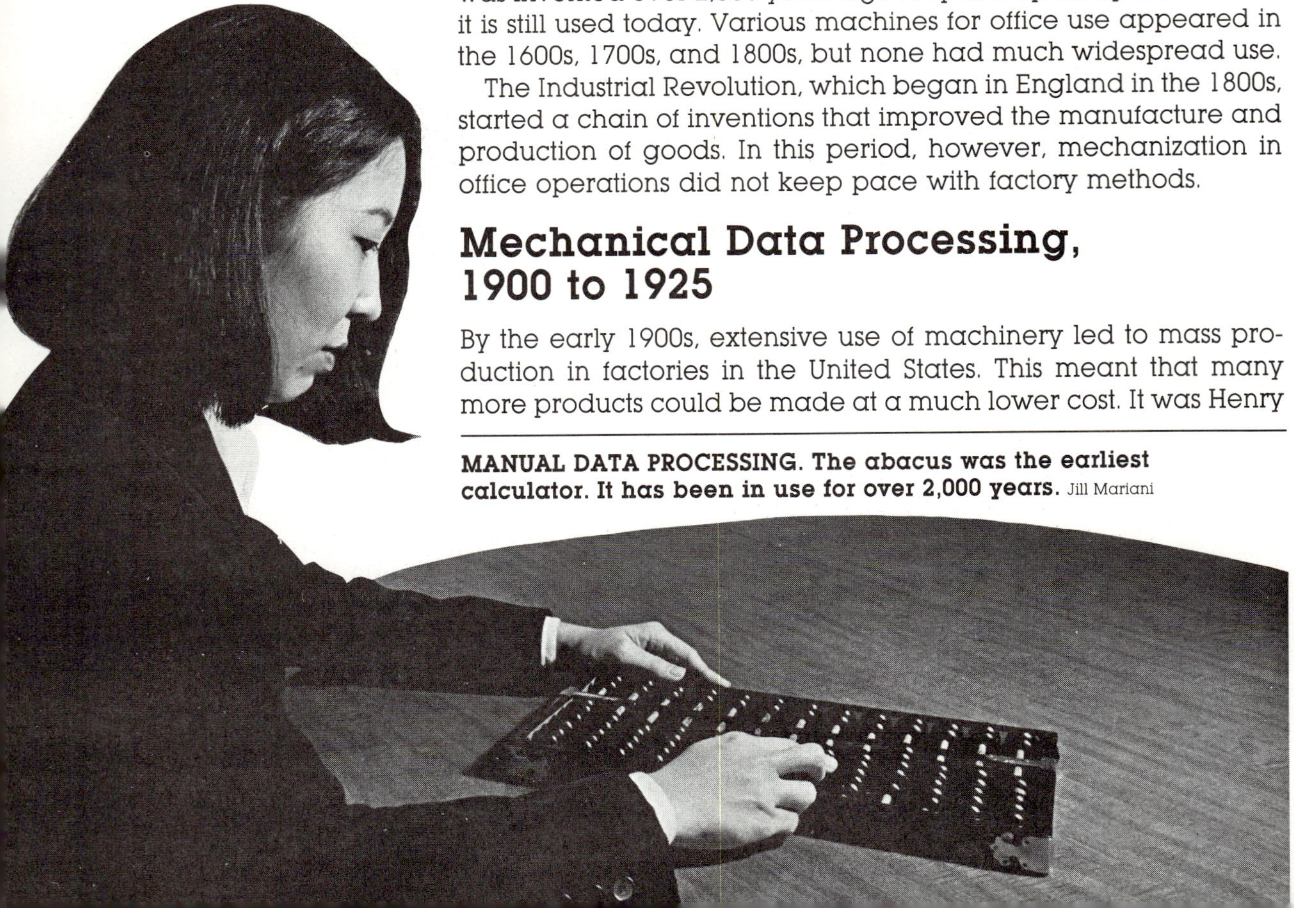

MANUAL DATA PROCESSING. The abacus was the earliest calculator. It has been in use for over 2,000 years. Jill Mariani

Ford's development of the production assembly line that made automobiles available to so many people.

Mechanization finally came to the office in the early 1900s. The typewriter, invented in 1714, gained widespread use. Machines to perform calculations and to summarize and post data gained in acceptance. However, the available office equipment performed only simple operations at slow speeds. Since the equipment was made with mechanical parts, the processing performed was called **mechanical data processing.** A great deal of manual effort was still required with mechanical data processing.

Mechanical data processing is using equipment with mechanical parts to do data processing.

Punched-Card Data Processing, 1925 to 1950

In 1924 the IBM Corporation was founded. Though IBM took over a type of office equipment that already had been available, the new company made the first real effort to extend the use of improved equipment in the office.

The IBM machines were punched-card machines, electromechanical in operation. These machines, which processed data recorded on punched cards, represented a significant improvement over other office equipment. They could perform many of the ten processing operations described earlier at faster speeds than in manual or mechanical data processing.

World War II particularly helped speed the development of improved equipment for the office because of the large increase in the quantity of business data that had to be processed and the shortage of workers to do the data processing.

When World War II ended, American businesses expanded greatly to meet the war-end demand for consumer products. The volume of data processing operations grew enormously, and the use of punched-card machines for data processing, called **punched-card data processing,** became very popular.

Punched-card data processing is using punched-card equipment to do data processing.

Computer Data Processing, 1950 to 1970

Through this period American business continued to expand. With this expansion, the demands for data processing multiplied. In the 1950s, the number of office workers increased rapidly, although factory workers still made up a greater share of the work force. But by 1960, the number of office workers in the United States was greater than the number of factory workers. By 1970, over 10 million people in the United States were office workers processing business data.

This tremendous increase in office work and office employment stirred interest in developing new techniques to process office data more efficiently. New types of adding, calculating, posting, and punched-card machines were developed to reduce the amount of human effort needed in business data processing. At the same time, great technological advances were being made in the development of high-speed calculating machines that were originally invented to solve problems in engineering and science. These machines were the prototypes of business computers.

In the 1950s, businesses began to look to scientific data processing machines for solving business problems. In 1954, the General Electric Company started to use a large-scale scientific computer, called the UNIVAC, for processing payroll data. It was the first time a computer was used to handle business data processing.

After the first successful attempt to utilize a computer for business data processing, concentrated efforts were made to develop and use computers specifically designed to handle business data processing needs. By 1960 over 50 models of computers were available.

Automation means performing work without human effort, except that of telling a machine what to do and when to do it.

At first, the use of computers in business was referred to as *automated data processing* (ADP) or *office automation*. In a strict sense this is not correct. **Automation** means performing work without human effort, except that of telling a machine what to do and when to do it. An example of automation is the bottling of pickles. Machines automatically wash, sterilize, fill, cap, and pack the bottles. The packaged bottles are moved automatically by machine directly to a truck for delivery to stores.

Computer data processing or electronic data processing refers to the use of computers to process business data.

Computers cannot automate office work to this degree. Thus the terms **computer data processing** and **electronic data processing** (EDP) are more accurate words when referring to the use of computers to process business data.

Many improvements in computer equipment were made in the three decades of the 1950s, 1960s, and 1970s. These have set the stage for business data processing as it now exists in the 1980s.

Computer Data Processing in the 1980s

Modern business data processing in the 1980s has five characteristics that distinguish it from data processing activities in the previous periods just described.

1. **Computer data processing is used in many types of businesses, large and small.** When computers were first brought into the business offices in this country, they were used only by the very largest corporations. By the 1970s the availability of

AUTOMATION. Robotics is an industrial example of automation. Here robot welders perform repetitive tasks with great accuracy and consistent quality. Courtesy Chrysler Corporation

less expensive computers made it possible for smaller companies to afford computers. By the start of the 1980s it became possible for all business organizations, small and large, to use computers in an economical way. One of the ways that many smaller businesses can use computers is by renting computer processing time on a machine owned by someone else.

2. **A variety of devices and machines simpler than computers are used in every office, large and small.** In virtually every office a variety of equipment simpler than a computer is used to perform operations either independent of or related to computer processing. Part 1 of this book is devoted to descriptions of the simpler office equipment used in modern business data processing.

The office of the future is an office where certain functions such as filing and mailing are done by machine.

3. **Computers and word processors are used to handle office functions which so far have not been mechanized.** In the 1970s much was written about the office of the future, also called the paperless office. These terms are used to describe the result when certain administrative functions such as filing and mailing are mechanized. It is only in the 1980s that mechanization of these functions has advanced beyond the experimental stage.
4. **Almost every office worker is involved in some aspect of computer processing.** There is a popular though untrue belief that the use of computers means peopleless offices. All of the

evidence indicates that this is not true. In fact, in the 1980s more people than ever before are employed in office activities in spite of the increase in the number of computers. Though computers have eliminated a great deal of human effort, the growth in the volume of work and the increase in governmental regulations for business reporting have added to the total data processing requirements of business. This situation, combined with the fact that people are needed to operate computers, means that people will always be needed in business.

In the 1980s almost every worker in an office will be involved in some aspect of computer data processing. This work may be in one point or in all points of the data processing cycle. The work may be in the input or starting point of the cycle, the processing phase, or the handling of the output or the results of the processing. Part 4 of this book will describe the career options open to you in each part of the data processing cycle.

5. **Business data processing is having a greater impact on society as a whole than ever before.** Technological developments in the 1970s provided both government and private businesses with new means for influencing the lives of individuals throughout society. For the first time, it became possible to collect and maintain huge volumes of information about individuals throughout the country. Such information stored in electronic form is referred to as a **data bank.** In the 1980s data banks are rapidly expanding. Every citizen must be concerned about the information contained in the data banks as it concerns his or her own privacy. The final chapter of this book shows more fully the impact of modern business data processing on you as a member of society.

Large volumes of information stored in electronic form are called data banks.

CHECK YOURSELF

Supply the missing words.

1. Processing data by hand is called __?__ data processing.
2. The type of data processing performed by simple machines has been called __?__ data processing.
3. In the period 1925 to 1950 the most advanced data processing used in business was __?__ - __?__ data processing.
4. The computer was first used to process business data in the year __?__ .
5. The office of the future is also called the __?__ office.
6. The type of data processing used in the 1980s in almost all offices is called __?__ data processing.
7. Large volumes of information stored in electronic form are called __?__ __?__ .

Review Questions

1. Businesses have three primary needs for processing business data. Name them, and give an example of each.
2. Name the three parts of a business data processing cycle.
3. There are ten different types of data processing operations. Name them, and give an example of each.
4. Define the terms *data, data processing, business data processing, input,* and *output.*
5. How was data processed prior to 1900?
6. What type of equipment was used in offices starting about 1900?
7. What type of data processing equipment became available for use about 1925?
8. When were computers first used for processing business data?
9. Describe five characteristics which make business data processing in the 1980s different from that of previous periods.
10. In the 1980s almost every office worker is involved in one or more stages of the data processing cycle. Name these three stages.

Comparing Ideas

1. Give an example of data handled by each: banks, telephone companies, insurance companies, airline offices, and schools.
2. Name business machines that you have seen at home or in business. Which data processing operations do they perform?

Data Processing Activities

Now you can try out the kinds of data processing activities business workers perform. Below is a summary of the work you will do. You will find the actual information and business forms you need in your *Data Processing Work Kit.*

Activity 1. You will be a secretary to a data processing manager. You will be asked to process data about eight trainees studying to be data-entry clerks.

Activity 2. As an assistant to a systems analyst, you will be responsible for checking the accuracy of output reports. You will review credit card slips for completeness.

BASIC Project 1
Introduction to Programming

Many business people look at a computer as the ideal worker. It is fast, accurate, and tireless. But to employ this worker, you need to speak its language. One language that many computers understand is BASIC. Like all languages, BASIC has a structure (syntax) and a vocabulary. Because this language uses English words, you can learn it quickly. The BASIC projects in this book will show you how to make a computer work for you. Each project consists of instruction, a sample program, sample output, and activities to reinforce the material just covered.

Commands and Program Statements
The NEW Command and the PRINT and END Statements

The computer can be told what to do by typing in certain BASIC words known as **commands.** The command NEW, for example, clears the computer's memory of any program that was there so that it is ready for a new program to be entered. The word READY will appear on the screen or paper.

As you type the word NEW, it will be displayed on the computer screen or paper. Pressing the key marked RETURN (ENTER on some computers) tells the computer that you are done typing the command and that it should be carried out.

If the computer understands the command, it will be executed. If not, an *error message* will be printed.

For example, if you typed in the word MEW instead of NEW and then pressed the RETURN key, the computer would not know what you meant. It would print an error message and then wait for you to give it another command. You could then repeat the command correctly, and it would be carried out as if you had not made the error.

In order for the computer to do something useful, it must be given a series of instructions which it remembers and then carries out when told to. This list of instructions is called a **program.**

In BASIC, each instruction is made up of a *line number* and a *statement.* The sample program shown uses two common BASIC statements: PRINT and END.

NEW The NEW command clears the computer's memory and makes it ready to accept a new program.

PRINT The PRINT statement starts with the word PRINT and is followed by letters, numbers, or spaces enclosed within quotation marks.

END The END statement ends the program. It is the last statement in a program.

Sample Program

To enter this program into the computer's memory, you would first type the number 10, then the word PRINT, then the word GREETINGS in quotation marks. When you press the RETURN key, the computer reads the line and includes it as part of the program being stored in memory.

The BASIC program consists of two instructions. The first tells the computer to print whatever is between the quotation marks. The second instruction indicates that the program is over and the computer should stop processing it.

```
10 PRINT "GREETINGS"
20 END
```

The line numbers do not have to be consecutive (for example, 1, 2, 3, and so on). Programmers usually number by tens to make the program easy to read and to allow new lines to be added later on. When the RUN command is given, the instructions will be carried out in order of their line numbers, from lowest to highest. The END statement should have the highest line number.

Output
The LIST and RUN Commands

To cause the computer to *execute,* or carry out, the program, you must give the command RUN. When you do this, the word GREETINGS will appear on the screen or paper because that is what the instructions of the program say to do. If you made any errors in the program statements you entered, for example, misspelling the word PRINT, the computer would print an error message. The word GREETINGS would not be printed.

Another important BASIC command is LIST. This causes the instructions of the program to be displayed on the screen or printed on paper so that the programmer may examine them.

It is important to be clear about the difference between RUN and LIST.

LIST The LIST command tells the computer to print the statements, or instructions, that make up the program.

RUN The RUN command tells the computer to execute, or carry out, the instructions in the program.

As long as the program remains in memory, you may give the RUN or LIST command as often as you wish. This ability to repeat a task again and again is one of the features of computers that make them so useful. Giving the NEW command erases the program from the computer's memory.

The LIST command will cause the computer to display the program like this.

```
10 PRINT "GREETINGS"
20 END
```

The RUN command will cause the computer to process the program, and the result will look like this. READY means that the computer is waiting for your next command.

```
GREETINGS
```

Keyboarding Activities

1. Enter the program shown in the Sample Program section.
2. Use the RUN command to cause the program to be executed, and examine the output.
3. Keyboard the following program line.

```
15 PRINT "TO YOU!"
```

Give the LIST command, and examine the program listing to see that line 15 has been inserted between lines 10 and 20.

4. RUN the new version of the program, and examine the output.
5. Keyboard this program line.

```
15 PRINT "TO EVERYONE!"
```

Now LIST the program. The new line 15 replaced the old line 15. RUN the new version of the program, and examine the new output.

6. Keyboard this line.

```
15
```

That's right, just the line number with no statement after it. LIST the program. Line 15 is now gone. Entering a line number with nothing following it is a way of removing a line from a program. When you RUN the program, the output should be the same as when the original program was RUN.

Enrichment Activities

1. Give the NEW command to erase the previous program from the computer's memory, and write a new program telling the computer to print your name, address, age, and school name. LIST and RUN the program.
2. Change the program so that it causes the computer to print out the school address also. LIST and RUN the program.
3. Change the program again so that your age is no longer printed when the program is RUN. LIST and RUN this version of the program.
4. Give the NEW command again, and write a new program to print out any message you wish.

CHAPTER

2

Basic Office Equipment for Data Input, Processing, and Output

DATA PROCESSING TERMINOLOGY

Business form
Forms register
Imprinting device
Time clock
Data collector
Sorting device
Optical scanner
Pocket-sized calculator
Desk-sized display and/or printing calculator
Programmable electronic calculator
Cash register
Point-of-sale terminal
Accounting machine
Microform
Aperture card
Microfiche
Recorder
Reader
Micrographics
Copying machine
Duplicating machine
Burster
Decollator
Teletype transmission
Facsimile communication

PERFORMANCE GOALS

- **Recognize four types of forms used for data input and output.**
- **Name four different types of basic data input devices, and give an example of how each is used in business.**
- **List three types of basic calculating machines.**
- **Name two machines used for multiple data processing operations.**
- **Name two types of equipment used to store and retrieve business documents.**
- **Distinguish between low-volume and high-volume copying machines.**
- **Name three devices used to communicate data.**

Prior to this century most business data processing was done by hand. This is called manual data processing. Today, almost no work is done in an office without the aid of some kind of equipment. The use of simple office machines originally was called mechanical data processing. But because electronic components are now incorporated in most office machines, it is no longer accurate to refer to processing by equipment such as calculators or accounting machines as mechanical data processing. Instead, office machines that perform fewer functions than computers or punched-card and word-processing equipment can best be referred to as *basic office equipment.*

#1

Understanding the types and uses of basic office equipment is important because almost every office uses some of this equipment. And knowing how data can be processed with basic office equipment makes it easier to understand what a computer must do to process data.

Devices for Data Input and Output

Data input begins the data processing cycle. Data output ends the cycle.

Data input is the beginning of a data processing cycle. Data output is the end of a data processing cycle. A variety of business forms and basic equipment is used in recording data input and reporting data output.

Business Forms

Business forms are sheets of specially designed paper used for recording or reporting data. A business form designates specific areas for recording information. Four general types of business forms are shown below.

1. A single-sheet form. Each form is a single page. Copies are

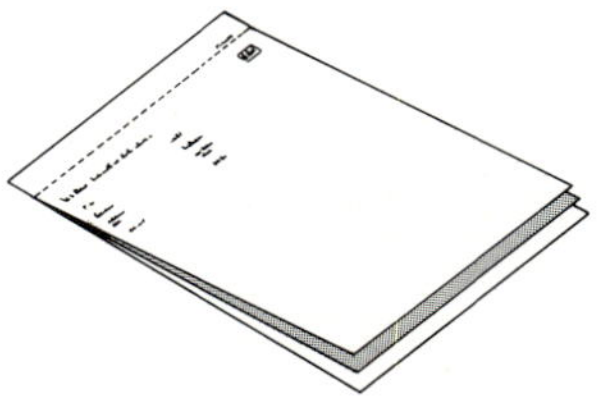
Single-Sheet Form

Pad of Forms

Single Set of Forms

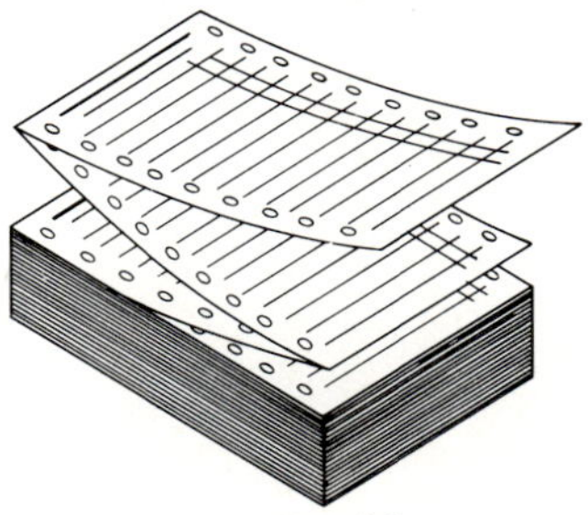
Continuous Set of Forms

made by manually inserting a sheet of carbon paper between two forms.

2. **A pad of forms.** This is a set of individual forms that are glued or stapled together. A copy can be made by manually inserting a sheet of carbon paper between two forms in the pad.
3. **A single set of forms.** Two or more individual forms, depending on the number of copies required, are glued together at the top. Each form may be a different color or have some other distinctive marking. Carbon paper may be inserted between the pages to make the copies, or the paper used for the forms may be a specially treated paper called *NCR* (no carbon required). NCR paper automatically makes copies of the data recorded on the top form.
4. **A continuous set of forms.** This is a group of identical forms that are linked together as a continuous strip of paper but separated from each other by perforations to permit easy tearing apart. Continuous-form sets may be made with extra paper strips interleaved with carbon paper or with carbonless masters to provide as many as 15 copies of the original form.

Basic Office Equipment

The types of business forms just described can be used with a variety of data input and data output devices when hard-copy recording or reporting is required. Some of the basic input recording and output reporting devices that use such forms are as follows.

1. Forms registers
2. Typewriters
3. Imprinting devices
4. Time clocks
5. Bursters
6. Decollators

Forms Registers. A **forms register** is a metal box that holds a supply of continuous office forms. Carbon paper may be placed between the paper strips so that the office worker or salesclerk can prepare as many as seven carbon copies at one time. Instead of using carbon paper, the forms can be made of carbonless paper. When one set of forms has been used, a new set can be moved into writing position by moving a hand lever or a button. Forms registers are often used in preparing source documents for sales in a store. The salesclerk writes a sales ticket on the forms register and gives the customer one copy. Duplicate copies of the ticket are often given to other departments to meet their needs for information. The last copy, called the audit copy, remains in the register. At the end of the day, the audit copies are used to prove cash and are then sent to the accounts receivable department.

The comparison of cash taken in during the day with the total cash receipts is called proving cash.

A forms register saves time by eliminating the need to arrange forms and carbon paper every time a transaction is posted. A

FORMS REGISTER. A forms register holds a supply of continuous office forms. Jill Mariani

DATA COLLECTOR. Complex time clocks record employee attendance data in machine readable form so that a computer can process the information.
Courtesy IBM Corporation

forms register also reduces the chance of making an error, since the information is written only once.

Typewriters. The manual typewriter was once the most commonly used office machine for recording business data. Over the years, the manual typewriter has been replaced by the more efficient electric typewriter. With this faster typewriter, 12 or more copies of a transaction can be prepared at one time.

Several typewriter attachments simplify the recording of data on business documents. One attachment is the typewriter form feeder, which feeds continuous, multiple-copy forms into the typewriter. The forms have holes along the edges, and the typewriter roller has pins that fit into the holes. The pins hold all the copies in position so that the data typed is in the exact same position on all carbon copies.

Another attachment is the typewriter line finder, which is similar to the carriage return on a manual typewriter. The attachment allows a typist, in a single motion, to move a continuous form from any line on one form to the first typing-stroke position on the next form. For example, after having typed the last line of one invoice, the typist can pull down the line finder to move the paper to the first line on the next invoice.

A regular office typewriter is used in different ways as a data input device. First, input data may be recorded on a single form, a set of forms, or a continuous-forms document. Any of these can serve as an input source document. For example, an order called in from a customer can be typed on a two-part customer order form, with one part sent to the warehouse for confirmation that the products are in stock. On the order form the warehouse records the availability of stock and the date on which it can be shipped. The order form serves as the input document for the billing processing cycle.

OPTICAL CHARACTER READER. This machine automatically reads data typed with an OCR element and converts it into machine-readable form. Courtesy Burroughs Corporation

Data recorded by typewriter can be used in another way for data input. The typed form can be placed in a machine called an *optical scanner*, an *optical character reader (OCR)*, or a *page reader*. Such a machine automatically reads the typed data and converts it into machine-readable form for input to a computer or a word processor.

Today much data output is prepared by computer equipment. But in every office there are still output reports prepared by more basic equipment. The typewriter in particular is widely used for the preparation of short reports. Statistical reports are much easier to prepare if done on electric typewriters equipped with devices to permit decimal alignment and the storage and correction of at least an entire line of type. Output data and documents also can be prepared on accounting machines.

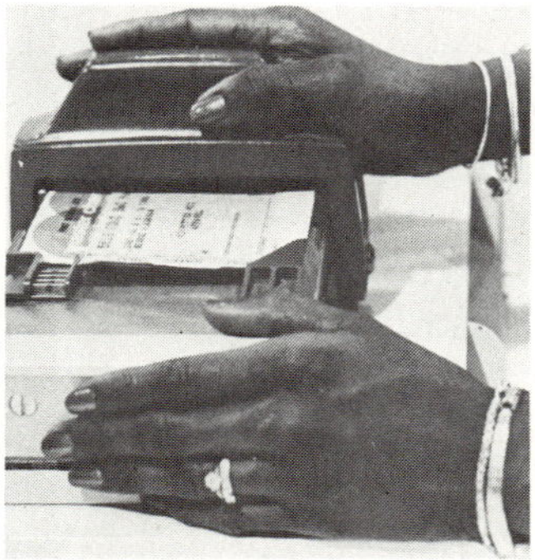

IMPRINTING DEVICE. An imprinting device is used to transfer data from embossed plates to business forms. Jill Mariani

Imprinting Devices. An **imprinting device** is used to transfer data from embossed plates to business forms. For example, if you buy gas and use a credit or charge card, the attendant puts your card and a sales slip in an imprinting device. When the attendant moves the printing handle across the sales slip, the data on the card is recorded on the sales slip.

The sales slip on which the amount of the sale and your signature are also recorded serves as a data input document for the monthly credit billing cycle. Here, too, an optical scanner can be used to read the imprinted sales slip and convert the data into machine-readable input.

Time Clocks. Many businesses use **time clocks,** devices that record the hours worked by each employee. When an employee arrives at or leaves work, he or she inserts a time card into the time clock. The clock records the date and time on the card. This record can be used in one of two ways as input for payroll processing. The time card itself can serve as a source document that the payroll department uses to prepare input data for the computer processing. More complex time clocks called **data collectors** record the attendance data in machine-readable form so the computer can read it.

Bursters and Decollators. Whether output documents are prepared by computer, word processor, typewriter, or other machines, two tasks must be performed to make the output usable. Multiple-copy forms must be separated, or *decollated,* to remove carbon paper and to arrange each set of forms into neat stacks. In addition, continuous forms and business documents are easier to handle when they are separated, or *bursted,* into individual sheets. There are specially designed office machines to perform the decollating and bursting tasks. **Decollators** perform only the copy-separating job, and **bursters** do the job of tearing continuous forms into single documents. A machine called a *decollator/burster* can perform both functions.

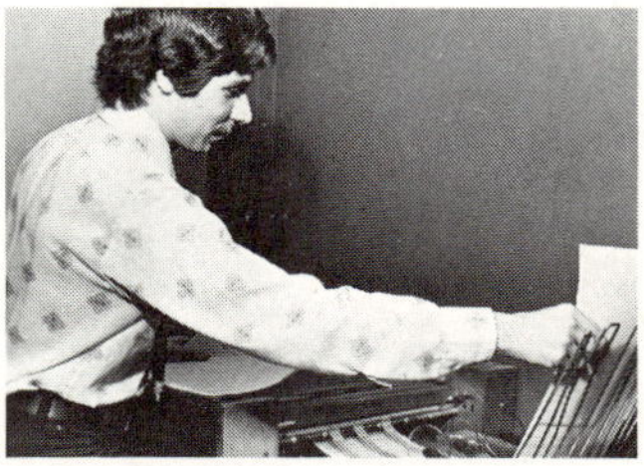

DECOLLATOR/BURSTER OPERATOR. A decollator/burster is used to separate and sort continuous forms and other business documents. Jill Mariani

Devices for Classifying

When business data is classified manually, a reference device is generally used to look up code numbers or other identifiers. The telephone directory is a reference tool because it enables us to identify individuals by telephone number. (Telephone numbers make up one type of code system.)

Reference devices are often needed to identify a specific person or item by code number. For example, a small gift shop may

STRIP RECORD. A strip record is used to refer to customer, product, or supplier information.
Courtesy Datastrip Corporation

keep the names and code numbers of the items it sells in a notebook with index tabs. In larger businesses that classify hundreds of items, a strip record may be more efficient. A *strip record* is used for referring to customer, product, or supplier information. Large metal panels are hinged together so that they can be turned like the pages of a book. Long strips of paper containing such data as customer names, addresses, and code numbers are inserted into each panel.

Devices for Sorting

Manual sorting of business documents can be made easier by sorting devices. **Sorting devices** provide containers for the physical arrangement of documents in numeric or alphabetic groupings. The best sorting devices allow workers to sit while sorting documents. Such devices consist of indexed dividers that form pockets into which copies of documents can be inserted. Circular sorting devices revolve to bring the correct pocket to the seated worker. Horizontal sorting racks slide backward and forward. Racks of different sizes are made to handle different document sizes and volumes.

So far no office appears able to eliminate the manual sorting of paper documents, so sorting devices are commonly used. The largest sorting operation in most offices is the one for handling incoming mail.

CHECK YOURSELF

Supply the missing words.

1. Identical forms linked together as a strip of paper but separated by perforations are known as ___?___ ___?___ .
2. A machine that can read typed copy is called a(n) ___?___ ___?___ .
3. A(n) ___?___ ___?___ records data when the printing handle of the device is moved across the sales slip.
4. To keep accurate records of time employees work, many businesses use ___?___ ___?___ .
5. A machine that converts typed data into ___?___ ___?___ form prepares data for processing by computer or word-processing equipment.
6. ___?___ typewriters have a device enabling the operator to store and correct data.

Devices for Calculating

Electronic calculators are in wide use in both offices and homes.

Many types of machines can be used for calculating. Even at home, many people calculate by machine rather than by hand to make out budgets, balance their checkbooks, and check their bills. By 1975 hand-held electronic calculators had become a must in many homes. As the prices of these calculators continue to fall, heavy demand for them increases. Dollar for dollar, the cost of electronic calculators continues to decline compared with the cost of earlier calculators. In 1965 a mechanical calculator that could do complicated arithmetic cost about $1,500 and took up about half a desk top. By 1980 a pocket-sized electronic calculator costing only $15 could do such arithmetic much faster than the older, more expensive machine.

Such improvements have led businesses to replace much of their older adding and calculating equipment with three types of electronic calculators.

1. Pocket-sized calculators
2. Desk-sized display and/or printing calculators
3. Programmable calculators

Even where computers are found, you will find many individuals using an electronic calculator to prepare controls on input data or to desk-check computer output results.

Pocket-Sized Calculators

These tiny calculators can be used for all the normal business computations involving simpler addition, subtraction, multiplication, and division. Typically, the pocket-sized calculator is the type

ELECTRONIC CALCULATOR. Desk-sized calculators are common in business. Here an employee uses a display and printing calculator.

of calculator used by the person who has an occasional need for machine calculations. Most pocket calculators do not provide a tape record of the computations.

Desk-Sized Display and/or Printing Calculators

Printing calculators provide a tape record of computations.

A standard-sized calculator is the most popular type for an individual such as an accounting clerk who has a frequent need for machine computations. A display section shows both the data entered and the results of the computations. Some models are also equipped with a printing device to provide a tape record.

Programmable Calculators

A program is a series of instructions for a machine to follow.

An even more sophisticated type of electronic calculator is the programmable type. Such a machine can be programmed to perform certain specified operations automatically. With some models, the operator transmits the program by pressing several keys in sequence. With others, the operator enters the program with a storage medium such as a punched card, a tape cassette, or a magnetic strip. The program provides step-by-step instructions for solving a common business problem. The data to be processed can also be handled by pressing buttons or inserting cards on which the data has been punched.

Programmable calculators are usually needed only by individuals involved in long sequences of complex arithmetic computations. Economists, insurance actuaries, and financial planning specialists are typical examples.

Devices for Multiple Operations

The summarizing step combines data items, reducing the amount of data shown.

In summarizing data, the basic recording, classifying, computing, and reporting operations are usually combined. Two types of machines can be used.

1. Electronic cash registers
2. Accounting machines

Electronic Cash Registers

More recent models of electronic cash registers are gradually replacing older models in a wide range of retail businesses including restaurants, supermarkets, and department stores. A **cash register** is used primarily to summarize sales transactions. This

POINT-OF-SALE TERMINAL. Point-of Sale (POS) electronic cash registers automatically transmit sales data to a central computer for further processing. Courtesy IBM Corporation

machine records customer purchases, computes the amount of sales tax, summarizes the amount due from each customer, and prints a receipt.

Many cash registers perform additional data processing operations. In supermarkets, for example, a cash register classifies each item by type. Daily sales totals are summarized by merchandise type or by the store's departments.

A point-of-sale terminal is an example of an electronic cash register.

In many department stores, electronic cash registers also store data, automatically transmitting it to a central computer for further processing. The data is used for customer billing, inventory, and sales analysis. This type of cash register is typically called a **point-of-sale (POS) terminal.**

Accounting Machines

Until the early 1970s, accounting machines were key-driven electromechanical devices. These machines performed recording, classifying, computing, summarizing, and reporting (or printing) operations relatively slowly. Because today's accounting machines are made with electronic components, they work faster and more reliably than the earlier machines they have replaced.

An accounting machine usually has a keyboard and a movable carriage similar to that of a typewriter. The documents on which data is to be recorded are inserted around a roller in the carriage. An accounting machine records a transaction on several forms at once. It can be programmed to compute and summarize data automatically. For example, an accounting machine used for billing prepares a bill by multiplying the unit price by the purchase quantity. Then it summarizes the purchases, providing the total cost.

Ledger cards are often used for recording data processed by accounting machines. Some such cards contain stripes of magnetized spots of coded data. An accounting machine automatically positions the card, reads the coded data, and then uses it for computations. Sometimes the data is printed. In a billing operation, for example, if the name and address of a customer are recorded on the stripe, the machine prints the invoice heading without any keyboarding.

Accounting machines are used in both small and large businesses to keep track of accounts receivable. The output may be used as computer input. For example, the billing information provided by an accounting machine can be captured in machine-readable form for input for computer sales analysis.

CHECK YOURSELF

Match each term with the word or phrase that best defines it.

1. Pocket-sized calculator
2. Program
3. Programmable calculator
4. Point-of-sale terminal
5. Display calculator
6. Accounting machine
7. Keyboarding
8. Printing calculator

a. An electronic machine that displays input data and the results of computations.
b. A machine that can be instructed to perform computing and summarizing operations automatically.
c. A small calculator capable of performing basic business computations.
d. A series of instructions.
e. An electronic calculator that can be instructed to perform specific operations automatically.
f. A basic computing machine equipped with a device for printing input data and results of computations.
g. A method of data input to basic machines that compute.
h. A machine that summarizes customer purchases, automatically transmitting them to a central computer.

Devices for Storing and Retrieving

The equipment used for storing data determines how the data will be retrieved.

Storing data and retrieving data are two separate operations that occur at different times. Business data placed in storage may remain there for less than a day, or it may stay there for several years before it is retrieved. The two operations are linked in that the type of equipment used for storage determines how information will be retrieved.

Hard-Copy Documents

Despite the efforts of technology to reduce paperwork, no one predicts a time when there will be a completely paperless office. Productivity specialists believe there will always be a need for some hard-copy documents. Since office workers store and retrieve a large number of paper documents, several types of filing cabinets and storage shelves have been manufactured.

If a large volume of documents are to be stored and retrieved often, files at which workers can sit are convenient. Five types of files are shown here.

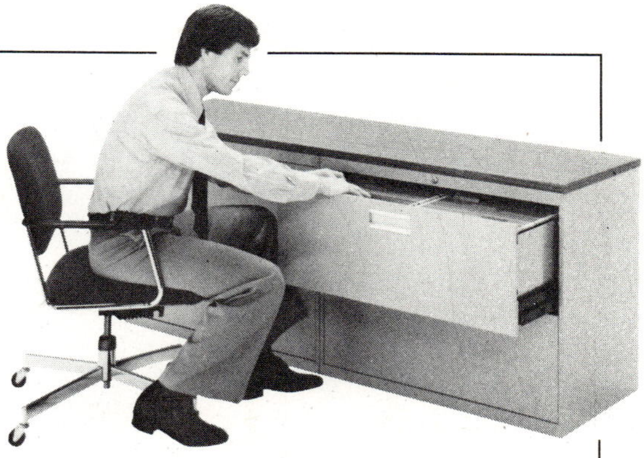

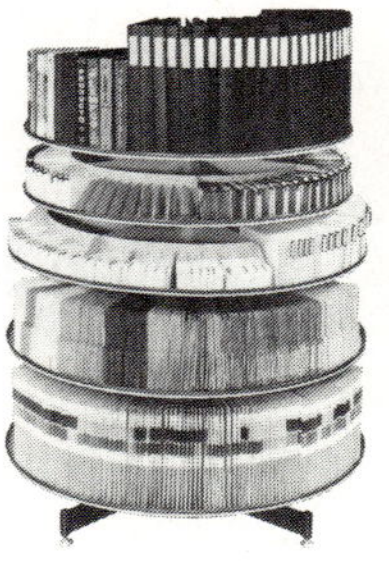

FILING CABINETS (*Clockwise, starting at top-left corner*). *Vertical filing cabinets* have drawers arranged so that an employee can easily reach all the files from the front. *Lateral filing cabinets*, usually with two drawers, are becoming more popular than standard vertical filing cabinets. *Document tub files* are bins that resemble large drawers without tops. Often, the tubs are equipped with wheels so that the tub can be moved to any work area. *Rotary files* are arranged so the items to be filled are placed on a rotating wheel. This device permits fast and easy access to the stored data. *Vertical shelf files* are open files usually containing no more than three or four shelves. Courtesy GF Business Equipment, Inc., Courtesy The Hon Company, Courtesy Wilson Jones Company, Courtesy Oxford Pendaflex Corp., Courtesy Delco Associates, Inc.

Microforms

Data stored as small images is called microforms or microimages.

A microfiche is a single sheet or card of film storing microimages. Many people use the abbreviated term *fiche*.

Banks, insurance companies, and other large businesses usually have huge numbers of business documents that must be stored for reference. Storing these in hard-copy form in the types of files just described would consume large areas of expensive office space. In addition, retrieving a document when needed from such large files would be slow.

For these reasons, many businesses are photographing key business documents to create small images called **microforms** or **microimages.** These images, too small to read without magnification, can be stored in a number of ways. Examples include strips of film in cartridges, cassettes, or aperture cards, and microfiche. An **aperture card** typically used for engineering drawings contains only one microimage. In contrast, a **microfiche** is a single sheet or card of film on which many different images are

MICROIMAGES. Microimages come in many forms, as is illustrated here.

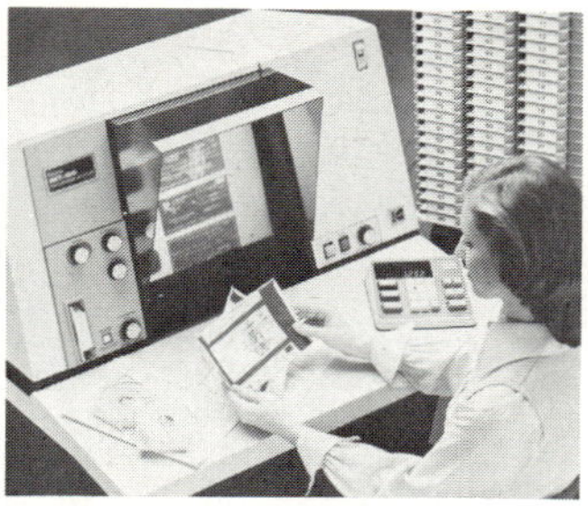

MICROFORMS. Many businesses photograph key documents to create microforms or microimages to reduce the need for expensive office space. Here a microimage terminal is used to read these documents. Courtesy Eastman Kodak Company

arranged in a gridlike pattern. A fiche is convenient for storing and retrieving information that must be referred to and duplicated as a unit. An example of such information is the payroll data for one pay period.

The use of microforms for storing data has increased with the use of computers. Often the output prepared in computer processing goes directly on microfilm. Each image is indexed so it can be easily retrieved. The equipment used in the office for storing and retrieving microimages includes both a recorder and a reader. A **recorder** photographs documents in miniature. A **reader,** also called a *viewer,* enlarges and displays a microimage so it can be read. Equipment is also available for indexing and retrieving and for duplicating microimages. The word **micrographics** describes all the equipment for creating or using microforms.

Devices for Copying

You read earlier about the ability of basic business machines to make copies of business documents. A special type of one-write copying process is a recordkeeping system in which different types of records are created by posting the data only once.

In the 1970s the availability of low-cost copying machines greatly decreased the use of the copying process while creating input documents. Copying machines have also contributed to the volume of paper documents. It is estimated that by the early 1980s over 100 billion pieces of paper were being created yearly by copying machines.

In business a distinction is generally made between two types of copying equipment.

1. Machines for low-volume copying
2. Machines for high-volume copying (duplicating)

Low-Volume Copying

Most offices have one or more **copying machines** for making a small number of copies of input documents, correspondence, or output reports. Such machines can normally be operated by anyone in the office. The definition of *low volume* varies from office to office. For example, in a small office or a gift shop the copying machine may be used to make up to 10 copies of each document. In contrast, bank workers may use copying machines to make as many as 20 copies of each document.

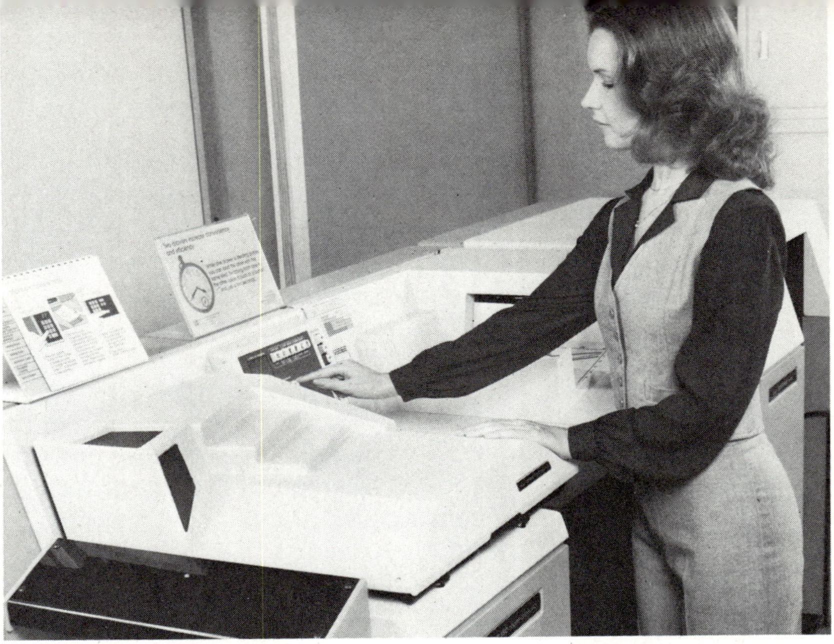

LOW-VOLUME COPYING. Copying machines are commonly used in offices for low-volume copying. Courtesy Eastman Kodak Company

Copying machines differ with respect to capabilities such as copying one or both sides, copying in color, providing a reduced image, and copying on plain paper. These machines also differ in the way in which they create a copy. One of the earliest copiers was a machine using an electrostatic process called *xerography* to transfer an image from the original to the copy paper. This process was so widely used that for a time the trade name *Xerox* was used interchangeably with the word *copy*. Copying machines incorporate more advanced technology such as fiber optics or laser beam printing processes.

Manufacturers of copying machines use advanced technology such as fiber optics or laser beam printing processes.

HIGH-VOLUME COPYING. Duplicating machines, such as the offset press shown here, are used for high-volume copying. Courtesy A.B. Dick Company

High-Volume Copying

When a large number of copies are required of one or more pages, **duplicating machines** are generally used for the copying operation. Duplicating machines are faster, more complex, and more expensive than copying machines. For these reasons, duplicating machines are generally operated by individuals specially trained in the machine's use.

A wide variety of duplicating machines are in use today. Besides the characteristics mentioned for copying machines, duplicators vary in speed of operation and in their ability to collate and staple together multiple pages of a report (output), as well as in the copying process. One group of older machines, called *ditto machines,* uses a spirit duplicating method for reproduction. This method requires the preparation of a special master. *Mimeograph machines* and *offset machines* require different types of master sheets for reproduction.

Devices for Communicating

In almost every data processing cycle, data must be communicated. *Communicating* data means sending data from one person to another, from one office to another within the same company, or from company to company. The data used as input for a data processing cycle may start with order information communicated by a customer. Computer-produced sales reports may be communicated electronically from retail stores around the country to the headquarters offices.

The U.S. postal system is used for much business communication. However, as that system becomes both slower and costlier for high volumes, businesses are using other methods as well. These include the following.

1. Document conveyors
2. Teletype transmission
3. Facsimile transmission

Document Conveyors

A simple means of transmitting data within an office building is by conveyor. A vertical conveyor, sometimes called a *tube,* carries mail and office documents from one floor to another. This means of sending data is handy when workers in one department need paper documents quickly. An example is the need for a department store to compute the day's sales from the transaction records made in each sales department. Typically, the last of the day's sales are made just before the store closes.

Teletype Transmission

TELETYPE MACHINE. Teletype transmission allows data to be transmitted quickly from an office in one part of the country to one or more offices in other parts of the country. The data is keyboarded, transmitted by wire, and printed out at a receiving station.
Courtesy Teletype Corporation

Data can be quickly communicated from an office in one part of the country to one or more offices in other parts of the country. A teletype machine, also called a teletypewriter, looks very much like a standard typewriter. During teletype transmission, data is keyboarded, transmitted by wire, and accepted by a receiving station. The receiving station prints out the data.

Facsimile Transmission

Facsimile transmission can also be used to communicate data quickly from one office building to another, whether the offices are separated by a few blocks or by thousands of miles. Unlike teletype transmission, *facsimile communication* does not involve the keyboarding of the information to be transmitted. Rather, an image of a hard-copy document in one location is transmitted

FACSIMILE TRANSMISSION. Fax machines work like TV cameras but more slowly. The image of a document is automatically sent from one location to another.
Courtesy Xerox Corporation

automatically by facsimile to another location. Facsimile transmission involves four steps. In the first step the business document, which may be a page of data, text, or graphic material, is placed in a facsimile transmitter, where a photoelectric scanning device is passed over it, converting the material into an electric current.

In the second step, the current is converted automatically into a form that can be transmitted over a telephone line. The third step takes place at the receiving station, where a facsimile receiver translates the current back into its original form. Then a printing mechanism is automatically activated to produce a hard-copy image of the original document. A hard-copy image is an exact duplicate of the original document on paper.

In the 1970s the cost of facsimile transmission decreased. Because facsimile transmission does not involve keyboarding, with possibilities for human error, it is a more reliable method than teletype transmission. For this reason many more companies are now using it for communicating high-priority reports, letters, and charts as well as other data.

CHECK YOURSELF

Supply the missing words.

1. A type of storage and retrieval system often substituted for paper documents in large businesses involves ___?___ .
2. Examples of devices for storing small images include strips of film, aperture cards, and ___?___ .
3. The increasing use of computers has led to the greater use of ___?___ in business.
4. Users of small images need to know how to use a(n) ___?___ .
5. In many large offices ___?___ have replaced paper documents stored in file cabinets.
6. Machines commonly used to make a few copies of a document are called ___?___ ___?___ .
7. Machines used to make a large number, or high volume, of copies are generally called ___?___ ___?___ .
8. An example of a duplicating machine is a(n) ___?___ ___?___ .
9. Three methods of communicating data from one office to another include document conveyors, ___?___ transmission, and ___?___ transmission.
10. Because of both decreasing cost and the need to keep the error rate down, business use of ___?___ ___?___ is increasing.

Review Questions

1. Name two reasons why understanding the types and uses of basic office equipment is important.
2. Describe four different types of forms used in modern business.
3. Name four different data input devices, and give an example of how each input device is used in business.
4. Describe the work done by an optical scanner or page reader.
5. Give two examples of devices used in classifying data.
6. Name one sorting operation that occurs in every business.
7. Name three types of electronic calculators, and describe each.
8. Describe two machines used for summarizing data, and give one example of how each may be used in a business.
9. Name the kind of equipment used for storing hard-copy documents.
10. Give two reasons for storing data in microform, and name two pieces of equipment used in handling the microforms.

Comparing Ideas

1. How do you think the installation of point-of-sale cash registers would affect the operation of a local supermarket? How would the salesclerks be affected? the customers?
2. Think of at least two business situations in which microforms are useful.

Data Processing Activities

Now you can try out the kinds of data processing activities business workers perform. Below is a summary of the work you will do. You will find the actual information and business forms you need in your *Data Processing Work Kit.*

Activity 1. You will be a salesclerk at the main store of a chain of department stores. You will be asked to record a mail-order sale.

Activity 2. You will be a credit clerk at the main store. You will be asked to check the credit rating for each customer placing an order.

Activity 3. As a credit clerk, you will be asked to prepare two summaries. The credit manager will use them as the basis for authorizing credit.

Activity 4. You will be an accounting clerk at the main store. You will be asked to compute the total sales each day.

Activity 5. You will be a duplicating clerk at the main store. You will be asked to determine the best method of reproducing documents.

Activity 6. You will be an assistant to the equipment analyst. You will research articles on the use of point-of-sale equipment.

BASIC Project 2

Introduction to Output: Mailing Labels

All businesses need to store and communicate data. BASIC can help reproduce needed customer information such as mailing addresses.

Program Statements

The REMARK and PRINT Statements

BASIC allows you to store and display data in various ways. The REMARK statement is used to identify programs or store information of interest for future use. The PRINT statement can be used to produce lines and boxes in computer output.

REMARK The REMARK statement starts with the word REMARK (REM for short) and is followed by letters, numbers, special characters, or spaces. REMARK differs from PRINT, since no sign of this statement will appear on the output when the program is RUN.

PRINT The PRINT statement can be used with special characters such as * to format or box computer output.

Sample Program

```
10 REMARK PRINT OUT THREE MAILING LABELS
20 PRINT
30 PRINT "************************"
40 PRINT "MS. JUDY R. CASHEO"
50 PRINT "1345 OLYMPIC BLVD."
60 PRINT "SEATTLE, WA 98940"
70 PRINT "************************"
80 PRINT
90 REMARK START MAILING LABEL 2 ON THE NEXT LINE
100 PRINT
```

```
110 PRINT "************************"
120 PRINT "MR. HALL R. ALEXANDER"
130 PRINT "P.O. BOX 7345"
140 PRINT "OMAHA, NE 68107"
150 PRINT "************************"
160 PRINT
170 REMARK START MAILING LABEL 3 ON THE NEXT LINE
180 PRINT
190 PRINT "************************"
200 PRINT "DR. MARION BANDLEY"
210 PRINT "845 SOUTH FRONT ST."
220 PRINT "SUITE 2156"
230 PRINT "SAN DIEGO, CA 90956"
240 PRINT "************************"
250 PRINT
260 END
```

REMARK statements are commonly used to identify the purpose of the program and identify specific areas.

The PRINT statement can be used to repeat special characters (*, -, .) to produce lines and boxes in computer output. You will see how special characters can be used to separate data on reports when you enter and RUN the program. Notice that PRINT statements without words in quotation marks (lines 20, 80, 100, 160, 180, and 250) produce blank lines.

Output

The program as provided will display three mailing labels if keyboarded and RUN. Notice that the REMARK lines (10, 90, and 170) do not produce output. To display the complete contents of the program, including the REMARK lines, you must type LIST and press the RETURN key.

When the computer program is RUN, the output on the screen or printer should look like the printout on page 44.

```
***********************
MS. JUDY R. CASHEO
1345 OLYMPIC BLVD.
SEATTLE, WA 98940
***********************

***********************
MR. HALL R. ALEXANDER
P.O. BOX 7345
OMAHA, NE 68107
***********************

***********************
DR. MARION BANDLEY
845 SOUTH FRONT ST.
SUITE 2156
SAN DIEGO, CA 90956
***********************
```

Keyboarding Activities

1. Enter and run the program given above.
2. Examine the output.
3. LIST the program; compare the listing with the sample RUN.

Enrichment Activities

1. Add a REMARK statement indicating the author and the date that the program was written.
2. Write a new program that will prepare an announcement for a grand opening for a bank in your neighborhood. (Use the NEW command to erase the

previous program from the computer's memory so that you will have a clean workspace in which to write this new program.)

So far, all the programs you have written for these BASIC projects have been erased from the computer's memory when the NEW command was given or when the computer was turned off. You might have saved a program by using the LIST command if your computer prints on paper or by copying the instructions onto paper yourself. In either case, to use the program later, you would have to enter the program into the computer's memory by keyboarding it again.

This is not very efficient. Businesses need to use the same programs over and over and cannot enter long and complicated lists of instructions into memory by keyboarding each time they are needed. Programs are saved by being copied from the computer's *main memory* to a *secondary storage device,* such as a *magnetic tape* or *disk.* When a program is needed again, it may be copied from the tape or disk back into the main memory.

Chances are the computer you are using is also able to do this. It may have a small *disk drive,* which may be used to store programs on and retrieve them from magnetic diskettes. An ordinary cassette tape recorder might be used for saving programs on tape.

After you have written a program, a command such as SAVE is used to record it on a tape or disk. When you want to retrieve a program you have saved earlier, you use a command such as LOAD or OLD to copy from the tape or disk into the main memory.

Each computer system works differently, so you will have to ask your instructor or read the manual that comes with the computer in order to learn the correct procedures for the system you are using.

Once you have done this, save the programs you write for each BASIC project so you can go back to them at a later date.

CHAPTER

3

Punched-Card and Word-Processing Equipment

DATA PROCESSING TERMINOLOGY

Punched card
80-column card
96-column card
Unit record
Card design
Data field
Keypunch
Data-entry operator
Keypunch operator
Verifying
Interpret
Control panel
Word processors
Magnetic memory
Stand-alone word processors
Shared-logic word processors
Electronic mail

PERFORMANCE GOALS

- State two uses of punched cards in business.
- Define the term *data field.*
- Code numeric and alphabetic characters on 80-column and 96-column punched cards.
- Discuss the equipment and process used to prepare punched-card data input.

- **Name seven types of punched-card processing machines.**
- **State the importance of word- and information-processing equipment, and describe the types of such equipment.**
- **State one difference between a stand-alone processor and a shared-logic processor.**
- **Distinguish between the terms *word processing* and *information processing.***
- **Describe a magnetic device that can be used as a storage device for word and information processors.**
- **State two characteristics of the office of the future.**
- **Distinguish between traditional mail service and electronic mail.**

PUNCHED CARDS

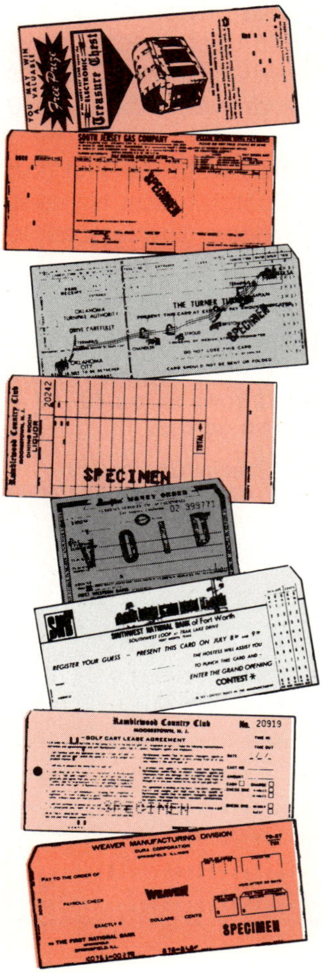

Punched cards have entered the lives of millions of Americans. Paychecks often come in the form of a punched card. Bills from telephone and utility companies are often printed on punched cards. Through the mail come punched-card renewal forms for magazine subscriptions and punched-card dividend payments.

Punched-card machines became the chief means of processing data in the 1930s and 1940s, although people first tried to apply the idea of punched cards much earlier. In 1801, a man named Jacquard used cards with punched holes to control the weaving of threads in looms.

Modern punched-card equipment, however, stems from the work of Dr. Herman Hollerith of the U.S. Bureau of the Census. Hollerith developed punched cards to enter data into an electric tabulating machine. This machine tabulated in five years the United States census of 1890. Without this machine, workers performing the census would have taken better than ten years to complete the task.

In the 1920s Thomas J. Watson, Sr., took over the management of a company called the Computing-Tabulating-Recording Company. This company included the company that Hollerith had founded for producing and marketing his card-operated tabulating machine. The firm was the beginning of what was to become IBM, for Watson optimistically used the name International Business Machines Corporation.

The Punched Card

A **punched card** is a rectangular form with numbered rows and columns in which data is recorded by punching holes. The use of punched cards for recording and storing data was a major step in the improvement of business data processing. Today, however, many businesses have replaced much of their punched-card data processing with computer systems. Even so, punched-card machines are still used to prepare input data for computer processing.

In punched-card processing, data is recorded as holes punched in specific places on a specially designed card. While there are several different types of punched cards, business data processing primarily uses two types: the 80-column card and the 96-column card. Because these cards were made popular by IBM, they are sometimes called IBM cards. The 80-column card is also called the Hollerith card.

Punched cards are often called IBM cards because they were made popular by IBM.

The 80-Column Card

The **80-column punched card** is the card most commonly used in business data processing. Cut from special paper, an 80-column punched card measures $3\frac{1}{4}$ inches (8.26 centimeters) by $7\frac{3}{8}$ inches (18.23 centimeters). When pressed together, about 150 cards take up 1 inch (2.54 centimeters) in a file drawer. About 4,000 cards can be filed in one drawer.

The 80-column punched card gets its name from the fact that it is divided into 80 vertical columns. Each column can be used to represent an alphabetic or numeric character. This is possible because each of the 80 columns has 12 positions (rows) in which a rectangular hole can be punched. Of these 12 positions, 10

80-COLUMN CARD. There are 80 columns and 12 rows on an 80-column card. Columns go up and down. Rows go across.

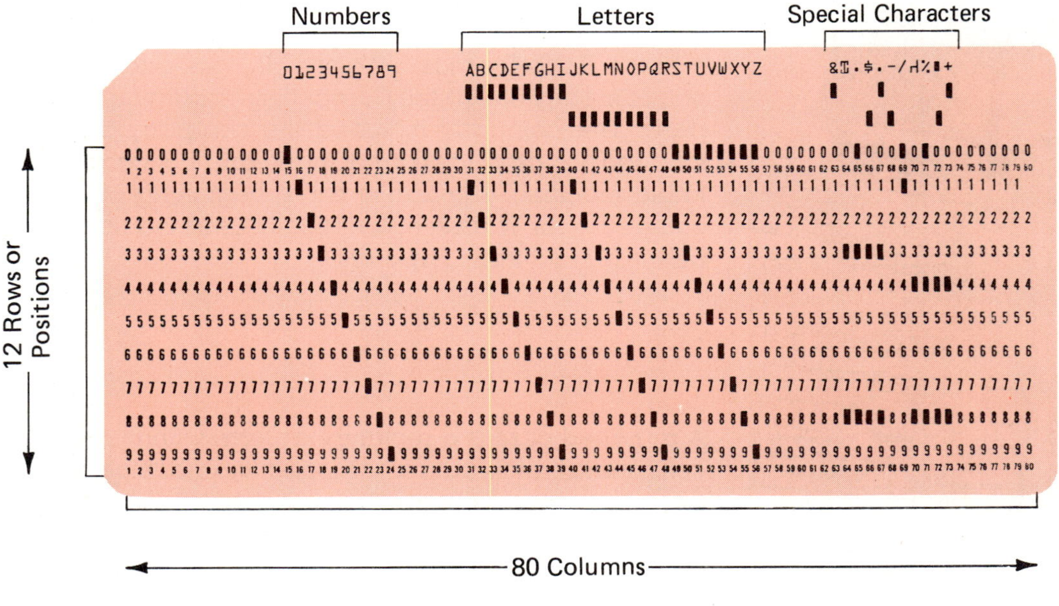

indicate the numbers 0, 1, 2, 3, 4, 5, 6, 7, 8, and 9. Above the 0-position are two unmarked positions: the 11- and the 12-positions.

Punched cards are often referred to by the number of columns they have.

The numbers 0 through 9 are represented by a single punch in a vertical column. For example, a 5 is represented by a punch in the 5-position of the column. The number of columns used to record data depends upon the size of the item. A number such as 5,703 would take up four columns. (The comma is not recorded.)

RECORDING CHARACTERS ON AN 80-COLUMN CARD

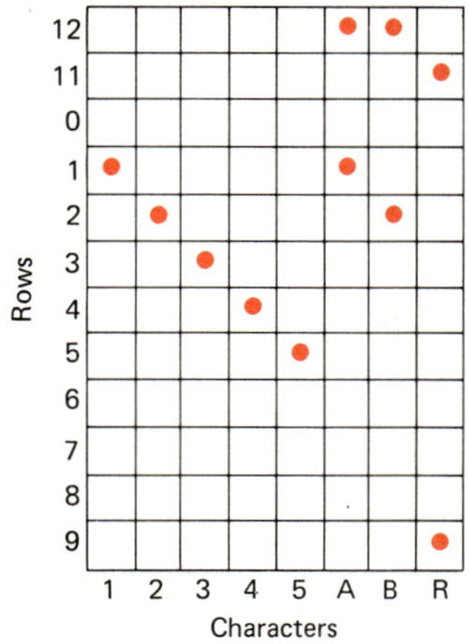

A letter can be recorded in a card column by punching a combination of two holes in the same column. Look at the figure to see how two punches record a letter. The combination consists of one punch in one of the 1- to 9-positions, plus a punch in the 0-, 11-, or 12-position. The positions labeled 0, 11, and 12 are called *zone positions*. The first nine letters of the alphabet, A through I, are represented by a combination of the 12-position and one of the 1- to 9-positions. The letters J through R are recorded by punching a combination of the 11-position and one of the 1- to 9-positions. The last eight letters, S through Z, are represented by a combination of the 0-position and one of the 2- to 9-positions.

Look at the 80-column card shown on page 48; it shows this code system. Special characters such as $, *, or % can be represented by other combinations of punches in a single column. The information punched in the card can be printed along the top edge of the card.

The 96-Column Card

In 1969 IBM introduced a punched card called the **96-column card.** Designed to be used with the IBM System 3 computer, the 96-column card can serve as an input document for several other small computers.

The 96-column card differs in four ways from the 80-column card. The 96-column card is smaller; it measures only 2.63 inches (6.68 centimeters) in height and 3.25 inches (8.26 centimeters) in length. Though smaller in size, the 96-column card can hold 20 percent more data than the 80-column card. A third difference is that on 96-column cards data is recorded by punching round holes rather than rectangular holes.

The 80-column card has twelve punching positions in each column; the 96-column card has only six.

The fourth difference between the two cards is in the method used to code numeric and alphabetic characters. On the 96-column card the columns for recording data are arranged in three tiers of 32 columns each; these are on the lower end of the card as shown in the illustration. In each of the 96 columns there are six punching positions (or rows) as contrasted with the twelve punching positions (or rows) on the 80-column card. Four of the

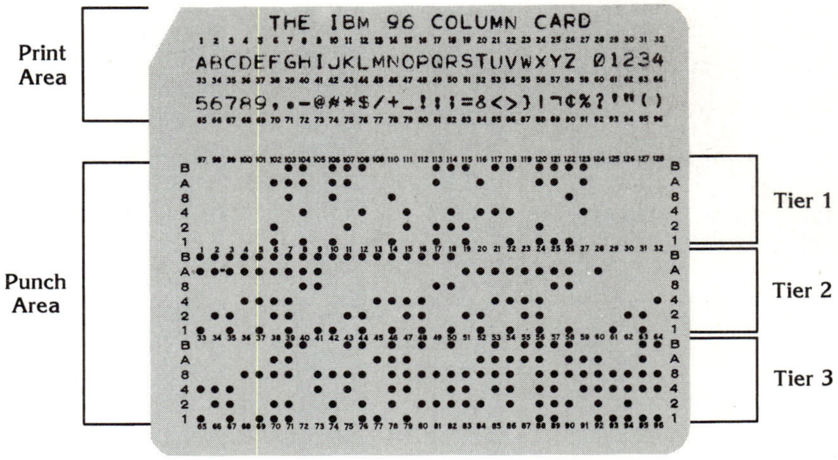

96-COLUMN CARD. The 96-column card is smaller than the 80-column card. Yet the 96-column card can hold more data.

RECORDING CHARACTERS ON A 96-COLUMN CARD

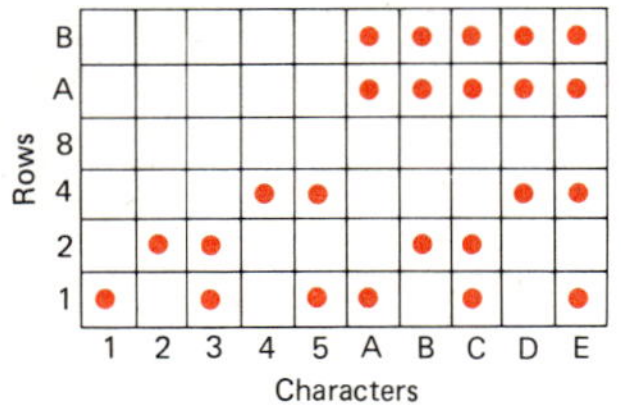

six punching positions are labeled with the numbers 1, 2, 4, and 8, and the other two positions are called A and B.

On the 96-column card, a number is recorded in a card column by punching the number or the combination of numbers that add up to the digit to be recorded. For example, a 1 is punched to record the digit 1, a 2 to record the digit 2, and a 1 and a 2 to record the digit 3. With combinations of the numbers 1, 2, 4, and 8, all the digits from 1 to 9 can be coded. Look at the figure shown here. Alphabetic and special characters are recorded on the 96-column card by combinations of the two zone punches, A and B, with the number positions. For example, the letters A to E are coded with both an A punch and a B punch and a number from 1 to 5 as shown.

The upper part of the 96-column card contains space for the printing of data punched in the cards. There are 128 printing positions arranged in four rows of 32 positions each.

CHECK YOURSELF

Supply the missing words.

1. The 80-column and 96-column cards are often called ___?___ cards.
2. The 80-column card can hold ___?___ characters of data, while the 96-column card can hold ___?___ characters.
3. The ___?___ -column card is larger than the ___?___ -column card.

4. The positions labeled __?__, __?__, and __?__ are zone positions on the 80-column card; the positions labeled __?__ and __?__ are zone positions on the 96-column card.
5. The code for the number 3 on an 80-column card is __?__, and on a 96-column card it is __?__ and __?__.
6. The letter R is represented on an 80-column card by the punches __?__ and __?__ and on the 96-column card by the punches __?__, __?__, and __?__.
7. The 96-column card has __?__ punching positions (rows) in each column, while the 80-column card has __?__.
8. Punched holes on the 80-column card are __?__ in shape, and those on the 96-column card are __?__ in shape.
9. The number 0 is coded on an 80-column card as __?__.
10. The letter O is punched on an 80-column card as __?__ and __?__ in the same column.

Punched Cards for Data Input

One punched card, whether 80-column or 96-column, usually contains data on only one business transaction. The punched card is sometimes called a **unit record** because it represents one of a group of business transactions. For example, if a customer order were recorded on punched cards, one card would be used for each item ordered. If three items were ordered, three punched cards would be prepared.

Each of the three cards would contain at least five pieces of data: a customer number identifying the customer placing the order, the date on which the customer order was received, an item number identifying the product ordered, an item description, and the quantity of the item ordered. A sample 80-column card designed to record this input data is shown on page 52.

Data Fields on Punched Cards

Card design refers to the grouping of columns on a card that identifies the data and where it is to be recorded.

Each punched-card document is specially designed to be a particular type of business record. The term **card design** means a grouping of columns on a card identifying the data to be recorded and the columns in which it is to be recorded.

Different card designs are needed for different card uses. One format may be used for sales data, another format for inventory data, and yet another for payroll. These formats help the operator read and handle punched cards. In every step of the data processing cycle, planning is very important if processing is to be

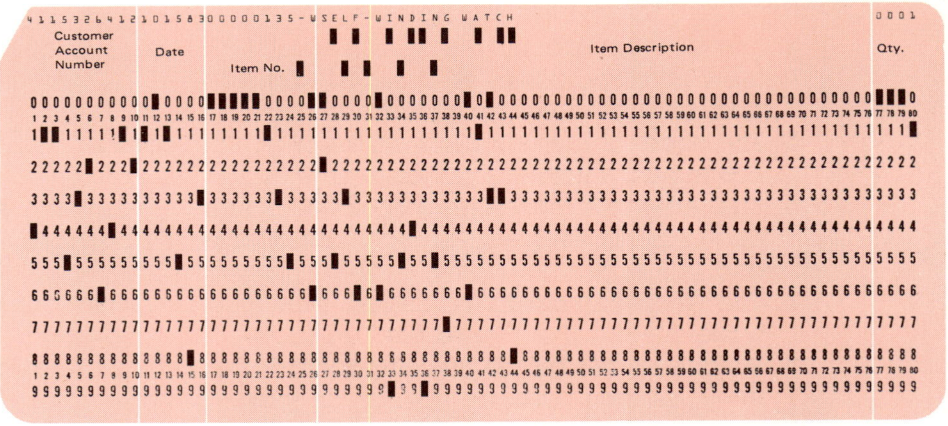

DATA FIELDS. Punched cards are formatted for specific uses. The cards are divided into data fields, which are used to record a certain group of data.

efficient. Card color codes, stripes, corner cuts, and special printing are also used to distinguish different types of cards.

How is data recorded on a card? Each data item is assigned a specific set of columns on a card. The columns assigned to each type of data are called a *field* or a **data field.** A data field is made up of one or more columns. The number of columns in a field is determined by the longest piece of data that must be recorded in the field. Suppose that of all a business's customers, the longest name and address takes 60 card columns. The field would be designed to hold 60 characters. An hourly payroll rate in dollars and cents may take only three columns, or it may take four columns. Look at the fields in the 80-column card shown.

The size of a field is determined by the largest piece of data that must be recorded.

Recording Data in Card Fields. Data recorded in a card field may be numeric, alphabetic, or alphanumeric, which is a combination of numeric and alphabetic.

In recording numeric data, the numbers are started with the units position in the rightmost column of a field. Zeros are usually recorded in any unused columns to fill up the field. In contrast, alphabetic data is started in the leftmost column of a field. No zeros are recorded in the unused columns. Alphanumeric data such as a street address is handled like alphabetic data. These concepts are illustrated in the card field shown here.

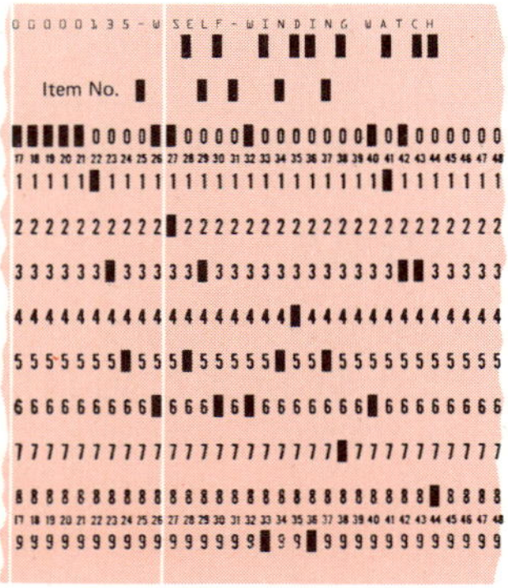

CARD FIELDS. Numeric, alphabetic, or alphanumeric data are recorded in card fields.

Preparing Punched-Card Data Input

When computers were first used for business data processing, data input was mostly in the form of punched cards. But in the 1970s

Punched cards are still used although newer forms of data entry are available.

many other forms of data input became available. Now punched cards are less widely used in computer processing. But punched cards are still often used for data input.

Punched-card input is done on a machine called a **keypunch,** a *card-punch machine,* or a *data recorder.* All modern keypunch machines have a keyboard with the letters arranged as on a typewriter. The numbers may be positioned as on a typewriter keyboard. However, since all letters on the punched cards are capital letters, numbers can be placed on these alphabetic keys instead of the lowercase letters found on a typewriter. Using the same keys enables the operator to use the touch system of the ten-key numeric card punch, since the operator does not have to reach up to a separate row of number keys.

Punching Input Data. The recording of data on punched cards is done by a **keypunch operator,** or **data-entry operator,** who reads numbers or letters recorded on a business document and presses corresponding keys on the keyboard of the keypunch machine. The operator starts by placing a stack of blank cards in the card hopper of the machine, which then automatically feeds and positions one card for the keyboarding step. The operator presses a key for the recording of a letter or number in one column. The card is then automatically positioned for the recording of data in the next column.

On older models as a key is pressed, data is recorded in the form of a punched hole. On modern keypunches, like the one shown here, actual punching is delayed until all the data has been keyboarded. This is done by storing the keyboarded data temporarily until the whole card can be punched at one time. The purpose is to permit a data-entry operator to correct a keyboarding error before a card is punched.

Verifying Input Data. Even with the new keypunch machines equipped with a data storage unit, an error may be punched on a card. For this reason, it is usually necessary to check the accuracy of the keypunched data by an operation called **verifying.** New models of keypunch machines can also verify input data. However, since older keypunch machines can only be used for punching, a separate machine called a *verifier* must be used. In either case, a second operator verifies the accuracy of the original card by reading from the same source data and pressing the keys of the verifier.

A verifier is used to check the accuracy of punches in a card. A notch at the top of a column means there is an error in that column.

The verifier compares the key pressed with the hole already punched on the card. A difference causes the verifier to stop. A notch in the upper right edge of the card indicates that it has been punched correctly and verified. However, a notch directly

KEYPUNCH. Data is recorded on punched cards using a keypunch machine. Courtesy Sperry/Univac Corporation. Photograph by Larry Keighley

above a particular column indicates that either the keypunch operator or the verifying operator has made an error in punching that column. A card with an error must always be repunched. Verifying should eliminate any errors except those due to inaccurate source documents.

Interpreting Punched Data. Newer models of keypunch machines may also be equipped with mechanisms to **interpret** the data punched. This is the operation by which all or any part of the data being keypunched can be printed at the top of the card at the same time the punching takes place. Interpreting makes it easier to refer to data that has been punched.

Data Input by Mark Sensing. There are several methods of punching cards automatically instead of typing in the data at a keypunch machine. In one such method, called **mark sensing,** a machine reads data recorded by hand with a graphite pencil. The marking operation, similar to that of marking a multiple-choice test, can be used only for limited amounts of data. One application might be to record the number of hours worked in a factory.

Punched-Card Processing Machines

Until computers became available, punched-card processing machines provided the fastest method of processing business data. These machines were called by several names, including *tabulating* (or *Tab*) *equipment* and *EAM*. EAM is an abbreviation of the term *electromechanical accounting machines*. Such machines have also been called IBM machines, from the name of the leading manufacturer of the equipment.

Although punched-card processing machines are no longer widely used, some offices still use the following machines.

1. A *sorter* arranges a set of punched cards in numeric or alphabetic sequence according to a particular data field punched in the cards.
2. A *tabulator (punched-card accounting machine)* lists and summarizes data recorded on punched cards. It can also produce printed reports such as invoices and checks.
3. A *punched-card calculator* reads the punched data, performs arithmetic operations, and records the results in punched form on the same card.
4. An *interpreter* reads punched data and prints that data on the card.
5. A *reproducer* copies all or selected data fields punched on one card onto another card or onto a set of cards.
6. A *collator* checks the sequence of a set of cards. It also merges two sets of cards into one set. Yet another step is a check of two sets of cards to ensure that the two sets match.
7. A *card communications terminal* electronically communicates data punched at one location to a terminal elsewhere.

Operating Punched-Card Equipment

From an operator's standpoint, there are two types of punched-card equipment. These are keyboard-operated machines used to punch or record data and other machines used to process data.

Keyboard-Operated Machines. Keypunches and key verifiers are operated at a keyboard from a seated position by data-entry clerks. The skills required to operate these machines are basically the same as those required for any keyboard equip-

The touch system used to operate a keyboard is called *fingering*.

ment. First, an operator must be trained in the key positions to learn *fingering*. Knowledge of the ten-key adding machine touch system is extremely helpful, and familiarity with the typewriter keyboard is essential. In addition to having fingering skill, an operator must know the following techniques.

1. How to feed the cards into the machine.
2. How to operate the control switches on the machine, such as the start-stop mechanism.
3. How to unload punched cards.

A program-drum card helps the operator prepare a set of punched cards faster.

A special punched card called a *program-drum card* is used to control the position of cards automatically. Thus a complete deck of cards will be punched in the proper columns. Operators must know how to prepare and use the program-drum card. A program-drum card is shown in the margin.

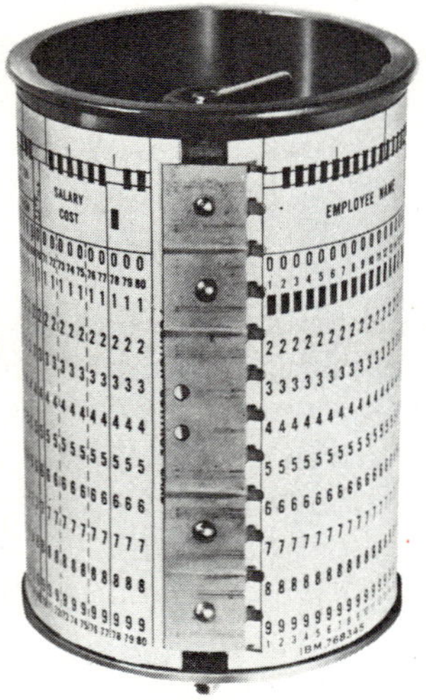

PROGRAM-DRUM CARD ON A PROGRAM DRUM Courtesy IBM Corporation

Punched-Card Processing Equipment. Punched-card processing machines are operated from a standing position by punched-card equipment operators. The operations include handling cards, loading or feeding cards into a machine, and unloading or removing the cards when the machine has completed its work. The operators of these machines must acquire a dexterity enabling them to align stacks of cards quickly and then to feed the cards into the machine properly.

In addition to skill in handling cards, a punched-card equipment operator needs some basic knowledge about each machine for which he or she is responsible. This can be a general understanding of the machine; it need not be a detailed knowledge of its internal workings.

Any operator must check a machine at regular times to make sure it is operating well and producing correct output. The more knowledgeable machine operator is able to detect problems in machine performance quickly and identify the causes. An error can result from poor input data, an operator mistake, or a machine malfunction.

Control-Panel Wiring. With the exception of the sorter, the operations of all punched-card data processing machines are directed by a **control panel,** also called a *plugboard*. The control panel tells the machine what to do, which card columns to read, and which columns to process, whether by adding or printing. A control panel is similar to a telephone switchboard. Wires are used to complete electrical circuits between parts of the machine. A control panel allows a single machine to perform numerous tasks. This external program is similar in concept to the stored program used to instruct a computer.

CHECK YOURSELF

Match each term with the word or phrase that best defines it.

1. Card design	a. The column(s) assigned to each type of data.
2. Data field	b. One who records data on punched cards.
3. Unit record	c. A means of distinguishing different types of cards.
4. Punched card	d. The name given to preparing input data at a keypunch machine.
5. Verifying	e. The operation in which data is printed at the top of a card to correspond to the hole punched on the card.
6. Interpreting	f. Another name for a punched card.
7. Mark sensing	g. A form of data input for computer processing.
8. Code or stripe	h. A grouping of columns identifying both the data to be recorded on a card and the columns to be used.
9. Data-entry operator	i. An operation performed to check the accuracy of punched data.
10. Keyboarding	j. A method by which a machine reads hand-recorded data.

Word Processing

Automatic typewriters have evolved into more powerful machines known as *information processors*.

Special types of machines, first called *automatic typewriters* and then **word processors,** were developed to aid typists in revising typed documents and in typing many similar letters. In the late 1970s these machines evolved into more complex electronic equipment. The newer word-processing machines, called *information processors*, can handle many of the ten processing operations described in the first chapter. They are especially designed to process data expressed in words *(text material)*.

Understanding word- and information-processing equipment is important for three reasons.

1. Word- and information-processing equipment is used to automate office functions that used to be done manually or with basic office equipment.
2. Word and information processors can serve as input devices for computer processing.
3. The input/output and other devices making up the newer word and information processors are similar to those making up

WORD PROCESSING. Word-processing equipment allows businesses to automate numerous office functions. Courtesy IBM Corporation

computer systems. The devices are so similar that many people believe that soon there will be no clear-cut distinction between the two groups of equipment.

Word- and Information-Processing Equipment

Early word processors were made up of electric typewriters with small magnetic memories. A **magnetic memory** is a device in which data, numeric or alphabetic, is stored in the form of magnetized spots that can be read only by machines. The memory stores a typist's keystrokes so the typist can later rekey only the copy needing change. Once the corrected data is stored in magnetic form, the typewriter can be instructed to print any of the stored data. With this automatic retrieval, data appears either on a display screen or as hard copy. The operator specifies in which form the output is to appear and the number of printed copies desired if the output is to be generated as hard copy.

Modern word- and information-processing equipment can be divided into two groups.

Stand-Alone Word and Information Processors. Many modern word processors are **stand-alone machines.** This means that each machine operates independently of other machines. At a minimum, a stand-alone system has four units. These include a keyboard for data entry, a memory, a logic unit, and a printing device.

The keyboard the typist uses to enter the data is usually similar to that of a standard electric typewriter. The memory unit may

DISKETTES. Flexible diskettes have become the most widely used storage medium for information processors. A diskette is sometimes called a *floppy disk*. Courtesy Radio Shack. A Division of Tandy Corporation

be in the form of magnetic cards, on which only a page of text is stored. A larger-volume storage device such as a tape cartridge, a cassette, a diskette, or a minidiskette may be used. Diskettes are most widely used at this time. These flexible, round plates about the size of 45-rpm phonograph records are sometimes called *floppy disks*. The logic and internal memory unit of a word or information processor is needed to instruct the machine in its operations. The printer may be similar to the mechanism on a standard electric typewriter. A faster, newer type of printer is now widely used. It is called a *daisy wheel* printer because of its pinwheellike print unit.

In addition to the four units just described, many stand-alone word processors have a cathode ray tube (CRT) display unit to display characters and lines of text as they are being typed or called up for revision.

A cathode ray tube display unit looks very much like a television set equipped with a keyboard. Such a display unit is often called a *CRT*.

Shared-Logic Word and Information Processors. Where there is a large volume of work to be handled and more than one word-processing unit is needed, a shared-logic system of equipment is often the most effective type for businesses to use. With this system there can be many, say 12 or more, individual input units with keyboards and CRT display devices connected to one central processing unit (CPU). Because one CPU is shared by the input units and one or more printers, these systems are known as **shared-logic systems.** A separate daisy wheel or faster printer is usually also shared.

Many other devices can be connected to or used with the newer word- or information-processing systems. One of these is the optical character reader (OCR). Such a machine can read a page typed in a common typeface and record the data on a magnetic medium for word processing (or for computer processing). Also, communication and calculating mechanisms and copying equipment can be connected to the more advanced information-processing systems to perform the functions described in the next section.

DAISY WHEEL. Many electronic typewriters and high-speed printers use a print wheel typing element. Courtesy Olivetti Corporation

Using Word and Information Processors in Business

Even the simpler word-processing machines perform important functions in modern offices when long business documents must be typed, revised, and reprinted. Continual updating of contracts is characteristic of law offices. And in engineering departments, there are often new specifications to be included in project plans or technical manuals.

A need to type similar letters, such as new-product announcements for customers, is also common in business. Word-processing equipment helps automate such functions by eliminating extensive retyping, storing, updating, and retrieving. For example, a large manufacturing company keeps shipping instructions and the names and addresses of its suppliers in memory. When the company has to reorder the raw material needed for its manufacturing process, a word-processing operator retrieves from memory the shipping information and the name and address of the desired supplier. The operator uses this information to prepare a purchase order for the supplier.

OFFICE AUTOMATION. One possible configuration for the "office of the future" is shown here. Courtesy IBM Corporation

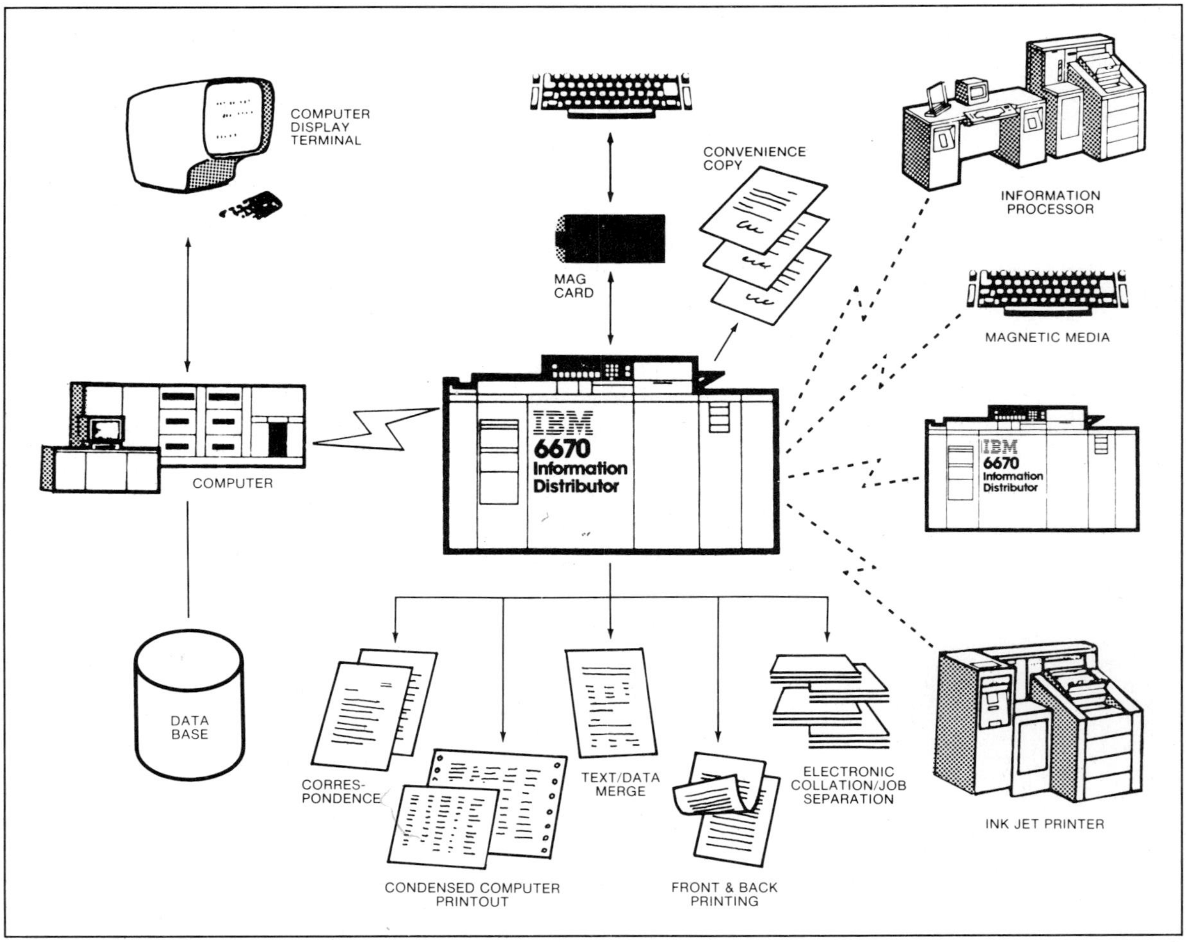

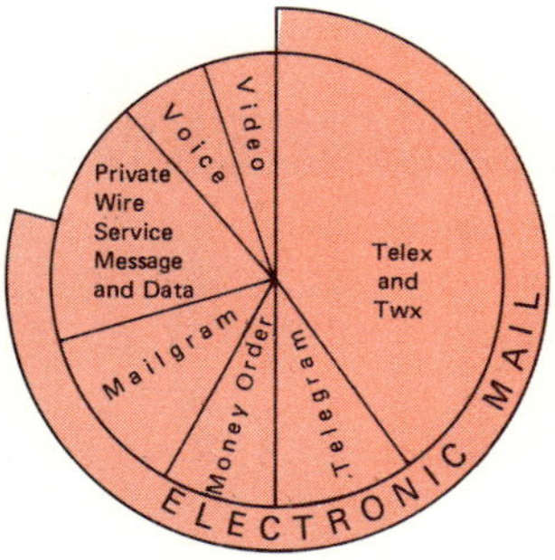

ELECTRONIC MAIL. Electronic mail is the communication of information automatically from machine to machine. Western Union uses electronic mail for mailgrams, money orders, telegrams, and other services.

In the late 1970s the capabilities of new word and information processors to reproduce and distribute business information electronically led to predictions of the office of the future. Already some of the characteristics of such an office have been demonstrated successfully. Many experts predict that by the end of the 1980s the office of the future will be a reality. In such offices there are likely to be fewer paper business documents. Lengthy business correspondence will be stored in electronic units. When the information is needed, it will be retrieved from storage and automatically revised and copied. In seconds it will be distributed electronically from point to point within an office building or from one building to another, sometimes many miles away.

The communication of information automatically from machine to machine is called **electronic mail.** Because it involves distributing information, it is also sometimes called *electronic distribution.* Its speed is to be contrasted with the relatively slow communication of information by the physical movement of business correspondence or documents from one point to another—what we have traditionally thought of as mail.

CHECK YOURSELF

Supply the missing words.

1. Newer, more powerful word-processing machines are called __?__ __?__.
2. Word processors can be used as __?__ devices for computers.
3. A magnetic __?__ is a medium or device on which data is recorded in the form of magnetized spots.
4. A word processor that has its own memory and logic device is called a(n) __?__ __?__ machine.
5. A shared-logic word processor shares its logic and memory devices with other __?__, __?__, and __?__.
6. A flexible, round magnetic storage plate is called a(n) __?__ disk or diskette.
7. A printer commonly used with word processors is called a __?__ __?__ printer.
8. The distribution of business information electronically is called __?__ __?__.
9. In the office of the future there will be __?__ paper documents.

Review Questions

1. Explain how numeric data is coded on an 80-column card and why zone punches are needed to code alphabetic characters.
2. Describe the code system used to represent numbers and letters on a 96-column card.
3. Explain why a punched card is sometimes called a unit record. Give an example of a punched unit record.
4. Define the terms *card design* and *data field*.
5. Describe how numeric and alphabetic data are recorded in a card field.
6. Describe two operations that can be performed on a keypunch machine.
7. Give three reasons why word- or information-processing equipment will become increasingly important.
8. Name the two types of word- and information-processing machines. Describe the features of each type of processor.
9. Give three examples of functions performed on word-processing equipment.
10. State two characteristics of the office of the future.

Comparing Ideas

The questions below are to help you think about what you have learned in this chapter. They are thought questions. There is no one correct answer.

1. How do you think the installation of word processing equipment would affect the work of secretaries in an advertising department? Assume that advertising copy is written in rough form, reviewed for content, rewritten, retyped, edited, and then retyped in final form. Do you think the new equipment would create any new job openings?
2. If you were going to work in the headquarters of a chain of retail stores, how would the office of the future be likely to determine your company's choice of office equipment? Explain your answer.

Data Processing Activities

Now you can try out the kinds of data processing activities business workers perform. Below is a summary of the work you will do. You will find the actual information and business forms you need in your *Data Processing Work Kit.*

Activity 1. As a data-entry clerk at a company that tests students for schools, you will be asked to classify test data and then design punched cards to use for the students' test records.

Activity 2. As a data-entry clerk you will record alphabetic and numeric data.

Activity 3. You will help write a word processing procedures manual.

BASIC Project 3

Formatted Output: Business Letter

Word processing needs are growing every day in the modern office. Programming can be used to store and retrieve routine correspondence. The following exercise will give you practice in preparing formatted output. Many reports and documents can be prepared in this way.

Program Statements

The PRINT and PRINT TAB Statements

We will expand upon our use of the PRINT statement in several ways in this exercise. The following program also introduces the PRINT TAB statement, which is used to tell the computer where (on a line) to start printing output. The statement always includes a number enclosed in parentheses. PRINT TAB (25) "HELLO" will cause the computer to print the word HELLO starting at the twenty-fifth space from the left margin.

PRINT TAB

Sample Program

```
10 REMARK SAMPLE LETTER
20 PRINT TAB(20)"MAY 11, 19--"
30 REMARK CHANGE THE NEXT FIVE LINES FOR NEW ADDRESS
40 PRINT "MR. ROBERT THOMPSON"
50 PRINT "112 SCOTT STREET"
60 PRINT "SCOTTSDALE, TN 31340"
70 PRINT
80 PRINT "DEAR MR. THOMPSON,"
90 PRINT
```

```
100 PRINT "    PLEASE CANCEL OUR MEETING SCHEDULED"
120 PRINT "FOR FRIDAY, MAY 21. I WILL CALL FOR A NEW"
130 PRINT "APPOINTMENT."
140 PRINT
150 PRINT
160 PRINT TAB(20)"SINCERELY,"
170 PRINT
180 PRINT
190 PRINT TAB(20)"MARTINA JONES"
200 PRINT
999 END
```

The PRINT TAB statement starts with the words PRINT TAB. These words are followed by a number in parentheses and whatever is to be printed within quotation marks. *NOTE:* If your computer system does not have a PRINT TAB command, use the print statement and space bar to begin printing at the desired position.

```
20 PRINT "                   MAY 11"
```

Notice that the date will be printed starting at position 20 on the line. The PRINT TAB statement will also make sure that the date will line up with the close and signature.

Output

```
                   MAY 11, 19--
MR. ROBERT THOMPSON
112 SCOTT STREET
SCOTTSDALE, TN 31340

```

```
DEAR MR. THOMPSON,

   PLEASE CANCEL OUR MEETING SCHEDULED
FOR FRIDAY, MAY 21. I WILL CALL FOR A NEW APPOINTMENT.



                                SINCERELY,


                                MARTINA JONES
```

Keyboarding Activities

1. Enter and RUN the program given above.
2. Examine the output.
3. Modify the program so that the date, close, and signature will start at print position 25.

Enrichment Activities

1. Prepare a program that will produce a daily sign-in sheet for all the individuals currently in your class or work group. Discuss what will take place when new individuals enter.
2. Prepare a program that will produce an office layout sheet. The output should show major furniture items (file cabinets, clocks, and so on) and their names. Use special characters, such as +, ( ), and -, to display the shape and location of each item.
3. Alter the letter to include the following.
   Today's date
   A company name above the date line
   A title for Martina Jones (for example, president)

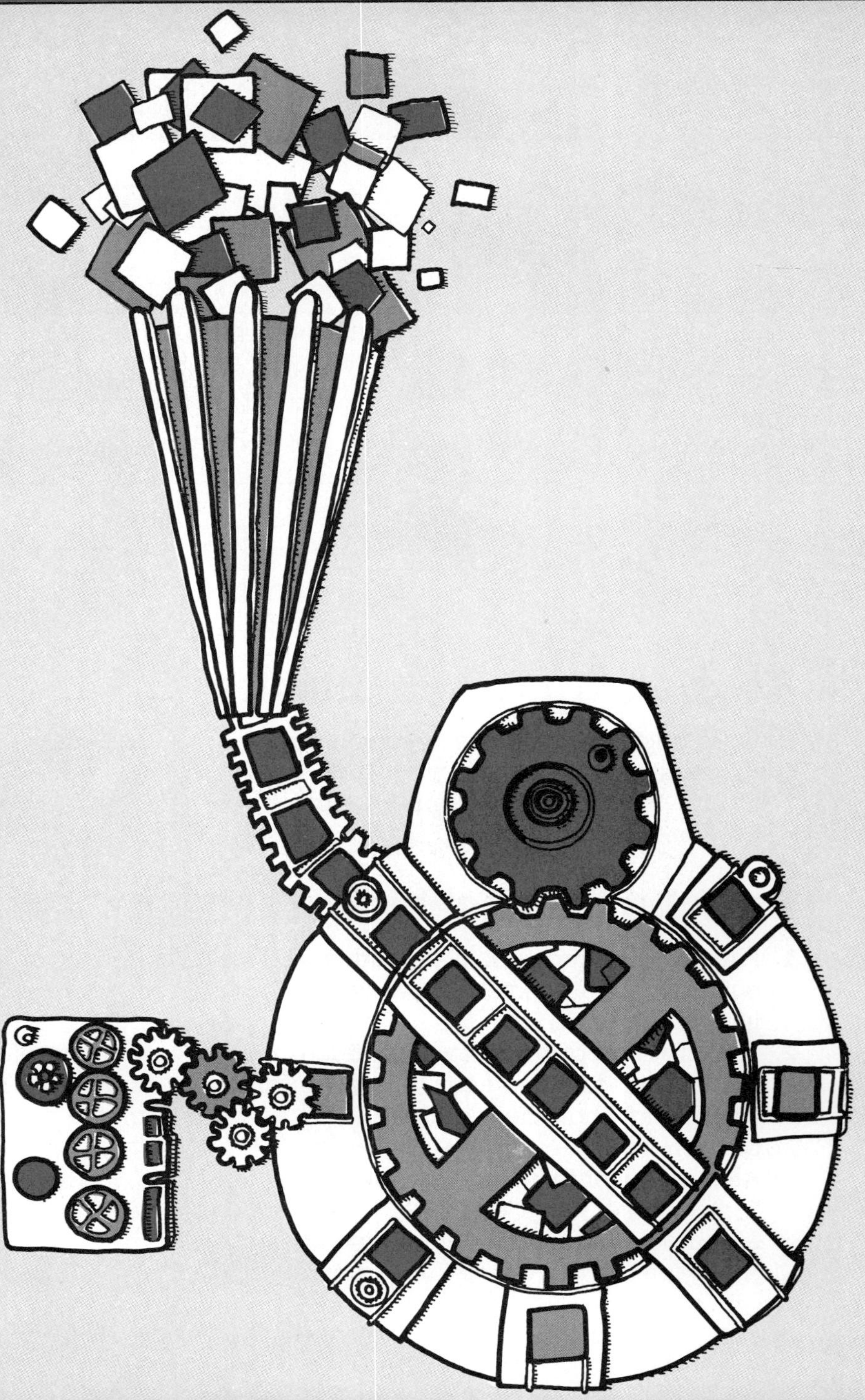

PART 2

Computers and Business

CHAPTER

4

Concepts of Computer Data Processing

DATA PROCESSING TERMINOLOGY

Computer
Computer program
Digital computer
Analog computer
Computer hardware
Computer software
Computer programmer
Programming language
Coding
Program library
Input device
Central processing unit (CPU)
Arithmetic/logic unit
Control unit
Storage device or memory unit
Output device
Computer operator
Decimal or base-ten system
Binary or base-two system
Bits
EBCDIC
ASCII

PERFORMANCE GOALS

- Name two ways in which computers differ from other business machines.
- Name three generations of business computers, and state the differences between the first business computers and today's computers.

- **List the advantages of computer processing.**
- **Distinguish between binary and decimal code systems.**
- **List the steps in preparing a computer program.**
- **Name four hardware components a computer must have to perform the various data processing operations.**
- **Discuss the work that must be done by people in computer data processing.**

Computers have become very common in the last 25 years. We seldom get through a day without reading or hearing the word *computer* or having a computer affect our lives in some way. Accurate forecasting of weather depends on computers. So does the guidance of satellites and spaceships through the solar system and of airplanes from city to city. Under computer control, traffic lights in a city may change to suit the overall traffic situation in a particular hour. Even your hamburger order at a chain restaurant may be recorded in a computer. Computer games and personal computers have become popular.

A computer is an electronic machine that does high-speed processing of data according to a program stored in the machine.

The word *computer* is often misused. By strict definition a **computer** is an electronic machine that performs high-speed calculating and other processing operations on input data. The operations are carried out according to a program of instructions stored in the machine.

The computer is the most advanced machine for business data processing. Computers designed to process business data differ from other business equipment in two respects. First, computers can perform at very high speeds nine of the ten data processing operations needed in business. These are the operations of classifying, sorting, computing, summarizing, storing, retrieving, reporting, copying, and communicating data. Only recording (or preparing of input data) is not done by computer. This step must be taken before the computer can start processing.

A computer program is a set of instructions telling a computer what work to do and how to do it.

The second difference between computers and other business equipment is that computers operate only if given a set of instructions telling them what to do and how to do it. Once given instructions, a computer automatically will do everything it has been told to do. It will even change the instructions during the processing if told to do so. The set of instructions telling a computer what work to perform and how to do it is called a **computer program.**

How the Computer Was Developed

In the 1830s a prototype computer was designed by Charles Babbage, an Englishman. He called this machine an *analytical engine*. Babbage's invention could accept data recorded on cards,

COMPUTER PROTOTYPE. A forerunner of the computer was Babbage's analytical engine. "It can do whatever one knows how to order it to perform." Courtesy IBM Corporation

perform computations, and place the results in a memory store. Lady Augusta Ada Byron, Countess of Lovelace, said of her friend Babbage's analytical engine: "It can do whatever one knows how to order it to perform." This can be said of a modern computer too. Babbage was so far ahead of his time that only a model of his analytical engine could be constructed.

No more significant progress was made in the development of computers until 1944. Then, a machine called the Mark I, or the Automatic Sequence-Controlled Calculator, was designed by Professor Howard Aiken of Harvard. It was converted into a working machine by IBM designers and engineers. The Mark I weighed 5 tons and had over 500 miles of wire. The wire linked its 3,300 electromechanical relays, allowing it to calculate and store data.

There soon were other large experimental calculating machines. One of these was named the ENIAC (Electronic Numerical Integrator And Calculator). It was developed to decrease the time spent solving ballistic problems for the military. The ENIAC was not only the first electronic calculator. It was also the first machine to be named by an acronym (a word that is formed by the initial letter or letters of each of the key words making up a term).

The ENIAC led to the development of the EDVAC (Electronic Discrete Variable Automatic Computer) under the guidance of John von Neumann, the well-known mathematician. Von Neumann's idea to store a program of instructions within the machine itself marked the change from electronic calculators to electronic computers.

Digital and Analog Computers

TYPES OF COMPUTERS

1. Digital (counting)
2. Analog (measuring)

From the experimental machines came commercial computers produced to process business data. Business computers are **digital computers,** which means they solve problems by counting, that is, by adding, subtracting, multiplying, or dividing numbers. A digital computer performs data processing operations sequentially and in a prescribed order. It has a memory in which it can store operating instructions as well as the results of its processing operations. Digital computers are most typically used for business data processing, although engineers and scientists also use these machines for complex computations.

Digital computers are most often used in business.

There is a special type of computer that is less common than the digital computer. The **analog computer** solves problems by measuring, that is, by determining the amounts or changes in amounts of physical units such as units of heat or speed. Analog

Analog computers are most often used in industry and science.

EARLY COMPUTERS. Mark I, the first electro-mechanical calculator to work successfully. It was first used in 1944. Courtesy IBM Corporation

computers are most typically used to control manufacturing processes in industry and in scientific research work.

Generations of Business Computers

Computer professionals speak sometimes of three or more generations of computer development since the 1950s, when computers were first used for business data processing. They mean that a completely new kind of machine was developed in each generation. But generation dates and definitions are not universally agreed upon. However, on the basis of vastly improved types

ELECTRONIC DIGITAL COMPUTERS. The first electronic digital calculator was ENIAC. This computer, completed in 1946, was able to perform 5,000 additions and subtractions a minute.
Courtesy Sperry Univac

of components used in the machines, at least three generations of computers can be identified. The improvements made in each generation over the previous one resulted in faster, smaller, more reliable, and cheaper computers.

First-Generation Computers

General Electric used a model of the UNIVAC in 1954 in its first application of computers to business data processing.

First-generation computers were made of thousands of vacuum tubes. These tubes were the size of TV tubes and produced so much heat that special air conditioning was required to cool off the computer rooms. The UNIVAC was the first electronic computer. The UNIVAC 1 and the IBM 701 are examples of these early business computers. They had small memory capacities, and the preparation of the program of instructions was difficult. The first generation of computers extended from about 1951 to 1958.

Second-Generation Computers

The second generation of computers appeared in 1958. These were distinguished by the use of transistors to replace vacuum tubes. Computers with transistors produced much less heat than those made of vacuum tubes. But even more important, the machines were much faster and smaller in size, and they made fewer processing errors. Also, the second-generation computers, such as the extensively used IBM 1401, the IBM 7070, and the UNIVAC 1107 machines, were easier to program and had larger memory capacities than the earlier machines.

FIRST GENERATION COMPUTERS. The UNIVAC I was the first computer to be made available commercially. It was used to process data at the General Electric Company. Courtesy Sperry Univac

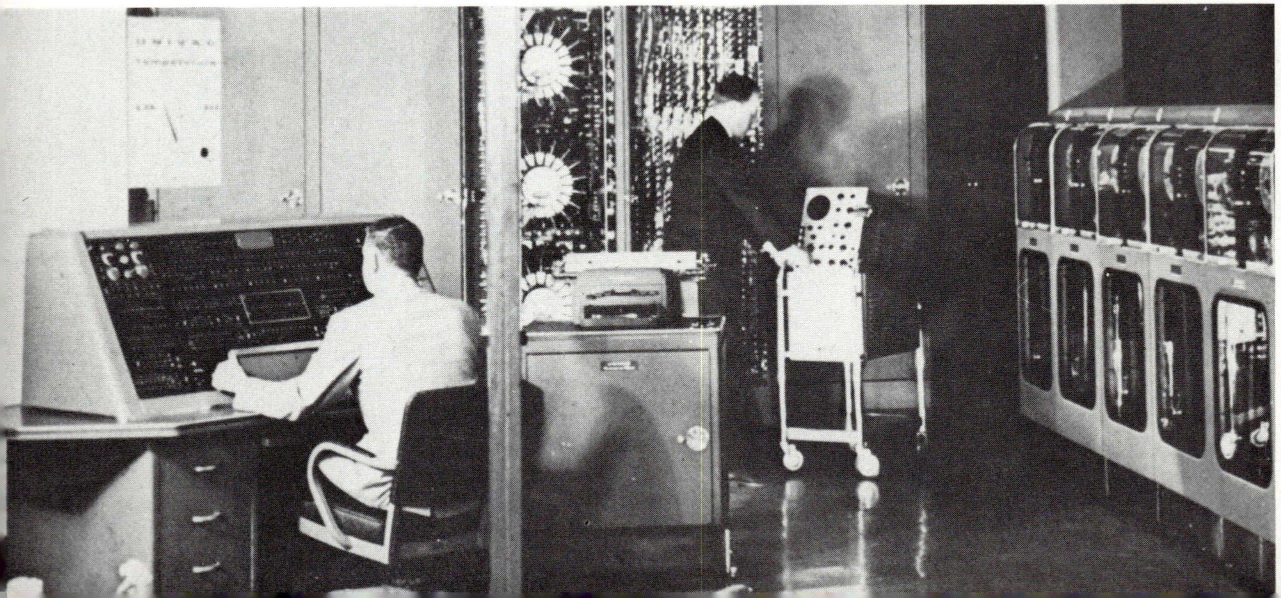

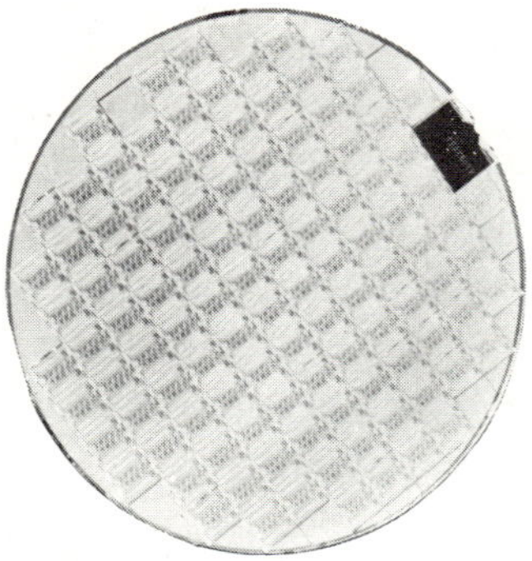

SILICON WAFER. This storage medium, 3¼ inches in diameter, holds more than 100 silicon chips. Each silicon chip can store 64,000 characters.
Courtesy IBM Corporation

In spite of inflation, computer processing is much less expensive than it was in the 1950s.

Third-Generation Computers

A third generation of computers became available about 1964. In these machines the electronic components are organized in microcircuits, originally called *integrated circuits* (IC). As improvements were made, the integrated circuits became smaller and smaller. They are now known as *large-scale integrated* (LSI) *circuits*, or *very large scale integrated* (VLSI) *circuits*. LSI and VLSI mean that thousands of transistors and other electronic components are placed on thin wafers or chips of silicon. Each wafer is as small as one-tenth of a square inch (0.254 square centimeters) in size. Computers made with these circuits are even smaller in size, faster, less expensive, and more accurate than the second-generation machines.

The widely used IBM 360 and 370 computers were among the early third-generation machines with integrated circuits, but these machines already have given way to newer, more advanced models of computers. One of the newer models of the third-generation computers, the IBM 4341, weighs only 22 pounds, but it can operate about 125 times faster than a first-generation computer weighing several tons. It has been estimated that 25 years ago it cost $1.25 to do 100,000 multiplications by computer. With today's computers it costs less than a penny.

Later Generations of Computers

Some industry observers refer to 3½ generations of computer developments; others call it four generations. The distinction is not important, for all experts agree that newer machines are faster, more reliable, smaller-sized, and cheaper. Also important is that recent emphasis has been on machines that simplify computer programming.

CHECK YOURSELF

Supply the missing words.

1. __?__ was the name of the first electronic computer.
2. A computer made of __?__ __?__ was slower and less reliable than one made with integrated circuits.
3. __?__ computers are the most commonly used type of computer in business data processing.
4. The __?__ computer solves problems of measuring by determining the amounts or changes in amounts of physical units.

5. The newer computers are both __?__ and less __?__.
6. __?__ computers solve problems by counting.
7. Industry experts disagree on the number of computer __?__ there have been.
8. Electronic components are organized in microcircuits now known as large-scale __?__ __?__.

Advantages of Computer Data Processing

A computer offers four advantages when compared with other types of office equipment.

1. More rapid data processing
2. More accurate data processing
3. More automatic data processing
4. More economical data processing

Rapid Data Processing

Until the computer was available, the fastest machines to process data were punched-card processing machines. The computer by far outperforms every punched-card machine. For example, a punched-card calculator can perform and record in punched-card form several thousand calculations an hour. By comparison, large computers can perform one million calculations a second.

Today's computers process data rapidly because electronic impulses travel through the circuitry almost at the speed of light.

Operating speeds of current computers are being measured in microseconds (millionths of a second) and nanoseconds (billionths of a second). A few giant computers execute instructions in picoseconds (trillionths of a second). The very fast speeds of computers come from the use of electronic impulses to represent data. These impulses travel almost at the speed of light through computer circuitry.

High-speed data processing is essential in businesses faced with large volumes of transactions. Insurance companies, banks, and utilities are just a few of the businesses in which customer files of millions of records must be kept up to date daily.

Accurate Data Processing

Computers not only process data faster, they produce more accurate results than other office equipment so long as they are properly instructed. Computers are also tireless: they can work around the clock every day of the year without even a coffee

PROCESSING SPEED. A computer can outperform every other machine that processes data. While using a computer, workers can process billions of pieces of data in a very short period of time.
Courtesy NCR Corporation

break. The accuracy of computer processing is improved by having the machine check on its own work. Special programs are written to help the computer do this. Errors found in the results of processing usually come from errors in either the computer program or the data to be processed.

Accurate processing is as important as speed in business data processing. Reliability in processing patient medical histories or in processing traffic control data for busy airports can result in the saving of lives.

Automatic Data Processing

Processing data by computer requires less human effort than manual, mechanical, or punched-card processing. Computer processing is more automatic because of two factors.

1. The computer's ability to accept and store a set of instructions in advance of its work.
2. Its ability to handle data in miniature form.

COMPUTER APPLICATIONS. Computers can save time and energy in almost every type of work. Engineers use computers to design highways, bridges, and dams. Courtesy Auto Club of Michigan

STATE-OF-THE-ART COMPUTER TECHNOLOGY. Sophisticated computers are used to make thousands of complex decisions required to control space flights. Courtesy NASA

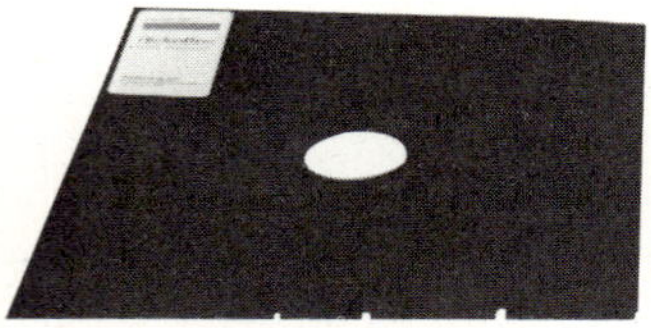

MAGNETIC DISK. Over a million characters of data can be stored on an 8-inch disk. Courtesy Nashua Corporation

In the early days of computers a master customer file might have contained two to three million punched cards.

Following instructions just like a robot, the computer performs the operations of data processing automatically and sequentially, in the order specified by the program. The ability to perform a large number of different operations with little help from the operator is not possible in other data processing methods.

The handling of data in miniature form also makes computer processing more automatic than if other types of processing are used. Imagine what a problem it was for large companies to handle millions of customer records on ledger cards or even punched cards.

In computer processing data is usually stored in miniature form such as magnetized spots on different types of magnetic material (or media). Magnetic disks are most commonly used. On a single 8-inch (20.3-centimeter) disk, over a million characters of data can be stored. Because data is compressed in such a small space in computer files, there are enormous savings in human effort in handling the files.

Even though less human effort is required for computer processing than for earlier, less automated methods, hundreds of thousands of people are employed in this industry. These workers prepare the data the computer processes, operate the computer equipment, and design and implement computer systems. Computers have not replaced people. Instead, they have eliminated many of the boring, repetitive tasks workers used to do themselves.

ECONOMICAL COMPUTER SYSTEMS. Data General's CS60 business computer can operate independently or as an adjunct to a larger system. It uses interactive COBOL. Courtesy Data General

Economical Data Processing

Even though the computer is more expensive than other types of office equipment, the advantages of greater speed, more accuracy, and more automatic data handling usually mean that savings can be realized from computer data processing. The larger a business and the greater its volume of transactions, the more economical computer use will be. In addition, the recent development of very small and less expensive computers has brought computers well within the reach of smaller businesses.

CHECK YOURSELF

Supply the missing words.

1. The computer can accept a set of instructions called a(n) __?__ telling it what to do and how to do it.
2. Computers can perform __?__ of the ten data processing operations.
3. Computer data processing requires __?__ human effort than other methods of data processing.
4. Only the operation of __?__ cannot be done by a computer.
5. Data is often recorded in the form of __?__ spots to reduce a large volume of business records to a small space.
6. A nanosecond is one __?__ of a second.
7. Four advantages of computer data processing over other methods are greater speed, more automatic data processing, __?__ __?__, and less expensive data processing.
8. A punched-card calculator can do several thousand calculations an hour. A computer can do one __?__ calculations per __?__.

Data Coding in Computer Processing

People generally count using ten digits: 0, 1, 2, 3, 4, 5, 6, 7, 8, and 9. Because this number system is based on ten digits rather than two digits or some other number of digits, it is called the **decimal system,** or the **base-ten system.** Math historians believe that the decimal system of counting came about from our having ten fingers on which to count.

Binary System

Computers do not use the decimal or base-ten system for computing or other processing operations or for the identification of data held in storage. Instead, data in computer processing is coded in the *binary system.* In this system all numbers (and letters) are represented by combinations of only two digits, 0 and 1. Because it is based on two digits, the binary system is also known as the **base-two system.** The reason why computers use the binary system is that the data processed and stored is represented electronically. The presence or absence of electronic pulses provides a computer with only two different conditions for the coding of data. As an example, the presence or absence of magnetized spots on a reel of tape or on a disk provides two conditions that can be used for a binary data code.

There are different types of binary coding systems used in computer processing, but all are based on the combination of the two digits of 0 and 1. These digits are called **bits,** short for *bi*nary digi*ts.* When an electronic pulse (or magnetized spot) is present, the computer recognizes a 1-code; the absence of the pulse or magnetized spot will be identified as a 0 by the computer. A binary code is based on different combinations of 1 and 0 to represent the numbers 0 through 9, all the letters of the alphabet, and special symbols used in data processing such as $ or *. The table in the margin shows how to represent the decimal numbers 0 through 9 by using a four-position (or four-bit) binary code.

Binary Codes for Decimal Numbers 0 to 9

DECIMAL	BINARY
0	0000
1	0001
2	0010
3	0011
4	0100
5	0101
6	0110
7	0111
8	1000
9	1001

EBCDIC System

One of the most commonly used binary code systems in newer models of third-generation computers is known as **EBCDIC** (pronounced "ebb-see-dic"). EBCDIC stands for Extended Binary Coded Decimal Interchange Code. EBCDIC has eight positions (or bits) of binary numbers that can represent 256 different letters, numbers (0 through 9), and special characters. The data representation for the numbers and letters of the eight-bit EBCDIC code is presented in the table shown on the next page.

EBCDIC and ASCII Code Representations for Decimal Numbers and Letters

DECIMAL NUMBER OR LETTER	EBCDIC EXTENDED BINARY CODED DECIMAL INTERCHANGE CODE (8 BITS)		ASCII AMERICAN STANDARD CODE FOR INFORMATION INTERCHANGE (7 BITS)	
	ZONE BITS	NUMERIC BITS	ZONE BITS	NUMERIC BITS
0	1111	0000	011	0000
1	1111	0001	011	0001
2	1111	0010	011	0010
3	1111	0011	011	0011
4	1111	0100	011	0100
5	1111	0101	011	0101
6	1111	0110	011	0110
7	1111	0111	011	0111
8	1111	1000	011	1000
9	1111	1001	011	1001
A	1100	0001	100	0001
B	1100	0010	100	0010
C	1100	0011	100	0011
D	1100	0100	100	0100
E	1100	0101	100	0101
F	1100	0110	100	0110
G	1100	0111	100	0111
H	1100	1000	100	1000
I	1100	1001	100	1001
J	1101	0001	100	1010
K	1101	0010	100	1011
L	1101	0011	100	1100
M	1101	0100	100	1101
N	1101	0101	100	1110
O	1101	0110	100	1111
P	1101	0111	101	0000
Q	1101	1000	101	0001
R	1101	1001	101	0010
S	1110	0010	101	0011
T	1110	0011	101	0100
U	1110	0100	101	0101
V	1110	0101	101	0110
W	1110	0110	101	0111
X	1110	0111	101	1000
Y	1110	1000	101	1001
Z	1110	1001	101	1010

EBCDIC is the code system used most often to record data on magnetic tape. Such tape is known as 9-track (or 9-channel) tape because there are nine-bit recording positions for each letter or number. Eight of the positions are the EBCDIC code bits, and the ninth position is called a *check bit.* The check bit is used to ensure the accuracy of the code recording. The eight EBCDIC code bits making up each letter or number on tape are called a **byte.**

Data can be recorded at different densities of bytes (or characters) per inch depending on the type of computer and magnetic tape being used. The acronym *BPI* stands for *bytes per inch.* Recording densities of 800 and 1,600 characters per inch are common, and a standard reel of tape is 2,400 feet long. This means that a standard reel of magnetic tape for recording 800 characters per inch could hold 9,600 characters per foot and a total of more than 23 million characters. This is equivalent to 300,000 fully punched 80-column cards.

ASCII System

Another binary code widely used for data transmission is known as **ASCII** (American Standard Code for Information Interchange). The number and letter representations for ASCII are also shown in the table. It is a seven-bit code, meaning that seven binary positions are needed to represent the numbers (0 through 9), letters, and special characters in the code.

In the early days of computers, operators of the machines and computer programmers had to understand the *machine language,* that is, the way in which the computer identified numbers and characters in all its processing operations. Fortunately, modern computers can, through their input devices, translate decimal numbers and alphabetic characters into machine language for processing. In addition, output devices translate the results of the processing operations back into numbers and letters that we can read.

CHECK YOURSELF

Match each term with the phrase that best defines it.

1. Bits
2. EBCDIC
3. Binary system
4. Check bit
5. Decimal system
6. Machine language

a. A code position used to ensure the accuracy of data recording.
b. Number system based on eight digits.
c. Binary code system used for data transmission.
d. Number system based on two digits, 0 and 1.
e. Two binary digits, 0 and 1.
f. A binary code system used in newer third-generation computers.
g. Number system based on ten digits, 0 to 9.
h. The way earlier computers identified numbers and characters in processing data.

An Illustration of Computer Data Processing

There are two essential parts to computer data processing. First, there is the machine, electronic in operation and made up of individual units or devices that are interconnected. The physical equipment used for computer data processing is called **computer hardware.** The second essential part is the set of programs needed to instruct the computer. Professionals refer to programs as **computer software** to distinguish them from equipment.

To become familiar with the use of computer hardware and software to process data, we will look at a specific business task—payroll data processing. A few important steps in this task include the following.

- Calculating the amount of each employee's earnings. This amount, called the gross (total) pay, is the sum of his or her regular and overtime earnings.
- Listing and calculating all deductions to be made from the gross pay.
- Computing the net (take-home) pay.
- Printing all the data needed for each employee's earnings statement and paycheck.

To save performing the same repetitive steps for each employee, the employer can use a computer. Computerized payroll processing requires the following.

1. Planning a computer program to instruct the computer in how to do the payroll work.
2. Preparing the input data so the computer can start its processing operations.
3. Making available computer hardware to perform the required processing work.
4. Providing human effort to operate the computer as it performs its work.

Each of these steps will be examined in relation to the payroll tasks so that you can learn better what a computer is supposed to do and how it does it.

Planning a Computer Program

The computer is supposed to accomplish all the payroll tasks without stopping to receive help from an operator. How? Before any of the payroll work can be given to the computer, someone must prepare a list of instructions specifying the work to be done, step by step. This list, a **computer program,** tells the computer what work to perform and how to perform it. The program is written in a language that the computer can read but that usually is very unlike ordinary English. The special language used in writing a computer program is known as a **programming language.** Written in English, the program would read something like this.

"Computer, each pay period you will be given a punched attendance card for each employee. Each card will show the number of regular and overtime hours the employee has worked. You will also be given a reel of magnetic tape, called the master payroll record file, on which the pay rates and the pay deductions for each employee are recorded. You are to read each attendance card and match it with the corresponding master employee record, which you can find on the magnetic tape. Select the data you need to compute the first employee's earnings. Then multiply the regular rate by the regular hours, and multiply the overtime rate by the overtime hours. Add the two amounts together to get the gross pay. Store the results temporarily.

"Next, read from the employee's record the data that tells you his or her withholding-tax class. Using this information, compute the amount of withholding tax to be deducted from the gross pay. Determine the amounts of all other deductions, and compute the employee's net pay.

"Next, computer, retrieve from storage all the results of your computations. Print them and the other reference data in the proper place on the employee's earnings statement and paycheck.

"Repeat all these operations for each employee on the payroll. Finally, computer, tell us in writing if you have not been able to balance the hours worked that you read from the attendance cards with the control figure prepared for you. If they have not balanced, prepare an error report. If they have balanced, stop processing."

A program flowchart uses symbols to show the sequence of instructions.

A programmer's translation of each instruction in a program flowchart into a programming language instruction is known as *coding.*

Each of these paragraphs includes several instructions to the computer. The best way to show the step-by-step instructions is with symbols in a diagram called a *program flowchart.* The meanings of the various shapes of the symbols used in a flowchart are shown on the next page. This flowchart summarizes the payroll instructions given to the computer. Once the instructions are in this form, the programmer needs to code them. **Coding** is the translation of each flowchart instruction into a programming language instruction. There are many programming languages. You will read about some of the most popular ones in Chapter 6.

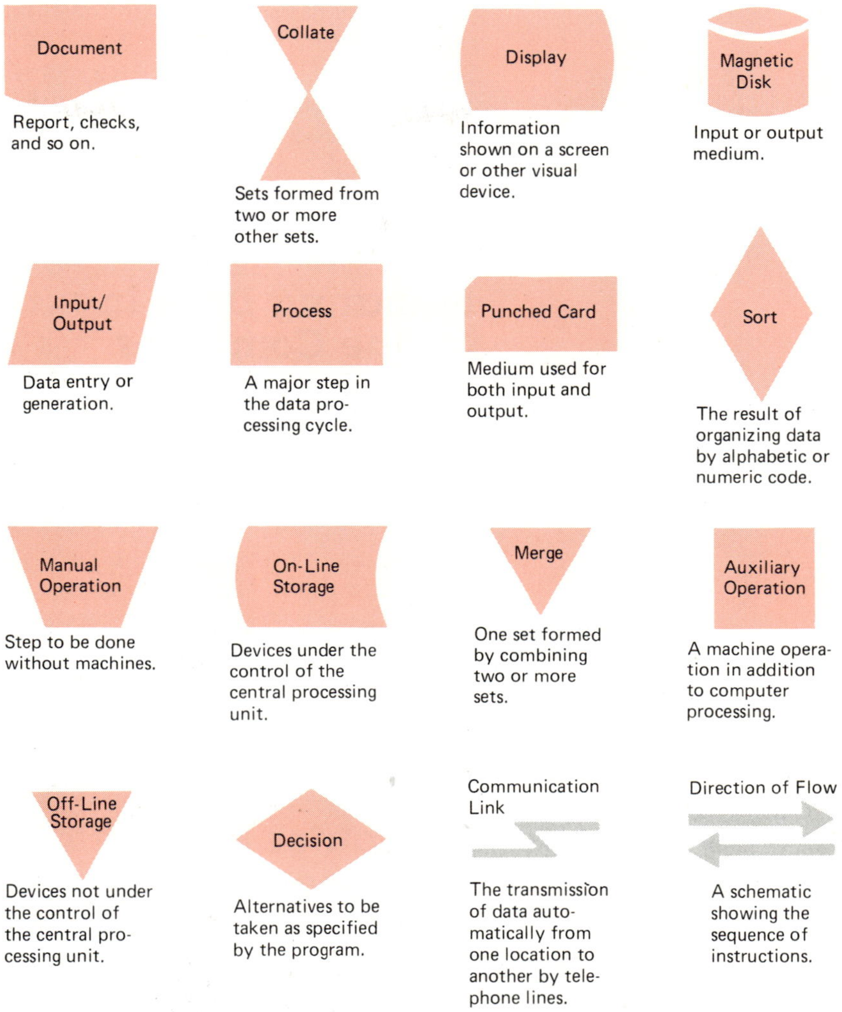

SYSTEM FLOWCHARTING SYMBOLS

The person who writes a computer program is usually called a **computer programmer.** First the programmer tests the program manually. When the program seems both complete and correct, he or she can test it on the computer. A test run is usually done with sample data representative of the data to be processed.

Once a program has been completely tested for accuracy, it is placed in the **program library,** a file of all the programs needed to perform the computer processing work in a business. When a program is needed for the actual processing of data, it is taken out of the library. It is returned when the processing is completed. For example, a program for payroll work is used for each pay period. Depending on how often employees are paid, this would be every week, two weeks, or month. All programs in the library are recorded in machine-readable form, often in the form of magnetized spots on disks. Written copies of the program instructions are always maintained in another location.

Preparing Data Input for the Computer

The computer can perform no processing work unless it is given data to process. This data is called **input data.** An example of input data is the payroll record of hours worked by each employee. To do the payroll processing, the computer also needs the master file data. This file must be kept up to date so it can be used each time the payroll is processed.

The computer must have its input data recorded in machine-readable form. This is why a data-entry operation is always needed for computer processing. In the payroll example described in this section, data-entry operators record the input attendance data in punched-card form. The master payroll file is recorded on a reel of magnetic tape, and the computer program for payroll processing is recorded on a magnetic disk.

Computer Hardware for Processing Data

Although people write the computer program and prepare the input data for each task to be performed by the computer, the computer does the processing. A computer must have hardware devices to perform four functions required in all business data processing applications.

1. Read input data.
2. Control and perform calculating and other processing operations.
3. Store data.
4. Report output data.

Hardware to Read Input Data. Every computer used for business data processing needs one or more **input devices** to read the input data to be processed. Different types of input devices are used to read data recorded on different kinds of input media. For example, in the payroll application, one type of input device (or card reader) is needed to read the employee attendance data recorded in the form of punched holes on cards. A second type of input device (magnetic-tape input device) is needed to read the master payroll file data that is recorded on a reel of magnetic tape.

Hardware to Control and to Perform Calculating and Other Processing Operations. A computer hardware component called the **central processing unit** (CPU) performs two important functions. First, the CPU acts as the manager over all the computer processing operations. Through a device called a **control unit,** the CPU interprets the instructions in the computer program and directs the operation of the other computer devices in the execution of the program instructions. The control unit also serves as a communication link between the person operating the computer and the machine itself.

A second unit of the CPU is the **arithmetic/logic mechanism.** It performs additions, subtractions, multiplications, divisions, and all other calculating operations included in the computer program. This unit also performs other processing operations such as sorting. Data is sorted when one record is compared with another to arrange the records in numeric or alphabetic sequence.

In the case of the payroll processing you read about earlier, the CPU is needed to see that all the steps in the payroll program are properly executed. It also assures that the calculations necessary for each employee's gross earnings and net pay are done accurately.

Hardware to Store Data. Every computer needs some type of **storage device** (or **memory unit**) to hold its program of instructions, plus the input and file data needed for processing. Also, the results of the processing operations must be stored until they are reported as output data.

Hardware to Report Output Data. At least one **output device** is always needed on a business computer to report the

INPUT/OUTPUT. An important decision is the form of input, reference, and output data in computer processing. Jill Mariani

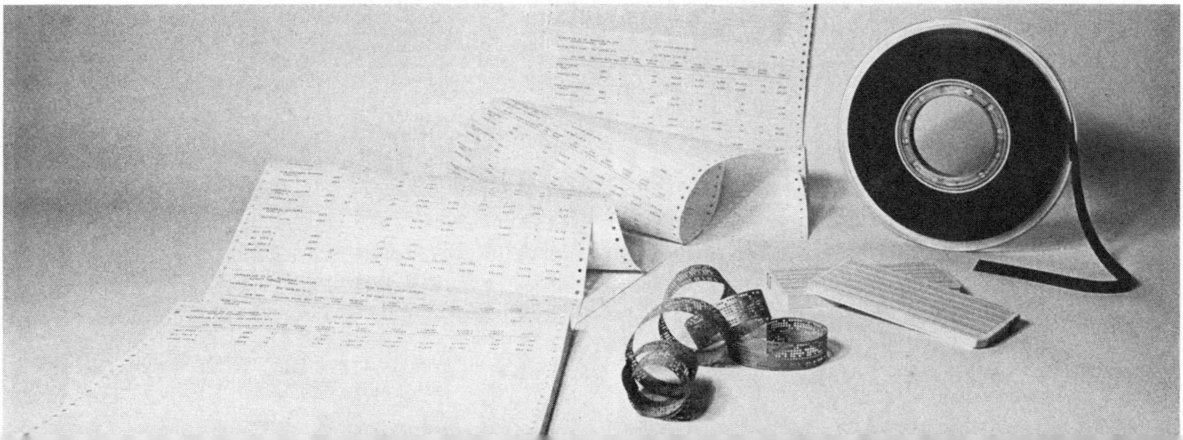

results of the processing operations. There are different types of computer output devices, many of which can be used interchangeably as input devices. Output printers report data in the form of printed copy, while CRT output terminals display output data on screens. To print paychecks and earnings statements, a computer doing payroll processing needs a printer as one output device.

Operating a Computer

Computer data processing is not completely automatic. People are needed to write the computer programs, to prepare the input data for each task to be performed by the computer, and to operate the computer.

A **computer operator** is responsible for both loading and unloading the input and output devices and for keeping an eye on the computer during processing. In setting up the computer for the payroll assignment, the operator places the computer program in a magnetic-disk storage device. Next, the operator places the master file, recorded on a reel of magnetic tape, in a magnetic-tape input device. The data to be processed must also be placed in an input device. For payroll processing, the punched-card attendance records are placed in a punched-card input device called a *card reader*. Then blank, continuous-form payroll statements and checks are loaded in a *printer*, an output device.

Once the computer is loaded, the computer operator can start the processing. When the start key is pressed, the computer automatically begins reading the first step of the computer program. The program may include hundreds or even thousands of steps that have to be performed to prepare each employee paycheck. Without any direct human intervention, the computer performs each part of its work assignment.

In one series of steps, for example, the computer performs all the computations necessary to determine an employee's net pay.

COMPUTER OPERATION. A computer operator loads and unloads the input and output devices. The operator also monitors the computer through processing. Jill Mariani

The results of each of these computations are stored while the next ones are being done. When the computer has finished all the computations for one employee, it retrieves the results from storage and prints them all at once on the employee's earnings statement and paycheck. The steps required to prepare one paycheck may take the computer less than a minute. After it finishes one employee's paycheck, it follows all the same steps to prepare a paycheck for every other employee. It continues preparing the paychecks without human intervention until the assignment is completed.

When the computer has printed the paychecks, the operator unloads the tape reel for the master payroll file and removes the storage disk containing the payroll program. The operator also unloads the punched-card attendance records and then removes the paychecks. Now the computer is ready to be loaded for another data processing job.

Another machine operator called a *burster* completes the processing of the payroll checks printed on continuous forms. These forms are passed through a bursting machine, which separates the forms into individual paychecks that can be distributed to employees.

CHECK YOURSELF

Match each term with the phrase that best defines it.

1. Computer programmer
2. Card reader
3. Computer program
4. Printer
5. Computer system
6. Computer operator
7. Central processing unit
8. Program flowchart

a. The several connected machines used in computer data processing.
b. A machine that measures and compares quantities in one operation.
c. A computer output device.
d. A component of the electronic computer that houses the arithmetic/logic unit and the control unit.
e. A computer input device.
f. The person whose job it is to load and unload the input and output devices and to monitor the computer through processing.
g. Instructions that can be entered into a computer system and used for processing.
h. The person who writes a series of instructions for the computer.
i. The best means for illustrating the step-by-step instructions of a computer program.

Review Questions

1. Define the word *computer*, and describe two ways in which computers differ from other business equipment.
2. List four advantages of computer data processing.
3. Explain why computer processing is more automatic than punched-card processing.
4. State the difference between digital computers and analog computers.
5. List three generations of computer equipment, and describe the improvements made in each generation.
6. Define the terms *computer program* and *computer software*.
7. Define the terms *programming language* and *program library*.
8. Name the four types of hardware components common to all business computers and describe their functions.
9. Give an example of a computer input device and a computer output device.
10. Explain three tasks that must be performed by people in computer data processing.
11. Describe the difference between decimal and binary code systems, and explain why computers use binary codes to represent numbers and letters.
12. List the steps needed to create a computer program.

Comparing Ideas

1. Why do you think some businesses prefer to rent, rather than buy, data processing equipment? Can you think of two possible explanations?
2. Try to think of a data processing application in a business with which you are familiar. Identify and discuss the four hardware components you observe.

Data Processing Activities

Now you can try out the kinds of data processing activities business workers perform. Below is a summary of the work you will do. You will find the actual information and business forms you need in your *Data Processing Work Kit*.

Activity 1. As an accounting clerk at a personnel agency, you will be responsible for preparing the billing data for processing.

Activity 2. You will verify the accuracy of a computerized expense report system.

Activity 3. As a storage librarian you will identify the appropriate storage diskette for use by computer operators.

BASIC Project 4

Computer Run Cards: Batch

Many people think of computers as good tools for working with numbers and doing mathematics. The following exercise shows how a computer may also be used with words. It produces a computer job request card while introducing a new BASIC tool: the string variable.

Program Statements

The LET and DIM Statements and String Variables

The LET statement allows you to assign the value of a data item to a variable name for the purpose of storage and processing. LET can be used with numbers or strings (also called character strings). A **string** is a series of letters, numbers, punctuation marks, or other symbols. Names, addresses, and telephone numbers are examples of strings.

The result of a LET statement is that an item can be referred to by the name that it was given in a previous BASIC statement. This can eliminate a great deal of data input, which is costly. The item is called a *constant* because its value does not change. The name is called a *variable* because its value changes when the LET statement is used.

For example, both these BASIC programs will produce the same output.

```
10 LET A$="FRED"
20 PRINT A$
30 END
```

```
10 PRINT "FRED"
20 END
```

The following program will print FRED and then print MARY.

```
10 LET A$="FRED"
20 PRINT A$
30 LET A$="MARY"
40 PRINT A$
50 END
```

The value of A changes, or varies, from FRED to MARY because of the LET statements. The LET statement assigns the value FRED and then the value MARY to the variable called A. The PRINT statements cause the value of the variable to be printed.

Since the computer stores numbers and strings differently in its memory, it must know which type of data will be assigned to a variable by a LET statement. String variable names always end with a dollar sign ($). If there is no dollar sign, the computer assumes that the data will be numeric.

Many versions of BASIC allow you to use words for variable names. This makes it possible to use variable names such as NAME, ADDRESS, and AGE that are descriptive of the type of data to be assigned with LET statements.

The maximum allowable length of variable names varies from one version of BASIC to another, and in some cases, only single letters may be used. Consult the reference manual for your particular system to find out what the limitations are in your version of BASIC.

In this exercise, single letters are used for variable names. Since the data assigned to the variables are strings, each single letter is followed by a dollar sign.

Some versions of BASIC require you to specify the maximum length of a string that could be assigned to a string variable by a LET statement. The DIMENSION (or DIM) statement is used for this purpose.

This statement means that the length of a string assigned to the string variable A may not exceed 25 characters.

```
100 DIM A$ 25
```

LET The LET statement starts with the word LET. This word is followed by a variable name, for example, a, x, y, or z; and a number or a string. A *string* is a series of letters, numbers, punctuation marks, or other symbols. The variable name assigned to a string must end with a dollar sign ($).

DIM The DIM statement starts with the word DIM. This word is followed by the name of the string variable and the maximum length of the string enclosed in parentheses.

DIM statements usually go at the beginning of a program because they must precede any use of the variable name in a LET, PRINT, or other statement. Most versions of BASIC do not use the DIM statement. Instead, a maximum length for strings is assumed. This maximum is generally quite large (often 256 characters), so the programmer need not be concerned about it.

Consult your instructor and reference manual to see if DIM statements are needed in your version of BASIC and, if not, what the maximum allowable string length is.

NOTE: Do not confuse this DIM statement with the DIM statement used to dimension *arrays*. Arrays are like lists or tables of related data items. The size of an array must be decided upon before it is used. Arrays are commonly found in most versions of BASIC.

Sample Program

```
110 LET A$="WRITE TAPE FOR J. CROWLEY"
120 LET B$="JAN 12, 19--"
130 LET C$="ACCOUNTING"
140 LET D$="19-142"
150 LET E$="DISKETTE"
160 LET F$="TAPE #953"
170 LET G$="MAIN COMPUTER"
180 LET H$="LINE PRINTER"
190 LET I$="ROOM 152"
200 PRINT
```

```
210 PRINT "************************************************"
220 PRINT
230 PRINT "   JOB REQUEST CARD"
240 PRINT
250 PRINT "JOB NAME:";A$;TAB(40)"DATE:";B$
260 PRINT "DEPARTMENT:";C$;TAB(40)"CHARGE NO.:";D$
270 PRINT "INPUT:";E$
280 PRINT "STORAGE:";F$
290 PRINT "PROCESSING:";G$
300 PRINT "OUTPUT:";H$
310 PRINT
320 PRINT "SPECIAL INSTRUCTIONS----------------------------------"
330 PRINT "-------------------------------------------------------"
340 PRINT "-------------------------------------------------------"
350 PRINT "ROUTE TO:";I$
360 PRINT
370 PRINT "************************************************"
999 END
```

Job request cards are prepared to give specific instructions to computer operators.

You will note that nine assignment or LET statements are made. Each variable is named by a letter (A through I) followed by a $.

The variable names (H$ is equal to LINE PRINTER) can be used in PRINT statements. This can save a great deal of data input and computer storage.

You will also notice in this program that more than one variable can be printed on a single line of output. On line 250, for example, you can see that the job name and the date will be printed on the same line. The TAB (40) will cause the date to be printed starting at space 40 on the line of output.

Notice that semicolons are used to separate the different components of the PRINT statement.

Output

```
*************************************************

    JOB REQUEST CARD

JOB NAME: WRITE TAPE FOR J. CROWLEY    DATE: JAN 12, 19--
DEPARTMENT: ACCOUNTING                 CHARGE NO.: 19-142
INPUT: DISKETTE
STORAGE: TAPE #953
PROCESSING: MAIN COMPUTER
OUTPUT: LINE PRINTER
SPECIAL INSTRUCTIONS--------------------------------------------
----------------------------------------------------------------
----------------------------------------------------------------
ROUTE TO: ROOM 152
*************************************************
```

Keyboarding Activities

1. Enter and RUN the program given above.
2. Modify the program to include the following: a second tape, number 407; and a special instruction, "MAKE TWO TAPE COPIES FOR SECURITY"

Enrichment Activities

1. Create a computer program that produces a letter of application for part-time employment. In your program use the LET statement and a string variable for the company name. In this way you can send the same letter to a new company by simply changing the contents of the string variable.
2. Produce two applications using your program.

CHAPTER

5

Computer Hardware

DATA PROCESSING TERMINOLOGY

Computer system
Off-line equipment
On-line equipment
Direct-data-entry equipment
Key-to-disk machine
Diskettes or floppy disks
Shared-processor data-entry device
Optical character reader (OCR)
Magnetic ink character reader (MICR)
Terminal
Intelligent terminal
Time-sharing
Magnetic-tape drive
Mainframe
Console
Primary storage
Secondary storage
Access time
Bubble memories
Telecommunications
Distributed data processing systems
Microprocessor
Microcomputer
Minicomputer
Medium- and large-sized computers
Throughput

PERFORMANCE GOALS

- Define the term *computer system.*
- Distinguish between off-line and on-line computer hardware.
- Name four methods of data entry.

- **List three computer input devices.**
- **Name the two parts of the central processing unit.**
- **List seven storage devices.**
- **List six computer output devices.**
- **Discuss the chief types of modern computer hardware.**

The computer of the early 1950s was expensive and little understood. Experts predicted its limited usefulness in business. But within one decade the price of computer equipment dropped significantly, and the programming and operation of the machines was greatly simplified. By 1965 over 20,000 computers were processing data in the United States. By 1980, more than 250,000 had been installed.

The term *computer hardware* is commonly used to include a broad variety of equipment associated with computer processing. It includes, for example, different types of machines used to prepare input data in machine-readable form. The term **computer system,** or simply the word *computer,* refers to a specific group of physically attached devices that perform processing operations. The parts that make up a computer or computer system generally include input, central processing, storage, and output devices.

A computer system is a group of interconnected machines or devices that perform data processing operations.

This chapter treats some of the more important types of computer hardware used in business data processing.

1. Input hardware
2. Central processing hardware
3. Storage hardware
4. Output hardware

Input Hardware

In order to operate, a computer must be given data to process and a program of processing instructions. Both the input data and the programs must be recorded in machine-readable form. Typically, about one-third of business processing dollars are spent to make data ready for computer input. The function of recording data in machine-readable form has become known as **data entry.** The employee who converts data from human-readable form to machine-readable form is often called a **data-entry clerk** or *data-entry operator.*

Data entry is the recording of data in machine-readable form.

In the early days of computer processing, all data and programming instructions to be entered into a computer had to be recorded in the form of punched holes either on punched cards or on paper tape. Today the use of punched cards for data entry has declined in popularity, and paper tape is rarely used for business data entry. Newer techniques have been developed to simplify the data-entry operation.

Four of the most common methods now used for recording business data as input for computer processing are as follows.

1. Punching data into cards.
2. Keying data on magnetic tape or disks.
3. Keying or marking data for machine scanning.
4. Keying data directly into computers from terminals.

Off-line devices are independent of the computer in operation. On-line devices are physically linked directly to the computer.

For each data-entry method, a variety of computer hardware devices can be used. Devices not linked directly to the central processing unit of a computer are called **off-line equipment.** In contrast, **on-line equipment** is physically linked directly with the central processing unit. Both off-line and on-line input devices have the same function: to translate input data into a form readable by a computer.

Off-Line Equipment

The card-punch machine is still used as a data-entry device.

Card-Punch Machines. Although its popularity is decreasing, the card-punch machine is still widely used as a data-entry device. Data recorded by means of punched holes in cards can be read by computer input devices and used in processing operations.

Punched-card machines were the chief means of processing data in the 1930s and 1940s. When businesses began to convert to computer data processing in the 1950s, 80-column cards were seen as a direct and simple means for preparing data for entry into computers. Today we continue to use the 80-column card as well as the 96-column punched card.

Although newer types of data-entry methods are usually better for handling large volumes of input data, there are still many cases where card-punch machines are more economical to use for data entry. It is very easy for an experienced card-punch operator to pick up a punched-card record, read it, and replace it if there is an error. As you read earlier, unlike card punching, recording data in punched/paper tape is no longer commonly used for data entry. However, punched/paper tape still plays a role in data communications, as will be described later in this chapter.

Key-to-disk and other direct-data-entry devices record input data directly on disks or magnetic media.

Key-to-Disk and Other Direct-Data-Entry Devices. Card-punch machines are being replaced as data-entry devices by a variety of key-to-disk, key-to-tape, and key-to-diskette devices. These devices are called **direct-data-entry equipment** because the machines are designed to record input data on magnetic disks, tapes, or diskettes rather than on punched cards.

Although there are many variations in these key-to-disk or key-to-tape devices, all have a keyboard similar to the keyboard of a card punch. Instead of recording data in the form of punched holes in individual cards, the data-entry clerk records data in the form of magnetized spots. These spots are recorded on a magnetic disk or on magnetic tape that may be rolled on a reel or contained in a tape cassette or a tape cartridge. The machines permit the operator to enter data into a storage unit as it is keyed. The operator transfers the contents of the storage unit for recording on a disk or tape only after an entire record has been keyed. Thus, merely by backspacing and rekeying, he or she can make any keying corrections that may be necessary.

More advanced direct-data-entry devices are equipped with visual display screens so that the data-entry operator can detect keying errors before the data is recorded. A display screen is like a small TV screen; the data is shown on the screen as it is keyed. Devices with TV-like screens are referred to as *visual display devices* or *CRT* (cathode-ray tube) *input devices.*

A CRT input device has a visual display screen that is like a small TV screen.

Large computer installations need many data-entry machines for input preparation. A type of **key-to-disk machine,** called a **shared-processor data-entry device,** is being used for these situations. With this equipment a group of individual data-entry stations (typically from 8 to 64) is connected to (or shares) a small computer processing unit. The shared processor permits editing functions to be performed at each data-entry station. This ability simplifies the data-input operation. Once recorded and verified, the input data keyed by all data-entry operators on a disk is transferred to magnetic tape for input to the computer.

The key-to-diskette machine records input data on small, flexible recordlike disks called *diskettes* or *floppy disks.*

Another type of direct-data-entry device, the key-to-diskette machine, is being widely used. The key-to-diskette machine, like the earlier direct-data-entry devices, operates independently of other equipment. It has a keyboard and a CRT display unit similar to the earlier machines, but the input data is recorded on small, flexible recordlike disks called **diskettes,** or **floppy disks.** On one side of a diskette it is possible to record over 250,000 characters, the equivalent of more than 3,000 80-column punched cards. Diskettes carry much more data than tape cartridges and cassettes, which hold 28,000 and 200,000 characters, respectively. Some equipment permits the recording of data at even higher densities and on both sides of the diskette. Diskettes can be used for data input directly in processing by smaller computers. For processing by larger computers, data recorded on diskettes is transferred to magnetic tape for input.

DISKETTE STORAGE
Courtesy IBM Corporation

The reason for the popularity of the direct-data-entry devices just described is the belief that they are much more efficient than card-punch machines. Their advantages over card-punch machines include the following.

1. They enable the data-entry clerk to move from record to record without waiting for the cards to drop and be registered (properly placed for punching).
2. They eliminate the need for loading the hopper with blank cards and for removing punched cards from the stacker.
3. They do not limit the user to a specified record length (for example, 80 characters).
4. They can duplicate and skip at much faster speeds.
5. They permit recording on magnetic tape for input to the computer.
6. They reduce operator fatigue and irritability because they run more quietly than card-punch machines.

Scanning Devices. A third way of accomplishing the data-entry task is to have input data printed, typed, or marked so it can be read by a scanning machine and recorded in machine-readable form. A variety of machines are designed to accomplish this function. All such machines can scan the input data and record it in machine-readable form, usually on magnetic tape. Data entry by machine scanning is done in two ways—by optical reading and by magnetic-ink scanning.

Optical character readers (OCR) can scan documents and read typed, computer-printed, or hand-posted data.

The most widely used data-entry scanning machines are called *optical scanners,* or **optical character readers (OCR).** These are more flexible than magnetic-scanning machines because they can scan documents and read numerals or letters that are typed, computer-printed, or even hand-posted. There are also optical readers (optical mark readers and optical bar readers). These machines scan and interpret combinations of marks and bar codes that represent input data. The scanned data is usually converted to magnetic tape or punched cards, though it may also be read directly into a computer. Some optical scanners can read only marks, numerals, or characters printed in a special typeface. Other optical scanners can read *any* typed or printed material. Optical scanners work at high speeds. They can scan up to 2,000 paper or card documents a minute.

Optical scanning is based on the use of a bright light source with a lens system to detect, in electrical impulses, the pattern of a printed character. This pattern is matched against a master character pattern to identify the numeral or letter.

Typically, data entry by optical scanning starts with a data-entry clerk typing the input data in a preselected typeface. The input data may be recorded on cards or on sheets of paper. The cards or sheets of paper are placed in a scanner. The scanner reads the typed data and records it on magnetic tape for later processing.

Optical scanners are also used for reading data on a variety of source documents, including gasoline credit cards. For a credit sale, the station attendant imprints the customer's name, address, and account number from a credit card onto a multiple-copy charge form. Then the attendant either hand-posts or machine-records the date and the amount of the sale. The attendant gives one copy of the charge form to the customer and forwards the other copies to a data processing center. If necessary, the sales amount is keyed or card-punched. The document is read by a scanner, and the data is recorded on tape for computer entry. Some scanning equipment operates on-line so that data can be entered directly into the computer without the additional step of recording the data on tape.

A more recent application of optical scanning is in supermarkets. A supermarket cashier scans product information by using a hand-held wand that is attached to an optical scanner or by passing the product over the optical scanner itself. In either method, the optical scanner reads a Universal Product Code (UPC). This code is made up of a series of vertical bars printed on the packaged goods. The customer tape that is produced at the end of the transaction varies with the computer system. The systems that are most likely to win customer approval are those that produce a tape listing each product purchased with its price. This system, in which data is entered into the computer system at the actual point, or location, of the sale, is an example of the use of *point-of-sale* data-entry equipment.

UNIVERSAL PRODUCT CODE

OPTICAL SCANNING. Optical scanners read numbers printed in a special type with regular ink. This scanner reads product data printed on packaged goods. The Universal Product Code is used to record this data. Courtesy Hobart Corporation

Magnetic ink character readers (MICR) read source documents on which data has been recorded with a special magnetic ink.

Magnetic-ink scanning was developed to help banks process the more than 30 billion checks that are written each year. Machines called **magnetic ink character readers (MICR)** read source documents on which data has been recorded with a special magnetic ink (iron oxide). A special typeface designed for documents to be processed by MICR machines has been adopted by the American Bankers Association (ABA) as a national standard for use by banks throughout the United States. Banks issue sets of blank checks printed with the customer's account number and the bank branch number in the lower left part. When the recipient of a check presents it for payment, a data-entry clerk imprints the amount of the check in magnetic ink. Then an MICR machine scans the check along with the many other checks being processed. This machine records the data on a magnetic tape or disk for computer input. Typical information includes the bank branch, account number, and amount.

In the past, bank employees sorted the checks themselves so that they could be returned to customers along with statements of their accounts. This tremendous sorting job can now be done by machines at the same time the input data is being recorded on magnetic tape.

DOCUMENT SORTER. This machine is sorting bank checks and recording data about each check at the same time. Courtesy Burroughs Corporation

CHECK YOURSELF

Match each term with the phrase that best defines it.

1. Off-line equipment
2. Data-entry operator
3. CRT device
4. Point-of-sale equipment
5. Direct data entry
6. Keypunch
7. Optical scanner
8. Magnetic ink character reader
9. Input device
10. Computer system

a. The employee responsible for converting data into machine-readable form.
b. Recording of input data on magnetic disks, tapes, or diskettes.
c. Equipment not linked directly to a computer system.
d. Input device to record data at the time of a sale.
e. Data-entry device with a TV-like screen.
f. Key-to-diskette device.
g. A type of off-line data-entry device.
h. Human-readable data.
i. A machine used for entering data on bank checks.
j. A device that can read typed data and convert it into machine-readable copy.
k. A group of machines physically attached to perform data processing operations.
l. The employee responsible for monitoring the operation of a computer.

On-Line Data Entry

By definition, a computer system is made up of electronic devices that are linked together. Therefore, with the exception of some types of scanning machines, the data-entry machines just described are not actually considered part of computer system hardware.

A computer on-line input device is linked physically to a computer processing unit. The device reads input data and transfers it for processing or storage within the computer system. The three types of computer input devices now most commonly used are on-line terminals, punched-card input devices, and magnetic-tape input devices. (Punched-tape input devices, which were frequently used with early computers, are now rarely used in business computer processing.)

The three major types of computer input devices are punched-card input devices, magnetic-tape input devices, and terminals.

On-Line Terminals. The machines used in the three data-entry methods previously described (keypunches; key-to-disk, key-to-tape, or key-to-diskette devices; and scanning machines) are usually completely independent of the computer. Since these devices are not physically attached to the computer, they are said to be off-line.

With each of the three off-line methods, input data is usually recorded in machine-readable form on a punched card or magnetic disk or tape for later entry into a computer. In contrast, data entry by terminal permits on-line input data entry directly into the storage or processing unit of a computer. A **terminal** is a keyboard device that is connected to a computer system for the input (and usually output) of data. On-line terminals are connected directly to the computer either by cable or by ordinary telephone lines or a special data communications network.

A terminal is a keyboard device that is connected to a computer system for the input of data.

ON-LINE DATA PROCESSING. An on-line terminal allows for the processing of transactions as they occur. This ticket agent is processing airline reservations. Ticket agents all across the country share processing time on a single mainframe computer. Sepp Seitz/Woodfin Camp & Associates

A data-entry clerk operating a terminal reads the data from a source document. On a keyboard that is typically similar to that of a card punch, the data-entry clerk keys the data for entry into the computer. Many on-line terminals are also equipped with visual display or CRT screens similar to those described for key-to-disk devices. The screens allow an operator to check the data as it is being keyed. Other on-line terminals provide only a typed copy of the data entered into the computer. The touch-tone telephone may also be adapted for use to transmit numeric input data to a computer.

The terminals used for data entry may be located in the same office building as the computer, in a building in the same city, or in a building thousands of miles away. For example, an airline reservations clerk in a ticket office on the West Coast can enter data about passenger reservations on a terminal keyboard. Almost instantaneously, this data is read into a computer on the East Coast. The use of terminals for data entry in computer processing is an example of computer **time-sharing.** This term is used because the terminal operators are sharing the computer processing time.

Intelligent terminals perform data editing and similar processing operations independently of the computer's central processing unit.

A special type of terminal called an **intelligent terminal** has a small memory and processing unit in addition to the keyboard and the display unit typical of other terminals. This terminal is intelligent because it can perform data editing and similar processing operations independently of the computer's central processing unit, to which it is connected.

It is the direct connection to the computer that makes all terminals different from the other data-entry devices described earlier. One disadvantage of on-line terminals is that all the keyboard devices sharing a particular computer come to a stop whenever there is a computer failure. Also, the operation of on-line terminals is generally more expensive than that of the off-line data-entry devices.

Punched-card input devices use a photoelectric cell to read data recorded as punched holes in cards.

Punched-Card On-Line Input Devices. Punched-card on-line input devices read data recorded as punched holes in 80- or 96-column cards. Using a photoelectric cell to sense the punched holes, a punched-card input device, known as a *card reader,* can transfer all or any part of the data to the computer's storage or central processing unit. The very early computers were equipped only with punched-card input devices. Until the late 1960s, smaller computers could accept data only in punched-card or punched paper-tape form.

Punched-card on-line input devices are attached by cable to the computer's central processing unit. These devices vary in the speed at which they can read punched holes; they have speeds ranging from 300 cards a minute to 2,000 cards a minute. A typical reading speed is 600 cards of 80-column information a minute. This means that 48,000 characters are read each minute (600 × 80 = 48,000). Several smaller computers are equipped with card input devices to read 96-column cards. These cards can be read at a speed of 300 to 600 cards a minute.

Magnetic-Tape Devices. A common input device on modern business computers is the **magnetic-tape drive,** also called a *magnetic-tape input/output device.* This device reads input data recorded on reels of magnetic tape and transfers the data to the processing or storage units. The magnetic-tape input unit operates in the same manner as a home tape recorder. This means that data can be read off the tape for processing, and new data can be written onto the tape. Thus, a magnetic-tape device serves as both an input and output device. The data can be recorded

MAGNETIC-TAPE DEVICES. Magnetic tape drives read the magnetized spots on magnetic tapes and translate them into electronic impulses. The systems analyst and the operator review computer output as programs are being run. Courtesy American Management Associations

at different densities of characters for each inch depending on the computer and the magnetic tape being used.

In business data processing, magnetic-tape units have replaced many punched-card and punched-tape input devices. There are several advantages of magnetic tape over punched cards and paper tape.

Some advantages of magnetic tape are that it is reusable, can be read at high speeds, and can store large amounts of data in a small area.

1. It is reusable.
2. It can be read at much higher speeds.
3. It can store significantly larger amounts of data in a smaller area.

The typical magnetic-tape unit reads about 60,000 characters a second. More powerful units can read up to 350,000 characters a second. Usually two or more tape-drive devices are attached to each computer processing unit.

CHECK YOURSELF

Supply the missing words.

1. A keyboard input device with a memory and processing unit is called a(n) ___?___ ___?___.
2. A(n) ___?___ ___?___ device reads data on punched cards for input into a computer.
3. A magnetic-tape unit is an example of a computer ___?___ device.
4. An on-line terminal is used to enter data into a computer ___?___ or processing unit.
5. The use of many on-line terminals simultaneously is an example of computer ___?___ ___?___.

Central Processing and Storage Hardware

An important unit of a computer system is the central processing unit (CPU). The central processing unit, often called the **mainframe,** includes a control unit and an arithmetic/logic unit. In today's computers, storage units are no longer included as part of the central processing unit. This is in contrast with early computers, when storage was physically part of the mainframe.

Central Processing Unit

The control unit interprets the instructions in a computer program.

Control Unit. The *control unit* of the central processor interprets the instructions in a computer program that has been read on an input device. It calls on the input mechanisms, the storage unit, the arithmetic/logic unit, and the output mechanisms as needed to have the instructions carried out.

The control unit acts as the traffic director of computer operations. It contains the electric circuitry and registers necessary for supervising the execution of each instruction in the computer program in proper sequence. Another part of the control unit is the **console,** which enables the computer operator to communicate with the central processing unit. A console often includes a panel board of switches and push buttons that start, stop, and otherwise control the operation of the computer. Flashing lights on the console indicate the operation of each part of the computer.

On medium- or large-sized computers, consoles are usually separate units equipped with an electric typewriter and one or more visual display terminals. The console can be used by the computer operator to enter small amounts of input data, such as the date, an accounting code, or a processing option. The computer can also issue messages to the operator on the console typewriter or visual display terminal. Such messages tell the operator about computer-detected errors that may interfere with executing the instructions on the computer program. Such errors can include the operator's failure to make available to the computer the input and output devices needed for that program. Printing consoles can provide valuable printed records that serve as a system log.

An important part of the central processing unit is the arithmetic/logic unit. It enables the computer to compute.

Arithmetic/Logic Unit. The arithmetic/logic unit is one of the important parts of the computer. It enables the computer to calculate—that is, actually perform the arithmetic operations of addition, subtraction, multiplication, and division and the logical operations of comparing two or more numbers, letters, or special characters. A typical comparison might be to look at two numbers and identify one as the lesser or the greater of the two. Arithmetic/logic units vary mainly in the speed at which they carry out the arithmetic or logic operations specified in a computer program.

Storage

Without an internal storage or memory device, a computer could not accept a program of instructions and then perform the operations specified. There are many different types of computer storage units, but in all such units data is stored in binary coded form. You can think of the storage unit as an arrangement of storage areas that can be identified by numbers called addresses. To indicate where data is stored, the programmer uses a storage address, just as you use a street address to indicate where you live. Storage units are distinguished first by the function that they

A primary storage unit houses data that is used often and that must be retrieved quickly.

perform. **Primary storage,** *main storage,* and *internal storage* are interchangeable words used to describe a memory unit housing data that is used often and that must be retrieved quickly. For example, input data to be processed, program instructions required for processing, and in-process calculations are stored in primary memory.

Because a primary storage unit is an expensive part of the modern computer, manufacturers have developed other storage devices to supplement the primary storage capacity of computers. These storage devices are called **secondary** (or *auxiliary* or *external*) **storage** devices. The purpose of secondary memory units is to store data that is used less frequently, that does not need to be retrieved immediately, and that, therefore, can be kept outside primary storage. When the data in secondary storage is needed, it must be moved to primary storage.

Programming instructions are read from magnetic tape, disks, or punched cards into the primary storage unit. The computer retrieves one or more instructions at a time from storage, performs the operations called for, and returns the instructions to the storage unit so that they are available when needed again. Besides holding the instructions, the computer storage unit must also hold data processed by the machine. In a payroll application, for example, the computer stores the computations for a given employee so that all the data for one paycheck can be printed at one time.

Some data is stored in the computer for a long period of time because the computer needs this data again and again. For example, think of the multiplication tables stored in your mind for frequent reference. Most data in the computer, however, is erased after it has been used. Think of your throwing away the scratch paper used in solving a difficult math problem.

Computer storage devices vary in their capacity to hold numerals and letters. Small storage devices can hold only several thousand characters. Very large storage devices can hold billions of characters.

Storage devices also vary in the length of time needed to retrieve data from storage, that is, to locate the data required and transfer it out of storage. The length of time it takes a computer to store data or to retrieve data from storage is called **access time.** Some computer storage units provide an access time so short that it is measured in microseconds (millionths of a second). The four most common devices now used for storing data in computers are semiconductors, magnetic cores, magnetic disks and diskettes, and mass storage systems. Magnetic drums that were formerly used as large secondary storage units are no longer widely used.

Four common devices for storing data in computers are semiconductors, magnetic cores, magnetic disks and diskettes, and mass storage systems.

Semiconductors. Semiconductors are used for primary storage in the most recent models of computers. They are more compact than other storage devices, and they permit faster access to data in storage at a lower cost. Semiconductor memories consist of small chips of silicon on which memory circuits and support circuits are etched. Current can be conducted or not conducted through these circuits to represent data that is coded in binary form.

Semiconductors, made of small chips of silicon, are more compact and permit faster access to data than other storage devices.

Magnetic Cores. Slower access time is provided by less expensive magnetic cores, although access time is still relatively fast. Until the development of semiconductors, *magnetic cores* were the most common primary storage device. These cores consist of a large number of tiny doughnut-shaped rings made of iron. Wires are woven through each core. Current passing through these wires magnetizes the cores in either of two directions. One direction is said to have a value of 0; and the opposite direction, a value of 1. These two values are called *binary digits,* or *bits.* The computer uses groups of bits to identify numbers or alphabetic characters in storage.

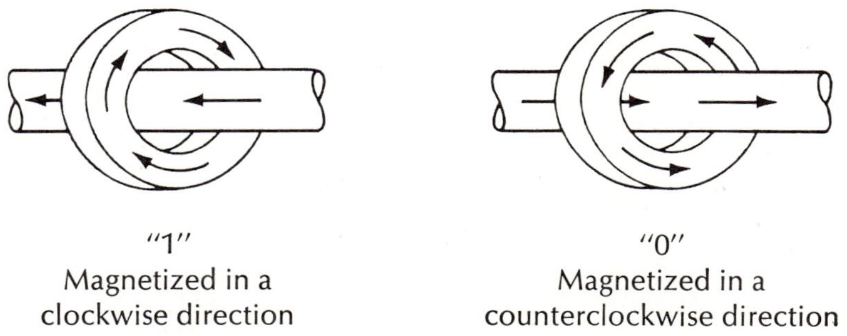

CORE STORAGE. Magnetic cores are given a value of "0" or "1" according to the position in which they are magnetized. The two values are called binary digits, or bits.

Magnetic cores, made of tiny rings of iron, are usually used to store programming instructions and to hold data items that are to be processed immediately.

Because of its fast retrieval time, magnetic-core storage usually is used to store programming instructions and to hold data items that are to be processed immediately.

Magnetic Disks and Diskettes. Thin metal disks, coated on each side so that data can be recorded in the form of magnetized spots, are called **magnetic disks.** They are generally used as secondary storage devices. The disks are mounted in a group on a vertical shaft so that they look like a jukebox full of records. As the disks spin around like records, data can be stored on them or retrieved from them. For ease of handling, disks are often

Data is recorded on magnetic disks as small magnetized spots on round tracks.

DISK STORAGE. Magnetic disks are used as secondary storage devices. A typical magnetic-disk pack can hold nearly eight million characters of data. Courtesy NCR Corporation

grouped in removable packs; each pack has six or more separate disks.

On each side of a disk are hundreds of separate round tracks on which data is recorded in the form of very small magnetized spots. The number of tracks and the density of data recording on disks vary, but a typical disk pack can hold nearly eight million characters of data. Data can be stored on or retrieved from disks at speeds ranging up to 500,000 characters a second.

Diskettes (or floppy disks) are smaller and less expensive than the typical disk storage units. For these reasons, they are used for small computer systems.

Mass Storage Memories. In business data processing involving large volumes of file data, access to billions of characters of stored data may be needed. For example, an insurance company with five million customers may require a 2,000-character record for each customer or a total of 10 billion characters of data to be stored. Mass storage units combining both magnetic-tape and magnetic-disk devices are now available with capacities to store hundreds of billions of characters.

Magnetic-Bubble Memories. Magnetic-bubble memories (MBM) are a new type of secondary storage device. They

MASS STORAGE. Mass-storage devices are capable of storing hundreds of billions of characters. Courtesy IBM Corporation

BUBBLE MEMORY. Bubbles stand for ones, and a lack of bubbles stand for zeros. Courtesy A.T.&T. Company

are made up of tiny, cylindrical, magnetic bubbles, and they are housed in a thin, crystallike magnetic film. Bubble memories can be densely packed with data.

Bubble memories represent just one of many new developments designed to provide computer memories at larger capacities, in smaller sizes, and at less expense. A magnetic bubble is a tiny magnetic area less than 1/10,000 inch (or 1/4,081 centimeter) in diameter; it is contained in a thin layer of crystal. About five million bubbles have been stored on a crystal chip about the size of a dime.

The presence or absence of bubbles represents bits of information. Bubbles stand for ones. A lack of bubbles means zeros. Bubbles can be moved about at high speeds to perform storage and logic functions.

Because the bubbles hold their contents even when power is shut off, users can enter data at a terminal during the day and transmit the data at night. The advantage is that data communication rates are substantially lower at night. Although savings can result from such use, this type of data storage is still not competitive in price with other forms of storage.

CHECK YOURSELF

Match each term with the word or phrase that best defines it.

1. Card reader
2. Magnetic core
3. Primary storage
4. Magnetic disks
5. Access time
6. Semiconductors
7. Floppy disks
8. Bit
9. Secondary storage
10. Computer system

a. Main memory.
b. The length of time it takes a computer to locate data and retrieve it from storage.
c. Computer input device.
d. A value of 0 or 1.
e. Small chips of silicon containing memory circuits and support circuits.
f. Storage used to hold data that is not used frequently.
g. A tiny ring of iron that can be magnetized in either of two directions.
h. Diskettes.
i. Thin, round metal devices on which data can be stored in the form of magnetized spots.
j. An on-line terminal used for real-time processing.
k. Interconnected input, central processing, memory, and output devices.

Output Hardware

The mechanisms the computer uses to report the results of its processing are known as *output devices* when they are physically connected to the computer. The most popular output device is the printer, which reports processing results in printed form on paper or card documents in a range of printing speeds. Output devices also include magnetic-tape and magnetic-disk units, card punches, terminals, computer-output microfilm devices, and voice-response systems. Paper-tape output devices are no longer commonly used in business data processing.

Printers

A widely used output device is the *printer,* the computer mechanism for printing hard copy on business reports or documents. Printers used with computers generally print a complete line at one time. Such printers are usually classified as either "impact" or "nonimpact."

Impact printers produce print by the striking of a metal character against an inked ribbon. Nonimpact printers print with a jet stream of ink.

An *impact printer* produces printed results by the striking, or impact, of a metal character against an inked ribbon. The impact of the ribbon on paper results in the printing of characters on the paper. A newer, ribbonless printer, called a *nonimpact printer* or *page-printing system,* can produce business forms and reports in a variety of typefaces. The nonimpact printers use standard business letter-sized paper instead of the oversize paper used by the impact printers. Nonimpact printers print with a jet stream of ink. They are generally faster and quieter than impact printers are. Some nonimpact printers produce copy by a thermal process, using specially treated paper.

PRINTERS. Printers provide hard-copy output of business documents and reports. Instructions about the form of the output are included in the program. Courtesy IBM Corporation

Printing speeds vary with the printer. Depending on the model, impact printers generally produce from 300 to 2,000 lines a minute. A nonimpact printer can produce up to 20,000 lines a minute. A printed line is usually 120 characters long but can vary from 80 characters to as many as 160 characters. The number of characters printed out for each line is specified in the computer program that is being executed. This is true whether the printing takes place on-line (as data is manipulated by the central processing unit) or off-line. With large volumes of data, off-line printing, done on a printer not attached to a computer, is usually less expensive than on-line printing because there is no charge for computer time with off-line printing.

The computer programmer includes instructions in the computer program that tell the printer in what form data is to be printed. A carriage-control system in the printer makes different formats possible. This system assures the user the flexibility needed in positioning data on the various types of continuous forms used in business. Such a system, which is one of the features of the new printers, eliminates the need for a carriage-control tape.

Magnetic-Tape and Magnetic-Disk Units

Magnetic-tape units are always made to serve as both input devices and output devices. The computer can write data out on tape at the same speed at which it reads data from tape. As new information is recorded on tape, old information on the tape is destroyed. There are many, many models of magnetic-tape units, which vary in the density of data recording and in the speed of operation. A magnetic-disk unit may also be considered an output device when results of computer processing are stored on the disk for future use.

Card Punches

The output device for producing punched cards from the results of computer data processing is called a *card punch*. It can either be combined with a punched-card reader or be a separate device. Card punches work much more slowly than card readers. One of the newest combined models—a card read/punch—is an input/output device that can both read data on punched cards into the computer and punch into cards the results of computer processing. A card read/punch reads cards at speeds of over 1,000 cards a minute and punches cards at speeds up to 300 cards a minute. Both combined models and separate card readers and card punches have input hoppers and output stackers.

Terminals

There are two types of terminals used as computer output devices. One type of output terminal has a keyboard like that of a typewriter. It records output from computer processing in printed form on paper. Such a terminal is similar in appearance and in operation to a teletype machine, which also automatically types one character at a time as received. Because the printing time is much slower than that of a printer, such a terminal is used only for printing small amounts of output data. It usually also serves as an input device to the computer.

The second type of terminal provides for a visual display of computer processing results. This CRT type of terminal has a small

The CRT type of terminal has a small screen for the display of computer processing results.

screen on which data can be displayed as needed. For example, the current amount of inventory in stock may be available for display on a visual display screen. Also, some terminals are designed to display data in different colors in graphic form, such as ten-year financial data in chart form. A visual display terminal may serve both as an input device to enter data directly into the computer and as an output device to receive the results of the preceding operations.

Computer-assisted instruction (CAI) gives students aid in learning school lessons.

Input-output terminals are popular in schools, where they are used for a variety of applications. One application is **computer-assisted instruction (CAI).** A student is aided in a lesson or unit of instruction by the display or printing of instructional material and tests on terminals. Students work at terminals chiefly in business, technical, and language areas, although computer-assisted instruction can be used for any subject area.

Another popular educational application of the terminal is for career guidance. The Computerized Vocational Information System (CVIS) provides information on more than 400 types of careers. The student enters his or her name or student number at the terminal. The computer checks the CVIS records to determine whether that student has ever used CVIS. If not, the terminal prints out a statement about the purpose of CVIS. Next, the terminal prints out several questions for the student and then provides career information that is consistent with the student's responses. If the student's career interests are unclear or if they are inconsistent with the achievement indicated by the student's records, the terminal prints a message suggesting that the student talk with a school counselor for additional career guidance.

Computer-Output Microfilm Devices

COM converts data on magnetic tape into data on a microfilm cassette or microfiche.

Microfilm records can be produced by a special computer output device. The device—often called COM, for *computer-output microfilm*—converts data on magnetic tape into data on a microfilm cassette or microfiche. COM can record 10,000 lines a minute on microfilm. Another advantage of COM is that it helps reduce record storage space; a small microfilm cassette can contain photos of 2,400 pages of hard copy. COM is suited particularly to the handling of a large number of sequential records. Such records can then be referred to by desk-top microfilm readers. Some COM devices operate on-line, while others operate off-line.

Voice-Response Devices

Computers now have a limited capacity to provide output in the form of a human voice. A computer *voice-response device* con-

A voice-response device converts data received from computer processing into a spoken message.

verts data received from computer processing into a spoken output message. Voice-response units are used, for example, in the banking industry. A bank teller keyboards an inquiry at a computer terminal and hears as a response the account number and account balance of a particular customer. The voice-response unit constructs its message from a library of prerecorded numbers, words, and phrases. The telephone company also uses computer voice-response systems to tell callers about changes in telephone numbers.

CHECK YOURSELF

Match each term with the phrase that best defines it.

1. COM
2. Impact printer
3. Voice-response device
4. Page-printing system
5. Card punch

a. A type of nonimpact printer used for output of business forms.
b. A device to read punched cards.
c. A computer-output microfilm device.
d. A device to record output on punched cards.
e. A printer that operates by the striking of metal characters against an inked ribbon.
f. A type of output device used by the telephone company to redirect wrong-number dialing.

Modern Computer Hardware

Businesses now have their choice of a tremendous selection of computer systems. In addition to a central processing unit, all computer systems have at least one input, storage, and output device. Most computer systems have more than one of each of these devices.

Because a computer system can be made up of a variety of hardware units for input, storage, and output, a business can select the particular combination of devices that can perform its work most effectively. The selected devices linked together with a central processor become its computer system. This choosing and linking together of computer devices is similar to the process of selecting a record turntable or tape deck and connecting it with stereo speakers.

Minicomputers and Microcomputers

A minicomputer is smaller and less expensive than medium- and large-sized computers.

In the 1960s a company named Digital Equipment Corporation introduced a computer system that was much less expensive than the small computers then made by IBM and other manufacturers. Because of their low cost, the new computers were introduced as **minicomputers.** The disadvantage of minicomputers when they were introduced was that they could be equipped only with input devices to read either data or computer instructions recorded on punched cards. Also, the results of the processing operations were recorded mostly as output on punched cards. Only a limited amount of printing could be accomplished through a computer-controlled typewriter operating as an output terminal device. This is no longer true.

Today's minicomputers use integrated circuits, may weigh less than 50 pounds, and require no special surroundings. In addition to the central processing unit, a typical minicomputer system may have a CRT terminal unit, a combination card reader and card punch, a disk or diskette storage unit, and a line printer for hard-copy output. Examples of powerful minicomputers are the IBM System 34 and System 38 computers, which were introduced in 1978 as replacements for the older, widely used IBM System 3 computers.

MINICOMPUTERS. Minicomputers are small computer systems that perform data processing for a wide range of applications. Courtesy Burroughs Corporation

Besides IBM, other manufacturers of larger computers (Burroughs, Honeywell, NCR, and Sperry Rand) also make minicomputers. There are many other manufacturers of minicomputers, some of which have specialized in smaller computers. Such manufacturers include Data General, Hewlett-Packard, Wang, and the Digital Equipment Corporation (DEC). DEC manufactures the widely used machines known as the DEC PDP-8 and PDP-11.

In the 1970s the development of large-scale integrated (LSI) circuitry for computers made it possible for the first time to reduce in size a central processing unit so that it would fit on a single silicon chip only 1/10 inch (2.5 millimeters) square. Because of its tiny size and low cost, the reduced CPU has been called a **microprocessor.** A microprocessor is an arithmetic/logic unit combined with circuits. It contains over 50,000 transistors and can perform more than 100,000 operations a second.

A microcomputer is a microprocessor linked to simple input, storage, and output units.

Microcomputer is the name given to a very small, low-cost computer system with a microprocessor linked to simple input, storage, and output units. Manufacturers of microcomputers include IBM, Apple, Radio Shack, Commodore, and Atari. These small computers are often called *small business* or *personal computers.* You will learn more about them in Chapter 13.

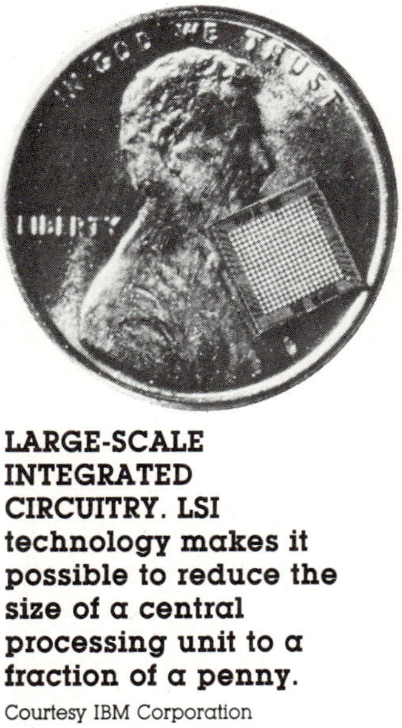

LARGE-SCALE INTEGRATED CIRCUITRY. LSI technology makes it possible to reduce the size of a central processing unit to a fraction of a penny.
Courtesy IBM Corporation

At the time of this writing, microcomputers could not perform effectively the large volume of input and other operations that typify business data processing. Instead, these computers, as well as the smaller-model minicomputers, have typically been used as *special-purpose* computers, depending on the software available. They are often designed to perform a single data processing task such as controlling the changing of a traffic light. Depending on the skill of the user or the software available, such single-purpose hardware may also be used to process federal income taxes or balance a checkbook. Microcomputers are used mostly in small, individually owned businesses. They are also becoming more and more popular in the home as a greater choice of input/output devices and software become available.

You are probably wondering how to distinguish between a minicomputer and a microcomputer. Unfortunately, there is no universally accepted definition for minicomputer. When the first minis were produced, they were smaller, less expensive processors than the medium- to large-sized computers available before that. Today, both minicomputers and microcomputers are considered small computers. In general, you can assume that a microcomputer is both smaller and less expensive than a minicomputer, but you may find exceptions to this rule.

One disadvantage of both minicomputers and microcomputers is that the computer manufacturers have provided far less software for these machines than for larger computers. Like most

MICROCOMPUTER. A microcomputer is a small, low cost computer system with a CPU microprocessor linked to simple input, storage, and output units. Courtesy Radio Shack A Division of Tandy Corporation

microcomputers, many of the smaller minicomputers are used only for a single business application, such as billing. Such single-purpose usage requires simpler programming, which is sometimes done by the computer manufacturer or by a company specializing in software services. More and more such companies are producing software for the small-computer user.

Medium-Sized and Large-Sized Computers

Medium- to large-sized computers have faster arithmetic and processing units, as well as larger storage units.

IBM and other manufacturers produce computers that are said to be more powerful than minicomputers. Such machines may be categorized as **medium-sized or large-sized computers,** depending on their cost. But the basic difference between these machines and the smaller ones is that they have much faster arithmetic and processing units. They also have the capacity to handle at high speed a larger number and a wider variety of input/output devices, and they have much larger primary and secondary storage units. For these reasons, data can be read in at higher speeds, business reports can be produced in a wider variety of formats at higher speeds, stored programs and data can be more efficiently retrieved, and throughput is faster.

Throughput is the cost efficiency of a computer system for a particular application.

Throughput is the cost efficiency of a computer system in handling a particular application that must be performed regularly. Throughput is a major factor in the selection of a computer system.

A computer system such as the IBM System 4300 Series, introduced in 1979, consists of several computer models of varying processing capacities. It is said to be a family of computers providing an easy way to expand computer capacity by upward growth in processing power. In addition, computer programs written for the older IBM System 370 machines can be used on the newer IBM 4300 Series of machines. This newer series can perform at one-fifth the cost the same amount of work as an equivalent System 370 computer. Thus it is also a simple task for System 370 users to transfer their data processing operations from an older family of computers to a newer, more powerful family. The movement from one computer model to another of the same manufacturer is often called *upward compatibility* because of the ease with which this transition can be handled.

Typically, medium- and large-sized computers have a central processor with a console typewriter for communication between the operator and the machine. CRT terminals may be used for on-line data entry, but large input volumes are handled by multiple-tape input-output units and by the storage of active file data and program libraries on magnetic disks. For the reporting of hard-copy output, high-speed line printers may be used on medium-sized computer systems and page printers on the larger systems. Typically, the larger the computer system, the larger its

MEDIUM AND LARGE-SIZED COMPUTERS. These computers are more powerful than minicomputers. They have much faster arithmetic and processing units. Courtesy Burroughs Corporation

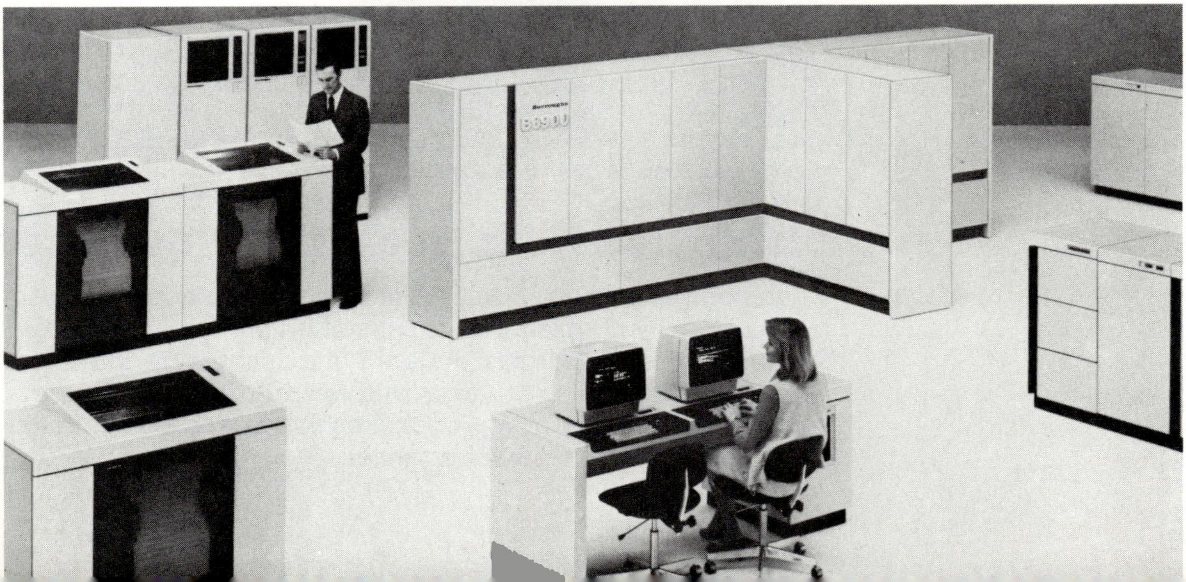

primary and secondary storage capacities and the faster its access and operating speeds. One type of disk storage unit used on larger computer systems holds 561 million characters; the storage unit is about the size of an electric typewriter.

The Burroughs 900 Series of computers and the Sperry UNIVAC 1100 Series of machines offer computer systems in the medium- to large-size range. NCR and Honeywell are two other well-known manufacturers. Control Data Corporation is known for its very large (super) computers, one of which is called the CDC Star-100. This computer can perform almost 100 million operations a second. A new family of large computers called the 3081 series was introduced by IBM in 1980.

THREE MAIN FEATURES TO CONSIDER IN CHOOSING A COMPUTER SYSTEM.

1. **Throughput**
2. **Expandability**
3. **Upward compatibility**

When considering which computer system to install, businesses typically think about their long-term processing needs as well as the throughput, expandability, and capabilities of the computer systems that are available for purchase or leasing. Then businesses consider other criteria such as initial purchase cost or annual rental costs, programming languages, and the availability of appropriate manufacturer-developed software. Each business must identify its own current data processing needs, project its long-range needs, and select the computer or other data processing system that most efficiently processes its data in relation to the estimated cost of alternative systems.

Approximate Cost of Each Instruction Executed Each Second*

YEAR	COST	YEAR	COST
1959	$20.00	1971	$2.25
1961	14.00	1973	2.00
1963	12.00	1975	1.75
1965	3.75	1977	0.80
1967	3.25	1979	0.33
1969	3.25		

*Adapted from *Fortune*, May 19, 1980, page 108.

Distributed Data Processing Hardware

When computers were first used in business, the computer and related equipment typically were centralized in one location. There was a good reason for this; the early machines were large, expensive, and difficult to program and operate. It was more effective to have a single group of experts within each corporation responsible for the computer activities.

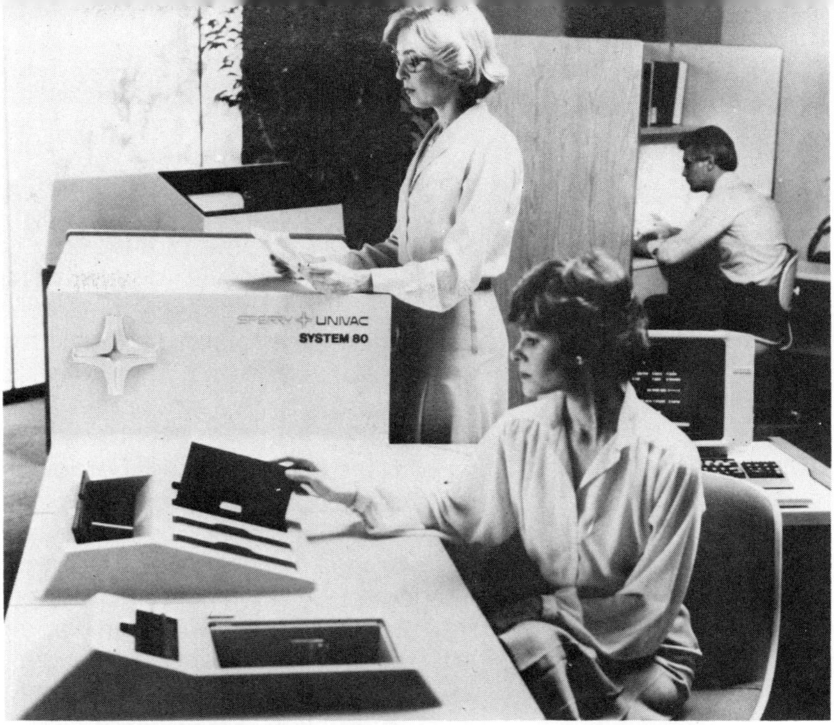

DISTRIBUTED DATA PROCESSING. In distributed data processing, intelligent terminals or minicomputers are located in separate physical sites but are connected by communications networks to a large, centrally located computer. Courtesy Sperry Univac

The availability of the less expensive minicomputer systems permitted those departments of a company having large computing requirements to use some decentralized computing equipment. The disadvantage of decentralized computer systems is that the decentralized equipment may not be needed 100 percent of the time by a single department and is therefore left idle.

An alternative to wholly centralized or decentralized computing is called distributed data processing. In **distributed data processing** intelligent terminals or minicomputers are placed in physically separated sites but are connected by communication networks to a large computer at a central site. The advantage of distributed data processing is that specialized data can be processed at a remote site in a company with a minimum of computer hardware. The results of the remote processing can then be sent electronically to the larger central computer for more complex processing. The IBM 8100 computer, introduced in 1978, is designed specifically for a distributed processing system.

Data Communication Equipment

The rapid growth in the use of computers for processing business data has resulted in the development of new data communication equipment and transmission facilities. As you read earlier, the data-entry function is often performed at a physical location far from a computer. This is because a modern corporation may have widely scattered plants and offices and may have a distributed computer processing system. Thus the company needs ways to send input data from remote areas to its computer center. It also needs ways to transmit back the results.

Data communication systems originated with the invention of the telegraph system by Samuel Morse in 1844. As only ten characters a second could be transmitted by telegraph, newer communication systems had to be developed to keep pace with the high-speed computer processing systems.

In the 1950s and 1960s it was possible only to communicate data from one teletype machine to another. Data to be communicated by teletypewriter was punched in coded form on a strip of paper tape. It was then communicated from a paper-tape transmitter in one place to a paper-tape receiver in another. It later became possible to communicate data from a punched-card transmitter in one place to a punched-card receiver in a second location. Now equipment is available for the high-speed communication of data between magnetic-tape units or directly between computers. Data recorded on magnetic tape at one location can be communicated to magnetic tape at another location faster than the same data can be transmitted by punched-card or punched-tape equipment. Data exchanges made between two computers in different places are also done at very fast speeds. With the use of telephone circuits, microwave networks, or satellite transmission, data can be transmitted at more than 100,000 characters a second. Transmitting data at these faster rates is, however, more expensive. Because telephone circuits were first used for the high-speed communication of data, all these methods are known as **telecommunications.**

There is a wide variety of communications terminal equipment available to businesses that need to communicate data. These include input communications terminals and receiving communications terminals, as well as combination input-output terminals. The input terminals provide alternatives to entering data by manual keying or by reading data recorded on punched tape, punched cards, or magnetic tape for transmission over a communications line. Special communications equipment is needed to allow the exchange of data between two computer systems over a communications line. Data can be received from a communications line by a terminal, which may record the data in printed form or in the form of punched tape, punched cards, or magnetic tape. Newly developed minicomputers often serve as multipurpose communications input-output terminals for larger computers.

Other Computer Equipment

In addition to the data-entry and data-output devices that may operate independently of the computer processing unit, there are other types of electronic equipment used by computer departments. This equipment is designed to perform only one or a few functions off-line. Some of these functions include the conversion of punched-card or punched-tape data into magnetic-tape data and the reverse operation.

Often the data recorded in punched cards or punched tape is needed for magnetic-tape computer processing. Like the devices that convert punched-card data into punched-tape data, there are electronic devices that convert punched-card or punched-tape data into magnetic-tape data. These devices reproduce on magnetic tape all or a selected part of the data recorded in punched cards or punched tape. Other devices convert magnetic-tape data into punched-card or punched-tape data.

CHECK YOURSELF

Supply the missing words.

1. A group of machines including input devices, storage devices, a central processing unit, output devices, and a control unit is called a(n) ___?___ ___?___.
2. Major advantages of medium- and large-sized computer systems over the smaller systems are speed of processing, greater choice of input/output devices, and larger ___?___ devices.
3. The ability of the computer user to easily move up from one computer system to another is called ___?___ ___?___.
4. The first ___?___ was developed in the early 1960s as a slower, lower-cost alternative to larger computers.
5. A computer system made up of minicomputers that are located in different places but connected to a central computer is called a(n) ___?___ ___?___ ___?___ system.
6. Paper tape was used for data input in communication by the ___?___ machine.
7. High-speed data communication is known as ___?___.

Review Questions

1. Describe the difference between on-line and off-line computer hardware, and define the term *computer system*.
2. Describe four common ways of recording business data as input for processing, and state which methods represent off-line data entry and which may be on-line data-entry operations.
3. List the devices that make up a computer system.
4. Name three types of computer input devices.
5. Describe the two parts that make up the central processing unit.
6. Define the term *primary storage*, and describe two such devices.
7. Describe two storage devices used for secondary storage.
8. Name six types of computer output devices, and describe each.
9. Explain the main differences between small and large computers. Define *microcomputer* and *minicomputer*.
10. Explain the purpose of a distributed computer system.
11. Explain why new means of data communication are important for business data processing.

Comparing Ideas

The questions below are to help you think about what you have learned in this chapter. They are thought questions. There is no one correct answer.

1. Name a local business that does not process its data by computer. Describe the business and the data processing system it has. If this business installed a computer, which size of computer do you think it would install? Why?
2. Who is affected most by the increased use of computer voice-response devices: Employees? Employers? Customers? Explain your answer.

Data Processing Activities

Now you can try out the kinds of data processing activities business workers perform. Below is a summary of the work you will do. You will find the actual information and business forms you need in your *Data Processing Work Kit*.

Activity 1. As a data input clerk in a large bank you will code data on mark-sense forms.

Activity 2. You will verify the accuracy of MICR coding on customer checks.

Activity 3. You will select the computer system (microcomputer, minicomputer, or larger) that should be used for some of the bank's data processing requirements.

BASIC Project 5
Inventory Project

Computer systems are made up of numerous machine components. In some businesses computer system components are treated like all other pieces of office equipment, and equipment locations must be accurately recorded and maintained. We can use BASIC to produce an equipment roster that can be easily updated when items are moved.

Program Statements

You used string variables (A$, C$, and so on) and set them equal to character strings (characters between quotation marks). We can use BASIC to create numeric variables. Numeric variable names do *not* have a dollar sign at the end. AGE, N, TOTAL, and B2 are examples of numeric variable names in BASIC. (Keep in mind that some versions of BASIC allow only single letters or a letter followed by a digit to be used for numeric variable names. Other versions allow longer names. Check your reference manual to find out what your system requires.) You will notice that the same variable can be given many different values in the same program. This is also true of string variables.

Sample Program

```
10 REMARK INVENTORY FOR TYPEWRITERS
15 REMARK CHANGE LINES 30,50,70,90,110, WHEN EQUIPMENT MOVES
20 REMARK TO NEW ROOM
30 LET N1=121
40 PRINT "SCRIPTOR MODEL 3R IS IN ROOM";TAB(30);N1
50 LET N2=122
60 PRINT "ADVANCE MODEL 5 IS IN ROOM";TAB(30);N2
70 LET N3=123
```

```
80 PRINT "SCRIPTOR MODEL 3S IS IN ROOM";TAB(30);N3
90 LET N4=151
100 PRINT "ADVANCE MODEL 6 IS IN ROOM";TAB(30);N4
110 LET N5=152
120 PRINT "ADVANCE MODEL 7 IS IN ROOM";TAB(30);N5
130 END
```

In this program string variables (N1$, N2$, and so on) could have been used instead of numeric variables because no arithmetic operations were done with the room numbers. In BASIC Project 7 we will see a program where numeric variables are required. Here the programmer may make the choice.

Output

The room locations will all be printed starting at print location 30 to make the report more readable.

```
SCRIPTOR MODEL 3R IS IN ROOM           121
ADVANCE MODEL 5 IS IN ROOM             122
SCRIPTOR MODEL 3S IS IN ROOM           123
ADVANCE MODEL 6 IS IN ROOM             151
ADVANCE MODEL 7 IS IN ROOM             152
```

Keyboarding Activities

1. Enter and RUN the program given above.
2. There is a shorter form of the LET statement. Oddly enough, it is formed by simply leaving out the word LET. The BASIC program line 30 N=121 is the same as 30 LET N=121. Change lines 30, 50, 70, 90, and 110 of the sample program, leaving out the word LET. Then run the program to verify that the output is the same as before. (The word LET is optional when this statement is used with string variables also.)
3. Modify the program to report the following changes.

```
ALL SCRIPTORS ARE NOW IN ROOM 123
THE ADVANCE MODEL G HAS BEEN DROPPED FROM INVENTORY
```

Enrichment Activity

Prepare an equipment inventory report for office equipment in your school or agency. Add serial numbers and the date purchased on a second line of print. (Do you need a string variable or a numeric variable for a serial number? What do you need for a date?)

CHAPTER

6

Programming a Computer

DATA PROCESSING TERMINOLOGY

Computer software
Mark sense
System specifications
Systems analyst
Program flowchart
Assembler language
Assembler
COBOL
BASIC
Pascal
Compiler
Diagnostics
ANSI
Documentation
Job request card
Data-base management software
Applications packages
Batch processing
Real-time processing
Interactive processing
Time-sharing
Service bureaus

PERFORMANCE GOALS

- Define *computer software*.
- List four key steps in completing a programming assignment.
- State the chief difference between a higher-level language and a symbolic language.
- List four programming languages used for business data processing.

- **List four key steps in operating a computer.**
- **Discuss the chief benefits of an interactive programming language.**
- **Distinguish between batch processing and real-time processing.**
- **List three reasons why a business might choose to use a service bureau for its data processing needs.**

You read earlier that a computer system processes data by following a list of instructions written by the computer programmer. The physical equipment that makes up a computer system is known as the **computer hardware.** The list of instructions and other procedures the computer system uses in processing data is often called the **computer software.** In this chapter you will learn more about the steps that must be taken to *program,* or develop instructions for, a computer. You will learn more about how to operate a computer, and you will read about recent developments in computer software that enable businesses to process data more efficiently. You will read about two types of computer data processing. You will also learn about the use of service bureaus to process business data.

Programming a Computer

The mystery and glamour associated with computers have made many believe that only those trained in college-level mathematics can work with a computer. It is true that complex mathematics formulas are often needed to develop detailed instructions for processing data in engineering, scientific, and research applications. Employers in these areas still tend to hire applicants with very strong mathematics backgrounds. Very few business data processing applications, however, require complex mathematics formulas. Now businesses are aware that such high school courses as business mathematics, data processing, recordkeeping, accounting, and retailing are sufficient background for most business applications. Usually, data manipulation calls for simple addition, subtraction, multiplication, and division, or a combination of these operations. For example, to find the average price of a calculator when the price has gone from $18 to $20 to $25, add the prices, divide by 3, and record the average price of $21.

Workers in scientific data processing usually need a much stronger background in math than workers in business data processing.

Defining the System Specifications

Programming is preparing a detailed and comprehensive list of instructions for a computer so that it can carry out a particular job. The programmer must have a very clear understanding of

Programming is preparing instructions for the computer to follow.

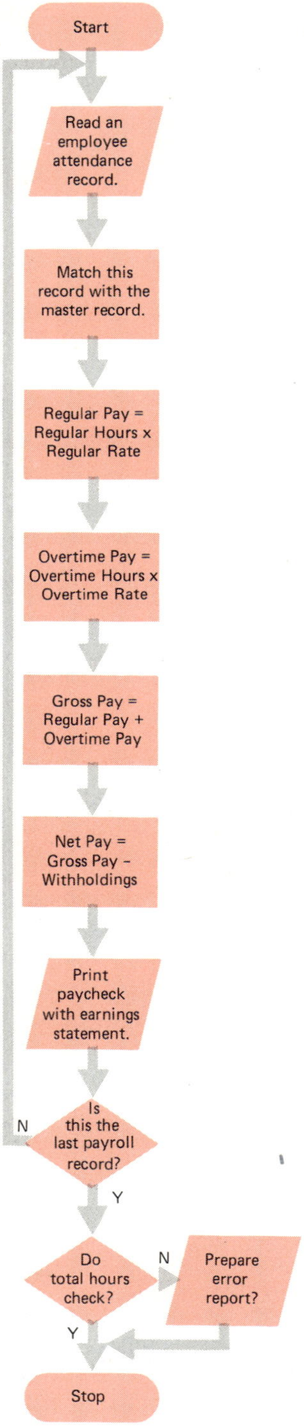

PAYROLL FLOWCHART

his or her work assignment and must think about the steps necessary to complete it. A skilled programmer usually thinks about the form in which the data to be processed will start out and the way in which it will appear after the processing has taken place.

If a programming assignment is for the payroll department, for example, much of the data will arrive on time cards that are either handwritten or punched on a time clock. The first step will be to design a procedure for changing the data into a form that is machine readable. This may be accomplished in several ways. The data on time cards may be put on punched cards and fed into a card reader. The time-card data may also be key-entered directly by video display terminals. It is even possible to design the time cards using **mark sense** or optical character entries that can be inputted directly using scanner equipment.

Developing the instructions themselves requires very careful and detailed planning and analysis. It takes a long time. Computers either do nothing or perform computations with errors if the programmer fails to do a good job. For example, telling a computer how to prepare payroll checks takes far more time and effort than explaining the same job to a payroll clerk. Programming need not be considered complex, though, because the rules to be followed do not require any advanced training in mathematics, electronics, or other subjects.

The job of the programmer does not begin until someone else has decided what data processing operations should be accomplished by the computer. A computer work assignment, usually referred to as a set of **system specifications,** is usually defined by a person called a **systems analyst.** In a typical payroll application, such specifications would be defined as follows.

1. The content and layout of the output data (the paycheck with the earnings statement).
2. The procedures to be followed in computing the gross pay, including the method for computing overtime pay.
3. The procedure for the preparation of the input data.

Creating the Program

Once the systems analyst has defined the system specifications and obtained the approval of management (in this case the manager of the payroll department), he or she turns the specifications over to one or more programmers who are assigned to write the program. The programmer performs four steps in sequence to complete the programming assignment.

1. Planning and flowcharting the program.
2. Coding the program.

```
Payroll Specifications
 1. Gather the employee attendance cards.
 2. Get each employee's pay rate from the master employee record.
 3. Compute each employee's regular pay.
 4. Compute each employee's overtime pay, if any.
 5. Get each employee's exemptions and voluntary deductions from
    the master employee record.
 6. Compute each employee's withholding tax and other deductions.
 7. Compute the net pay.
 8. Prepare each employee's paycheck with earnings statement.
 9. Prepare a payroll register for all the employees paid.
10. Verify the accuracy of the payroll by checking the total of
    all hours worked to the inputted control total.
```

PAYROLL PREPARATION PROCEDURE

3. Testing and debugging the program.
4. Documenting the program.

Before preparing a program, a programmer needs a set of system specifications.

Planning and Flowcharting the Program. A programmer must plan the computer execution of a program, step by step, from beginning to end. Planning is usually done by breaking down the broad specifications defined by the systems analyst into more detailed specifications. The way in which the programmer keeps track of what is happening to the input data as a result of each step is by drawing a flowchart. A **program flowchart** graphically shows each action to be taken by the computer. It enables the programmer to identify appropriate decisions each time there is a choice and then to follow the data through to check on whether the program will instruct the computer to process the data correctly and produce the desired results. Each flowchart is a series of rectangular, diamond, circular, or other shapes. These shapes are used as symbols for particular operations in the data processing cycle.

The illustration on page 83 shows the geometric shapes recommended for flowcharting by the American National Standards Institute. A *rectangular shape,* for example, specifies an operation (such as adding the hours worked each day to compute the number of hours worked in a particular week). A *diamond shape* indicates that the computer is to make a decision. In a payroll program, for example, for each hourly worker the computer would have to take action based on whether or not overtime hours had

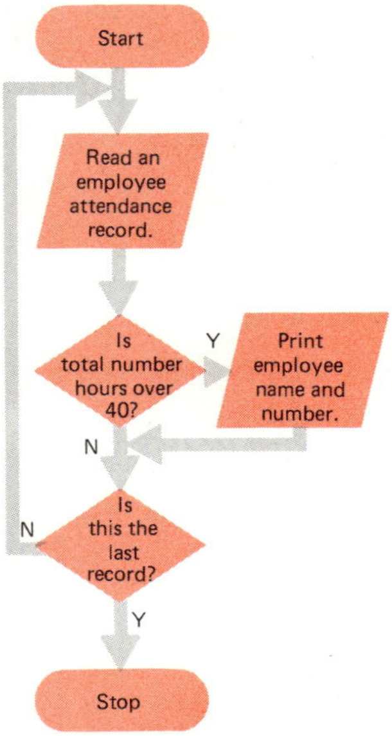

FLOWCHART FOR REPORTING OVERTIME WORK

been worked. The diamond asks the question, Overtime hours worked? The *parallelogram* represents clerical (nonmachine) steps.

In a flowchart, the rectangular, diamond, and other shapes are connected by arrows that show the sequence in which the instructions are to be carried out. The flowchart lists the instructions in order, just as you would instruct a payroll clerk to perform them. You can see that just a few spoken words can take a full page of flowcharting symbols.

Now think about the steps needed to prepare a flowchart for a simplified business data processing work assignment—a weekly payroll program. You are to review the data for each employee and then prepare a list of the names of the employees who worked overtime (more than 40 hours that week). To do this manually, you read the printout of payroll data, which shows each employee's social security number and name and the total number of hours he or she worked. In a few words, you could tell a payroll clerk to use the printout to prepare a list of employees who worked overtime.

To have a computer prepare a list of people who worked overtime, you would need to spell out every detail of the assignment. The flowchart a programmer could use would have two decision diamonds. The first diamond would ask the computer to decide for each employee whether the total hours worked exceeded 40. The second would ask the computer to decide each time an employee record is examined whether this is the last employee record. If the answer is yes, the computer has finished its work and must be told to stop. If the answer is no, the computer must be instructed to read another employee record.

The flowcharts a programmer would prepare for a typical business data processing work assignment are far more complicated than this example. To flowchart all the steps in a payroll or other business data processing application often requires many pages of flowcharting symbols. Each such flowchart, called a *program flowchart* or a *detail flowchart,* provides the programmer with a means of checking the flow of the data. It makes possible an early check on the completeness and logical order of a program. It also provides a framework for performing the next part of the programming task: coding or writing the program.

Coding means translating instructions into a form that the computer can understand.

Coding the Program. The word *programming* is sometimes used interchangeably with the word *coding.* Both words are used to indicate the programmer's use of a programming language to translate each instruction into a form that the computer can understand. Since a computer will process data only if it receives

FLOWCHARTING. Computer programmers prepare instructions for the computer to use in processing data. This programmer is preparing a flowchart. Hazel Hankin

instructions that tell it exactly what to do, coding from a flowchart can sometimes mean writing hundreds or even thousands of instructions for the computer. Each instruction tells the computer *which* operation is to be performed on *what* data. The program in the payroll example given earlier must include several sets of instructions. These include reading the overtime hours recorded on magnetic tape and multiplying the overtime hours by the overtime rate to obtain overtime pay.

Computers understand only machine language (numeric form). Instructions must be translated into machine language by the programmer.

Unfortunately, a computer can carry out the instructions in a program only if it receives instructions written in machine language, that is, in numeric form. This means that either the programmer must translate the programming instructions into numeric form or this translation must take place in some other way. As you read earlier, programmers using the first computer models had to understand machine language. Each computer manufacturer developed a numeric code suitable for its computer model. The programmer had to develop instructions in detail and then translate the instructions into numeric form. This meant that the programmer had to spend a great deal of time on each computer program.

As computers became more widely used for business data processing, the variations in numeric codes from manufacturer to manufacturer created difficulties and resulted in many errors. Programmers who had learned how to code instructions for one machine had to learn a whole new coding system in order to write computer programs for another machine. Another difficulty was that large businesses which might have used computers of different manufacturers could not use the same programs on different machines.

Computer manufacturers and large-computer users, such as businesses and government agencies, began sending representatives to meetings to develop standard language specifications that would work for all computer models. The goal was to enable programmers to write instructions in a form as close as possible to ordinary English. The first step that simplified the programmer's assignment was the development of *symbolic form*, which is a technique that enables programmers to write instructions in a combination of alphabetic and numeric codes.

TYPES OF CODING

1. **Machine language**
2. **Symbolic forms**
   Assembler language
3. **Higher-level languages**
   a. **COBOL**
   b. **BASIC**
   c. **FORTRAN**
   d. **RPG**
   e. **PL/1**

Although less detailed languages can also be used with newer models of computer systems, many programming departments prefer to write some programs in a symbolic language such as an **assembler language.** Because each programming instruction is so detailed, very little time is spent in telling the computer what is to be done. Even with such detailed language, however, the computer must be provided with a program called an **assembler** that translates each symbolic instruction into machine language. An assembler language program designed for use with an IBM computer is shown below.

A tremendous breakthrough in the simplification of programming came with the development of the so-called higher-level languages. Each such language, and now there are many, was designed to accomplish two things.

- To provide a means of writing computer instructions much like English.
- To enable computer installations to use programs more easily on the machines of different manufacturers.

COBOL is an effective higher-level language for business data processing.

1. **COBOL.** One of the most effective higher-level languages developed so far for business data processing is **COBOL** (com-

ASSEMBLER LANGUAGE. This is a printout of an asssembler language program for an IBM computer. Assembler language is a symbolic form of coding.

```
      SAMPLE PROGRAM-ASSEMBLER OUTPUT & DIAGNOSTICS                    PAGE   2
  LOC  OBJECT CODE    ADDR1 ADDR2  STMT  SOURCE STATEMENT          F08APR--  5/17/--
001000                             35  SAMPLE START    × '1000'            SAMP0020
                                   36  *                                   SAMP0030
                                   37  FIRST  ENTREE                       SAMP0040
001000 90EC  D00C 0000C            38+FIRST   STM     14,12,12(13)-SAVE CALLER'S REGS IN SAVEAREA
001004 05C0                        39+        BALR    12,0-SET UP ADDRESSABILITY (BASE REG 12)
001006                             40+        USING   *,12-TELL ASSEMBLER REG 12 IS BASE REG
```

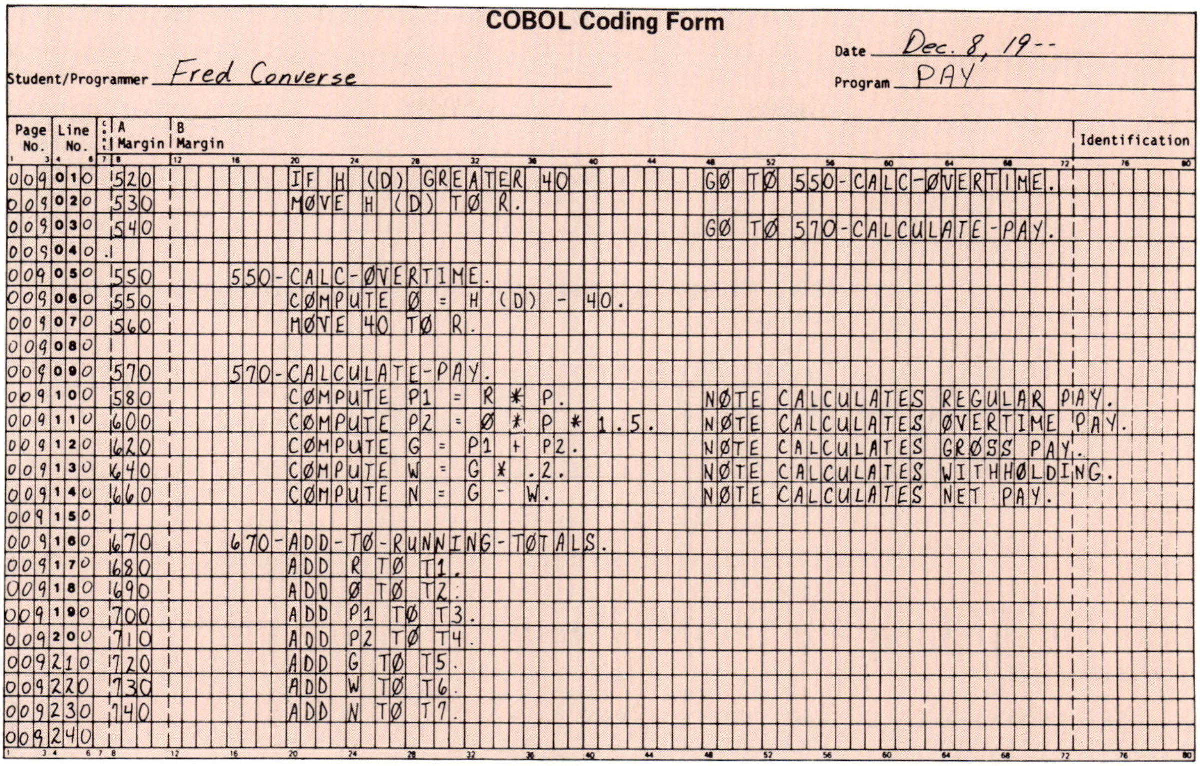

COBOL Coding Form

Student/Programmer *Fred Converse*
Date *Dec. 8, 19--*
Program *PAY*

Page No.	Line No.	A Margin	B Margin		Identification
009	010	520	IF H (D) GREATER 40	GØ TØ 550-CALC-ØVERTIME.	
009	020	530	MØVE H (D) TØ R.		
009	030	540		GØ TØ 570-CALCULATE-PAY.	
009	040	.			
009	050	550	550-CALC-ØVERTIME.		
009	060	550	CØMPUTE Ø = H (D) - 40.		
009	070	560	MØVE 40 TØ R.		
009	080				
009	090	570	570-CALCULATE-PAY.		
009	100	580	CØMPUTE P1 = R * P.	NØTE CALCULATES REGULAR PAY.	
009	110	600	CØMPUTE P2 = Ø * P * 1.5.	NØTE CALCULATES ØVERTIME PAY.	
009	120	620	CØMPUTE G = P1 + P2.	NØTE CALCULATES GRØSS PAY.	
009	130	640	CØMPUTE W = G * .2.	NØTE CALCULATES WITHHØLDING.	
009	140	660	CØMPUTE N = G - W.	NØTE CALCULATES NET PAY.	
009	150				
009	160	670	670-ADD-TØ-RUNNING-TØTALS.		
009	170	680	ADD R TØ T1.		
009	180	690	ADD Ø TØ T2.		
009	190	700	ADD P1 TØ T3.		
009	200	710	ADD P2 TØ T4.		
009	210	720	ADD G TØ T5.		
009	220	730	ADD W TØ T6.		
009	230	740	ADD N TØ T7.		
009	240				

CODING FORMS. A form for coding a payroll program in the COBOL language is shown here.

mon business oriented language). The COBOL language, which has been expanded by its developers since its first specifications were released in 1960, has been standardized as American National Standard COBOL.

From time to time, the computer manufacturers provide additional capabilities for their equipment and develop the necessary COBOL language statements for these new operations. Every few years, the American National Standards Institute (ANSI) documents the changes in the language so that each new development can be evaluated by user groups from business and government and then incorporated in the standard language. The acronym **ANSI** appears a great deal in computer-related articles, magazines, and books. All computer manufacturers must provide the users of their equipment with language translators called **compilers,** which translate each statement written by the programmer into machine language. For example, a COBOL compiler translates COBOL programming instructions into several very detailed machine-lan-

PROGRAM LANGUAGE TRANSLATORS

1. Programmer
2. Assembler
3. Compiler

guage instructions. A page of a program in COBOL is shown on the coding form on page 133.

2. **Other higher-level languages.** Through ANSI committees, similar efforts are being made to standardize other higher-level languages. These efforts are based on the interest shown by programmers and the number of computer manufacturers

BASIC. One page of the input for the BASIC payroll program looks like this.

```
510 REM***** FIND REGULAR HOURS WORKED *****
520 IF H[D]>40 THEN 550
530 R=H[D]
540 GOTO 570
550 O=H[D]-40
560 R=40
570 REM***** CALCULATE REGULAR PAY *****
580 P1=R*P
590 REM***** CALCULATE OVERTIME PAY *****
600 P2=O*P*1.5
610 REM***** CALCULATE GROSS PAY *****
620 G=P1+P2
630 REM***** CALCULATE WITHHOLDING *****
640 W=G*.2
650 REM***** CALCULATE NET PAY *****
660 N=G-W
670 REM***** ADD TO RUNNING TOTALS *****
680 T1=T1+R
690 T2=T2+O
700 T3=T3+P1
710 T4=T4+P2
720 T5=T5+G
730 T6=T6+W
740 T7=T7+N
750 REM***** PRINT REPORT *****
```

who offer the languages for their equipment. Over the years many higher-level languages have been introduced. The more widely used programming languages are as follows.

LANGUAGE	APPROXIMATE DATE	USE OF LANGUAGE
FORTRAN	1957	Scientific and mathematical work
COBOL	1960	Business systems
BASIC	1965	General-purpose use
PL/1	1965	Business and scientific work
RPG	1966	Business systems
Pascal	1971	General-purpose use

Beginner's All-purpose Symbolic Instruction Code **(BASIC)** has grown in use as a language for computer processing. This is due to several features.

- BASIC is easy to learn.
- BASIC can be used for business and mathematical work.
- BASIC is available on many microcomputers and minicomputers.
- BASIC is interactive and therefore easy to test and debug.

Students often learn BASIC as their first computer language. One drawback of BASIC is that it may not be suitable for the large-scale data processing applications found in many businesses. A page of a BASIC program is shown on page 134.

Pascal programming language (named for the seventeenth-century philosopher Blaise Pascal) is a more recent general-purpose language. It has most of the advantages of BASIC. Other features include the following.

- Pascal is appropriate for both large and small applications.
- Pascal is structured (in sections) so that large programs can be distributed for team programming.
- The Pascal format makes it easier to understand and alter work done by another programmer.

The Pascal programming language has recently become available on a wide range of large and small computer systems. A portion of a Pascal program is shown on pages 136 and 137.

At the time of this writing, COBOL and PL/1 are the most widely used languages for the programming of business systems. RPG (report program generator) is used only for the programming of simple business routines, and FORTRAN is the

```
PROCEDURE COMPUTEPAY;
    BEGIN
        IF HOURS [COUNT] > 40.0
            THEN
                BEGIN
                    REGULARHOURS [COUNT] := 40.0;
                    OVERTIME [COUNT] := HOURS [COUNT] - 40.0
                END
            ELSE REGULARHOURS [COUNT] := HOURS [COUNT];
        REGULARPAY [COUNT] := RATE [COUNT] * REGULARHOURS
        [COUNT];
        OVERPAY [COUNT] := 1.5 * RATE [COUNT] * OVERTIME [COUNT];
        GROSSPAY [COUNT] := REGULARPAY [COUNT] + OVERPAY [COUNT];
```

PASCAL. This program is written in Pascal. Since ANSI has not yet standardized Pascal or BASIC, the details of these languages vary from manufacturer to manufacturer. The printout produced when this program is executed is shown below and on the next page.

```
EXECUTE PAY
LINK:    Loading
[LNKXCT PAY execution]
INPUT          : TTY:
OUTPUT         : TTY:
MASTER         : MASTER.DAT
PROGRAM REPORTS PAY INFORMATION FOR THE FOLLOWING PEOPLE.
NAME           NUMBER
------------------------------------------------------------------
MYRON FURTH    1234
JUDY SOKOL      4321
LARRY CHAN      2468
HELEN KELLY    1357
INPUT EMPLOYEE NUMBER 1234
HOURS WORKED 40
ARE THERE ANY MORE? (Y OR N) Y
INPUT EMPLOYEE NUMBER 4321
```

```
HOURS WORKED 42
ARE THERE ANY MORE? (Y OR N) Y
INPUT EMPLOYEE NUMBER 2468
HOURS WORKED 38
ARE THERE ANY MORE? (Y OR N) Y
INPUT EMPLOYEE NUMBER 1357
HOURS WORKED 40
ARE THERE ANY MORE? (Y or N) N
HOURS FOR ALL EMPLOYEES HAVE BEEN ENTERED.
                              PAY REPORT
NAME          HOURS              PAY
                                                GROSS     WITH-      NET
             REG    OVR     REG        OVR      PAY       HELD       PAY
MYRON FURTH  40.0   0.0   220.00      0.00    220.00     44.00    176.00
JUDY SOKOL   40.0   2.0   180.00     13.50    193.50     38.70    154.80
LARRY CHAN   38.0   0.0   171.00      0.00    171.00     34.20    136.80
HELEN KELLY  40.0   0.0   190.00      0.00    190.00     38.00    152.00
TOTAL       158.0   2.0   761.00     13.50    774.50    154.90    619.60

INPUT CONTROL VALUE FOR TOTAL HOURS
WORKED THIS WEEK BY ALL EMPLOYEES
160
NO ERROR HOURS CHECK
```

language used where the processing involves many mathematical calculations. ANSI has not yet reached agreement on standards for either BASIC or Pascal. Slight differences in the language from one manufacturer to another require changes to use a program on different computers. The development of ANSI standards for these programming languages, as there are for COBOL and FORTRAN, will make it easier for the user to go from one computer to another.

Testing and Debugging the Program. When a program has been written and recorded on punched cards, punched tape, or a magnetic disk or tape or at a terminal device, it must be tested, or run through the computer. The skilled programmer checks his or her work throughout the work assignment

```
          IBM SYSTEM/34 RPGII COMPILER   RELEASE 06   12/03/--
               17.42
                                                       PAGE 1
     0001 H       024                                   PAYRPT
0001 0002 FPAYROLINIPF   80   80          CONSOLE       PAYRPT
0002 0003 FPAYREPO O  F 132  132    2     PRINTER       PAYRPT
0003 0004 IPAYROLINJH 01    1 CP                        PAYRPT
0004 0005 I                                2   30 NAME      PAYRPT
0005 0006 I                               31   34 EMPNO     PAYRPT
0006 0007 I                               35   382REGHRS    PAYRPT
0007 0008 I                               39   422OVEHRS 02 PAYRPT
0008 0009 I                               43   462RATE      PAYRPT
0009 0010 C    01       REGHRS   MULT RATE    REGPAY   62H  PAYRPT
0010 0011 C    01       RATE     MULT 1.5     OVERAT   62H  PAYRPT
0011 0012 C    01       OVERAT   MULT OVEHRS  OVEPAY   62H  PAYRPT
0012 0013 C    01       REGPAY   ADD  OVEPAY  GROPAY   62   PAYRPT
0013 0014 C    01       GROPAY   MULT .20     WITHEL   62H  PAYRPT
0014 0015 C    01       GROPAY   SUB  WITHEL  NETPAY   62   PAYRPT
0015 0016 C    01       REGHRS   ADD  TOTREG  TOTREG   82   PAYRPT
0016 0017 C    01 02    OVEHRS   ADD  TOTOVE  TOTOVE   82   PAYRPT
0017 0018 C    01       REGPAY   ADD  TORPAY  TORPAY   82   PAYRPT
0018 0019 C    01 02    OVEPAY   ADD  TOOPAY  TOOPAY   82   PAYRPT
0019 0020 C    01       GROPAY   ADD  TOGPAY  TOGPAY   82   PAYRPT
0020 0021 C    01       WITHEL   ADD  TOTWIT  TOTWIT   82   PAYRPT
0021 0022 C    01       NETPAY   ADD  TOTNET  TOTNET   82   PAYRPT
```

RPG II. The language known as RPG II is a newer version of RPG. This printout shows a section of a program called PAYRPT for *payroll report*. See if you can figure out what the programmer intended.

to make sure that the assignment will be completed accurately in the time allowed. This means that the program will be up and running, or performing accurately all the operations specified in the programmer's work assignment. It also means that the computer output will be in the proper form. The programmer needs to learn that there may be more than one correct way to write a program but that one way may be faster than another for the computer.

```
10 REM THIS PROGRAM ILLUSTRATES THE
20 REM USE OF THE OR STATEMENT
30 LET A=10
40 LET B=20
50 LET C=30
60 IF A=B/2 or C=A+B THEN 80
70 STOP
80 IF B=C-A OR B=A*2 THEN 100
90 STOP
100 IF A=10 or B=20 OR C=30 THEN 120
110 STOP
120 END
```

BASIC. A REM statement is used in BASIC to document the program. Each part of the message is introduced by the keyword REM, standing for the word *remark*. A listing of the program shows the message "This program illustrates the use of the OR statement."

Each time the programmer has completed a phase of the work assignment, there must be a careful self-check on whether that phase is both accurate and clear. This self-check is a manual process called **desk debugging.** In this way, many errors can be found before the program is tested on the computer. This is true for both errors in the *logic* of the program (the plan itself) and errors in the *syntax* used in coding the instructions.

A computer can print out diagnostics, that is, messages that help the programmer and operator detect errors.

Because of the great detail of a computer program, no amount of care in desk debugging catches every error. A coded program must be read into the computer, translated into machine language, and tested. The computer itself issues error messages, often called **diagnostics,** that identify mistakes in coding. When the programmer has corrected all coding errors, the entire program is run on the computer. Then the programmer must check the output to see whether the results are those expected and whether they are printed or punched in the correct form. For a long, complex program, it may take several weeks to find and correct all the errors made in planning and coding the program. But only after the testing operation has resulted in a complete and accurate program can a computer process real business data. This means that a great deal of time and money may be required before a computer can be used to process business data.

A computer program must be tested many times to ensure its accuracy.

Documenting the Program. Illustrations and explanations, called **documentation,** must be prepared for each working

Documentation for a program should include the purpose of the program, its estimated running (computing) time, descriptions of the input and output, and other helpful information.

program. Documentation typically includes flowcharts and written explanations (narrative) of the purpose of the program and each routine in it, sample input and output, and a test run. Documentation is prepared to meet two needs.

1. To give the information a computer operator would need to run the program or to give the information that a programmer might need later if the program had to be updated (for example, to compute overtime pay after 35 hours instead of after 40 hours). The person who is asked to update a program needs detailed program flowcharts and explanations for each section of coding. Without clear and complete documentation for such a project, a programmer might be forced to "reinvent the wheel." This duplication of effort would waste valuable time and energy.
2. To give the general information that the user of the program would require (for example, the information that the payroll department would need). The user for whom the processing work is done needs information such as the requirements for the data-entry operations and descriptions of each printout prepared by the computer.

CHECK YOURSELF

Supply the missing words.

1. The business programmer should have one or more courses in __?__ __?__, data processing, recordkeeping, accounting, and retailing.
2. The task of developing appropriate instructions for computer data processing is called __?__.
3. In the early days of computers, programming instructions were written in __?__ language.
4. The person who defines the system specifications is called a(n) __?__ __?__.
5. To graphically show the steps in the computer program, the programmer prepares a(n) __?__.
6. The flowcharting symbol that is used to show that a decision must be made has the shape of a(n) __?__.
7. The type of flowchart a programmer draws for a typical business application is called a program or __?__ flowchart.
8. An example of a symbolic programming language is __?__.
9. An example of a higher-level programming language important in business data processing is __?__.
10. A language translator that is used with a higher-level programming language is called a(n) __?__.

11. The programmer's self-check is called __?__ __?__.
12. Computer-generated error messages are often called __?__.
13. The illustrations and explanations that should accompany the computer printout of a working program are called __?__.
14. The programming language known as __?__ may not be appropriate for applications found in many businesses.

Operating a Computer

After a program has been tested and debugged, the computer can be used to process business data. But like any other business machine, a computer needs an operator to run it. In many respects, operating a computer is like operating any piece of business equipment. The operator must know how to perform four basic steps.

Four key steps in operating a computer are listed here.

1. Setting up for processing
2. Keeping the system operational
3. Documenting system and job failures
4. Signing jobs in and out

Setting Up for Processing

Depending on the input medium the programmer has selected, the computer operator must work with one or more input devices. He or she loads punched cards into punched-card readers (usually called card readers) and magnetic tape into magnetic-tape input/output devices. The printers must also be loaded with the proper forms for recording the output data. If the data is to be recorded on punched cards, magnetic tape, or microfilm, then the operator must load the output devices with these supplies.

Keeping the System Operational

Once the programmer's instructions have been followed and the necessary supplies have been loaded, the computer operator must start the computer. All machines have conventional on-off and start-stop keys, but the additional operating controls for a computer make the operation of a computer more complex than the operation of other business machines.

While processing is taking place, the operator must continually check the control panel (also called the *computer console*) to ensure that all units are performing properly. Control lights on the control panel indicate the state of the computer system. In addition, the operator must check the console typewriter or the visual display terminal, on which messages are sometimes recorded. The purpose of such hardware is to simplify communication between the computer operator and the central processing unit. For example, if the operator has forgotten to mount a reel of tape that the programmer has specified, a message is printed on the console typewriter or visual display terminal. The message states that processing will not take place until the tape is mounted.

Documenting System and Job Failures

Careful records must be kept for every job that runs or fails to run.

In most computer installations, the computer operator is required to maintain a log sheet that specifies the jobs received, the time they take to run, and any problems encountered on that shift. Other details may vary with the installation. But there must be a record that can be checked to ensure an efficient operation. Sometimes, of course, either the computer system or the job itself fails to run as expected. Then the operator is usually expected to determine, with the help of the control panel and the console typewriter or visual display terminal, whether he or she must take action. Such action might be as simple as replacing paper or mounting a tape. Or the necessary action could be as serious as terminating a job, noting the failure on the log sheet, and going on to the next job. Since many computer centers operate on three shifts, business managers often plan to use the processing results of one shift as input data for the next shift's processing.

Signing Jobs In and Out

The department in which a job originates usually submits a list of instructions along with the job. These instructions, recorded on a form called a **job request card,** specify the computer model to be used, the estimated running time, the output device to be used, the output medium (continuous paper, continuous forms, labels, magnetic tape, punched cards, or microfilm), and the dates by which the output is needed.

When a job arrives, an input/output clerk signs it in, keeping the instructions on file for future runs of the job. When the processing is finished, the computer operator or some other worker must remove the computer output from the output device used for that job and check to make sure that the output is complete. An input/output clerk signs the job out and forwards the output to the person or department specified on the job request card. For a program being tested, the output is forwarded to the programmer. For a monthly payroll, the paychecks are forwarded to the payroll department for distribution. And for an inventory report, the output is forwarded to the inventory department for follow-up.

JOB REQUEST CARD

Name________________________________ Date________________

Department ____________________________ Charge No. ____________

Input
- ☐ Cards
- ☐ Tape

Processing (Check as many as apply.)
- ☐ Computer (Model_____)
- ☐ Accounting Machines
- ☐ Card-Punch Machine
- ☐ Reproducer/ Interpreter
- ☐ Sorter

Output (Check as many as apply.)
- ☐ Report
- ☐ Cards
- ☐ Tape
- ☐ Microfilm
- ☐ Continuous Forms
- ☐ Labels

Special Instructions____

____

____

Route to ____

JOB REQUEST CARD. To request work from the data processing department, it often is necessary to prepare a job request form like this one.

In some cases, additional tasks will be specified on the job request card, such as *bursting* (separating) a set of continuous forms or paper, *decollating* (arranging copies in sets), or reproducing a deck of punched cards. For these extra tasks, the larger computer departments usually employ additional workers called *peripheral* or *auxiliary operators.* An operator whose only tasks are to operate a burster and a decollator is usually called a *burster/decollator operator.*

CHECK YOURSELF

Supply the missing words.

1. A computer operator must know how to perform __?__ basic steps in operating a computer.
2. The control panel of a large computer is also called the computer __?__.
3. The computer operator records when jobs are received, the time they take to run, and any problems encountered on that shift on a(n) __?__ __?__.
4. A(n) __?__ __?__ __?__ has written on it the instructions for processing a job.
5. Separating a set of continuous forms is called __?__.
6. Larger computer departments employ extra people, called __?__ operators, to run burster/decollators and to reproduce punched cards.

Recent Software Developments

PROFESSIONAL LITERATURE. Magazines and newspapers help computer professionals keep up to date. Hazel Hankin

As you read earlier, in the 1960s and the 1970s the computer manufacturers improved on their hardware time and again. The improved hardware sparked interest among computer professionals who wanted to know more about the available equipment. Computer-oriented textbooks, trade books, encyclopedias, newsletters, and magazines all arose out of a need to know about computers.

Because of the concern of every business with trying to keep its own costs down and its prices competitive, there has been great interest in making both computer hardware and computer software more efficient. The hardware developers have produced computer systems that are often less expensive, more reliable, and faster than earlier and more basic methods of processing data. In spite of inflation, some computer systems cost considerably less than their more primitive predecessors. The software developers have also found better ways to use computer systems to produce the desired results at less cost to the user. Four major breakthroughs in computer software are the following.

1. Improved software (improvements in programming techniques)
2. The development of software standards
3. Expansion of available utility programs
4. Widespread use of applications packages

Improved Software

Computer software includes the computer programs and other people-written instructions that enable computer programmers and operators to communicate with the hardware. You read earlier about flowcharts and coding forms—the tools of the computer programmer. And you read about the assemblers and compilers that translate the programmer's coded instructions into codes that can be read and executed by machines. In recent years the use of assembler languages has been declining. It is much easier for programmers to code their instructions in English-like languages such as COBOL, FORTRAN, or PL/1 than in the very detailed, highly numeric assembler languages.

THREE FUNCTIONS OF OPERATING SYSTEMS

1. **Provide standard aids for programmers.**
2. **Assist operators in recordkeeping and in correcting errors.**
3. **Increase the number of jobs that can be completed.**

Another software breakthrough is the development of operating systems. An **operating system** is a set of manufacturer-developed programs that perform three functions. First, an operating system reduces the work of programmers because it contains coded instructions for certain repetitive operations that are required for every computer job, such as the instructions for entering data into the computer. Second, an operating system also makes the computer operator's job easier by performing tasks such as keeping track of the running time of each job. Third, an operating system makes it possible to maximize the use of the computer hardware. For example, an operating system will schedule the sequence of multiple jobs so that the work is performed in the shortest possible time.

Today's operating systems can acknowledge processing requests from remote terminals, allocate the resources for satisfying these requests, and still run the job submitted at the site of the central processing unit. (A *remote terminal* is a terminal that is located at a different site from the computer.) The terminal operator is able to store data, process data, and retrieve data by working at the terminal's keyboard. Telephone lines transmit the keyed data and instructions to the central processing unit of the computer.

IMPROVED SOFTWARE

1. **Higher-level languages**
2. **Operating systems**
3. **Data-base management software**

Data-base management software is another type of program package that can be purchased from computer manufacturers or software service companies. This is a set of standard machine instructions that make it easier for a programmer to write a program that handles the storage, updating, and retrieval of data in a file such as a customer file used for billing.

Computer manufacturers and computer users continue to work at developing more effective ways of communicating with the computer and thereby reducing the need for human intervention. This is necessary because while unit computer processing and storage costs have been decreasing rapidly, the systems and programming costs for designing and installing computer systems have risen steadily. Also, there is a shortage of skilled people to do the work.

Standards

As you read earlier, ANSI stands for the American National Standards Institute, a nonprofit organization. The more than 140 trade associations and professional societies and 750 companies that make up its membership participate on a voluntary basis. ANSI coordinates the standardization of methods, terms, procedures, and symbols. Thus business, government, and labor can communicate effectively on matters of mutual interest.

In recent years, standards have been developed in a large number of areas. Two of the areas relating to the computer industry are classified as X3/Computers and Information Processing and X4/Office Machines. The business and government representatives serving on ANSI committees have made it possible, for example, for flowcharting symbols to have universal meaning and for COBOL programs to be used on many computer systems with minor adjustments in the control statements. (A control statement, often called a *job control statement,* defines what must be done if a specific condition exists. Programs are made up of control statements that serve as a link between the computer and the job to be processed.)

The ANSI committees meet regularly to evaluate and update existing standards, develop new standards, and publicize the standards so that they will be effective. When you see the term *American National Standard COBOL,* you know that the language elements are not for just one computer model but are incorporated into other computer models by the manufacturers of the major computer systems. Thus an employee can learn to use computer-related terms, a programming language such as COBOL, and a set of flowcharting symbols with some assurance that the learning can be applied in most computer installations where he or she might work in the future.

Expansion of Utility Programs

Software utilities, often called *programming aids,* have been greatly expanded in recent years. These preprogrammed tools can save hours of programming time. A sorting utility program, for example, can be inserted in a program, eliminating the need to write hundreds of instructions to tell the computer how to sort data.

Cross-reference utility programs can examine hundreds of lines of program code and locate a trouble spot. This is useful in debugging. In general, these specialized utility programs are being developed to help programmers save time. They eliminate the need to write instructions for common types of operations which must be done in many programs.

Applications Packages

Applications packages (often called *canned programs*) currently exist for a wide variety of business data processing systems such as payroll, inventory, and accounts receivable/payable. These programs are purchased or leased from software houses or may be supplied by the hardware manufacturer. They are popular with some companies, particularly smaller businesses, because they eliminate the need to employ a programmer to write the computer instructions. Some applications programs can be used with natural-language keyboard entry. For most readers of this textbook, English would be the natural language. No specialized computer language is required. The operator merely gives answers to *prompts* (questions) provided by the computer program. Applications packages are available for use on all sizes of computers. When hardware and software are combined to perform a specific business task, the combination is referred to as a *turnkey package*. This arrangement is very common in small businesses making their first computer purchase. The drawback of an applications package is that it may not exactly satisfy the particular requirements of a user. Also, purchasing or leasing an applications package may be more costly in the long run than paying employees to develop the programs.

CHECK YOURSELF

Supply the missing words.

1. A(n) __?__ __?__ is a set of manufacturer-developed programs that make the programmer's job easier and make the computer hardware more useful.
2. __?__ __?__ __?__ is a set of standard machine instructions that make the computer easier to program.
3. __?__ is a nonprofit organization that works for the standardization of computer-related methods, terms, procedures, and symbols.
4. __?__ __?__ aid programmers by eliminating the need to program common types of operations.
5. Software houses and computer manufacturers can supply __?__ __?__, which eliminate the need to hire a programmer.

Computer System Alternatives in Data Processing

TWO TYPES OF COMPUTER DATA PROCESSING

1. Batch processing
2. Real-time processing

The way in which the computer is used varies tremendously from installation to installation. Some businesses accumulate data over a period of time and then process it all at once. Other businesses must process data as a particular event occurs. These two types of computer data processing are the following.

1. Batch processing
2. Real-time processing

Batch Processing

The traditional way to process business data is to accumulate information over a set period of time—daily, weekly, or monthly.

Businesses of all sizes have to prepare a payroll, but the pay period varies from company to company and even within a company from executives and managers to the people they supervise. A typical pay period may be, for example, two weeks. Payroll data is prepared for entry into the computer system, and then this batch of payroll data is processed. In **batch processing,** the data-entry operation (recording data in machine-readable form) is performed by a device independent of the computer. When the data-entry function takes place at the same location as the computer processing, the batch processing may be called *local job processing.*

Data to be entered for batch processing by computer can also be prepared at a different site and sent by mail or transmitted back to the remote terminals located at other sites. This type of computer data processing, in which data is accumulated in one place but batch-processed in another place, is called *remote job* (or batch) *processing,* or *remote job entry.* An example of remote batch processing might be the way in which a bookstore with several branches processes its data. When it comes time to take inventory, the inventory of each store would be sent by terminal to a receiving terminal in the central office. When all the data is received and batched together, the computer can perform the necessary processing steps. Copies of the output data can then be transmitted to the remote terminal located at each store. Such processing allows for a record of the total inventory as well as a record of the inventory at each store.

BATCH PROCESSING. At the end of each week, all the sales slips for that week are collected as a *batch.* This is an example of batch processing, because the slips are processed in one batch instead of singly, as they are created.

Real-Time Processing

Operators enter data directly into the computer in real-time processing.

In **real-time processing,** data about a particular event is keyed into a computer as the event occurs, and the data is immediately processed. For this purpose, the terminal keyboard device is attached directly to the computer by cable or by telephone lines.

The best example of real-time processing was mentioned in an earlier chapter—it is the handling of airline reservations. Under a real-time system, a complete inventory of the seats available on all flights is kept in a computer storage device located in one place in the country. Agents throughout the country can communicate by keyboard directly with the computer to inquire whether seat space is available on a particular flight. Within a few seconds, the computer checks its inventory and sends back to the agent a response indicating whether or not the customer can be accommodated. If the customer then approves, the ticket agent presses keys to confirm the reservation. With this confirmation, the computer subtracts one seat from its inventory and records the passenger's name. There may be as many as 600,000 passenger records held by the computer.

On-line terminals are sometimes used to enter data into computer storage for processing at a later date. This is not an example of real-time processing.

When a user of a remote terminal can request information from a computer by keyboarding questions and obtain results speedily, this form of computer data processing is sometimes called **interactive processing** instead of real-time processing. An example of interactive processing is computer-assisted instruction. Also, the use of the Computerized Vocational Information System (CVIS) involves interactive processing. (CVIS is a source of career information on more than 400 jobs.) In these computer uses, many terminals may be active at any one time. When a number of users of real-time or interactive processing can share the same central processor, this is called **time sharing.**

Interactive processing has advantages for the programming staff. Many computer languages can be written interactively. This means that a programmer can enter program codes directly from coding sheets without the use of an intermediate document such as cards or magnetic tape. Although the typing speed of a programmer may be slower than that of a data-entry clerk, time can be saved in other ways when the programmer works at a terminal. The fact that many interactive programming languages check each line of the program as it is entered and reject many common errors may result in an overall reduction in turnaround

```
INPUT EMPLOYEE NUMBER 2468
HOURS WORKED 38
ARE THERE ANY MORE? (Y OR N) Y
INPUT EMPLOYEE NUMBER 2222 ILLEGAL EMPLOYEE NUMBER
ARE THERE ANY MORE? (Y OR N) Y
INPUT EMPLOYEE NUMBER 1357
HOURS WORKED 40
```

INTERACTIVE PROGRAMMING. A user of an interactive program has made an error and corrected it at the computer's request. See if you can pick out the error message.

time (the time from program request to program completion). Since the introduction of BASIC as the first commonly used interactive language, a number of higher-level languages have become available with interactive versions.

Service Bureaus

Service bureaus are companies that provide data processing services for a fee. This fee is based on equipment, software, and personnel usage. Service bureaus have proved to be ideal for many businesses small and large. They offer several advantages.

1. Companies can gain valuable experience with electronic data processing procedures.
2. A business is charged only for the equipment and support it uses; no equipment purchase is required.
3. Utilizing a service bureau may not require hiring additional employees.

These advantages generally benefit a small company more than a larger, well-established firm. Each company must consider the costs and benefits of a service bureau against the costs and benefits of an in-house computer.

A drawback to a service bureau may be inflexibility in scheduling work. That is, it may be difficult to get work processed when the company needs it.

Batch service bureau applications typically include source document conversion, processing, report bursting and decollating, and electronic media storage (disks and tapes), as well as the preparation of detailed usage reports by individual departments.

With on-line service bureau applications, input and/or output devices may be located at the user site. A company may perform all data-entry tasks using computer terminals provided by the service bureau. These terminals may be interactive, or they may merely perform remote-job-entry tasks. This arrangement gives the user better quality control and a shorter turnaround time.

CHECK YOURSELF

Supply the missing words.

1. Processing data after it has been accumulated over a set period of time is called __?__ __?__.
2. __?__ __?__ processing is processing that takes place at the same location at which the data is accumulated.
3. Batch processing that takes place at a location that is different from the location of the data-entry operation is called __?__ __?__ __?__.
4. Time sharing is a method of processing data that allows a number of people to share the same __?__ __?__.
5. Real-time processing is often called __?__ processing.
6. A(n) __?__ package is the combination of hardware and software needed to solve a particular business problem.
7. The time from program request to program completion is called __?__ time.
8. Interactive programming languages check each __?__.
9. Companies that provide data processing services for a fee are known as __?__ bureaus.
10. On-line terminals are sometimes used to enter data into computer storage for __?__ processing.

Review Questions

1. What is computer software?
2. What are the four major steps in completing a programming assignment?
3. What is the difference between a higher-level language and a symbolic language?
4. Which four programming languages are commonly used for business data processing?
5. What are the four main steps in operating a computer?
6. What are the major advantages of an interactive programming language?
7. What is the difference between batch processing and real-time processing?
8. What are the advantages and disadvantages of using a service bureau for business data processing?

Comparing Ideas

The questions below are to help you think about what you have learned in this chapter. They are thought questions. There is no one correct answer.

1. Think about the data processing activities of a local bank. What activities are done in batch? What activities are done on-line?
2. Do you think there are more job openings in your area for computer programmers or for computer operators? What about data-entry clerks? What effect has the increased use of microcomputer systems had on employment opportunities?

Data Processing Activities

Now you can try out the kinds of data processing activities business workers perform. Below is a summary of the work you will do. You will find the actual information and business forms you need in your *Data Processing Work Kit.*

Activity 1. You will work as a programmer trainee in a large computer service bureau. You will develop a flowchart for a check approval procedure.

Activity 2. You will sort and classify customer requests matching the requirement with the appropriate computer language.

BASIC Project 6
Computer Run Cards: On-Line

The use of computer languages like BASIC can greatly simplify the development of computer software. Interactive languages make coding and testing much easier. The following exercise improves the program developed after Chapter 4 by allowing for on-line data input.

Program Statements

The value of a BASIC computer program greatly increases as the program becomes more flexible. In Project 4 we were able to prepare a job request card by changing the values of the string variables stored in the program. The INPUT statement allows us to alter the value of a string variable by keyboarding in data when the program is RUN. This means that values of variables may be changed without altering the program itself.

INPUT The statement starts with the word INPUT. This word is followed by a numeric variable (for example, A) or a string variable (for example, C$). Using the INPUT statement, we can enter a numeric variable (INPUT A) or a string variable (INPUT C$). This statement usually follows a PRINT statement, which explains to the user what kind of input is expected.

The semicolon is used after the PRINT statement to keep the computer from going to the next line. The INPUT statement then causes a question mark to be printed to show that the program is waiting for the user to key in data.

Sample Program

The program on pages 154 and 155 will wait at nine separate lines for user input (115, 125, 135, 145, 155, 165, 175, 185, 195). When the RUN command is given, the computer will first look like the printout shown in the middle of page 155.

```
10 REM INTERACTIVE VERSION OF BASIC PROJECT 4
100 REM PRINT JOB CARD FROM STRING VARIABLES
110 PRINT "JOB NAME";
115 INPUT A$
120 PRINT "DATE";
125 INPUT B$
130 PRINT "DEPARTMENT";
135 INPUT C$
140 PRINT "CHARGE NO.";
145 INPUT D$
150 PRINT "INPUT";
155 INPUT E$
160 PRINT "STORAGE";
165 INPUT F$
170 PRINT "PROCESSING";
175 INPUT G$
180 PRINT "OUTPUT";
185 INPUT H$
190 PRINT "ROUTE TO";
195 INPUT I$
200 PRINT
210 PRINT "*********************************************************"
220 PRINT
230 PRINT "        JOB REQUEST CARD"
240 PRINT
250 PRINT "JOB NAME:"A$;TAB(40)"DATE: ";B$
260 PRINT "DEPARTMENT:"C$;TAB(40)"CHARGE NO.: ";D$
270 PRINT "INPUT:";E$
```

```
280 PRINT "STORAGE:";F$
290 PRINT "PROCESSING:";G$
300 PRINT "OUTPUT:";H$
310 PRINT
320 PRINT "SPECIAL INSTRUCTIONS -----------------------------------"
330 PRINT "--------------------------------------------------------"
340 PRINT "--------------------------------------------------------"
350 PRINT "--------------------------------------------------------"
360 PRINT "ROUTE TO:";I$
370 PRINT
380 PRINT "********************************************************"
999 END
```

The words JOB NAME were printed because of the PRINT statement in line 110. The question mark was produced by the INPUT statement in line 115. The program will not continue to line 120

```
JOB NAME?
```

until data is keyed in. When you type in WRITE TAPE FOR J. CROWLEY and press the RETURN key, the string you just typed is assigned to the variable A$. The program then continues on to line 120, which causes the word DATE to be printed. Line 125 then causes a question mark to be printed. You will see this on your screen or paper.

```
DATE?
```

If you type in JAN. 12, 1982, the value of B$ becomes JAN 12, 1982, just as it would if you included the program line 120 LET B$

= "JAN. 12, 1982" instead of using the INPUT statement (see Project 4).

The program will continue, waiting for data at each INPUT statement. After the last INPUT statement at line 195, the program continues, printing out the job request card. If you supply the same data that was used in the LET statements of Project 4, the output will be the same.

Keyboarding Activities

```
***********************************************************************

    JOB REQUEST CARD
JOB NAME: WRITE TAPE FOR J. CROWLEY    DATE: JAN 12, 19--
DEPARTMENT: ACCOUNTING                 CHARGE NO.: 19-142
INPUT: DISKETTE
STORAGE: TAPE #953
PROCESSING: MAIN COMPUTER
OUTPUT: LINE PRINTER
SPECIAL INSTRUCTIONS----------------------------------------------
------------------------------------------------------------------
------------------------------------------------------------------
------------------------------------------------------------------
ROUTE TO: ROOM 152

***********************************************************************
```

1. Enter and RUN the program given above.
2. Provide input data for each of the input questions. Use the data from Project 4.
3. RUN the program again, using different data. Compare the two outputs. RUN it a third time with a third set of data.

Enrichment Activity

Prepare a label-making program that produces an identification label for any user. It should include the name, street address, city and ZIP Code, and phone number. Use a special character such as the asterisk (*) to form a box around your label output.

PART 3

Systems and Procedures

CHAPTER

7

Business Data Processing Systems

DATA PROCESSING TERMINOLOGY

Source document
Systems analyst
Data processing system
Procedure
Management information system
Administrative support system
Service bureaus
File
Data base
Integrated systems
File maintenance
Data-base management system
Record
Data field
Systems design
Systems flowchart
Forms design
Data-base administrator

PERFORMANCE GOALS

- Define the term *data processing system.*
- Name at least eight data processing systems.
- Define and give examples of *data files, data bases*, and *file maintenance tasks.*
- State five key steps in setting up a data processing system.

- **List four factors that should be considered in selecting a data processing system.**
- **List five conditions under which a computer system may be cost effective.**
- **Name five parts of a systems design.**

You have read about both the purpose and the methods of data processing. To review, the purpose of business data processing is to produce information that can be used to: (1) operate a business, (2) control a business, and (3) satisfy outside needs for data. To ensure its success, a business must plan continually; it must learn from the past, evaluate the present, and make decisions about the future.

Data processing methods are only as effective as the managers, analysts, programmers, data-entry clerks, and operators who work with them.

In Chapters 1 through 6 you read about business data processing methods and equipment. These methods and the equipment are only as effective as the people involved with them—the business managers who identify the objectives for their data processing activities, the systems analysts who design the systems to meet the user's needs, the computer programmers who develop programs to instruct computers, the data-entry clerks who prepare the input data, and the computer or other machine operators who monitor and operate data processing equipment. Any data processing application must be *systematic* (performed step by step), or the information it produces will not serve its purpose.

All businesses need to develop efficient data processing systems.

Whether a business is large or small, its owners or managers must develop data processing systems and procedures to process data properly and efficiently. A business must have equipment that is appropriate for the amount and type of data that must be processed. It must also have employees who are skilled in instructing the equipment so that the output data is in a form that is acceptable to the user. A large insurance company, bank, utility, or government agency may need to process data for millions of accounts in one day. These transactions may be in the form of benefit or interest checks. Or they may be in the form of invoices for policy payments, charge cards, gas or electricity usage, or taxes. The business form on which the data for a particular transaction is recorded is often called a **source document** because it starts a process.

SOURCE DOCUMENT. Data for a particular business transaction is recorded on a form called a source document. Courtesy Eastman Kodak Company.

A drugstore, delicatessen, or specialty shop may have relatively few customer accounts; therefore, it may need only simple office equipment to perform its data processing tasks. A chain of drugstores or other shops may have much more data to process and either have its own data processing equipment or rely on the services of on-call data processing centers, commonly known as **service bureaus.** The owners and managers of any business, small

Small businesses may rely on service bureaus for their data processing needs.

or large, must keep track of the latest selling price, cost price, and quantity of each item the business sells.

Data Processing Systems

A data processing system consists of people, machines, and procedures.

A **data processing system** consists of people, machines, and procedures. It is the organization of all the manual and machine data processing operations required to produce information about a particular activity. A payroll data processing system, for example, consists of the many operations that produce the payroll information needed by a business. An effective data processing system is a system that provides the data needed in the form desired and at a minimum cost. To be cost effective, a data processing system should produce only the information that is considered to be worth its cost.

An effective data processing system is a system that provides the data needed in the form desired and at a minimum cost.

Within each system, the data processing operations are grouped into one or more procedures. A **procedure** is made up of the manual and machine operations that must be performed step by step to accomplish a particular task. In preparing payroll checks, for example, payroll clerks follow specific procedures each pay period. These procedures ensure that employee paychecks are prepared accurately and on time. One payroll procedure is the series of steps for recording the time worked by each employee in the pay period. Another procedure consists of the steps for computing gross and net pay, and still another consists of the steps for preparing payroll checks. Each such series of steps is known as a data processing procedure. The steps must be performed in a definite order. Thus a data processing procedure is a series of steps performed in a specified order.

A procedure is a series of steps performed in a specified order to accomplish a particular task within a data processing system.

Each business has several data processing systems, and each system provides data about a particular activity. At a minimum, the typical business requires data processing for eight activities.

1. Customer billing
2. Accounts receivable
3. Inventory
4. Sales and marketing
5. Purchasing
6. Accounts payable
7. Payroll
8. General accounting

In recent years businesses have started to recognize the importance of using modern systems for certain office activities that previously used only simple office equipment. The term **administrative support system** is the name given to a system that electronically links together office typing, filing (storage and retrieval), copying, and mailing functions.

An administrative support system electronically links typing, filing, copying, and mailing functions.

There are also special data processing systems for certain types of businesses. Banks, for example, have a system called demand-

A management information system provides information for management when needed.

deposit accounting; it is the organization of all manual and machine operations required for producing information about customers' checking accounts. Data processing systems that provide information for management for planning and control are called **management information systems** (MIS). Since each data processing system provides information on a particular business data processing activity, the objectives of each system are different. For example, the objective of a customer billing system is to do the paperwork required for goods to be shipped to customers and for invoices to be prepared for customers who do not pay in advance. The chief objective of an inventory management system is to ensure that there are enough goods on hand to fill customers' orders promptly. A payroll system usually has several objectives, but its chief objective is to pay employees for work done.

The owners or managers of a business specify the form of the output data to be produced by the various data processing systems. For example, one company may pay employees in cash, and another may pay by check. In a cash payroll system, the pay envelope must contain information on the employee's total earnings and deductions. A check stub would show the same information in a different form.

MIS REPORTING SYSTEM. A financial analyst at an on line terminal is retrieving management information from a data base. Courtesy IBM Corporation

Files Used in Data Processing Systems

To operate a business data processing system, there must be one or more files containing data about the particular aspect of the business for which the system is designed. The data in the files must be updated continually.

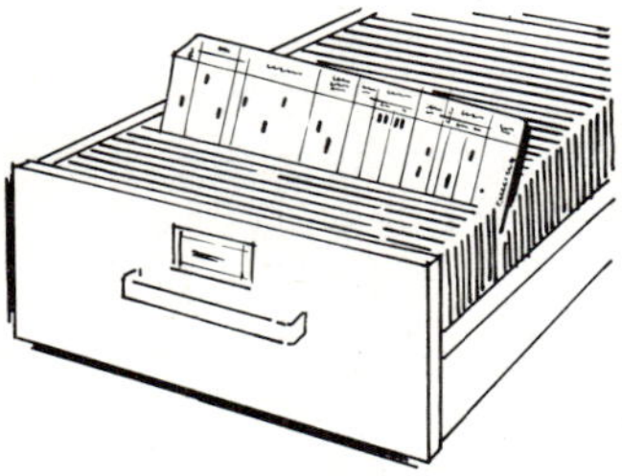

FILES. A file is a collection of records about an activity of a business, such as payroll. The master file is the main file of records in a data processing system.

A **file** (or a master file) is a collection of records about a particular activity of a business. Data is stored in a file and retrieved from a file regardless of the type of storage device used. Data may be stored on punched cards, magnetic tape, or magnetic disks and diskettes.

Sometimes the information needed by one data processing system is also needed by another. For example, the quantity a customer orders of each item is needed not only for customer billing but also for sales analyses and inventory management. Prior to the use of computers for data processing, separate files of data were usually established for each business activity. When the same information used for one data processing activity was needed for another, information had to be recorded and maintained in a second file. With the use of today's computers, one file of data can be used for several data processing activities. A file of data that is shared often is called a **data base.** Systems sharing data files are said to be **integrated systems.**

File Records and Data Fields

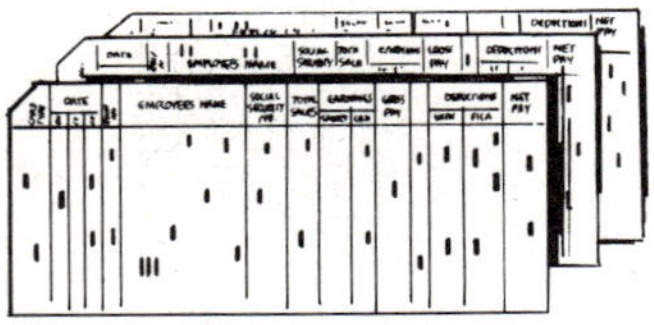

RECORDS. Records in a file contain data about particular items. A payroll file contains a record for each employee.

All the data in a file, or data base, for a particular product, customer, supplier, or employee is considered a **record.** For example, the inventory department of a paper products manufacturer maintains a master file. This file contains a record for each product kept in inventory.

METHODS USED TO UPDATE A MASTER FILE

1. **Real-time processing**
2. **Batch processing**

In a computer system, the master file can be updated in either of two ways: through real-time processing (as transactions occur) or through batch processing (after the transactions have been held for a particular period). The updating of the master file of available seats on an airline flight is an example of real-time processing. As customers purchase their tickets or check in at the terminal, the seat information (master file) is updated. In a batch processing system, on the other hand, the master file is not updated as transactions occur. Instead, the transactions are held (batched) for file updating at a regularly scheduled time, which may be daily, weekly, or monthly.

Each record in a file is divided into several areas called **data fields** or *fields* for recording data. A data field consists of one or more characters that make up an item of data. For example, in a payroll file *employee name* and *pay rate* are two important

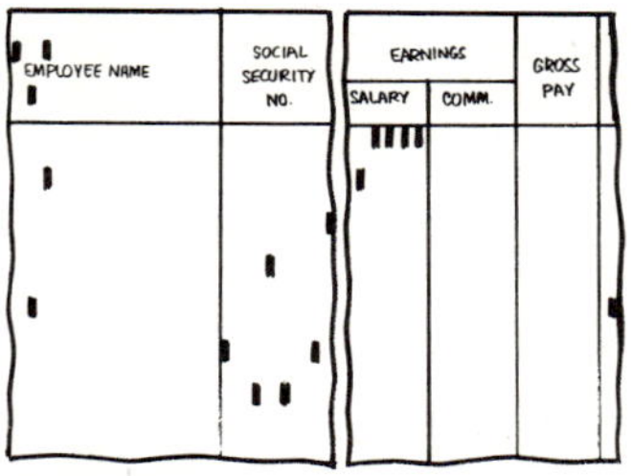

FIELDS. Records are divided into fields. Each field is an area in which specific data is recorded. An employee's wage rate is a data field.

data fields. Data recorded in a field may be alphabetic only, numeric only, or alphanumeric (both alphabetic and numeric). The word *character* in data processing means a letter (A through Z), a numeral (0 through 9), or an asterisk (*) or some other special symbol.

File Maintenance

Information in files must be kept up to date.

File maintenance is the task of updating records in a file or data base so that the file contains the latest information. In the file maintenance operation, whether done manually by a file clerk or automatically by a computer, new records are inserted in the master file, data in existing records is changed, and inactive records are removed from the file. Input data (any item of data entered into a system) is needed to update records in a file. Computer software programs designed to organize and maintain the information in data bases are called **data-base management systems.** A **data-base administrator** has the responsibility for seeing that the information in a data base is kept current and accurate.

The details of transactions in both business and government must be recorded accurately and reflected in the master file. A manufacturer may have to record customer transactions every day, payroll transactions every pay period, and tax transactions every quarter. Each of the transaction records differs in length, but they all have one task in common—the data for each transaction must be recorded accurately and stored so it is available when needed. As we said earlier, either a file can be updated as transactions occur, or the transactions can be held for later updating of the master file. Good file maintenance ensures that a master file or data base can be used for retrieving current data when it is needed for billing customer accounts, making payments, or preparing reports. Examples of file maintenance in two data processing systems follow.

1. A savings account data processing system
2. An automobile inventory data processing system

A Savings Account Data Processing System.

Keeping track of daily balances in savings accounts is a major task for a savings bank. In its data processing system, the bank sets up a complete file for customer accounts. To maintain a current record of each account, bank employees and machines process many input transactions daily. These transactions include amounts deposited by customers, amounts withdrawn by customers, and changes in customers' addresses.

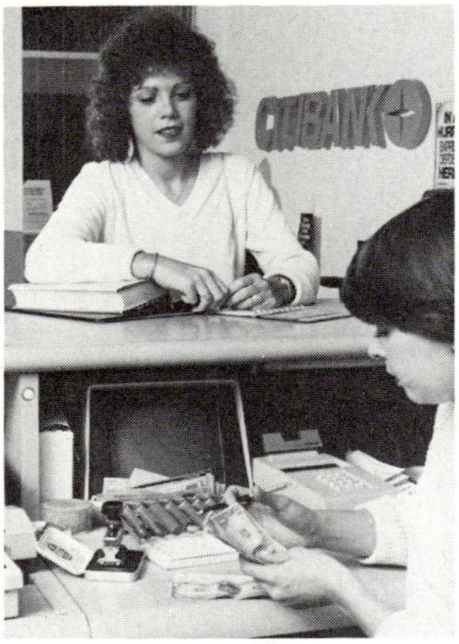

REAL-TIME PROCESSING. Banks use real-time processing to keep savings and checking account records up to date. Courtesy Citicorp

For each customer account, a savings bank must update two different records when a transaction occurs. One record belongs to the customer—the savings passbook (or bankbook). The other is the bank's record for the customer, which is in the file with all the other customer records. The file is usually maintained on magnetic disks or magnetic tape. When a customer makes a deposit or withdrawal, the bank teller keys into a computer terminal the date, the account number, and the amount deposited or withdrawn. A computer calculates the new balance in the account, including interest if any is payable. Then the computer records in the form of magnetized spots on the bank's master file the date, amount deposited or withdrawn, interest, and new customer balance. At the same time, duplicate information is recorded in print form in the customer's passbook. This imprinting is done when the bank teller inserts the passbook in the terminal.

An Automobile Inventory Data Processing System. Regardless of its size, an automobile dealership selling new and used cars maintains an inventory of automobiles for sale. There is one record for each car in the file. The data fields on each such record include the items that make up the description of the car—its make, model type, serial number, and color, as well as any optional features and their suggested selling prices.

The file maintenance task in keeping the automobile inventory up to date sounds easy. Each time a car is sold, the record for that car must be removed from the file. Each time a new car arrives from the factory, a record for that car must be added to

INVENTORY DATA PROCESSING. Computers may be used for summarizing customer preferences, for keeping inventory balances up to date, and for cataloging prices of items. Courtesy Mercedes-Benz of North America

the file. Also, if a customer trades in an old model of a car when buying a newer model, information about the used car must be added to the inventory. Though this file maintenance task may be simple, it must be done very accurately. It is important that the correct features and prices be recorded for each car. Also, it is important that the inventory be up to date so that one sales representative does not try to sell a car already sold by another sales representative. Very large automobile dealerships may keep their inventory records on computers, while smaller dealerships may use hand-posted or typed inventory file records.

CHECK YOURSELF

Supply the missing words.

1. A data processing system consists of people, machines, and ___?___.
2. A series of steps performed in a specified order is called a data processing ___?___.
3. The business form on which the data for a particular transaction is recorded is often called a(n) ___?___ ___?___.
4. An effective data processing system is one that provides the data needed in the form desired and at a minimum ___?___.
5. Data processing systems that provide information for management are called ___?___ ___?___ systems.
6. The typical business has ___?___ basic data processing systems.
7. In the office of the future, electronic equipment will be used in ___?___ ___?___ systems.
8. A collection of records about a particular activity of a business is called a(n) ___?___.
9. A file used in more than one system is called a(n) ___?___.
10. The updating of records so that they contain the latest information is called ___?___ ___?___.
11. A field that contains both alphabetic and numeric characters is said to be ___?___.
12. All the data in a file for a particular item, customer, supplier, or employee is called a(n) ___?___.
13. A record is divided into areas for recording data called ___?___.
14. Computer software programs for file maintenance are called ___?___ ___?___ ___?___.
15. Processing data periodically after transactions have been held is called ___?___ ___?___.
16. In data processing, any letter (A through Z), any number (0 through 9), or any special symbol is called a(n) ___?___.
17. The person responsible for data-base maintenance is the ___?___ ___?___.

Steps in Setting Up a Data Processing System

The systems analyst's main responsibility is finding the most effective way to get work done.

In most businesses and government agencies, employees called systems analysts develop the necessary data processing systems and procedures. The chief responsibility of the **systems analyst** is to determine the most effective way of doing work. Part of the job is to decide on the most efficient equipment for processing data. Should the simpler office machines be used, or should computers be used—or, more likely, a combination of both?

When a systems analyst begins work on a data processing system, he or she studies the business's needs for output data. System needs are often designed in reverse. Starting with the required output ensures that the input elements will be complete. Next the systems analyst decides which operations, if any, should be performed by machine and which should be performed by people. This decision is based on such considerations as the amount of data to be processed, the time and number of employees available for performing the data processing operations, the type of output data desired, and the expected cost.

SYSTEMS ANALYSIS WORK. One task of the systems analyst is to decide what form input and output data will take: punched cards, punched tape, printout, magnetic tape, or magnetic disk. Susan Muller

All data processing systems require people to perform some of the data processing steps. For example, data-entry clerks are needed to carry out the input operations in specific computer procedures, and computer operators are needed to run the equipment. Of course, computer programmers would have had to prepare written instructions for processing. These employees work together to operate the data processing system that the systems analyst develops. This is the kind of specialization that is found in large data processing organizations. Each member of the data processing team plays a vital and clearly defined role in the business activity. Smaller businesses may require one or only a few employees to perform the many specialized tasks that a system such as payroll requires.

The steps in setting up a data processing system are these.

1. Defining system objectives and requirements.
2. Selecting data processing equipment.
3. Developing a systems design.
4. Preparing computer programs.
5. Installing the system.

Defining System Objectives and Requirements

The systems analyst must meet with managers from each department that the data processing system is to serve. The man-

SYSTEMS ANALYST. The systems analyst must consult with management on the input to be recorded. Courtesy Burroughs Corporation

ager and the systems analyst must come to an agreement on the types of output documents needed, how often they will be needed, and the best way of recording the input data. Often the form of output needed will determine the input method. The plan the systems analyst develops for a new or improved data processing system must provide obvious benefits. These benefits might include the following: the availability of new data, the faster processing of data, more reliable performance of the system, and a reduction in operating expenses.

Once the basic system objectives are identified, the systems analyst must in detail write the requirements of the system. This includes studying the work already being performed—what is being done and how it is being done. Such a study also includes information on the availability of input data, the need for coding data, the files and records that must be maintained, the policies that must be followed in processing the data, and the output data being produced. All reports and other output documents produced must be evaluated as to whether they are needed. The study must also include statistics (numeric data) on the present volume of work and estimates of the volume of work that will need to be handled in the future.

Selecting Data Processing Equipment

Once the systems analyst has defined the system requirements and obtained management's agreement to them, he or she evaluates the data processing equipment that could be used to perform the work. Four factors are important in evaluating the advantages and disadvantages of different types of data processing equipment.

The four factors listed here are important in deciding which data processing equipment is best for procedural needs.

1. The speed at which the operations can be performed.
2. The accuracy and reliability of performance.
3. The types and costs of the people required to operate the equipment.
4. The costs of the machines required for the system.

The decision of management to set up a computer data processing system or some other system depends on the number of transactions to be processed, the number of file records to be maintained, and the complexity of the operations that must be performed to produce the necessary output documents. The use of simple equipment is the most sensible for a small amount of input data and simple operations. An example of an effective manual data processing system would be the weekly payroll processing of a small business such as a neighborhood drugstore. An owner-managed drugstore employing a pharmacist and two clerks would probably pay the pharmacist the same amount of money each week, and each of the clerks would be paid an hourly rate. Thus the payroll data would be recorded in a work log, and the computations would be performed with the aid of a calculator and reference tables for federal, state, and local taxes.

For more complex payroll data that might include a greater number of employees and perhaps a benefit plan, the employer would be likely to select a computer system. A summary of the thinking that should go into the selection of a computer system follows.

Choosing a Computer System. Thanks to the declining costs of small computer systems, more and more businesses are finding it cost effective to use a computer either by buying computing time from a service bureau or by installing a computer. Computer equipment requires fewer workers to operate, but its cost is generally higher than that of simpler data processing equipment. In addition, the computer programmers and computer operators needed to support the computer operation are normally paid higher salaries than the operators of other office machines.

Whether or not a computer system is cost effective in a particular situation depends on several conditions.

In general, a computer system may be cost effective under several conditions.

1. **Volume.** A large volume of file records, of complex processing operations, or of input and output data may justify a computer data processing system. For example, a department store, an insurance company, and a utility company (such as a telephone company) need to handle a large number of customer records for billing.
2. **Integration.** When information from the same source document is used for several types of processing, computer data processing may be the most efficient method. Input data from customer orders can be used for order fulfillment, for customer billing, for handling accounts receivable, for inventory management, and for sales analysis. This would be an example of common-source data.
3. **Complexity.** When there are many computations, each computation building on another, computer processing may be the only efficient method. Consider, for example, the work of a financial analyst. The analyst must assess many different statistics (such as income/profit ratios) about the current and past performance of a company in order to make an intelligent guess about its future performance.
4. **Speed.** When status reports or output documents must be produced quickly, computer data processing may be essential.

Banks, for example, need up-to-date information about the balance in each customer account. Nowadays almost every bank uses a computer to record deposits and withdrawals and has up-to-date customer balances available.

5. **Accuracy.** When data must be very accurate, a computer processing system is extremely helpful. It allows for an assembly-line approach to entering data, validating data, and checking data for reasonableness. And it ensures consistent processing. Also, when a large number of repetitive operations such as calculating or printing have to be performed, workers may become tired and make errors, while machines will not. For example, in the computation of gross pay (hours worked times pay rate) for a payroll of 10,000 employees, it is essential not to have any calculating errors.

The systems analyst evaluates alternative methods of performing work and determines which method will be the most cost effective for a particular system.

When the systems analyst recommends a selection of data processing equipment to management, he or she usually submits a written report based on the study. Many systems analysts include in this report a recommendation for the type of computer system to handle the data processing work. This recommendation includes the pros and cons of using a service bureau as against the installation of a computer within the business. Also, the alternatives of in-house (within the business) computers on a centralized, decentralized, or distributed computer basis are evaluated. These alternatives are discussed in Chapter 6.

In the report to management, the systems analyst also includes cost analyses that specify both the one-time costs and the continuing costs for the proposed system. One-time costs are the costs of putting a system into operation. The report includes a comparison of the estimated costs with the costs of the work already being done. It provides work schedules that show when particular operations will be performed. And it lists both the advantages and disadvantages, if any, of the recommended system.

Developing a Systems Design

A systems flowchart is a diagram of all the operations in a data processing system.

If management approves the selection of equipment recommended for the system, the next step is for the systems analyst to develop the **systems design.**

The systems analyst designs human and machine procedures.

The first step in systems design is the preparation of a **systems flowchart** by the systems analyst. Using standard systems flowchart symbols, the analyst identifies in pictorial form the series of manual and machine steps that make up the particular system being designed. In addition to the flowchart, the systems analyst prepares a written description of each step in each procedure of the system and of the data fields in each file.

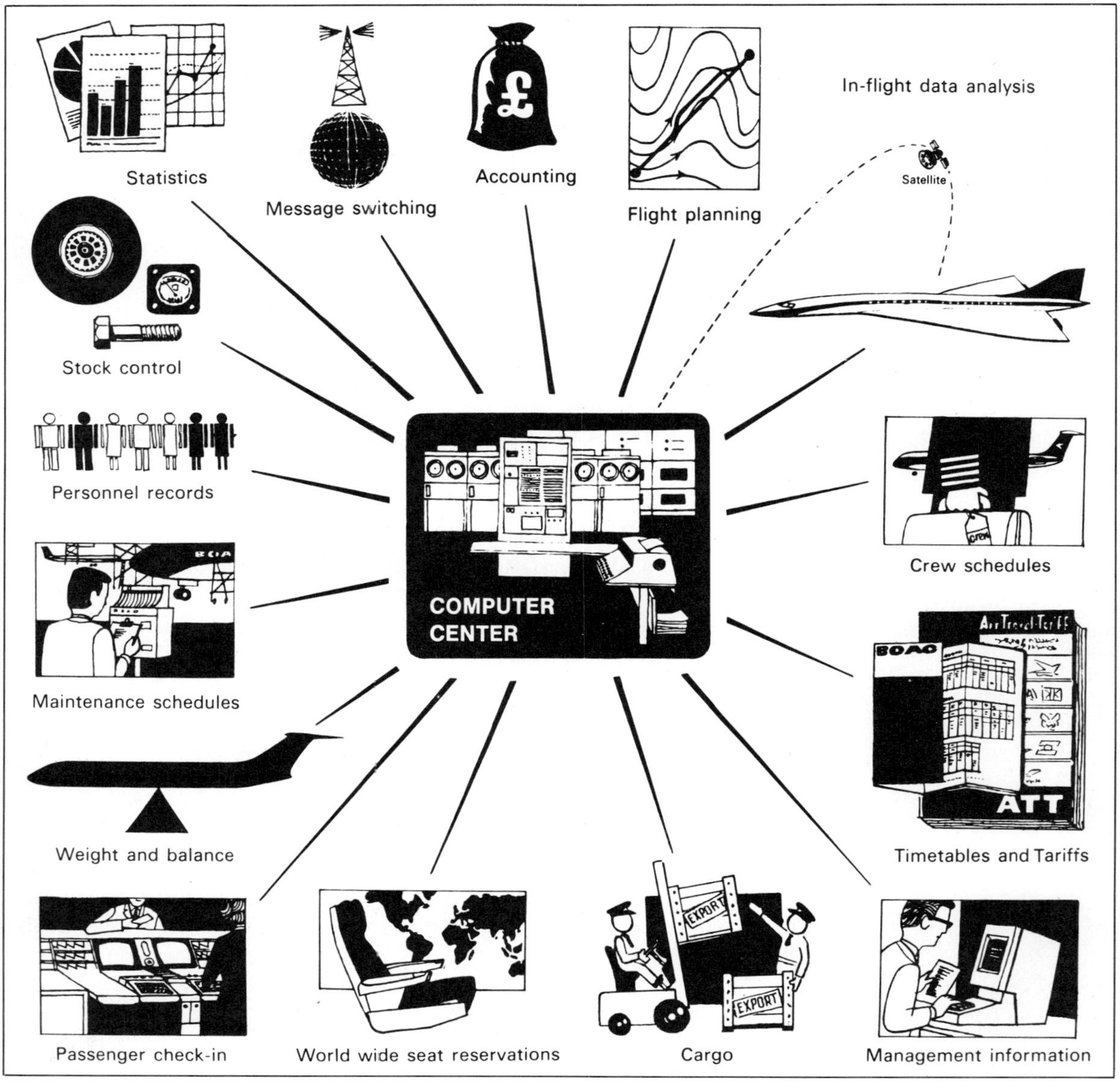

INTEGRATED DATA PROCESSING. A computerized data processing system is cost effective for an airline company because it can provide integrated data processing. Courtesy British Airways

The systems analyst must decide with management on the form in which the input data will be recorded. Data to be processed must be in a form that will be easy for a data-entry clerk to convert into machine-readable form.

Regardless of the processing method used, the systems analyst must provide for entering all the input needed to operate the

Planning forms to communicate data is called forms design.

system. For example, in a payroll data processing system based on employee names, each employee's name must be included as part of the pay period input data. But in a payroll system based on identification numbers, such as social security numbers, each number must be included in the data input. The idea is to ensure efficient data preparation as part of a cost-effective data processing system. Such considerations are part of a business process called forms design, which is vital for efficient data flow. **Forms design** is the planning of forms that will communicate the data needed for particular transactions.

SYMBOLS USED IN FLOWCHARTING

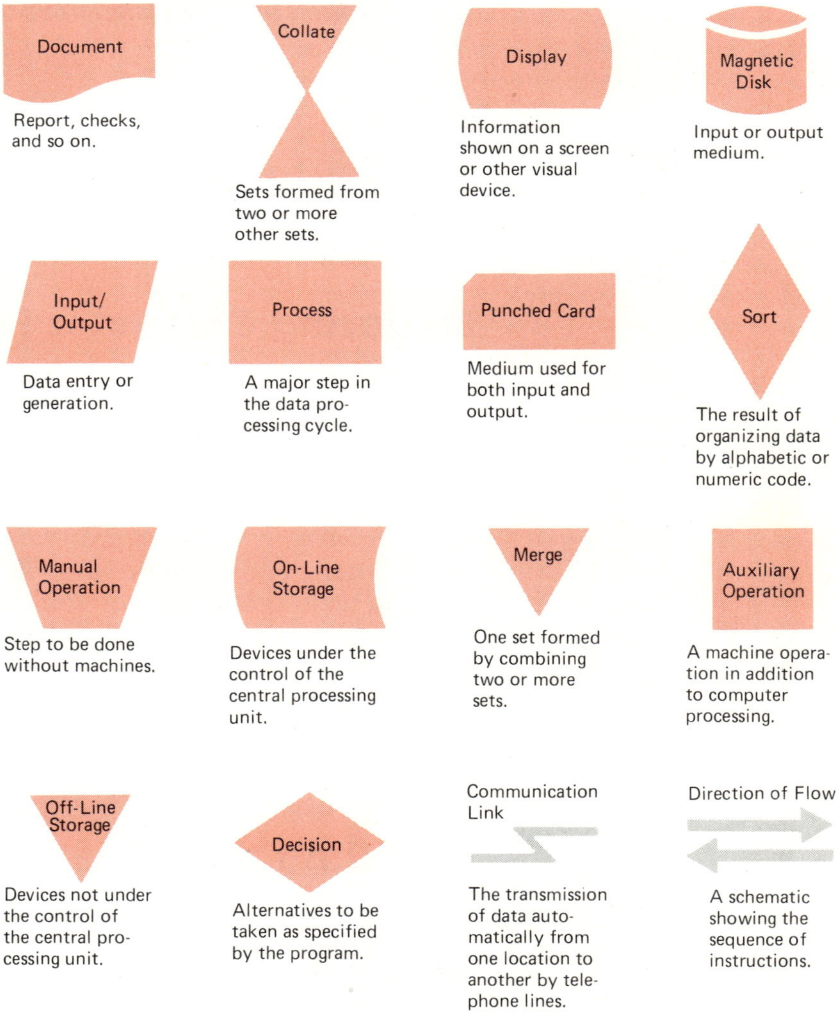

Just as the systems analyst must work out an efficient means of obtaining input data and having it read and processed, he or she must design the output documents needed. In a payroll data processing system, at least two output documents are needed. These are paychecks and tax reports. One business may want the earnings statement to include the employee's total pay and deductions for that year. Another business may want it to include the employee's pay and deductions for just that pay period. These details must be part of the overall systems design.

Depending on the data that management wants included in the output documents, the reporting procedure may be simple or require a great deal of output information. In either case, the systems analyst is responsible for ensuring that the various procedures produce the output documents specified.

A completed systems design usually covers the following items.

1. Descriptions of the files or data bases used in the system and the methods of file maintenance.
2. Design of formats for data input.
3. Descriptions of the processing steps that take place from input to output (flowcharts and narrative).
4. Design of formats for data output.
5. Specifications for computer programs.

Preparing Computer Programs

If a computer is to be used, the systems analyst prepares system specifications for the computer programmers. The task of translating these specifications into programs of instructions for the computer is described in Chapter 6. Depending on the complexity of the system, one or more computer programmers may be asked to write a computer program for a particular procedure in the system. For example, a computer programmer may be asked to write a program for computing the gross and net pay for each pay period. Another programmer may be asked to program the procedure for the preparation of paychecks and employee earnings statements. Another may be asked to program the procedure for preparing the quarterly tax reports required by the federal government. Each of these programs will be part of the payroll data processing system.

Installing the System

When the procedures for operating the new system are complete and the computer or other machine programs required are tested and up and running, the systems analyst assists the departments that are to use the system in converting to it. This step

SYSTEM FLOWCHART. A systems analyst developed this flowchart to depict the operations making up a typical payroll system.

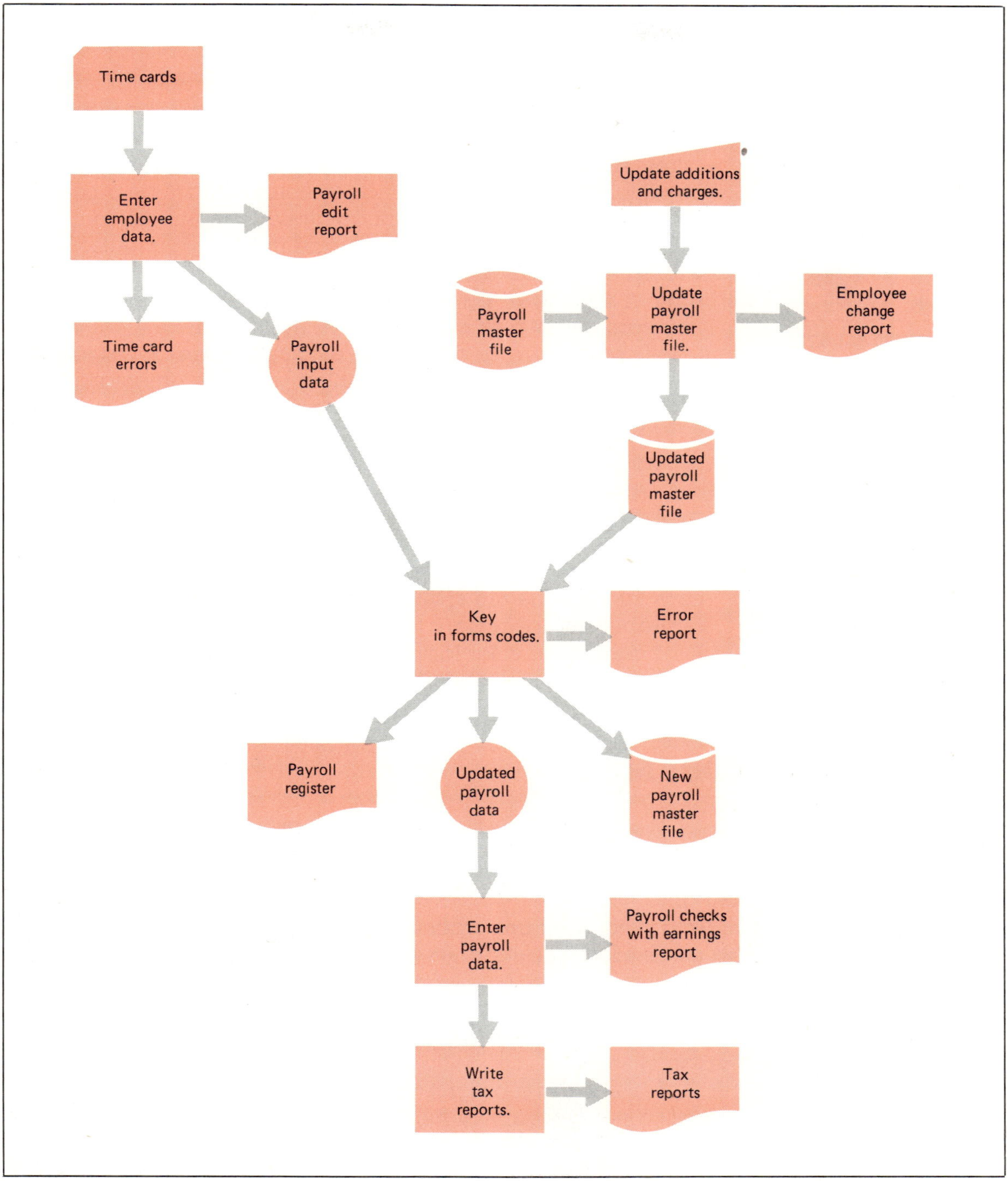

SYSTEM INSTALLATION. Manufacturers of data-entry equipment provide training sessions and reference materials for operators.

often includes the development of job training manuals for the employees who will be part of the organization of people and machines making up the system. Manuals of this kind ensure that a business can continue to function when employees leave or are promoted.

In addition to providing training programs, the systems analyst must thoroughly test and debug a system before it can be used to perform work. Testing should include all input, processing, and output steps of the data processing cycle. In testing for all possible conditions, first sample data (not the actual data to be processed) should be used. The feedback obtained from this test may show that some changes need to be made in the system. After testing with sample data, a second series of tests is made using actual data. If it is shown by this testing that the new system produces accurate output results, then the system is ready.

Setting up a simple data processing system that is cost effective may take minutes. But the planning and implementation of a sophisticated computer data processing system can take months, sometimes even years. The work that goes into a minicomputer processing system lies somewhere in between.

A business must think carefully about the amount of time it has available to plan, test, and install a system. While it is getting a computer system up and running, the business may have to pay its workers to process data the old way, temporarily incurring costs for both the old system and the new. Such overlap is both desirable and necessary to avoid interruption of service. A systems analyst will refer to the two systems as *parallel systems* and try to keep the best of both in the final system.

CHECK YOURSELF

Supply the missing words.

1. A(n) __?__ __?__ designs a data processing system that will provide the desired output data.
2. The results of data processing are produced on a(n) __?__ __?__.
3. A series of steps needed to perform a data processing task is called a(n) __?__.
4. A user's data processing needs are defined by the __?__ __?__.
5. A(n) __?__ __?__ shows the step-by-step operations to be performed in a data processing system.
6. A(n) __?__ __?__ writes a program for a particular procedure.
7. An old system and a new system that function together for a while are called __?__ __?__.

Review Questions

1. Define the terms *data processing system* and *procedure.*
2. Name eight data processing systems that are typical in business.
3. Define *management information system* and *administrative support system.*
4. Name the five steps involved in setting up a data processing system.
5. Describe the step of defining system objectives and requirements, and give an example of a system objective.
6. Define the terms *file, data base, file maintenance,* and *data-base management.*
7. Name four important factors in evaluating data processing equipment.
8. Name five reasons why computers may be cost effective for a business to use.
9. Describe the five parts to a systems design.
10. Define the function of forms design.
11. List some of the activities needed to install a system in a business.

Comparing Ideas

The questions below are to help you think about what you have learned in this chapter. They are thought questions. There is no one correct answer.

1. How do you think the installation of visual display terminals would affect the work of clerks at an automobile rental counter? Assume that the current system is a combination of telephones and adding machines. (*Hint:* Think about the steps that need to be taken in reserving a car for a customer, in checking a customer's credit, and in charging the customer when the car is returned.)
2. Which of the following reasons do you think businesses use most often to justify the cost of installing a computer system?
   - **a.** Need for new data.
   - **b.** Need for faster processing.
   - **c.** Need for more reliable performance.
   - **d.** Need to cut costs.

Data Processing Activities

Now you can try out the kinds of data processing activities business workers perform. Below is a summary of the work you will do. You will find the actual information and business forms you need in your *Data Processing Work Kit.*

Activity 1. As an administrative assistant at a major bank, you will convert questions about the bank's staffing needs into system objectives.

Activity 2. You will be asked to evaluate a new recruiting system. You will check the completeness of a system flowchart.

Activity 3. You will post job transfer requests using an on-line computer terminal.

BASIC Project 7
Savings Deposit Project

Even the simplest data processing system will include objectives and requirements. The following exercise produces the minimum output for a useful savings deposit information system. It is not the complexity of the calculations that matters. It is the value of the information the program produces.

Program Statements
The Plus and Asterisk Signs and Parentheses

It is difficult to think of business data processing without thinking of handling financial transactions. Most processing requires the use of fundamental arithmetic operations.

A PRINT statement can contain an expression using any of the four mathematical operations (addition, subtraction, multiplication, and division). The operations of addition and multiplication are indicated by using the symbol + for addition and the asterisk (*) for multiplication.

- \+ The plus sign stands for addition.
- * The asterisk sign stands for multiplication.
- ( ) Parentheses can be used to tell the computer to perform the arithmetic operation within the parentheses first.

When the computer *evaluates* (figures out the value of) an expression, it does multiplication and division first, then addition and subtraction. The expression 3+4*2 would be evaluated by first multiplying 4 times 2 to get 8 and then adding 8 to 3 to get 11.

You can change this order by using parentheses. The computer evaluates what is in parentheses first, so (3+4)*2 would be evaluated as 14. First 3 is added to 4 to get 7. Then 7 is multiplied by 2 to get 14.

Variables may also be used in expressions, as we will see in the sample program.

Sample Program

In this program the user will enter the values for B (balance) and D (deposit). Since the input must be numeric, there is no dollar sign after the variable names.

This program shows that BASIC can be used to print both stored information and the results of an expression that is evaluated in the program.

```
10 REMARK PROGRAM TO CALCULATE SAVINGS ACCOUNT INFORMATION
20 PRINT "TYPE BEGINNING BALANCE";
30 INPUT B
40 PRINT "TYPE DEPOSIT AMOUNT";
50 INPUT D
60 PRINT "TOTAL NOW IN ACCOUNT IS"; B+D
70 PRINT
80 PRINT "INTEREST (9.5%) IN 1 YEAR WILL BE";(B+D)*.095
90 PRINT
100 END
```

Output

The following output would be produced if a balance of 125 (no $, please) and a deposit of 33 were inputted.

```
TYPE BEGINNING BALANCE?125
TYPE DEPOSIT AMOUNT?33
TOTAL NOW IN ACCOUNT IS 158
INTEREST (9.5%) IN 1 YEAR WILL BE 15.01
```

As you RUN this program, you should be aware of the possibility of making an error when data is entered into the program. At line 30, for example, the computer waits for you to type in a value for BALANCE. What if you typed in HARRY? Since BALANCE is a numeric variable (no $ at the end), the string HARRY would not be accepted, and an error message would be printed. You would have to start the program over from the beginning by typing RUN again.

Remember that if a string variable is used, any string of letters, numbers, or other characters may be assigned to the variable. A or LIZ or 128 or AL3-6767 may all be used with string variables; 128 could also be used with a numeric variable.

Also remember that only numeric variables may be used in arithmetic operations.

Keyboarding Activities

1. Enter and RUN the program given above.
2. Input the following transaction amounts.

BALANCE	DEPOSIT
296	107
380	600
159	10

3. Modify the program to calculate the current savings interest rate in your area.

Enrichment Activity

Create a savings deposit program that accepts the following input data.

Your name	Beginning balance
Account number	Deposit
Today's date	Savings rate

Construct this program so that it will display or print two copies of a savings deposit receipt.

NOTE: You can repeat any BASIC statements in a program as long as each use has its own line number. For example, this will print HI twice.

```
10 PRINT "HI"
20 PRINT "HI"
```

CHAPTER

8

A Billing and Inventory System

DATA PROCESSING TERMINOLOGY

Sales slip
Shipping order
Inventory
Customer invoice
Packing slip
Shipping label
Reorder point
Balance on hand
Input prompting format
Net inventory position
Available inventory
Net available inventory
Open orders
Checkpoints
Operational
Conversion
Parallel systems
System test
Inventory exception report

PERFORMANCE GOALS

- List five steps in setting up a billing and inventory system.
- List four objectives of an integrated billing and inventory system.
- State the master files required for a billing and inventory system.
- Name the input and processing steps of a billing and inventory system.

- **Name two of the output documents from billing and inventory processing.**
- **Name alternative equipment that may be used for billing and inventory processing.**

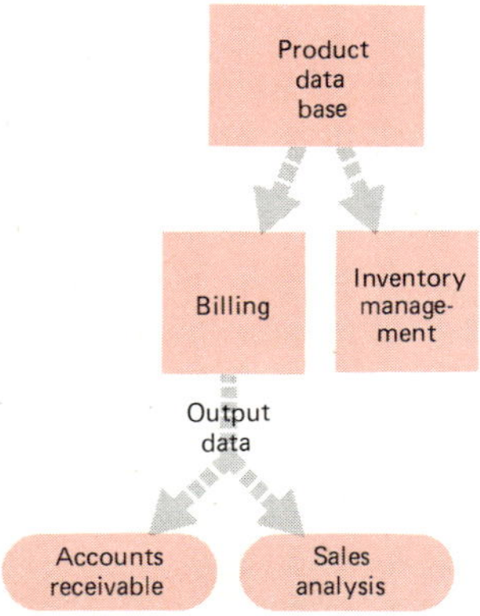

INTEGRATED DATA PROCESSING. An example of integrated data processing is the use of a single data base for processing both billing and inventory. Inventory data is updated at the same time that billing data is prepared.

Chapters 8 and 9 deal with actual business data processing systems. These chapters will show how business objectives and requirements are met by computer data processing. They will also further explain the role of a data processing system in business and will give examples of the input and output media used by many companies.

First you will study a system designed to handle the processing of billing and inventory data for the Good Times Paper Company, a manufacturer of greeting cards, writing papers, and other paper goods. This is an integrated system designed so that a data base of product information can be shared for both billing and inventory activities. The system provides for the updating of inventory data at the same time that billing data is prepared. Billing and inventory recordkeeping activities are important in both small and large businesses.

An order and billing system produces the paperwork needed to fill customer orders.

Billing is important because it produces the paperwork that is necessary to get merchandise to the customers who order it and to bill customers who have not paid in advance. Every business must have a billing system, however simple. In a small business such as a drugstore, the billing system may mean just having a salesclerk record cash purchases in a ledger while ringing them up on the register. Or it may mean recording credit sales on sales slips provided by an international credit service such as Visa or MasterCard. In a larger retail business such as a department store, a customer may select items, ask that they be delivered, and charge them to the account he or she has at the store. A filled-in **sales slip** provides a record of a particular transaction. In preparing a sales slip, the salesclerk is performing the first step in the billing system. A copy of the sales order, known as a **shipping order,** is sent to the shipping department, where the merchandise is packed and shipped to the customer. After delivery, the store's billing department prepares a bill and mails it to the customer.

All types of businesses need an order and billing system.

The telephone company and the gas and electricity suppliers must also have a system to handle customer orders and bill each customer for the telephone units or power used. A large telephone company must process a great volume of order and billing data when it treats each long-distance telephone call as an order.

Inventory data processing also is important. A company must try to have enough on hand of each product to fill customers'

INVENTORY UPDATING. Some sophisticated computer systems allow a salesclerk to ring up a sale and, through communications lines, update the inventory records at the same time. Courtesy NCR Corporation

THREE TYPES OF INVENTORIES

1. **Raw materials**
2. **Work-in-process**
3. **Finished goods**

orders promptly. The number kept on hand of each product is that product's **inventory.** There are different types of inventories. An automobile manufacturer, for example, has at least three types of inventories: a raw materials inventory (steel), a work-in-process inventory (parts such as auto bodies, gas gauges, and tires), and a finished goods inventory (automobiles ready for sale). The automobile manufacturer must have steel to start producing automobiles, parts to assemble the automobiles, and finished automobiles to make sales and earn a profit. The same data processing system can be used for any of these three types of inventories.

Since any inventory or combination of inventories represents a financial investment, the owner or manager keeps inventories as low as possible. The objective is to have just enough items to satisfy manufacturing needs or to fill customers' orders but not so many as to create excess or unusable supplies.

For any business, efficient billing and inventory processing is vital to good customer relations. It assures customers that their orders will be handled promptly and accurately and that the charges for which they are billed will truly reflect the merchandise or service purchased.

Your study of billing and inventory data processing will follow the outline used by systems analysts. As you learned in Chapter 7, the systems analyst must perform the following steps for each system under study.

1. Defining system objectives and requirements.
2. Selecting data processing equipment.
3. Developing a systems design.
4. Preparing computer programs.
5. Installing the system

INVENTORY MANAGEMENT. The manager of a business strives to keep inventories low, but not so low as to have insufficient merchandise for sale. A balance is important to keep customers happy and costs down. Courtesy Mohawk Data Services

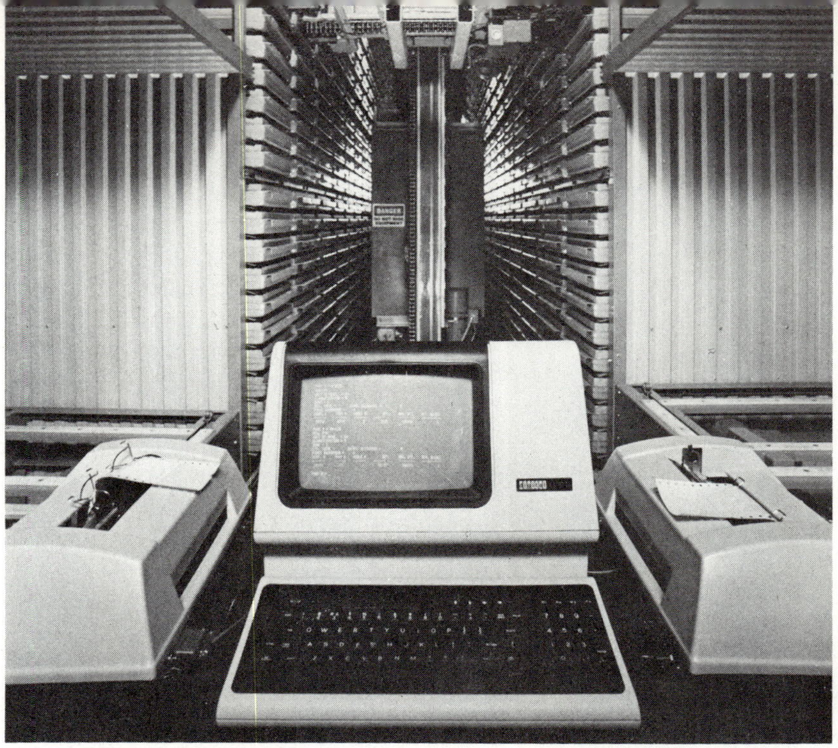

INVENTORY MANAGEMENT. Here a completely automated parts-storage facility helps management keep inventory costs down.
Dick Durrance II/Woodfin Camp & Associates

Defining System Objectives and Requirements

OBJECTIVES OF A BILLING AND INVENTORY SYSTEM

1. **Shipping merchandise**
2. **Billing customers**
3. **Maintaining good inventory levels**
4. **Providing data for follow-up**

The systems analyst at the Good Times Paper Company has talked with members of management to identify the objectives to be met with a new billing and inventory system. These objectives are defined as follows.

1. To ship merchandise to a customer within a short time after receipt of the customer order.
2. To bill promptly customers who do not pay in advance.
3. To keep accurate and current inventory records so that there is enough inventory on hand to fill incoming customer orders.
4. To provide current sales information for departments that need to follow-up after customer orders have been filled.

The data processing requirements to fulfill each of these objectives are defined by the systems analyst. The requirements for the Good Times Paper Company are similar to those in many businesses.

Shipping Merchandise to Customers

Units of merchandise will be shipped to a customer only if the shipping department is given appropriate instructions. A shipping order is typically used as an authorization for shipping. When a shipping order is received, the shipping department selects from the company's inventory the quantities of each type of merchandise ordered, packs or bundles the items, and arranges to have the merchandise delivered to the customer. The shipping department encloses in each package a **packing slip,** which lists the description and quantity of each item in the shipment. This slip serves as a checklist for the customer when the merchandise arrives. On the outside of the package, there must be a **shipping label,** which gives the name and address of the customer.

Billing Customers

If the customer does not pay for the merchandise when ordering it, the shipping department may enclose a bill in the package. But usually the bill is mailed to the customer after the goods have been shipped. The bill, often called a **customer invoice,** must contain at least three types of information: (1) standard information, such as the name and address of the company, which is printed on all invoice forms; (2) data identifying the customer being billed—the name, address, and charge account number;

BILLING. A customer invoice must always contain at least three types of information: (1) the company making the sale, (2) the customer, and (3) the products the customer has ordered. This invoice shows that in the current billing period, the customer purchased three products.

GOOD TIMES PAPER COMPANY
610 West 23d Street
New York, NY 10011

Account No. 84239
Invoice Date 11/15/-
Terms of Sale 30 DAYS
Late Payments 1.5 PERCENT INTEREST

Sold To
CONSUMER NOTES
950 JEFFERSON DRIVE
WASHINGTON, DC 20560

Item Number	Item Description	Transaction Code	Quantity	Unit Price	Total Price
401	WRITING PAPER	1	12	12.00	144.00
225	DESK CALENDARS	1	10	7.50	75.00
334	DESK SETS	1	24	50.00	1,200.00
				TOTAL	1,419.00
		SHIPPING CHARGES			15.00
Please pay this amount.					1,434.00

Transaction Codes

1. Charges
2. Payments
3. Credit Memos
4. Miscellaneous Debits
5. Miscellaneous Credits
6. Returned Check

and (3) data about the particular products the customer has ordered. A copy of the format of the customer invoice required at Good Times Paper is shown on page 185.

One system requirement for Good Times Paper is that the billing department prepare a customer invoice before the shipping department selects and packs goods and ships them to a customer. Under this system, the shipping copy of the invoice is used to instruct the shipping department to make the shipment. Another copy is used as a combination packing slip and shipping label. The original invoice is mailed to the customer after shipment.

Reporting Inventory Information

Inventory is merchandise on hand.

Sales forecasts help to keep inventory at an adequate level.

The number of products a company has available is usually called the *inventory balance* (or **balance on hand**). A small clothing store is faced with determining an inventory balance at the end of each day. Each morning the store's inventory system starts with the number of outfits available. As the day moves on, clothing is sold (orders are subtracted from inventory); some patrons may return clothing (items are added to inventory). The day ends with a new number (balance) of outfits available. If the inventory balance is kept too low, customer orders cannot be

INVENTORY REPORTS. An inventory stock report shows the balance on hand of the company's products. Here you see just one page of the company's current stock report.

INVENTORY STOCK REPORT

GOOD TIMES PAPER COMPANY 03 31 19--

PRODUCT CODE NO.	PRODUCT DESCRIPTION	OLD BALANCE	QUANTITY SOLD	QUANTITY RECEIVED	BALANCE ON HAND
1201	BIRTHDAY CARDS	10,514	4,301	2,500	8,713
1202	NOTE PADS	5,642	3,241		2,401
1203	PLACE CARDS	2,105	900		1,205
1204	NOTEPAPER	22,405	12,000	10,000	20,405
1205	CONGRATULATORY CARDS	7,032	1,252	100	5,880
1206	SYMPATHY CARDS	5,160	2,050		3,110
1207	THANK-YOU NOTES	76,210	11,000	40,000	105,210
1208	ANNOUNCEMENT CARDS	29,212	13,500		15,712
1209	ANNIVERSARY CARDS	38,011	25,611		12,400
1210	GIFT CARDS	1,500	1,200		300
1211	AIRMAIL PAPER	24,251	10,000		14,251

Merchandise must be added to stock when inventory reaches the reorder point.

filled and sales will be lost. If the inventories are kept too high, there is the danger that some of the merchandise will not be sold. A report form showing typical inventory stock data is shown on page 186.

The systems analyst must talk with management to identify the factors that go into deciding whether the number of items of merchandise kept on hand is adequate. What are some of these factors? One factor is the estimate of future sales for the merchandise. A company must estimate sales far enough in advance to ensure that customer orders can always be filled. As the inventory gets low, the company can usually manufacture or order additional quantities. Most companies have a reorder point for replacing sold merchandise. The **reorder point** is the estimated amount of merchandise needed to cover sales while additional inventory is being obtained. This means that when the inventory gets down to the reorder point, merchandise will have to be added so that the company can be fairly sure of its ability to fill customers' orders. The sales estimate needs to be made only for the time it takes to add merchandise to the inventory. It takes Good Times Paper one month to reprint a particular card. To be sure, the company should keep a balance greater than the sales estimated for one month.

An inventory management reporting system, which we will discuss in detail later in this chapter, can simplify the job of maintaining adequate inventories. In planning the system, the systems analyst must work with management to assign an appropriate reorder point to each item stocked.

PREPARING INVENTORY STOCK REPORTS (A COMPUTER SYSTEM)

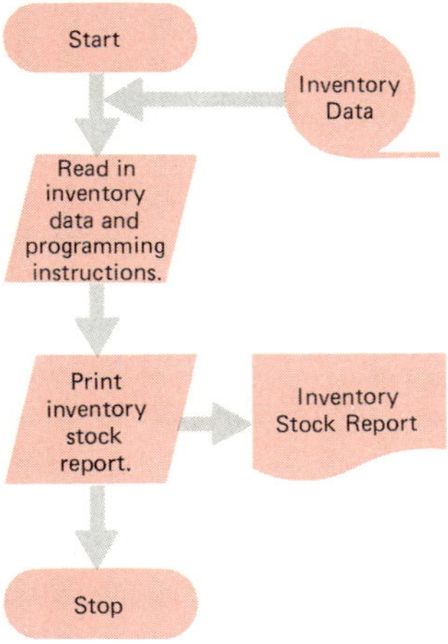

RECORDING SALES INFORMATION. A pharmacist processes a sale and records the type of product sold, the quantity sold, and the unit price. Courtesy IBM Corporation

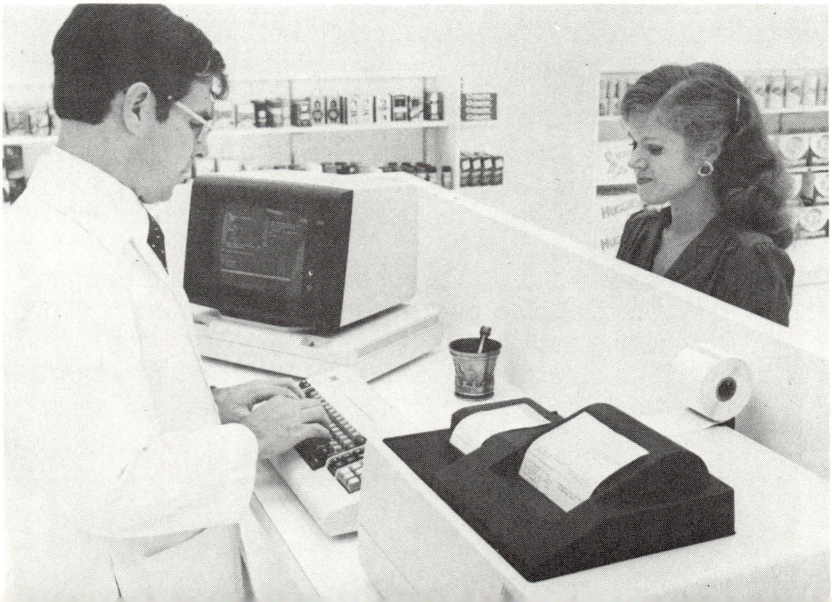

Providing Sales Information for Follow-Up

A billing and inventory system needs to supply current information about sales.

The fourth objective of the Good Times Paper billing and inventory system is to provide current information about each sale for at least two of the company's other departments: the accounts receivable department and the sales department. Each of these requires some, but not all, of the data on a customer invoice. The required data should be recorded in machine-readable form so that it does not have to be rerecorded for additional processing.

1. **Updating the accounts receivable data.** As soon as a customer invoice is sent, the billing amount must be recorded on the customer's account as an amount due. It is the function of the accounts receivable department to follow-up with customers on payments. The data required for this update includes the invoice number and date, the customer number or name, and the billing amount.
2. **Updating the sales information data.** When a sale is made, it may be necessary to compute a sales commission for the person who made the sale. Moreover, data about the sale must be combined with the data for other sales so that the sales department knows how much is sold of each item, how much is sold to each customer, and which sales representatives sell the most in dollar amounts. The sales information data must include the invoice number and date, the customer number or name, the sales representative's number or name, the item number, the quantity sold, and the billing amount.

CHECK YOURSELF

Supply the missing words.

1. The number of products a business has on hand is called the __?__ __?__.
2. The Good Times Paper billing and inventory system is said to be __?__ because file data is shared.
3. A bill for merchandise or services is often called a(n) __?__ __?__.
4. The __?__ point is the estimated amount of merchandise needed to cover sales while additional inventory is being obtained.
5. The shipping department encloses in each shipment a(n) __?__ __?__ listing the items shipped.
6. The objective of accurate and current inventory reporting is to have __?__ items on hand to fill customers' orders but not so __?__ as to create unusable supplies.

Selecting Data Processing Equipment

In our case study of the billing and inventory requirements of Good Times Paper, the systems analyst determines that some type of computer processing is needed to meet the four objectives outlined by management. Only with a computer can the billing and inventory system be integrated so that both billing and inventory activities share the same file data. In addition, when the computer is preparing a customer invoice, it can at the same time subtract from the inventory balance the quantity of each item ordered by the customer. And it can record on an output device, such as a terminal, any instances of inadequate inventory that need immediate attention.

Alternative Computer Systems

The analyst evaluates several alternatives for accomplishing the computer processing. One alternative is to install in Good Times Paper a minicomputer to be used only for processing billing and inventory data. A second alternative calls for the installation of a medium-sized computer that could be used for the company's other computer processing needs. A cost analysis shows that the second alternative is the most economical way for Good Times Paper to handle its data processing requirements. Management approves the purchase of a computer system with a central processor powerful enough to handle all the company's projected computing needs.

For handling the billing and inventory work, the selected computer system has twelve CRT display terminals, four magnetic-tape input/output devices, two disk secondary-storage units to supplement primary storage, a high-speed line printer, and the central processing unit. Ten of the CRT display terminals are used by data-entry operators in the billing department for the input of customer orders and file data. The remaining two terminals, located in the inventory management department, are used to key in data about inventory receipts and product file changes. These terminals are also used to display inventory information. The disk storage units are used to store the two master files (customer information and product information) needed for processing and for the computer programs. The magnetic-tape devices are used primarily as output devices to record information needed for special inventory and sales analyses, accounts receivable, and backup copies of file data. The line printer, attached to the computer, is used for the preparation of customer invoices, inventory reports, and other documents.

BILLING AND INVENTORY PROCESSING. A data-entry clerk in the billing department of the Good Times Paper Company enters customer orders.
Courtesy NCR Corporation

Developing a Systems Design

When management approves the selection of equipment recommended for the billing and inventory system, the next step is for the systems analyst to develop the systems design. This should include the following.

1. A description of the files or data bases used in the system.
2. Formats for data input.
3. A description of the processing steps from input to output.
4. Formats for data output.
5. Specifications for computer programs.

Setting Up and Maintaining Files

In defining the system requirements, the systems analyst must begin with this question: What pieces of information, or data, would be kept in the billing and inventory system files for Good Times Paper? The first data file has customer information, and the second file has product information.

The customer master file must include the *bill to* name and address and the *ship to* name and address (in case the shipment is to be made to a location different from the billing address). It must also include instructions on how to ship the merchandise, code numbers for both the customer and the sales representative, and the customer's credit rating (to allow for the possibility of charge sales). The order department must have the approval of the credit manager to fill orders for customers who have failed to pay previous bills or who have paid them very slowly. The code numbers for the customer and the sales representative are needed if the order department must process a great many sales.

The second master file (or data base) is required for both billing and inventory processing. This file has one record for each product that the company carries in inventory and is available for sale to customers. In the Good Times Paper system this file contains data about particular greeting cards, writing paper, and other products sold. The product data must include the name or description of each product (or set of related products), its code number, its unit price, the customer discount allowance, the inventory balance of the item, and its reorder point.

In the Good Times Paper system, both the customer file and the product file are recorded on magnetic disks. Data-entry operators in the billing department are responsible for keeping the customer file up to date. As customers move, their addresses must be changed in the file. Also, data on new customers must be added daily to the file.

A data-base administrator keeps files up to date.

A data-base administrator in the inventory department is assigned the task of keeping the reference data in the product file current. This means that each time the company offers a new greeting card or some other new product, a record has to be added to the product file. The task of updating the inventory balance for each product in the file is done by the computer in its processing of the billing and inventory receipts input data. As customer orders are keyed in, the inventory balance for each item is reduced by the quantity the customer has ordered. As inventory receipts are recorded by data-entry operators, the computer automatically increases the inventory balance. The hard-copy computer output is an *inventory stock report.*

Formatting Data Input

The customer order is the source document for input to the billing operation. An order may come in directly from a customer, or it may be called in by the sales representative for the customer's account. In either case, the order is routed to a billing data-entry operator for input to the computer. A format called an **input prompting format** is displayed on the CRT terminal screen so that the operator will key in all the required information in the correct sequence. This format is created by the systems analyst to guide the operator in using the correct sequence for data entry.

POINT-OF-SALE PROCESSING. A new IBM point-of-sale system provides cash register functions and also stores sales and inventory information for later processing. Courtesy Sweda International, Inc.

In addition to the order input data, billing clerks must also key into the computer terminals any changes that must be made in the customer files. The systems analyst designs special change forms for this input.

The systems analyst designs another format for recording additions to inventory. When the inventory balance on hand falls below the reorder point, an order may be placed to manufacture or purchase additions to inventory. As the additional inventory arrives, it must be recorded by a data-entry operator. Another addition to inventory takes place when a customer returns items. All returns must be keyed in so that the recorded inventory balance on hand is up to date.

Defining Processing from Input to Output

In the billing and inventory system designed for Good Times Paper, hundreds of processing steps must take place to meet the requirements of the system. The systems analyst shows these in a flowchart as described in Chapter 7. In addition, a narrative description is usually prepared as a supplement to the flowchart. A general description of the work flow in the billing and inventory system follows.

Processing starts with the receipt of a customer order assigned to one of the billing data-entry operators. Using a CRT display terminal connected to the computer, the operator keys in the cus-

BILLING AND INVENTORY PROCESSING. The terminal screen on the left shows the display before inventory receipt data is entered. The screen on the right shows the display after the data-entry operator has processed the receipt data.

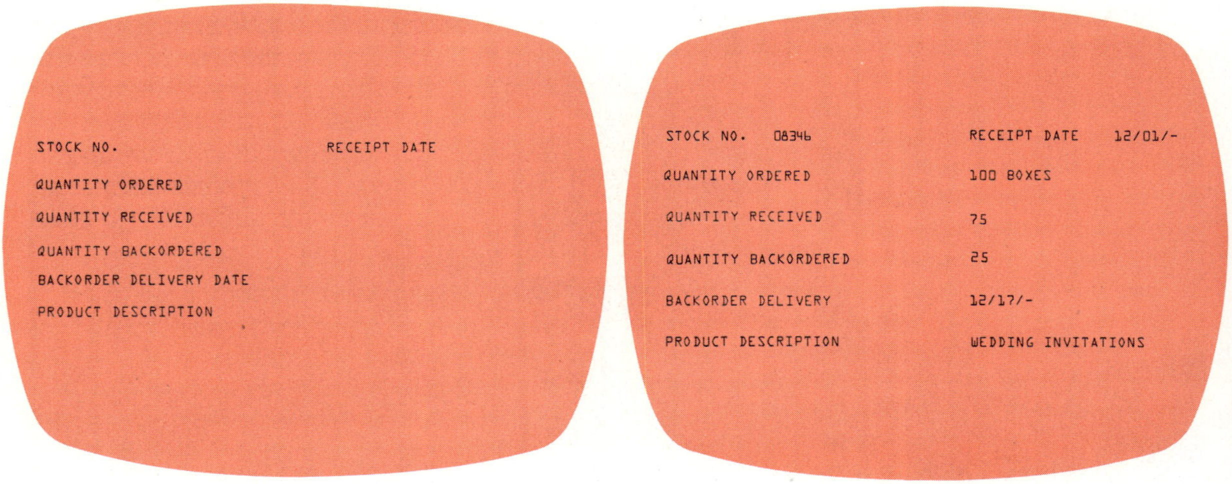

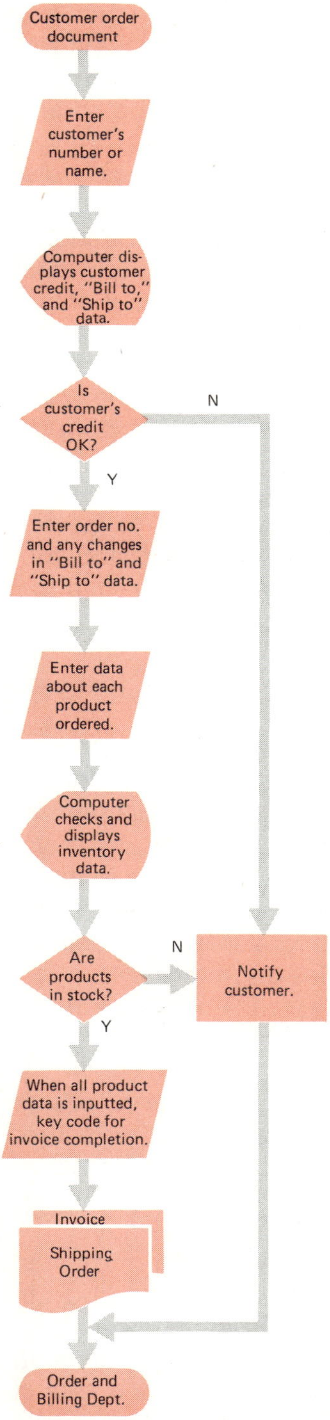

A CUSTOMER BILLING SYSTEM

tomer number. If no customer number is available, the operator keys in the full name of the customer. The computer matches the keyed data with data in the customer master file, which is stored in a disk unit. The machine then extracts from the customer file a code that indicates whether the order requires the approval of the credit manager before it can be processed. This code is displayed on the CRT screen. If necessary, the data-entry operator routes the order to the credit manager. In this case, the operator enters the next order for processing.

If no credit approval is necessary, the computer displays for the data-entry operator the *bill to* and *ship to* addresses, the shipping instructions, and the code number of the sales representative who sold the merchandise to the customer. The data-entry operator checks this data against the data listed on the customer order. If any of the data needs to be changed, the changes are keyed into the computer. If no changes are required, the operator keys in a code asking the computer to store the customer information in a pending-invoice file.

The next step is for the data-entry operator to key in the item code number and quantity for each product ordered by the customer. The computer matches the order quantity for each item against the inventory balance for the item which is contained in the product data base, stored on a disk. If a merchandise item is not available, the computer displays on the CRT screen a message notifying the data-entry operator. The operator then arranges for the customer to be told that there will be a delay in the delivery of that item.

For each item that can be shipped to the customer, the computer subtracts the quantity from the inventory balance and stores the new inventory balance in the product file. The computer adds to the customer information stored in the pending-invoice file the product item number, description, quantity ordered, and unit price for each item that can be shipped.

Once the data for all the products ordered is keyed in, the computer automatically makes all the calculations that are necessary to complete the customer invoice. As shown on page 185, this includes the extension (number of items times unit price) for each product shipped. Shipping costs to be billed to the customer are calculated on the basis of standard shipping charges per package according to the customer's geographic location. The addition of the extensions and the shipping charges results in the total billing amount. The results of the calculations are stored in the pending-invoice file.

When the input for all customer orders is completed for the day, the computer is programmed to print the customer invoices from the data in the pending-invoice file. In this billing system, the original invoice and five copies are prepared at one time. Once the invoice is completed, the order and billing department separates the invoice copies and forwards two copies to the shipping department. The order and billing department holds the original invoice and the three other copies in a pending file.

When the shipping department receives the two invoice copies, it selects and packs the merchandise ordered. One of the copies of the invoice the shipping department receives is a combination shipping label and packing slip. The packing slip is torn away from the shipping label and inserted into the package. Next the shipping label is attached to the outside of the package. The package is now ready to be shipped to the customer. The shipping department records the shipping date on the shipping copy of the invoice and returns this copy to the order and billing department.

When the order and billing department receives the shipping copy, it knows that the package has been shipped to the customer. It mails the invoice to the customer, files the shipping copy of the invoice with the customer order by the customer's number or name in the customer order file, and files another invoice copy by invoice number in the invoice reference file. The order and billing department routes the other two invoice copies to the accounts receivable and sales departments.

After completing the customer invoices, the computer automatically prints an out-of-stock report for each product item for which the inventory balance has fallen below the minimum requirement (the reorder point). The out-of-stock reports are sent to the inventory control managers responsible for adding to the inventory. Finally, the computer records on magnetic tape customer sales information that will be used for further processing in systems for accounts receivable and sales analysis.

Formatting Data Output

Each time output is reported by a computer, whether as printed copy, as a display on a CRT terminal screen, or as magnetized spots on a tape or disk, the information must be in the form most helpful to the user. It is the responsibility of the systems analyst to work with each user to identify the desired output formats.

A weekly inventory management report outlines a company's inventory position.

Two of the most important outputs from the billing and inventory system just described are the customer invoice and an inventory management report. (This report is printed weekly by computer.) Let us examine the Good Times Paper inventory management report to learn more about the formatting of output information for a user.

What is inventory management data? Reading from left to right, note that for item 1201, the balance on hand is 8,713. In the next column, the reorder point is given (5,000). This is the number of items the company expects to sell in one month. The column headed **Net Inventory Position** shows the difference between the balance on hand and the reorder point (3,713).

If the balance on hand is more than the reorder point, the net inventory position shows how many extra items there are for one month. If the balance on hand is less than the reorder point, a minus number must be recorded for the net inventory position. This shows how many items will be missing in inventory for one month. Look at the figures for item 1202. The net inventory position shows −2,599 (5,000 − 2,401 = 2,599). Each of the items coded 1205, 1209, and 1210 also has a minus net inventory position. Now the inventory management department needs to know whether to order additional quantities of these items. Action may already have been taken to add to the inventory. But we do not know for sure, and this is the reason for the column of the report that shows open orders.

OUTPUT FORMAT. Inventory management reports show the quantity of available inventory as well as the balance on hand.

INVENTORY MANAGEMENT REPORT

GOOD TIMES PAPER COMPANY 03 31 19--

PRODUCT CODE NO.	PRODUCT DESCRIPTION	BALANCE ON HAND	REORDER POINT	NET INV. POSITION	OPEN ORDERS	NET AVAIL. INV.
1201	BIRTHDAY CARDS	8,713	5,000	3,713		3,713
1202	NOTE PADS	2,401	5,000	-2,599		-2,599
1203	PLACE CARDS	1,205	1,000	205		205
1204	NOTEPAPER	20,405	10,000	10,405		10,405
1205	CONGRATULATORY CARDS	5,880	6,000	-120	5,000	4,880
1206	SYMPATHY CARDS	3,110	2,000	1,110		1,110
1207	THANK-YOU NOTES	105,210	100,000	5,210		5,210
1208	ANNOUNCEMENT CARDS	15,712	15,000	712		712
1209	ANNIVERSARY CARDS	12,400	20,000	-7,600	15,000	7,400
1210	GIFT CARDS	300	1,000	-700	500	-200
1211	AIRMAIL PAPER	14,251	10,000	4,251	10,000	14,251

Open orders are the quantities ordered but not yet delivered to inventory. In most cases, the balance on hand plus that on order (the **available inventory**) will be greater than the reorder point. This is true of the item coded 1205 (which has an open order of 5,000) and the item coded 1209 (which has an open order of 15,000). No further action is required on these items. The sum of the balance on hand and the open order less the reorder-point quantity is called the **net available inventory.** The last column of the inventory management report shows the net available inventory for each item. If the available inventory is not large enough to bring the inventory balance above the reorder point, the owner or manager must consider ordering merchandise to add to the inventory. A minus sign or some other symbol printed in the column labeled *Net Available Inventory* points out this condition. For example, look at the net available inventory figure for the item coded 1210 in the inventory management report.

Companies with large inventories may have a special reporting system in which inventory positions are reported on an exception basis. An **inventory exception report** mentions only the items for which inventory is inadequate. In such a system, no reports are made on items for which the inventory appears to be adequate.

An advantage of using a computer for billing and inventory processing is that the current demand for and availability of selected items of merchandise can be accurately reported to management. Whenever the inventory of an item of merchandise is inadequate for meeting the company's needs, a stock report is printed for that item. Thus management is assured that it will always be informed of an item that requires some decision making on its part.

INVENTORY EXCEPTION REPORT. An inventory exception report lists only those items with an inadequate inventory.

INVENTORY EXCEPTION REPORT

GOOD TIMES PAPER COMPANY 03 31 19--

PRODUCT CODE NO.	PRODUCT DESCRIPTION	SALES YEAR TO DATE	SALES PREVIOUS YEAR	SALES SECOND PREVIOUS YEAR	BALANCE ON HAND	OPEN ORDERS	REORDER POINT	EST. QTY. TO REORDER
1202	NOTE PADS	15,000	57,000	48,500	2,401		5,000	2,599
1210	GIFT CARDS	4,200	11,000	8,000	300	500	1,000	200

Creating Specifications for Programming

The final part of a systems design contains detailed specifications needed by the computer programmers who are to write the computer processing instructions. These specifications define the organization of individual programs that make up the system and clarify the logic to be followed in the processing steps. When developing the procedures and system specifications for a computer data processing system, the systems analyst tries to allow for the various **checkpoints** (checking operations) needed to ensure accuracy. Then the computer programmers assigned the job of writing the computer programs for each subsystem must build these and perhaps other checking operations into the programming instructions and documentation. Good system specifications decrease the chance of error in interpreting the work to be done and reduce the time needed for preparing computer software.

CHECK YOURSELF

Supply the missing words.

1. The Good Times Paper Company maintains master files on __?__ and __?__.
2. A product file used in an integrated billing and inventory system is an example of a(n) __?__ __?__.
3. Inventory receipts are recorded by employees called __?__ __?__.
4. So that information will be keyed into the computer in the correct sequence, an operator responds to a(n) __?__ __?__ __?__.
5. Two output documents from billing and inventory processing are the customer invoice and a(n) __?__ __?__ __?__.
6. The difference between the balance on hand and the reorder point is called the __?__ __?__ __?__.

Programming and Installing the System

Every system begins with this question: What are we trying to accomplish? Members of the team charged with making the system work must answer this question to the satisfaction of management. Then they must plan, test, document, and implement the necessary steps.

Preparing and Testing Programs

COMPUTER PROGRAMMER. This programmer for the Good Times Paper Company is helping to develop a program manual for the billing and inventory system.
Hazel Hankin

Depending upon the complexity of the business, the time needed for preparing programs for a billing and inventory system may range from 6 to 24 months. The programming work for the Good Times Paper system took about one year. During this time a group of programmers coded and tested each program in the system and then prepared a program manual. The program manual describes (or documents) the functions performed in each program and provides operating instructions for running the program.

System Installation

The way in which a changeover to a new system is planned and executed will have a major impact on the system's performance and acceptance. For this reason, systems analysts spend a good deal of time to ensure the effective installation of a new system. The more sophisticated the equipment selected for a system, the longer it can take to make it **operational** (working properly).

The changeover from the old billing system in Good Times Paper to the new system is called a **conversion.** During the conversion period, a systems analyst supervises the **system test,** or checkpoint; the computer programs are run first with sample input data and then with actual data. It is important to find out quickly whether or not the system produces the output documents needed in the format specified. In the case of Good Times Paper, the customer invoice data that the system prints out must be exactly in the right position to fit on the continuous forms.

Most of the companies that install a new system continue to use the old system along with the new one for some time. Two or more systems used at the same time for the same purpose are called **parallel systems.** The accuracy and effectiveness of the new system can be tested by comparing its results with the results of the old system. Employees have to be trained to work with the new system. The systems analyst must work with all the employees who will be part of the total system to ensure the efficient flow of information and documents from one part of the system to another. During the system test, employees are often asked to suggest improvements in forms and procedures.

Employees are frequently asked to suggest improvements for a data processing system.

Examples of Other Billing and Inventory Systems

A company with many warehouse distribution centers located around the country may use a distributed computing system for its billing and inventory processing. A distributed computer system is made up of many remote minicomputers (or intelligent terminals) connected by telecommunications to a central computer. In such a system, customer order and inventory data may be keyed in at an intelligent terminal (or minicomputer) located in each distribution center. The input data is telecommunicated to headquarters, where invoice processing is done on the centralized computer.

If a medium-sized business cannot support the cost of even a small computer, it may use a less expensive accounting machine for preparing customer invoices. Such a machine has several advantages. It can handle all the calculations needed for invoice preparation, and it can be equipped with devices to record sales data in machine-readable form for the processing of accounts receivable, inventory, and sales analysis data.

If a business has only a small number of customer bills to prepare each day, as may be the case with a local retail specialty store, a simple billing system can be used. Only one employee probably would be needed to type the invoices. The employee could maintain the customer and product files, and he or she could use a calculator to check, edit, and price incoming orders. But if there were an increase in either the number of customer orders or the number of products ordered by each customer, this system would require more employees to make it run smoothly. How many invoices do you think you could process in one day?

In a simple, low-volume system, inventory records are usually hand-posted. If there are few product items to keep track of, the inventory records are not difficult to keep up to date. But as a business grows, the number of items stocked in inventory usually increases. That is the reason why successful retail shops often use computer service bureaus for the handling of their inventory records even though they continue to do their own billing.

CHECK YOURSELF

Supply the missing words.

1. Programming of the Good Times Paper Company computer billing system took about one __?__.
2. The billing and inventory system is described in words and diagrams in the __?__ __?__.
3. Getting a new system to work properly is called making it __?__.
4. The changeover from an old system to a new system is called __?__.
5. Computer programs are run first with sample input data and then with actual data during a(n) __?__ __?__.
6. Two systems used at the same time for the same purpose are called __?__ __?__.

Review Questions

1. List four objectives for an integrated billing and inventory system, and give examples of the requirements for each objective.
2. Describe the units of computer hardware selected for the Good Times Paper billing and inventory processing.
3. List the five parts of a systems design.
4. Describe the two master files used in a billing and inventory system.
5. Explain why a product file may be called a data base.
6. Name four types of input formats needed for the Good Times Paper billing and inventory system.
7. Describe the contents of an inventory management report and its purpose.
8. Explain the purpose of system specifications for programmers.
9. Give examples of other equipment that may be used for customer billing and inventory processing.

Comparing Ideas

The questions below are to help you think about what you have learned in this chapter. They are thought questions. There is no one correct answer.

1. Select a local manufacturer. Describe the type of billing and inventory system this manufacturer uses. What business changes might prompt this manufacturer to look into the possibility of installing a new system? Why?
2. What types of computations are required in preparing invoices? How would a change in sales tax affect an order and billing system?

Data Processing Activities

Now you can try out the kinds of data processing activities business workers perform. Below is a summary of the work you will do. You will find the actual information and business forms you need in your *Data Processing Work Kit.*

Activity 1. As a programming trainee at a store that sells motorbikes and motorcycles, you will assist in preparing a system flowchart for a new computer order entry system.

Activity 2. You will help train employees in the operation of on-line terminals.

Activity 3. You will help prepare a customer master file and a product file.

Activity 4. You will develop some of the program specifications for the exception report.

BASIC Project 8
Loan Payments

Computers are often used to count. Machines can count automobiles and concert tickets as easily as dollars and cents. Businesses and consumers will find BASIC very useful in performing the kind of arithmetic that is required when buying and selling goods. The following exercise shows all the common arithmetic functions.

Program Statements

As in addition and multiplication, symbols are used to represent subtraction and division.

- – The minus symbol stands for subtraction.
- / The diagonal symbol stands for division.

We can now create a BASIC program that uses all four math operations to calculate report data.

Sample Program

If your version of BASIC allows it, use long descriptive variable names such as AMOUNT for A, TOTAL for T, and BALANCE for B.

```
10 REMARK CALCULATE LOAN REPAYMENT
20 PRINT "HOW MUCH DO YOU WISH TO BORROW";
30 INPUT A
40 PRINT "AT 16.5% SIMPLE INTEREST, YOUR 4 PAYMENTS WILL BE"
50 T=A+A*.165
60 B=T
70 PRINT "PAYMENT 1";T/4
80 B=B-T/4
90 PRINT "BALANCE IS";B
```

```
100 PRINT "PAYMENT 2";T/4
110 B=B-T/4
120 PRINT "BALANCE IS";B
130 PRINT "PAYMENT 3";T/4
140 B=B-T/4
150 PRINT "BALANCE IS";B
160 PRINT "PAYMENT 4";T/4
170 B=B-T/4
180 PRINT "BALANCE IS";B
190 END
```

Output

The following output would be produced if the amount of 1,000 were inputted as the amount to be borrowed.

```
HOW MUCH DO YOU WISH TO BORROW?  1000
AT 16.5% SIMPLE INTEREST, YOUR 4 PAYMENTS WILL BE
PAYMENT 1    291.25
BALANCE IS 873.75
PAYMENT 2    291.25
BALANCE IS 582.5*
PAYMENT 3    291.25
BALANCE IS 291.25
PAYMENT 4    291.25
BALANCE IS 0
```

*Some systems may not show extra zeros.

Keyboarding Activities

1. Enter and RUN the program listed above.
2. Enter the following data.

AMOUNT
1,000
1,450
600

3. Modify the program to calculate the current loan interest in your area.

Enrichment Activity

Create a program that will produce a report for any number of payments.
WORKING TIP: Use the INPUT statement.

CHAPTER

9

A Payroll System

DATA PROCESSING TERMINOLOGY

Pay period
Pay statement
Overtime
Net pay
Nonexempt employees
Exempt employees
Tax exemptions
Payroll register
Employee earnings record
Time card
Pay envelope
Pay statement
Payroll staff-change notice

PERFORMANCE GOALS

- Name four objectives of a payroll system.
- Tell why computers are cost effective for payroll processing.
- Name the five steps involved in developing a payroll systems design.
- List at least seven items of data that must be in a payroll master file.
- Name three payroll output documents.
- State the reason for parallel-testing a new system.

The computation of pay was once very simple. The pay given to most workers did not include time and a half for **overtime.** There were few, if any, deductions from an employee's earnings.

The computation of pay has become increasingly complex because of government regulations and employee benefit plans.

Over the last 40 or so years, however, the U.S. government has set up complex systems for ensuring that employees are paid fairly and for collecting taxes. In addition, many state and a few local governments require employers to deduct taxes from their employees' earnings.

EMPLOYEE BENEFIT PLANS

1. Insurance
2. Retirement
3. Stock-purchase
4. Savings and loan

Additional payroll deductions vary with the company. Many companies, particularly the larger ones, offer special benefit plans to their employees. Through these plans, employees can get low-cost medical insurance and life insurance, as well as a retirement income. Sometimes employees can also participate in a stock-purchase plan that enables them to buy shares of the company's stock. Employees pay into these plans by having deductions made from their earnings.

Because of the many types of pay plans and payroll deductions, businesses study their payroll needs carefully. A payroll data processing system must deal with all the normal payroll tasks. It must also be able to deal with preparing paychecks for new employees, for terminating employees, and for sick or vacationing employees. As with the customer billing system that you read about earlier, a payroll data processing system must be carefully planned. As with the other systems, the steps are as follows.

1. Defining system objectives and requirements.
2. Selecting data processing equipment.
3. Developing a systems design.
4. Preparing computer programs.
5. Installing the system.

Defining System Objectives and Requirements

The chief objectives of any payroll system are to pay employees and to account for all payroll deductions. Other system objectives are to provide information for government and to generate information for internal use. Several objectives that a payroll system must meet are as follows.

1. Paying employees for work performed.
2. Accounting for total earnings and for all deductions from total earnings.

3. Providing payroll data required by government agencies.
4. Providing payroll data needed by the company itself.

Many data processing operations are required to fulfill each of the four objectives. The more important of these will be described.

Paying Employees for Work Performed

A **pay period,** which is the time covered by a particular paycheck, may be a week, two weeks, or a month. At the end of this period, each employee receives a paycheck (or, in some cases, cash) for the work done during that period. The employee also receives a **pay statement,** which shows the total earnings, the deductions, and the **net pay** (the payment received). A typical paycheck with a pay statement is shown below.

To compute the total earnings shown on the pay statement, the payroll department must know the company's pay policies. For example, company policy defines the workweek. Is it a five-day

PAYCHECK WITH PAY STATEMENT. This paycheck and pay statement are for two weeks' work at 35 hours a week.

GOOD TIMES PAPER COMPANY 610 West 23d Street New York, NY 10011

1-500 / 260

DATE 3/24/--　CHECK NO. 1018

PAY TO THE ORDER OF MICHELLE ROTHFELD ------　296.53

TWO HUNDRED NINETY-SIX AND 53/100 ---------------- DOLLARS

SKYLINE TRUST
650 West 23d Street
New York, NY 10011

George T. Rey
Controller

⑆:0260⋯0500:⑆

GOOD TIMES PAPER COMPANY　PAY STATEMENT

PERIOD ENDING	REGULAR HRS. WORKED	REGULAR PAY	OVERTIME HRS. WORKED	OVERTIME PAY	GROSS PAY
3/24/--	70	525.00			525.00
FED. WITH. TAX	**STATE WITH. TAX**	**FICA TAX**	**MEDICAL INSURANCE**	**LIFE INSURANCE**	**PENSION PLAN**
77.12	27.88	88.30	2.50	4.75	17.25
OTHER DEDUCTIONS CODE	**OTHER DEDUCTIONS AMOUNT**	**SOC. SEC. NO.**	**CHECK NO.**	**DATE PAID**	**NET PAY**
NYC	10.67	298-13-5586	H5023	3/24/--	296.53

workweek, Monday through Friday, 8:30 to 4:30 with an hour off for lunch? This is a workweek of seven hours a day, five days a week, for a total of 35 hours.

Nonexempt employees receive pay for overtime. Exempt employees do not.

For over 40 hours of work, the U.S. government requires overtime pay for **nonexempt employees** (those not having managerial or professional positions). Managerial and professional employees are called **exempt employees** and are ineligible for overtime pay. This means that no matter how many hours these employees work in a week, they do not earn overtime pay. Their paychecks are always the same unless they receive a pay increase or their deductions change.

Overtime means hours worked in excess of 40 hours a week.

By law, nonexempt employees receive overtime or time and a half (1½ times their regular hourly rate) for all hours worked over 40 in a week. This means that depending on a company's payroll system, employees may be paid the regular hourly rate for hours worked over 35 and up to and including 40 hours.

Whether a job is exempt or nonexempt depends upon the level of responsibility involved and the amount of training required.

All jobs are considered either exempt or nonexempt depending on their level of responsibility and the training the employees must have. In each company, the payroll department must know which jobs are considered exempt and which are considered nonexempt. Company policy also instructs the payroll department on how employees are to be paid for time not worked, that is, for time off the job because of holidays, vacations, illness, or personal business.

The federal government checks to be sure that employers pay their employees properly for time worked. A federal law requires employers to keep records of the actual time worked by employees in nonexempt jobs. Companies meet this requirement by asking their nonexempt employees to fill out an attendance card (often called a **time card**) for each pay period. Some companies require their employees to record the time worked by using a time clock. Others accept time cards filled in by hand.

Accounting for Total Earnings and Deductions

In most cases, the payroll is the largest expense of a business.

The payroll is usually the largest expense of a business. If a company wants to know its profits by product line, the total payroll expense must be broken down by product. To do this, the payroll department prepares accounting entries to charge payroll expenses by product account.

Accounting entries must also be recorded for all deductions made from an employee's total earnings. On the pay statement shown earlier, there are sections for recording six types of deductions. Each of these deductions must be recorded as money the company owes, because the company does not own the money it withholds from employees' earnings.

The deductions made from employees' earnings for taxes are turned over to federal, state, and local governments. The deductions made for medical insurance, life insurance, and pension plans are turned over to the insurance companies and banks handling the company's benefit plans. Deductions for company stock-purchase plans are turned over to the stock brokerage firm handling the stock purchases. And the deductions made for company savings and loan plans are turned over to the bank handling these funds.

PAYROLL DEDUCTIONS

1. Income tax
2. FICA tax
3. Insurance
4. Pension plan
5. Stock-purchase plan
6. Savings and loan plan
7. Union dues

SOCIAL SECURITY. Both employees and employers contribute to social security so that employees can collect benefits if they are disabled or when they retire. Jill Mariani

Providing Payroll Data for Government Agencies

Employers must prepare reports for the federal, state, and local tax deductions made from employees' earnings. Employers themselves must also contribute to the social security payments credited to each employee under the FICA system. And employers may be the only contributors to other benefit plans such as those for unemployment or disability insurance.

At the end of each calendar quarter (March 31, June 30, September 30, and December 31), an employer must prepare a form for federal income tax withheld. This form, called the Employer's Quarterly Federal Tax Return (Form 941), shows each employee's name, social security number, and quarterly taxable FICA wages (earnings). The completed form also shows the total federal income tax withheld from employees' wages and the total FICA taxes payable. (FICA taxes are paid by both employer and employee.) A withholding tax statement (Form W-2) must also be prepared for each employee annually.

Providing Payroll Data for Company Use

The type of payroll data a company needs varies from company to company. Larger companies often need more information from the payroll system than small to medium-sized companies. Think of a company having 25 employees and one having 5,000 employees. The owner or manager of the smaller company does not usually need a written report to be aware of the overtime hours employees have worked. In the larger company, though, the employees may work in several different buildings. They may even work in different cities or states. Since the owners or managers of a company this size cannot personally be aware of the hours

Employers must report data quarterly about FICA taxes and the total federal income tax withheld from employees' wages.

These data-entry clerks are processing social security data and other tax deductions for government reporting.
Jill Mariani

worked by each employee, there must be a more formal record-keeping system. The overtime hours must be summarized by the payroll data processing system.

Overtime hours are only one example of the payroll data a company needs. Most large companies also need payroll data so that they can compare the typical earnings of their employees with those of employees in other companies in the same type of business. Employers must compare the pay rates of employees within their own companies so that one manager pays his or her employees as well as another manager. And employers need payroll data so that they can project departmental budgets for a year at a time as part of computing the cost of running the company.

CHECK YOURSELF

Supply the missing words.

1. Federal, state, and some local governments deduct amounts of money from an employee's paycheck as a means of collecting __?__.
2. Special benefits include __?__ insurance, life insurance, and retirement plans.
3. The chief objectives of any payroll system are to pay the employees and to __?__ for all payroll deductions.
4. A payroll system must also provide payroll data needed by __?__ agencies and by the company itself.
5. The time covered by a particular paycheck is called the __?__ __?__.
6. A payroll system must compute the difference between an employee's total earnings and his or her __?__.
7. This difference is called the __?__ __?__.
8. Payroll workers must know the company's policies about __?__ and non-exempt employees.
9. The attendance card a company usually requires its nonexempt employees to submit regularly is called a(n) __?__ __?__.

Selecting Data Processing Equipment

Suppose that the Good Times Paper Company has been using an accounting machine for handling the payroll. It expects to expand its line of paper products and hire more employees. In addition, management is considering the possibility of improving the company's medical benefits and offering membership in a profit-sharing plan. Both the addition of new employees and the new benefit plans would make the computation of payroll deductions more difficult. The systems analyst must decide with management whether to make changes in the existing payroll system or install a new, more sophisticated system.

Payroll master files may often be used by personnel departments to find candidates for job openings, to compare the salaries of similar jobs, and to guard against discrimination.

The systems analyst determines through cost comparisons that computer processing would be the most cost-effective method for doing the payroll work. One of the reasons for this determination is that the management of Good Times, as is true in most businesses, requires many special analyses of the payroll data. For example, one such analysis is an across-the-board study to verify that employees with similar responsibilities in different departments and locations have comparable earnings. In addition, management requires that a data base be established containing employee information such as job skills, long-range career interests, and job performance ratings. This data could be retrieved by the computer to identify employees who might be promoted to positions open elsewhere in the company. One of the benefits of such a companywide data bank is the guarantee that job openings will be available to employees on the basis of their interests and their skills. Such a system minimizes the possibility of denying an employee a job opportunity because of age, sex, race, or national origin.

Alternative Computer Systems

The systems analyst investigates the use of a computer service bureau for the handling of the Good Times payroll processing. The cost analyses indicate, however, that it would cost less to do the computing within the company. The same computer used for the processing of customer orders and billing and inventory control in the Good Times Paper Company could handle the payroll system requirements, although additional devices would have to be added to the system.

As described in Chapter 8, the computer system used for billing is of medium size. In addition to the central processor, the computer system has twelve CRT terminal input devices, four magnetic-tape input/output devices, two disk storage units, and a line printer. To handle payroll processing, four additional CRT terminals would be required for payroll data-entry operators who have to input data to keep the payroll master file current. A card reader input device would be needed to read payroll attendance records recorded on 80-column cards. An additional disk storage unit would be required for storing the payroll master file data and for storing the payroll computer programs. The equipment just described is on-line equipment connected to the central processor. Off-line computer hardware would also be needed for payroll processing such as keypunch equipment for keying in attendance hours and a tape-to-punch converter for preparing attendance cards each week.

Developing a Systems Design

The next step is to develop the systems design for payroll processing. As you remember from the study of the billing system, the five tasks to accomplish in systems design are as follows.

1. Setting up and maintaining files.
2. Formatting data input.
3. Defining processing from input to output.
4. Formatting data output.
5. Creating specifications for programming.

Setting Up and Maintaining Files

A payroll data processing system is like the other data processing systems you have studied in that it requires a master file. To set up a payroll system or to update an existing system, the systems analyst must know what information the company needs for each employee and what documents will supply that information.

PAYROLL MASTER FILE

1. **Name**
2. **Address**
3. **Social security number**
4. **Date employed**
5. **Employing department**
6. **Job title**
7. **Pay rate**
8. **Amounts of deductions**

The master file of payroll data must include the name, address, social security number, date employed, employing department, and job title of each employee. Many employers also assign a payroll code number to each employee. Other employers find it convenient to use an employee's social security number as his or her payroll code number.

The master file must also contain the employee's pay rate, whether it is hourly, weekly, or yearly. It must make clear whether the employee is exempt or nonexempt, and it must list the deductions to be made from the employee's total earnings. In Good Times Paper Company, a special form called a **payroll staff-change notice** serves as the basis for the master record for each new, terminating, or other employee for whom the master file must be updated.

Each new employee must fill out an Employee's Withholding Allowance Certificate (Form W-4). A copy of the Form W-4 for an employee at the Good Times Paper Company is shown on page 212. On this form the employee records the withholding **tax ex-**

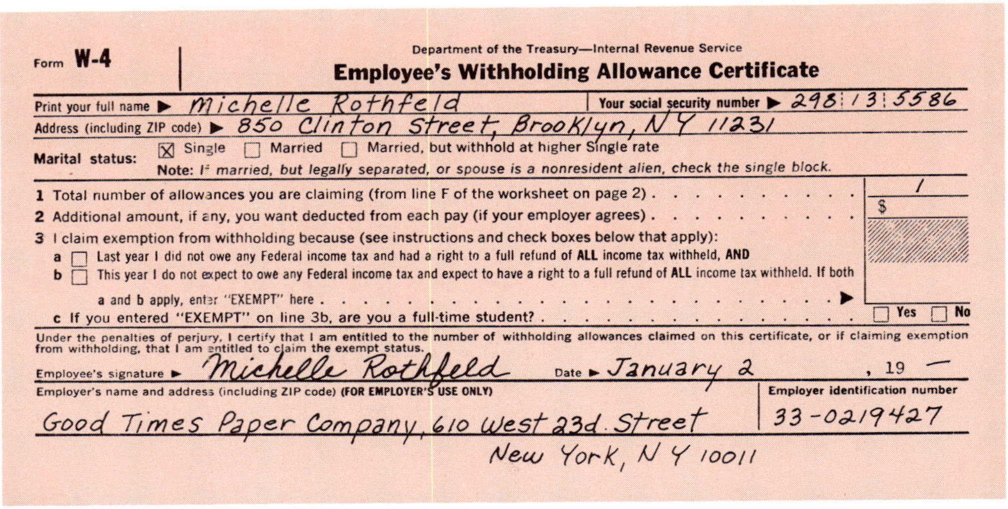

Form **W-4**

Department of the Treasury—Internal Revenue Service

Employee's Withholding Allowance Certificate

Print your full name ▶ Michelle Rothfeld | Your social security number ▶ 298 13 5586

Address (including ZIP code) ▶ 850 Clinton Street, Brooklyn, NY 11231

Marital status: ☒ Single ☐ Married ☐ Married, but withhold at higher Single rate

Note: If married, but legally separated, or spouse is a nonresident alien, check the single block.

1 Total number of allowances you are claiming (from line F of the worksheet on page 2) 1

2 Additional amount, if any, you want deducted from each pay (if your employer agrees) . . . . $

3 I claim exemption from withholding because (see instructions and check boxes below that apply):

a ☐ Last year I did not owe any Federal income tax and had a right to a full refund of **ALL** income tax withheld, **AND**

b ☐ This year I do not expect to owe any Federal income tax and expect to have a right to a full refund of **ALL** income tax withheld. If both a and b apply, enter "EXEMPT" here . . . . ▶

c If you entered "EXEMPT" on line 3b, are you a full-time student? . . . . ☐ Yes ☐ No

Under the penalties of perjury, I certify that I am entitled to the number of withholding allowances claimed on this certificate, or if claiming exemption from withholding, that I am entitled to claim the exempt status.

Employee's signature ▶ Michelle Rothfeld Date ▶ January 2, 19 —

Employer's name and address (including ZIP code) (FOR EMPLOYER'S USE ONLY) | Employer identification number

Good Times Paper Company, 610 West 23d Street, New York, NY 10011 | 33-0219427

FORM W-4. An employee records the number of exemptions he or she claims on a Form W-4.

emptions (the number of people for whom the employee provides financial support). The number of tax exemptions determines the amount of federal, state, and local tax the employer must deduct from the employee's total earnings. The amount of each employee deduction for medical insurance, life insurance, retirement, and other company plans varies by the amount of coverage the employee has requested. For example, a single person pays less for medical insurance than a married person who requests medical coverage for his or her family.

Once the master file includes all the information needed for preparing employee paychecks and pay statements, there must be a way to keep it up to date. As employees are promoted and receive pay increases, the master file must be updated to show the new job titles and pay rates. Similarly, when an employee marries, it may be necessary to record a change in his or her number of exemptions. There may also be changes from time to time in the amount of medical insurance or life insurance for which an employee requests coverage. Each time, a form must be filled out to indicate that one or more changes must be made in the payroll master file.

PAYROLL PROCESSING. Data-entry operators at Good Times Paper Company update payroll files at CRT display terminals. Courtesy Wang Laboratories, Inc.

The systems analyst for Good Times has determined that the payroll master file will be recorded and maintained on magnetic disks. All additions and changes for the file will be entered on CRT display terminals by data-entry operators in the payroll department. Once the data is keyed in, the computer will automatically update the master file information on the disks.

Formatting Data Input

Federal law requires employers to keep records of the actual time worked by nonexempt employees, mostly for the protection of those employees. But these records also serve another purpose: to provide the payroll department with the number of regular hours and overtime hours worked by each nonexempt employee in a given pay period. This information is used in computing the regular earnings and the overtime earnings of each nonexempt employee.

In the Good Times payroll system, the time worked each day is recorded by employees on an attendance card that the systems analyst has designed in the format of an 80-column punched card. At the end of the week the cards are sent to the payroll department, where the total hours for the week are recorded on the cards. A data-entry operator then keypunches the total hours worked into each attendance card, which is already prepunched with the employee's name, social security number, department, and pay period date.

Defining Processing From Input to Output

Many different procedures are needed to accomplish all the processing in the payroll system. Each procedure may have hundreds of operations that have to be performed. Let us look at just those processing operations involved in the computation of an employee's net pay.

Overtime earnings = overtime hours × overtime rate.

If a nonexempt employee has worked the company's standard workweek (35 hours at the Good Times Paper Company), the employee's total earnings, deductions, and net pay can be read from the payroll master file. For a nonexempt employee who has worked overtime, the overtime earnings must be computed (overtime hours multiplied by the overtime rate) and added to the regular earnings (regular hours multiplied by the regular rate). The sum of the overtime earnings and the regular earnings is the employee's total earnings. Computations must also be made for the employee who has not worked the standard number of hours in the pay period and is not to be paid for the time not worked. Once the total earnings have been computed for each employee, the amounts of income tax and social security tax to be deducted from each paycheck must be computed. Also, the amounts of other deductions must be subtracted from total earnings to determine the *net pay*.

The general objectives of a payroll system are the same for all companies, but each company has specific needs as well. Thus payroll procedures vary from company to company depending upon the complexity of the payroll system and the type of equipment used for processing. In the same way, the basic principles of systems design are universal, but the specific steps may be different from company to company. The systems analyst must therefore describe in both flowcharts and words all processing steps from input to output so that the parts of any one systems design are very clear.

Formatting Data Output

Forms must be designed for all output documents produced in the payroll system. The most important of these is the employee's check and **pay statement,** an example of which is shown below. When an employee is paid in cash, a **pay envelope** is used instead of the pay statement to record the employee's total earnings, deductions, and net pay.

The systems analyst must also design other forms that may be needed for payroll recordkeeping activities. These include the payroll register and the employee earnings records. The **payroll register** is a detailed list containing the names of all employees;

COMPUTERIZED PAYROLL SYSTEM. Specially designed continuous forms are used in a computerized payroll system.

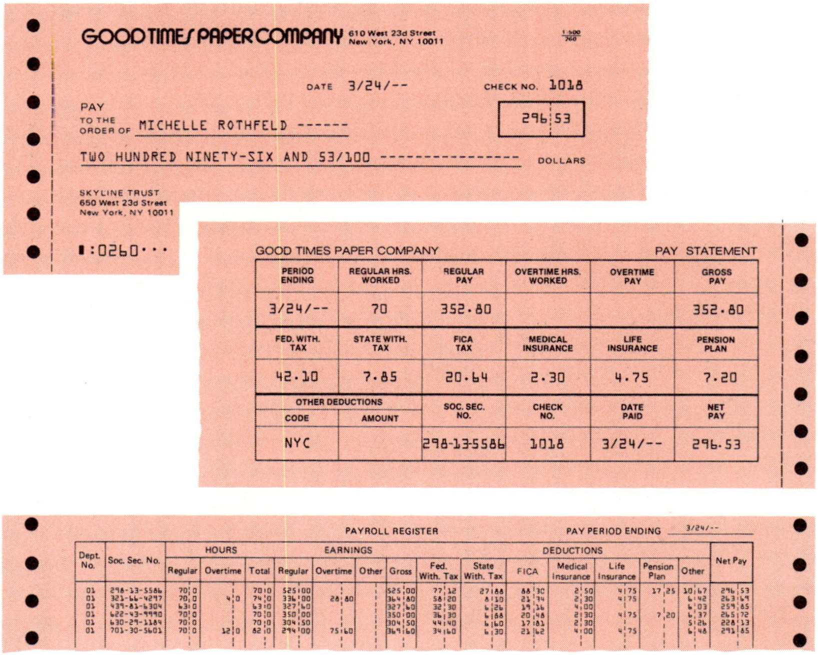

GOOD TIMES PAPER COMPANY 610 West 23d Street New York, NY 10011

1-500 / 260

DATE 3/24/--

CHECK NO. 1018

PAY TO THE ORDER OF MICHELLE ROTHFELD ------

296.53

TWO HUNDRED NINETY-SIX AND 53/100 ---------------- DOLLARS

SKYLINE TRUST
650 West 23d Street
New York, NY 10011

⑆:0260···

GOOD TIMES PAPER COMPANY — PAY STATEMENT

PERIOD ENDING	REGULAR HRS. WORKED	REGULAR PAY	OVERTIME HRS. WORKED	OVERTIME PAY	GROSS PAY
3/24/--	70	352.80			352.80
FED. WITH. TAX	**STATE WITH. TAX**	**FICA TAX**	**MEDICAL INSURANCE**	**LIFE INSURANCE**	**PENSION PLAN**
42.10	7.85	20.64	2.30	4.75	7.20
OTHER DEDUCTIONS CODE	**OTHER DEDUCTIONS AMOUNT**	**SOC. SEC. NO.**	**CHECK NO.**	**DATE PAID**	**NET PAY**
NYC		298-13-5586	1018	3/24/--	296.53

PAYROLL REGISTER — PAY PERIOD ENDING 3/24/--

Dept. No.	Soc. Sec. No.	Hours: Regular	Hours: Overtime	Hours: Total	Earnings: Regular	Earnings: Overtime	Earnings: Other	Earnings: Gross	Deductions: Fed. With. Tax	Deductions: State With. Tax	Deductions: FICA	Deductions: Medical Insurance	Deductions: Life Insurance	Deductions: Pension Plan	Deductions: Other	Net Pay
01	298-13-5586	70.0		70.0	525.00			525.00	77.12	27.88	88.30	2.50	4.75	17.25	10.67	296.53
01	321-66-4297	70.0	4.0	74.0	336.00	28.80		364.80	58.20	8.10	21.34	2.30	4.75		6.42	263.69
01	439-81-6304	63.0		63.0	327.60			327.60	32.30	6.26	19.16	4.00			6.03	259.85
01	622-43-9990	70.0		70.0	350.00			350.00	36.30	6.88	20.48	2.30	4.75	7.20	6.37	265.72
01	630-29-1184	70.0		70.0	304.50			304.50	44.40	6.60	17.81	2.30			5.26	228.13
01	701-30-5601	70.0	12.0	82.0	294.00	75.60		369.60	34.60	6.30	21.62	4.00	4.75		6.48	291.85

A payroll register contains data about all the employees in a business. An employee earnings record contains data about just one employee.

totals for hours worked, earnings, and deductions; and net pay. The employees are usually listed in the sequence of their payroll numbers within each department. Total hours worked, total earnings, total deductions, and net pay are accumulated for each department and then for the company as a whole.

An **employee earnings record** is a list of one employee's earnings, deductions, and net pay for the year to date. Each line of an employee's earnings record has the same payroll data shown on the pay statement the employee receives with the corresponding paycheck.

Finally, if output data is to be displayed on CRT terminal screens instead of being printed as hard copy, the systems analyst designs the format for the presentation of this information to make it most helpful to the user.

Creating Specifications for Programming

As described in Chapters 6 and 7, in order for the computer programmer to write the programs for payroll processing, the systems analyst must include as part of the systems design the specifications for each program. It is estimated that for the Good Times Paper Company payroll system, there may be as many as 25 programs to be written, including those needed to produce printed reports for special analyses of payroll data.

PAYROLL PROGRAM. The systems analyst for Good Times Paper Company created the company's payroll program specifications to yield the screen display shown here.

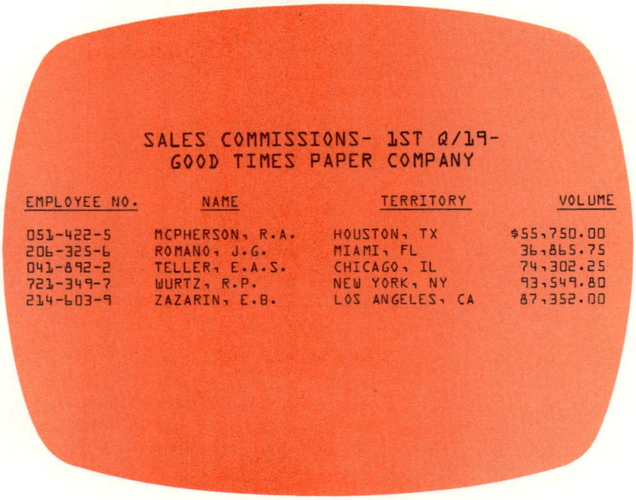

PAYROLL SYSTEM. The systems analyst for Good Times Paper Company developed this flowchart of the company's payroll system.

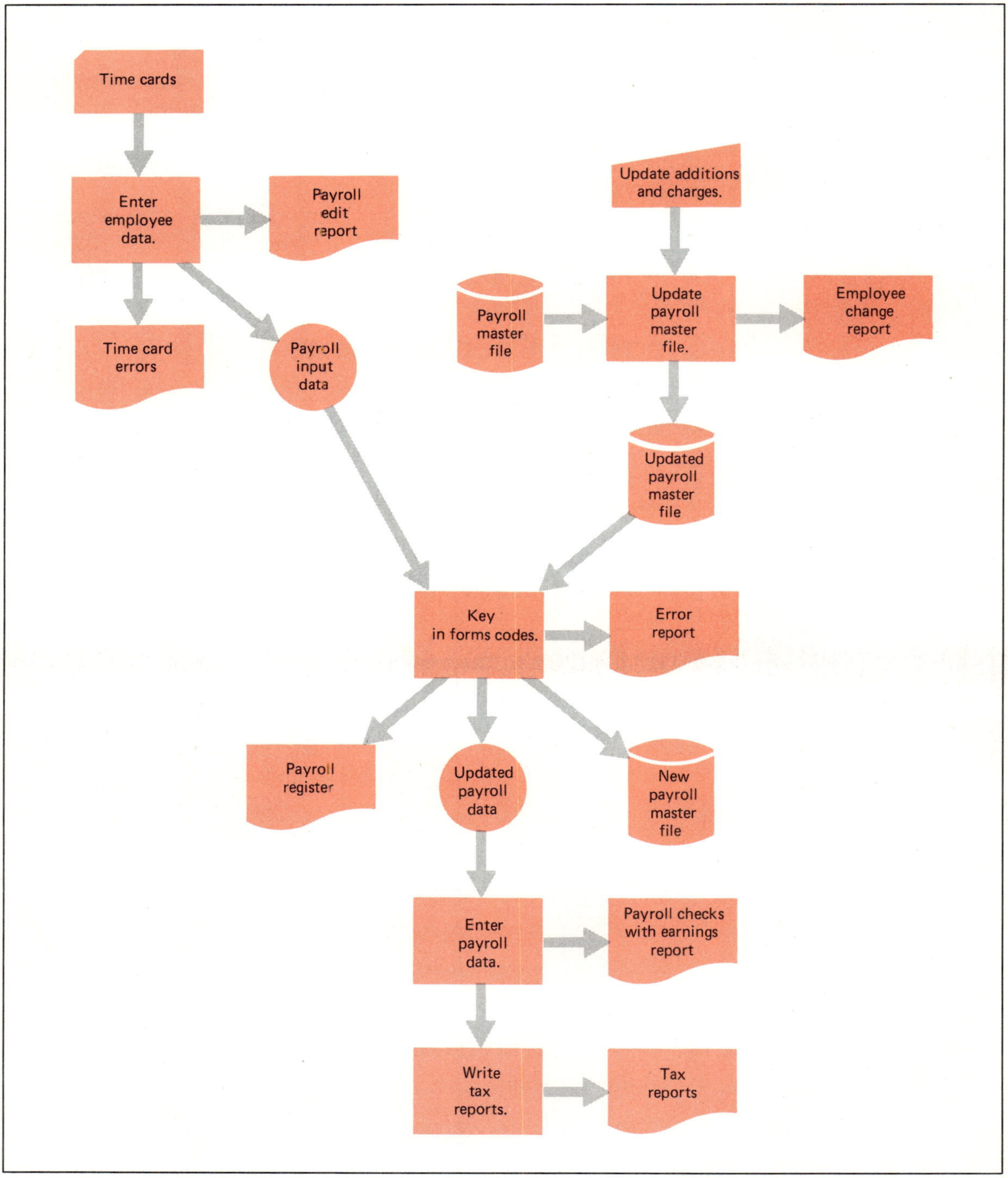

CHECK YOURSELF

Supply the missing words.

1. A computer is cost effective for payroll processing because Good Times Paper requires many special analyses using __?__ __?__.
2. On-line equipment has to be added to adapt the Good Times Paper Company computer to payroll work; a keypunch and a tape-to-punch converter must also be added, and these are __?__ __?__.
3. The file containing comprehensive payroll information is the __?__ __?__.
4. Attendance data on punched cards is one type of __?__ __?__.
5. Total earnings minus taxes and other deductions equals __?__ __?__.
6. When an employee is paid in cash, a record of the employee's total earnings, deductions, and net pay is made on the __?__ __?__.
7. A company record listing an employee's earnings, deductions, and net pay for the year to date is the __?__ __?__ __?__.

Programming and Installing the System

A payroll system is a prime example of a system that must be secure. The programmers need to code the programs in such a way that only authorized persons have access to the employee master file.

Preparing and Testing Programs

Packaged software may be purchased to take care of some data processing functions.

Although some of the requirements of payroll processing remain similar from company to company, there are usually enough variations to make it necessary for each company to prepare its own payroll programs. Packaged computer software can be purchased, however, to accomplish some of the standard payroll functions such as the calculation of federal income taxes and any state and city payroll taxes that must be deducted from employee pay.

As you read in Chapters 6 and 7, all computer programs that are written must be thoroughly tested for their accuracy. Before the present payroll system in the Good Times Paper Company can be replaced, each of the new payroll programs must be tested to ensure that it performs the specified processing operations and produces the desired output information in the correct format.

System Installation

Once the individual computer programs are tested and job training manuals are prepared, the operation of the entire new system from input through output must be tested before the new system replaces the old system. Usually it is necessary to operate the new system parallel to the existing system to check its accuracy and completeness.

The test period gives the data-entry operators and the computer operators an opportunity to learn their roles in the processing of payroll data. This is important to the success of the new system. Only after the results from the new computer system have proved to be accurate and reliable should the new system replace the old.

Examples of Other Payroll Systems

Depending upon the number of employees to be paid and the complexity of the required payroll analysis, a minicomputer or even a larger computer than that selected for the Good Times Paper Company may be appropriate. In addition, the computer system may be designed for different types of data input. For example, key-to-diskette or key-to-disk equipment could be used for keying in changes for the payroll master file data and for payroll attendance data. This would eliminate the need for the payroll CRT display terminals and for the card reader input device.

For a company with a very small number of employees (fewer than 25), it may be feasible to use a simpler system of payroll processing. Such a system may involve the use of a posting board. With the posting board, payroll forms can be mounted and properly aligned with one another for the recording of payroll data. Then the payroll clerk performs the computations, using reference tables for tax and benefit deductions and a calculator for other payroll computations.

A more advanced payroll system would use an electronic accounting machine that performs all the payroll calculations once the data is keyed into the machine. When payroll data is processed on accounting machines, usually the paychecks and pay statements, earnings records, and payroll register contain the same data used in the other payroll systems. However, the forms are designed so that the results of the payroll computations can be printed out by the accounting machine. The paycheck and pay

COMPUTERIZED PAYROLL PROCESSING

statement are laid out with the pay statement appearing at the left or right of the check; thus all the data for one employee can be recorded on one printing line. The forms are backed with carbon strips that align so that information can be recorded on all forms in one operation. Additional data about cumulative totals of earnings and deductions is also machine-posted on the earnings records and the payroll register.

Machine operations ensure accuracy and legibility in posting. An advantage that accounting machines have over a posting board is that they automatically provide cumulative totals of pay deductions and earnings. With a posting board, the payroll clerk must compute these cumulative totals and hand-post them on the employee earnings record.

Even small companies are now finding advantages in using computer processing for their total payroll requirements. Although a company may be too small to support the costs of installing a simple minicomputer, it may find it economical to have its payroll work processed at a local computer service bureau. Input data can be delivered to the service bureau for processing, or it can be keyed in at an in-house terminal linked to the computer in the service bureau.

CHECK YOURSELF

Supply the missing words.

1. Before a new computer system replaces an old system, the new system must first be ___?___.
2. A company with fewer than 25 employees may process its payroll data with a device called a(n) ___?___ ___?___.
3. An accounting machine has an advantage over a posting board in that it provides cumulative totals of pay deductions and ___?___.
4. Even small companies may use local computer data processing operations called ___?___ ___?___.
5. Input data can be delivered to a service bureau, or it can be keyed in at an in-house ___?___.

Review Questions

1. List four objectives for a payroll system, and give examples of the requirements for each objective.
2. Describe the units of hardware needed for the Good Times payroll processing.
3. Describe the contents of a payroll master file.
4. Explain the purpose of an employee attendance card.
5. Explain the calculations that are necessary for computing an employee's net pay.
6. Explain the purpose of a pay envelope.
7. Describe the contents of a payroll register, and compare it with an employee earnings record.
8. Explain the purpose of parallel-testing a new system.
9. Describe a manual system for preparing paychecks.
10. Explain the advantages of using an accounting machine instead of a manual system for payroll processing.

Comparing Ideas

The questions below are to help you think about what you have learned in this chapter. They are thought questions. There is no one correct answer.

1. If you had a part-time job, how would your rate of pay most likely be computed? What factors would be considered in preparing your paycheck?
2. How would the procedures for recording time worked in a large business differ from those used in a small business? How would these differences affect the preparation of paychecks?

Data Processing Activities

Now you can try out the kinds of data processing activities business workers perform. Below is a summary of the work you will do. You will find the actual information and business forms you need in your *Data Processing Work Kit.*

Activity 1. You will prepare a flowchart for the commission pay plan used by an insurance company.

Activity 2. You will prepare payroll data for computer processing.

Activity 3. You will code payroll data for entry using a touch-tone telecommunications system.

BASIC Project 9
Salary Schedule

Paying employees is a very important function in any business. Computers are used to process payroll data because they are accurate and reliable and because they can perform a variety of processing operations. The following exercise will show how BASIC can be used to calculate daily wages under a variety of working conditions.

Program Statements
The IF . . . THEN and GOTO Statements

In previous programs the INPUT statement was used to allow the user to keyboard variable input data as the program was run. Very often different processing operations are required for different types of input data. A computer program can include a list of choices for the different processing operations (called a *menu*). The user makes a selection (called an *option*) from the list of choices, and the program alters the processing operations on the basis of the choice the user makes.

The IF . . . THEN statement allows for decision making with respect to processing operations with a BASIC program. An example of an IF . . . THEN statement is 50 IF T = 1 THEN 600. If the value of T is 1 (as the result of an INPUT or LET statement before line 50), the program will *branch,* or jump, to the line number following the word THEN in the statement. If T has a value other than 1, the program will continue at the next line after line 50. The branch is called a *conditional branch* because it occurs only when a certain condition is met; in this case it is that T = 1.

The equals sign (=) is not the only relationship symbol that can be used in an IF statement. Any of the following symbols can be used.

=	Equals	>=	Greater than or equals
>	Greater than	<=	Less than or equals
<	Less than	<>	Not equal

These relationships make it possible for a program to make decisions on alternative processing operations on the basis of the input data a user provides.

BRANCHING. This program flowchart demonstrates the use of conditional branching in BASIC.

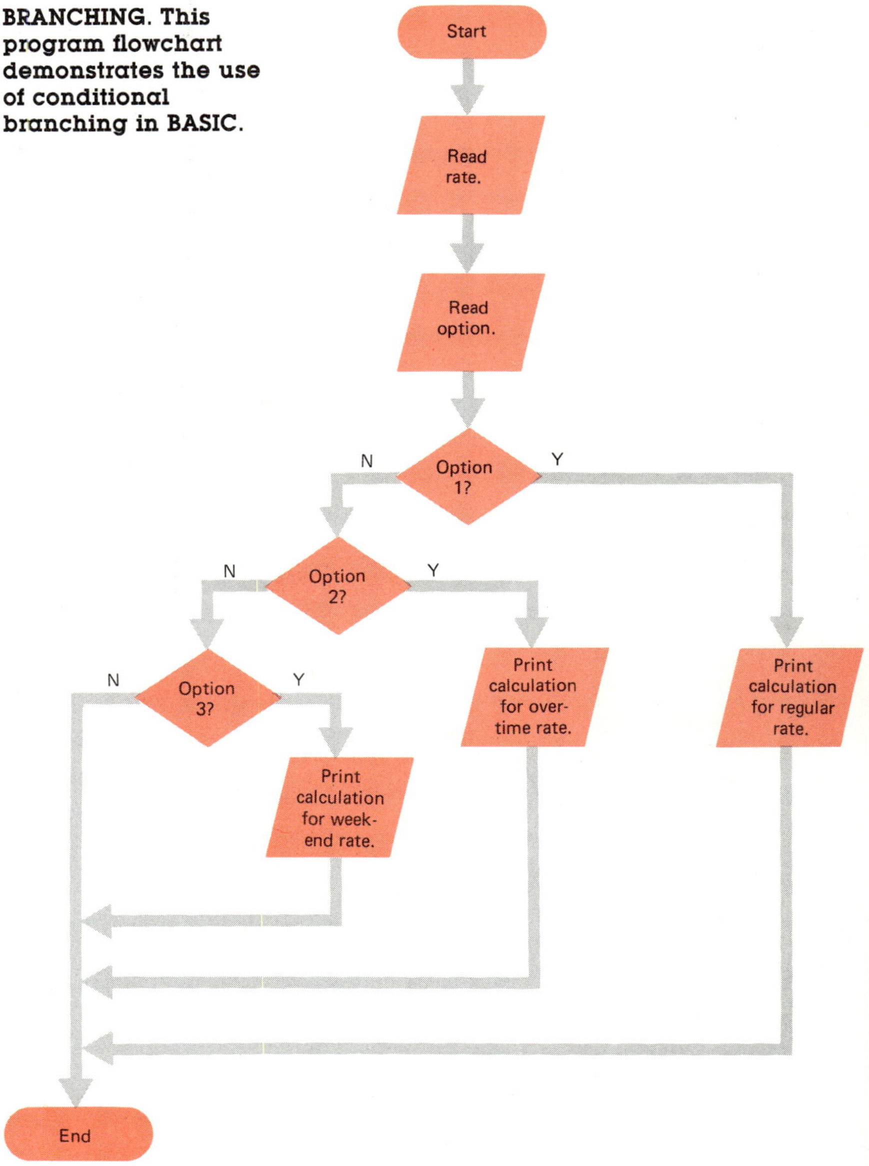

Another type of branch is called an *unconditional branch* because it will always occur. In BASIC, the GOTO statement causes a jump to a specified line number. For example, 10 GOTO 90 will always cause the program to continue at line 90 after line 10. We will see in the sample program how this can be useful.

As the flowchart on page 222 shows, a program may follow one of several paths by using conditional branching.

Sample Program

```
10 REMARK CALCULATE DAILY SALARY FOR VARIOUS POSSIBLE SHIFTS
20 PRINT "INPUT WEEKLY WAGE RATE";
30 INPUT R
40 PRINT "TYPE 1 FOR REGULAR TIME"
50 PRINT "      2 FOR OVERTIME"
60 PRINT "      3 FOR WEEKENDS"
70 INPUT T
80 IF T=1 THEN 200
90 IF T=2 THEN 300
100 IF T=3 THEN 400
110 GOTO 410
200 PRINT "DAILY WAGE FOR REGULAR TIME IS";R/5
210 GOTO 410
300 PRINT "DAILY WAGE FOR OVERTIME IS";(R/5)*1.5
310 GOTO 410
400 PRINT "DAILY WAGE FOR WEEKENDS IS";(R/5)*2.0
410 END
```

At line 70, a value for T is INPUT. The IF . . . THEN statements check this value and then direct the program along the appropriate path.

If T = 1, the IF . . . THEN at line 80 will cause a branch to line 200. If T does not equal 1, the program continues at line 90, where a test is made to see if T = 2. If this condition is met, there is a branch to line 300. Otherwise the program continues at line 100. If T = 3, there is a jump to line 400. If not, line 110 is the next line to be executed.

The GOTO statements are used to branch to the END of the program following a PRINT statement, thus assuring that only one message is printed for each value of T. Notice that if a value for T other than 1, 2, or 3 is INPUT at line 70, no branching will result from the IF . . . THEN statements in lines 80, 90, and 100. The program will reach line 110, where the GOTO statement will cause a branch to the END without any message having been printed out.

IF . . . THEN statements can compare alphabetic as well as numeric data, but the variable names must follow the rules for string variables. For example, 50 IF NAME$ = "JOE" THEN 600 is a perfectly good BASIC program line.

Output

The following output would be produced if the amount of 280 were inputted for weekly wages and a 2 for type of pay.

```
INPUT WEEKLY WAGE RATE? 280
TYPE 1 FOR REGULAR TIME
     2 FOR OVERTIME
     3 FOR WEEKENDS
?1
DAILY WAGE FOR REGULAR TIME IS 56
```

Keyboarding Activities

1. Enter and RUN the program listed above.
2. Input the following data.

WAGE	OPTION
250	2
290	1
310	3

3. Modify the program to give *triple time* (3.0) for weekend work.
4. To see clearly how the GOTO statements work in this program, remove them and RUN the program using the same data as you did in Activity 2 above. Also, RUN the program again and type in 4 for the option. Examine the output.

Enrichment Activities

1. Modify the sample program so that the message INVALID OPTION NUMBER is printed if a number other than 1, 2, or 3 is provided by the user.
2. Modify the sample program so that a string variable (T$) is used instead of T. Instead of numbers, the user would enter the word REGULAR, OVERTIME, or WEEKEND. The IF. . . THEN statements would also have to be changed so that tests are made for the strings instead of for numbers.
3. Create a BASIC program to produce a wage report that includes daily and monthly pay. Assume that the current week's schedule is repeated 4 times to calculate the monthly total.
4. Deduct (subtract) 1 percent of the monthly total for union dues, and show this deduction on the wage report output.

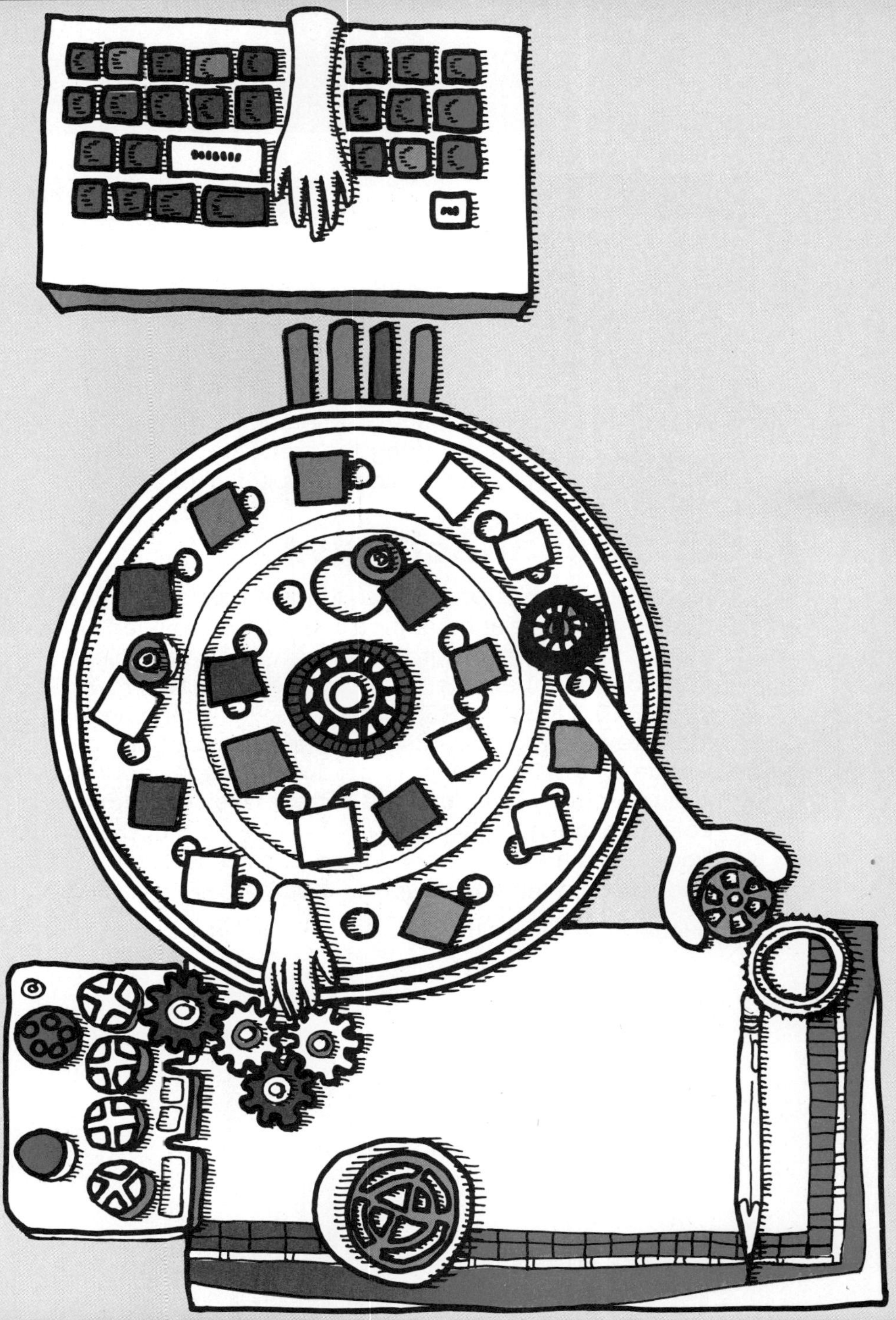

PART 4

Preparing for a Career in Data Processing

CHAPTER

10

Preparing for a Career

DATA PROCESSING TERMINOLOGY

White-collar occupations
Fortune 500
Specialization
Division of labor
Continuous work flow
Standardization
Turnover
Debugging

PERFORMANCE GOALS

- **List three basic elements of employee productivity.**
- **State three desirable characteristics of data processing employees.**
- **List seven entry-level skills important for success in data processing employment.**

The first step in preparing for a career is to be aware of the outlook for different types of jobs. The U.S. Department of Labor predicts an increase of 16 million jobs in the 1980s. More than half of these jobs will be in office work, or **white-collar occupa-**

tions. The fastest-growing white-collar group includes computer technicians, programmers, systems analysts, bank tellers, bookkeepers and accounting clerks, cashiers, secretaries, and word-processing specialists. Just the opposite prediction is made for the white-collar group that includes file clerks, keypunch operators, and other machine operators. These jobs are likely to decline during the 1980s.

The next step is to think about potential employers. The 500 largest companies, called **Fortune 500** employers, all use computers, as do most financial institutions, such as banks, savings and loan associations, and brokerage houses. Insurance companies and hospitals also depend on computers, as do large manufacturing companies, hotel chains, airlines, car rental companies, oil companies, wholesalers, shipping companies, and retail chains. The federal government and all 50 state governments use computers. Major city and county governments do also. About 15 percent of Americans work for the government. Think what this statistic means in terms of job opportunities.

JOB OPPORTUNITIES. The map shows projected job growth in the 1980s.

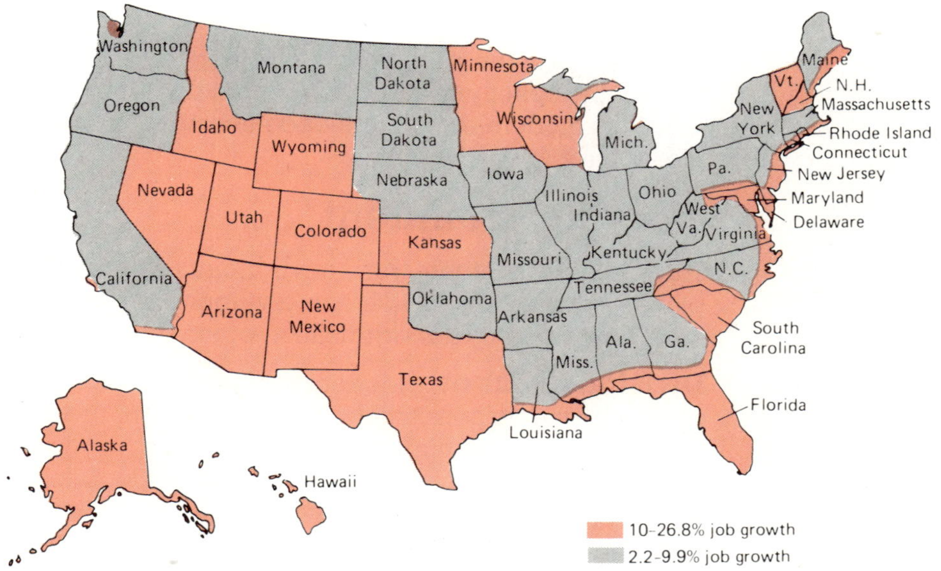

Job openings are expected to be most plentiful in the states with the fastest-growing populations. In general, greater job opportunities exist in cities, but there are more and more jobs available in industrial parks, manufacturing plants, and shopping centers in suburban and rural areas. In addition, the U.S. Department of Labor predicts a 92.5 percent increase in the number of computer technicians needed to service both large and small computers in business, in government, and in the home. As you will discover in Chapter 11, there are a variety of occupational specialties to choose from in the computer field. You will learn about jobs in several important career ladders. And in Chapter 12, you will read about opportunities in large companies and small ones and about opportunities in industry and in government.

Data processing requires special characteristics, skills, education, and training.

Before you can decide whether a career in business data processing might be right for you, you will need to know more about the special characteristics that different data processing systems and methods require in people. In this chapter you will learn about these basic characteristics. You will also learn about the special skills, education, training, and experience that are necessary or helpful in preparing for a career in data processing.

Characteristics for Career Success

The decline in the productivity of American industry can be reversed by better manufacturing and data processing systems aided by modern equipment and effective performance by people.

Work Environment

Three elements of the work environment that are basic to employee productivity are (1) the division of labor, (2) continuous work flow, and (3) standardization of job functions.

***Specialization* is focusing on one skill area.**

Division of Labor. Modern business systems are all too complex to be the responsibility of a single person. Teams of workers, each with a limited number of specialized tasks, make up a data processing work force. Such **specialization** (focusing on one skill area) by workers is called **division of labor.** Division of labor may require today's business worker constantly to learn new job skills as machines and procedures change. A student considering a data processing career may want to develop skill in one of the many specific entry-level jobs as a starting point. Once employed, the student will find that effort and the desire to learn more about other jobs will make opportunities for advancement possible.

Continuous Work Flow. Data processing procedures involve a detailed, step-by-step flow from the first data-entry operation to the last output operation. This is known as **continuous work flow.** Whether dealing with input, processing, or output, each employee is a vital link in the performance of the overall business operation. A single employee who fails to perform a task properly may cause the entire system to suffer. Hence, as a data processing employee, you could be the difference between success and failure in a team effort.

Standardization of Job Functions. Most people will change jobs during their working careers. They may be promoted to another job within a particular business, or they may move to another business. This is often called **turnover.** In business data processing, employee turnover has an important effect on how a job is performed.

***Turnover* refers to employees switching jobs.**

Standardization refers to the process of making procedures and job responsibilities uniform within a single business and similar from business to business. Effective standardization makes the replacement of employees easier. Employment standards also make it possible for workers to find employment in their field of interest in almost any part of the country. They can apply the years of training and experience they have to jobs in any geographic area. This may explain why specific skills and operations are described in such detail in job descriptions and employment handbooks. Most companies adopt standard procedures so that today's business operations are not disrupted by worker turnover.

Just as procedures are standardized, equipment is also standardized. The typewriter keyboard, for example, is standard on various pieces of equipment and would not vary from company to company. This keyboard is also the basis for both computer terminals and word-processing equipment.

Employee Characteristics

Success in any career is due to many factors. To name them all would be impossible. One can suggest, though, certain characteristics that are extremely desirable in all employees. Consider the three *p*'s: (1) patience, (2) persistence, and (3) precision.

Patience. Computers and electronic calculators can solve problems with incredible speed, producing vast amounts of output. But such speed can be misleading. Data processing systems often require years of development. Data to be processed may include the results of interviews or surveys that have taken months to collect and record.

The help that you receive and that you give is important to success.

As a member of a data processing team, you will work closely with many people. The help that you receive and that you give to others will be an important part of succeeding in your job. You must be patient when you give and receive this help, because in data processing, just as in any job, haste makes waste.

Persistence. We have discussed continuous work flow as a major element in any system. As a data processing employee, you may be one link in a chain of responsibilities. For this reason, failure to complete your work on schedule could seriously delay an operation. Since the requirements for data processing can be extremely precise, you may find that errors require tedious reworking. Payroll procedures, invoice forms, and computer programs are adopted for use only after numerous tests and reviews. Testing and evaluation are vital to data processing operations. The whole concept of feedback requires continual efforts to debug operating procedures and programs until every detail has been perfected. (**Debugging** refers to the operation of correcting errors in logic and other errors.) If you are discouraged easily, a data processing career may not be for you.

TEAMWORK. Members of a data processing team must communicate well with one another and with their user groups.
Courtesy Sperry Univac

Precision. Working with automated systems, particularly with mechanical and electronic devices, puts great responsibility on the human operator. It is the operator who must supply accurate information and detect machine errors. For example, a mistake in arithmetic, keyboarding, or programming can be greatly magnified through mechanical or electronic processing. Consider what could happen if a computer were instructed to *subtract* overtime pay from regular pay instead of to *add* overtime pay. In a large company, there would be hundreds of very angry employees!

Machines can greatly increase human productivity. Careless use of these machines, however, can greatly increase human wastefulness. Accuracy in human effort is richly rewarded by speed in machine production.

CHECK YOURSELF

Supply the missing words.

1. Focusing on one skill area is called __?__.
2. A distribution of responsibilities among teams of workers, with each team assigned a limited number of specialized tasks, is __?__ __?__ __?__.
3. When procedures call for work to move step by step from one operation to another, this is known as __?__ __?__ __?__.
4. A term that refers to workers changing jobs within a business or moving to jobs within another business is __?__.
5. The process of making procedures and job responsibilities uniform within a business and similar from business to business is __?__.
6. The three *p*'s for success in a career are __?__, __?__, and __?__.
7. The operation of correcting errors in logic and other errors is __?__.

Skills You Will Need

Data processing activities continue to require skilled workers and responsible decision makers. New techniques and equipment are constantly being introduced. Countless jobs are emerging that center around the operation, maintenance, and servicing of today's automated equipment as well as the varied input and output activities needed to support automated systems. Joining a data processing team means having an opportunity to work closely with a variety of specialists. You should try to learn from these specialists and to develop your employment skills while seeking advancement to higher levels of responsibility. The training offered for business data processing careers provides opportunities for both financial and geographic mobility.

There are seven entry-level skills.

What are the skills required for entry-level employment in the data processing field? We are going to look at seven basic skills you will need for success in business data processing. Your assessment of your own strengths and weaknesses will help you decide on both the type of career to pursue and the further education and training that may be helpful in achieving your goals. Think about your strengths and weaknesses in terms of the following skills.

1. Reading skills
2. Written communications skills
3. Oral communications skills
4. Problem-solving skills
5. Math skills
6. Keyboarding skills
7. Clerical skills

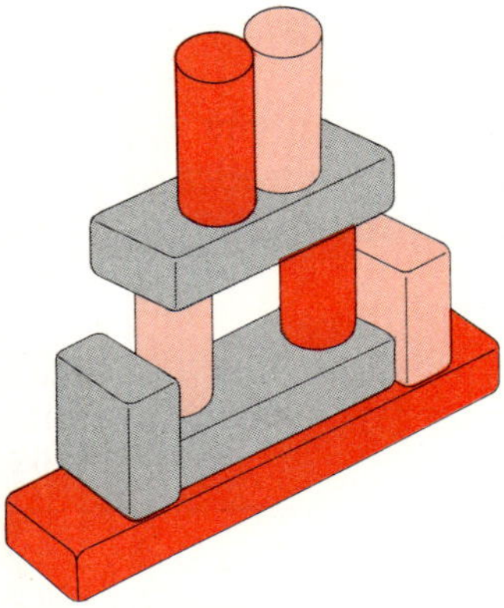

CAREER SKILLS. A successful career in data processing is based on well-developed skills. Each basic skill serves as a block on which a higher-level skill can be built. Without strong basic skills, the foundation for a good career is weak.

Reading Skills

The basic skill of reading will be very important to you as you prepare for a career. Not only must you be able to absorb, understand, and apply what you read in your courses, but you must be able to do the same with what you read on the job. Using reading skills means both keeping up with what you need to read and applying it on the job or in your personal life.

Reading words rather than complete thoughts is a problem for many people. They read paragraph after paragraph, only to find that they remember little if anything. You are the best judge of whether you need to develop your reading skills. An important clue is whether you remember enough to answer correctly the questions in the "Check Yourself" exercises in this textbook. If not, then you need to read more carefully. Make a reading plan for yourself. Choose a subject of special interest, and spend the same amount of time each day reading. Ask yourself questions as you read each paragraph to check your concentration and to be sure you are absorbing the ideas. Use the same approach as you read assigned sections in your textbooks.

Written Communications Skills

The ability to write clearly and neatly is an important skill.

In business it is important to write simply and clearly. Remind yourself as you are writing, whether in a course, in a personal letter, or on the job, that you are trying to share one or more ideas with someone else. On the job, you may often be asked to prepare a written report on the work you have accomplished. A clear report enables another employee to continue processing from the point at which you stopped. If you have difficulty making yourself understood on paper, make an outline first so that you have a plan to help get your points across. Be sure the points are listed in a logical sequence.

Content is one important aspect of written communications. Legibility is another. The constant need for manually communicating data makes the ability to write legibly an important employment skill. Certain input documents may be misread or misinterpreted because of illegible entries. Neat, readable handwriting will help ensure accurate communication.

Oral Communications Skills

The ability to speak clearly should be developed.

Speaking clearly and coherently is essential to success in business. Whether you are explaining something to someone else or asking for help yourself, you must make yourself understood. Use basic English; avoid slang, ethnic jokes, and other expressions that might offend the listener. Strive for a pleasant, tactful manner as well. Since teamwork is an important part of any business transaction, careful attention to the spoken word is a must. Both participating in small-group discussions and taking courses in public speaking are excellent ways to develop good speaking skills.

The ability to listen is an important skill.

Good listening skills are also important. The failure to pay attention to what is being said is commonplace in both our business and personal lives. Unfortunately, such failure leads to misunderstandings that are hurtful not only to the job at hand but also to ongoing relationships. Whether you are in a hurry or you are thinking about something that interests you more than what is being said, it is usually obvious when you are not paying attention. Make an effort, both in conversation and in your courses, to listen carefully. Just as you should check yourself on your reading skills, you should also check yourself on your listening skills.

Problem-Solving Skills

Problem-solving skills are important in almost every type of data processing job. In the simpler entry-level jobs, you will be given full instructions on how to perform the work. But there are almost always exceptions to take care of. You need to exercise good judgment in making decisions on how to process the exceptions for which you have no instructions.

An active curiosity indicates an ability to solve problems.

Often there is more than one way of doing something. Being a good problem solver means that you think through the problem

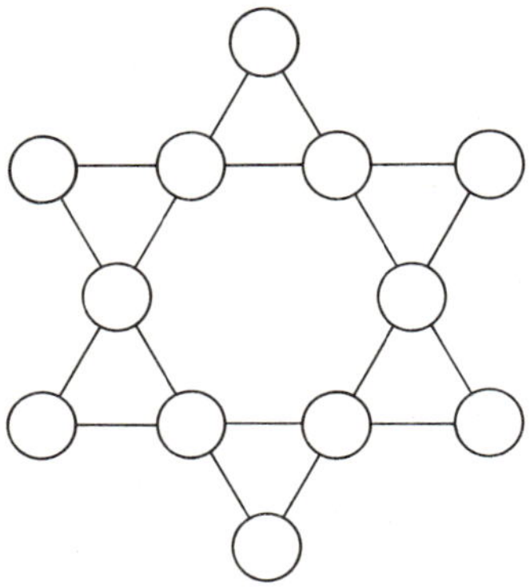

MATH SKILLS. Math puzzles provide valuable experience in problem solving. See if you can place the numbers 1 to 12 in this diagram so that the four numbers along each of the six lines add up to 26. Now try it with the added restriction that the numbers in the six points of the star must also add up to 26.

or situation, forcing yourself to consider the results of each option open to you. It means making your own judgments instead of waiting for others to make them for you. And it means using good communications skills, written or oral, to express your judgments and the reasons for them. It also means, of course, that you need to be open to the possibility that someone else's reasons are better than yours because he or she has thought of something important that you have not thought of.

In the development of any system—manual or automated—many obstacles must be overcome. Certain areas of data processing, such as systems analysis, computer programming, and equipment analysis, require skill in logic and a strong interest in problem-solving experiences. Many logic games, such as checkers, chess, and math puzzles, can provide valuable problem-solving exercise. Various learning games, particularly computer simulations, are also helpful. An active curiosity is probably one of the best indicators of a problem-solving capacity.

Math Skills

Basic math skills are essential for most jobs.

Since a wide range of business data processing tasks deal with the processing of numeric data, a firm foundation in basic math skills is highly desirable. Basic business mathematics (including addition, subtraction, multiplication, and division) should be sufficient for most entry-level jobs. Except for data processing applications in science and engineering, an extensive background in higher mathematics is not required for successful employment in the data processing field. Students have numerous opportunities to develop their math skills. Business mathematics, accounting, or other applied math courses can provide excellent employment preparation.

Well-planned work habits develop accuracy.

In addition to polishing your math skills, be sure to develop the habit of checking your work. Many business workers, however skilled they are at understanding how to do accounting and business math, make careless mistakes. Such mistakes can cause serious problems on the job. Whether these errors result in incorrect paychecks, the wrong discounts, overlooked bill payments, or an incorrect analysis of costs, there will be complaints.

Keyboarding Skills

A number of automated devices require keyboard entry. This is true whether we are talking about jobs in a computer room or jobs in a business office, a bank, an insurance company, or a department store. Keyboarding skills are also useful to the manager or professional who uses a computer or a computer terminal. Consumers who have a home computer or a hand calculator

JOB SKILLS. Keyboarding and math ability are just two of many skills that you will probably use in your career. Courtesy Victor Comptometer Corporation

are also well served by good keyboarding skills. Business students should acquire as many keyboarding skills as possible. Typing, in particular, machine calculation, or cash register operation can all be considered excellent preparation for the keyboarding needed in business data processing.

Clerical Skills

You will find that clerical skills are valuable whether you are in an entry-level job or are farther along in your career. Manual filing, collating, and sorting are important skills for the business worker to develop. Clerical skills include posting data and checking the posting done by others to ensure that names and numbers are recorded properly. These skills can be acquired in the various school courses offered in office practice and office procedures.

As stressed earlier, business data processing requires high standards of accuracy in both input and output stages. Students showing careless work habits and a low capacity for precision will find little success in a data processing environment. Most data processing aptitude tests include rigorous tests of clerical accuracy. Work experience, self-discipline, and good work habits can develop accuracy in a willing student. Remember, inaccuracies in input result in unreliable and often useless output. You may have read in other courses about the GIGO principle (garbage in, garbage out).

CHECK YOURSELF

Supply the missing words.

1. For success in business data processing, ___?___ skills are needed.
2. If you have difficulty making yourself understood on paper, make a(n) ___?___ first.
3. Careful listening is a(n) ___?___ skill.
4. Thinking through a difficult situation clearly until you arrive at a solution is a(n) ___?___ ___?___ skill.
5. Only data processing applications in science and engineering require extensive ___?___ skill.
6. The data processing skill that can grow out of an ability to type is ___?___ skill.

Education and Training

Although many people think of the computer industry as an industry that requires extensive education, there are more career opportunities that do not require a college degree than there are those that do. In Chapter 11, you will learn about the specific education and training requirements for typical entry-level jobs in data processing, as well as for higher-level jobs. After taking the appropriate courses in school and earning a high school diploma or recognized equivalent, individuals can usually start in an entry-level clerical job, in a data-preparation job, or in a job as an operator of simple office equipment.

Schools and Colleges

If you are interested in a career in data processing, you should enroll in computer courses available at the high school and college levels. Perhaps your school offers courses in data entry, computer operations, and computer programming. If not, you may be able to arrange to take one or more of these courses at another school.

Previous educational training is an indication of career interests.

Employers often consider previous educational training a clear indication of a student's career interests and of his or her ability to work successfully toward a career goal. Always work closely with your guidance counselor in selecting courses. Once the counselor is aware of your interest in a data processing career, the two of you can work as a team. Your instructors are also a valuable source of help; be sure they are aware of your career interests. Either your counselor or your instructors may be able to suggest summer courses, work experience, or a local computer club.

Many community colleges and industries have worked together to create cooperative work programs. In these programs, students spend part of their time taking courses at a local college and part of their time working in a local business and earning a salary. These students have a better chance for obtaining a full-time career with the business upon the successful completion of the cooperative work program.

Individuals who have a certificate in data processing from a community college may be considered for jobs as computer programmer trainees or computer operator trainees. Individuals with a degree from a four-year college or from a graduate program may be considered for more demanding jobs as systems analysts or programming analysts. The specific opportunities will depend on the type of industry or government agency and the education and training opportunities in different parts of the country. You can check the opportunities in your area by looking at the classified advertising in the local newspapers.

Job Training

Your data processing career may be greatly helped if you investigate any of the following sources for job training.

1. Specialized programs
2. Technical schools
3. Industrial training
4. Military service

Specialized Programs. Many schools, colleges, and federal government training programs maintain regional training centers that are specially equipped to provide apprentice computer training. The growth of such programs has been rapid in recent years. Often students enrolled in a standard career program may attend a specialized training center to add to their regular instruction. Your counseling staff should be consulted to determine if such opportunities exist. These programs are generally provided on a tuition-free basis and may be offered in both day and evening sessions. Government-sponsored programs can be located through local employment development offices.

Technical schools prepare students for immediate employment.

Technical Schools. A number of private technical schools offer entry-level instruction for data processing occupations. This instruction, on a fee basis, is designed to prepare students for immediate employment. But before considering enrollment in any technical school, you should examine your long-range career objectives carefully. Before making a decision, be sure to investigate the courses offered under general education in your area's vocational/technical program.

Equipment manufacturers provide extensive training.

Industrial Training. Those employed on a full-time or part-time basis in various job categories may qualify for industry-sponsored training in data processing. Equipment manufacturers provide extensive training courses for their own employees or for employees whose employers pay for their training. Many companies have closed-circuit TV or video instruction for computer operation and for some programming tasks. If you are an employee of a business that makes use of data processing services, you should investigate educational assistance programs. Check to see whether your firm has an employment or career counselor. If training or promotional opportunities are available, the counselor can tell you how to apply.

Military Service. Enlistment in the military services provides an excellent opportunity for training in data processing. During recruitment, investigate the many military occupational specialties (MOS) dealing with data processing. Before enlistment, you may be tested for aptitude in these areas; this can increase your chances of obtaining extensive training and work experience.

Experience

Either work experience or after-school activities in areas related to business will increase your eligibility for jobs of interest to you. You should also be familiar with both vocational and employment testing. Many employers look for related experience, a good work record, and good test results when comparing applicants for a particular job.

Work Experience. Work experience in virtually any business area can help you set realistic career objectives, mainly because it will help you decide which assignments you like and do well. If you are interested in a data processing career, part-time or summer employment can provide an opportunity to assess both your interests and your potential. Look for work as a cashier in a supermarket, a salesclerk in a retail store, a file clerk or mail clerk in a business office, or a data-entry operator in a computer center. Experience in a business office or as an equipment operator is excellent preparation for a specific job. Take advantage of any work experience, course work, or after-school activities that help develop the necessary basic skills you will need in your career.

Experiences that develop entry-level skills will prove beneficial.

SPECIAL ABILITIES. The ability to speak a second language is often a plus when looking for a job. Courtesy Citicorp

---

Bear in mind that the job applicant who best meets the job requirements is generally the one selected.

Special Abilities. Every person is unique and may bring special skills to a work assignment. Personal development in any way may contribute to a successful data processing career. An employer has many needs that may require your basic skills. Foreign-language ability, interest in travel, or leadership ability should always be listed when you are applying for training or employment.

Testing. Many students entering an employment area are disappointed to find themselves right back in the classroom. You should not be surprised to find that reading assignments, formal lectures, and testing are as common in business as they are in school. Testing in particular is often used to screen employees for promotional opportunities. Any test should be considered your opportunity to demonstrate your qualifications for the job. Testing generally covers three areas: interest, aptitude, and achievement. Tests used for career counseling as well as for screening employees and applicants will be discussed in Chapter 14.

A test gives you a chance to show your qualifications for the job.

Today's students should consider carefully the educational training, work experience, and personal skills that will best prepare them for a career in business data processing. Chapter 11 will explore each of these areas in detail. As you read through

EXPERIENCE. Work experience and after-school activities in job-related areas increase your job eligibility in your chosen career.
Courtesy IBM Corporation

this next chapter, consider the physical activity, work environment, educational requirements, responsibility level, and job complexity of each of the data processing occupations described. You may wish to pursue one of these many careers in business data processing.

CHECK YOURSELF

Supply the missing words.

1. Many high schools and colleges offer courses in data entry, ___?___ ___?___, and computer programming.
2. Employers often consider previous ___?___ training as a clear indication of a student's career interests.
3. A student should always work closely with his or her ___?___ ___?___ in selecting courses.
4. Regional training centers are specially equipped to provide apprentice ___?___ training.
5. Specialized training programs are often offered on a(n) ___?___ basis.
6. Technical schools provide instruction that is designed to prepare students for immediate ___?___.
7. ___?___ manufacturers provide extensive training courses for their own employees.
8. Enlistment in the ___?___ ___?___ may provide an excellent opportunity for training in data processing.
9. Specific opportunities in data processing depend on the type of ___?___ or government agency.
10. ___?___ ___?___ in any way may contribute to a successful data processing career.
11. To screen job applicants, companies may often use interest, aptitude, and achievement ___?___.

Review Questions

1. List three elements basic to employee productivity.
2. Name three communications skills important in business. For each of these skills provide an example of an awkward situation that could have been avoided with better communication.
3. Name two elements of effective written communication, and explain why each element matters in businesses.
4. Name two elements important in business problem solving.
5. Give an example of a problem that can arise in business as a result of a math error.
6. Name three business machines equipped with a keyboard.
7. List two typical data processing jobs for which a community college graduate may be considered.
8. Name two data processing jobs that often require a degree from a four-year college or from a graduate program.

Comparing Ideas

The questions below are to help you think about what you have learned in this chapter. They are thought questions. There is no one correct answer.

1. Imagine that a data-entry clerk makes a typographical error in spelling a new employee's name. Discuss the company records that may be produced incorrectly due to this error in recording.
2. What are the characteristics of oral and written communication as input and output media? Divide up into teams of ten students each, and transmit numeric and alphabetic data from one person in the team to another. Do this using oral and then written communication. Discuss the advantages and disadvantages of both methods.
3. Divide up into groups, and discuss why you might be afraid of tests and how you can overcome such fears.

Data Processing Activities

Now you can try out the kinds of data processing activities business workers perform. Below is a summary of the work you will do. You will find the actual information and business forms you need in your *Data Processing Work Kit.*

Activity 1. As a supervisor at a company that sells office equipment and supplies, you will be responsible for routing customer orders to the proper clerk.

Activity 2. You will design a magnetic-tape label for the monthly sales summaries.

BASIC Project 10
Keyboarding Drill

A common expression used in computer system work is "garbage in, garbage out!" This is a reminder to all of us that input data must be as accurate as possible. The following exercise will give you practice in keyboarding and verifying sample business data using a BASIC data-entry program.

Program Statements

In the last project, conditional branching (using IF . . . THEN statements) and unconditional branching (using GOTO statements) resulted in the selection of one of several paths through a program.

Branching may also be used to cause a section of a program to be repeated any number of times. The repeated section is a *program loop.*

Sample Program

The sample program on page 246 selects a particular path using conditional branching in the same way as the program in Project 9. However, unless the option number is 3 (which causes a branch to the END of the program at line 999), the program will eventually loop back to line 20 and repeat. This is caused by the statement GOTO 20, which is found in lines 90, 120, and 270.

There is a second loop in this program. If the verification line and entry line do not match when they are checked at line 230, the program will proceed to line 240, where the message YOU MADE A MISTAKE, TRY AGAIN will be printed. At the next line, 250, control is returned to line 200 (by the statement GOTO 200), where the program again asks for the verification line to be typed. The only way to get out of this loop is to type in the line correctly.

NOTE: In earlier projects we encountered two kinds of errors. If a statement itself is incorrect and the computer can't understand it, the error is a *syntax error.* Even if there are no syntax errors, *run-time errors* may occur when the program is being executed.

LOOPS. This flowchart demonstrates the use of a program loop in BASIC.

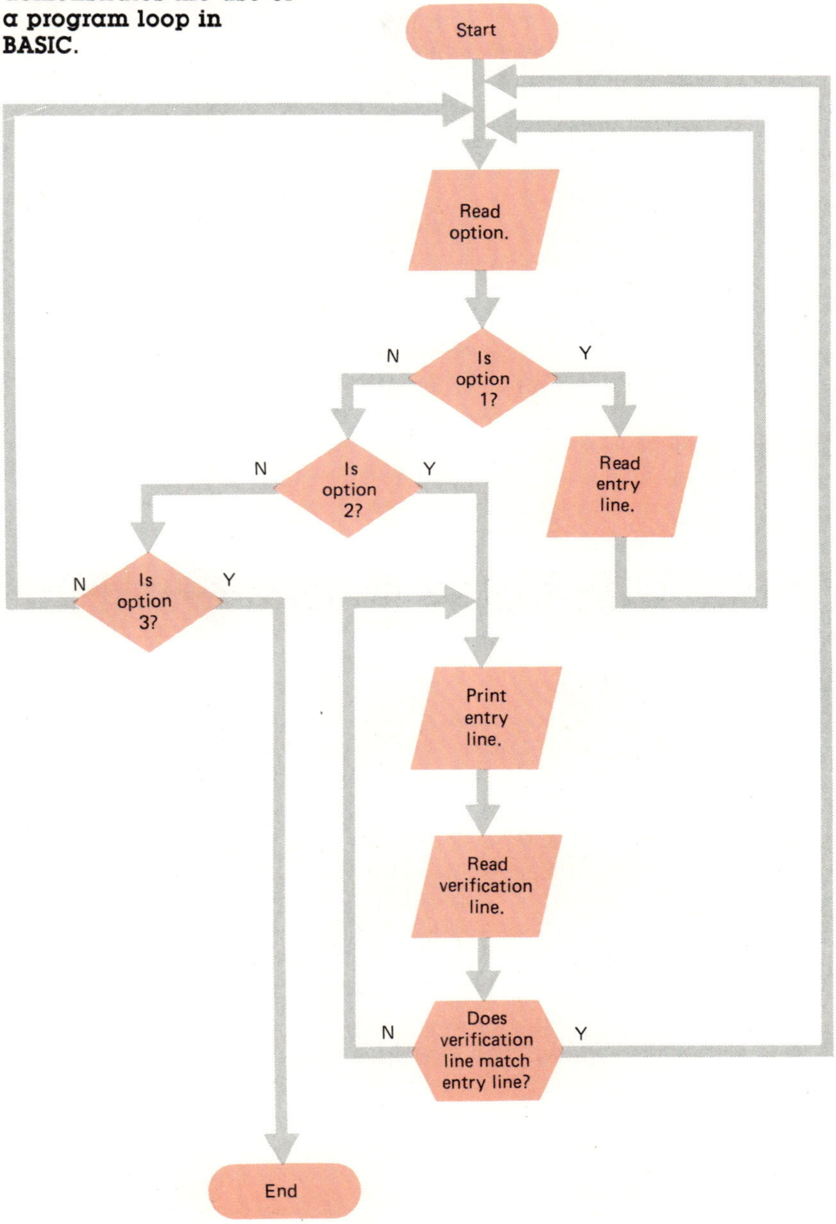

Trying to input string data for a numeric variable or attempting to divide a number by zero will cause such errors.

A third kind of error is known as a *logic error*. All the program statements may be correct, and the program may run smoothly, but it won't do what you want it to. From the computer's point of view, everything is fine.

As you become more experienced as a programmer, you will tend to make fewer syntax errors. Run-time errors and, in particular, logic errors will become your main concern as you write more complicated programs.

Logic errors sometimes cause a particularly sticky problem known as an *endless loop*. This can happen if the program does not provide a condition that allows an exit from the loop or if the program provides a condition that cannot be met.

```
10 REMARK KEYBOARDING PRACTICE DRILL
20 PRINT "TYPE 1 FOR ENTRY"
30 PRINT "      2 FOR VERIFY"
40 PRINT "      3 TO END"
50 INPUT T
60 IF T=1 THEN 100
70 IF T=2 THEN 200
80 IF T=3 THEN 999
90 GOTO 20
100 PRINT "TYPE A LINE OF DATA"
110 INPUT A$
120 GOTO 20
200 PRINT "TYPE THE FOLLOWING LINE OF DATA"
210 PRINT "  ";A$
220 INPUT B$
230 IF A$=B$ THEN 260
```

```
240 PRINT "YOU MADE A MISTAKE, TRY AGAIN"
250 GOTO 200
260 PRINT "VERY GOOD"
270 GOTO 20
999 END
```

What would happen to the sample program if line 80 were removed? You should know how to stop the RUN of a program in case you accidentally cause an endless loop. On many computers there is a key labeled BREAK that is used to stop a program. Ask your instructor about your system, or check the reference manual.

Output

```
TYPE 1 FOR ENTRY
     2 FOR VERIFY
     3 TO END
?1
TYPE A LINE OF DATA
?THIS IS A TEST OF ACCURACY NOT SPEED.
TYPE 1 FOR ENTRY
     2 FOR VERIFY
     3 TO END
?2
TYPE THE FOLLOWING LINE OF DATA
 THIS IS A TEST OF ACCURACY NOT SPEED.
?THIS IS A TEST OF ACCURACY NOT SEPED.
YOU MADE A MISTAKE, TRY AGAIN
TYPE THE FOLLOWING LINE OF DATA
```

```
 THIS IS A TEST OF ACCURACY NOT SPEED.
?THIS IS A TEST OF ACCURACY NOT SPEED.
VERY GOOD
TYPE 1 FOR ENTRY
     2 FOR VERIFY
     3 TO END
?3
```

Keyboarding Activities

1. Enter and RUN the program given above.
2. Input the following data (option 1)

```
PRACTICE MAKES PERFECT!
```

3. Verify the data (option 2) by retyping PRACTICE MAKES PERFECT!
4. Improve your keyboarding accuracy by entering and verifying data.

Enrichment Activities

1. Modify the keyboarding practice drill so that you can enter your name as input (prior to the menu) and have the program report the following on the basis of performance.

```
VERY GOOD, ROBERT
```

or

```
YOU MADE A MISTAKE, ROBERT
```

2. Modify the sample program so that the message INVALID OPTION NUMBER is printed when the user enters a number other than 1, 2, or 3.
3. Go back to Projects 7, 8, and 9. Modify each one so that it loops back to process another set of input data unless the user types in a signal to END.

CHAPTER

11

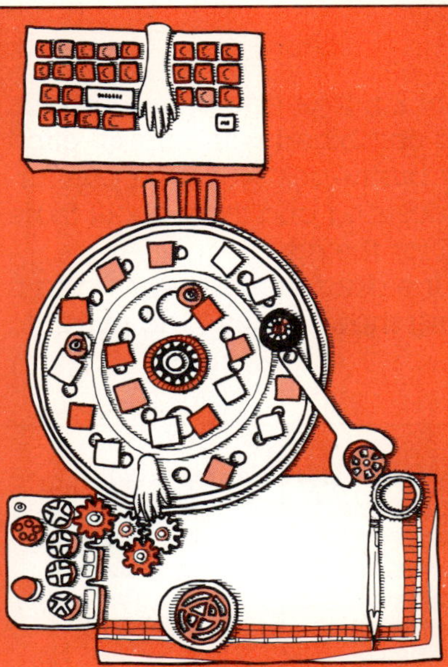

Choosing a Career

DATA PROCESSING TERMINOLOGY

Career ladder
Career pyramid
PEERS job rating system
Job characteristic

PERFORMANCE GOALS

- Name five characteristics that may be used to describe and compare data processing jobs.
- Name 20 different career opportunities offered in computer data processing.
- List nine other data processing jobs commonly found in business.
- Prepare a career ladder in data processing for yourself.

What role will you play if you decide to work in data processing? How will your career begin? What will your chances for advancement be? To find the answers to these questions, you must look closely at what people who work in data processing do. In this book you have read about different kinds of equipment used in business and how this equipment is combined with human effort to produce information needed by businesses. Now you can further explore various jobs in data processing and think about those you would like. Then you can plan for the future.

As a start, it may help to think of the data processing field as a **career pyramid.** Look at the drawing shown below. The pyramid

CAREER PYRAMID. The base of this pyramid shows entry-level positions in electronic data processing departments and other departments requiring basic processing skills. As you move up the pyramid visually, you are looking at positions that require more education, training, responsibility, and analysis. The top jobs are far more complex than those shown at the base of the pyramid.

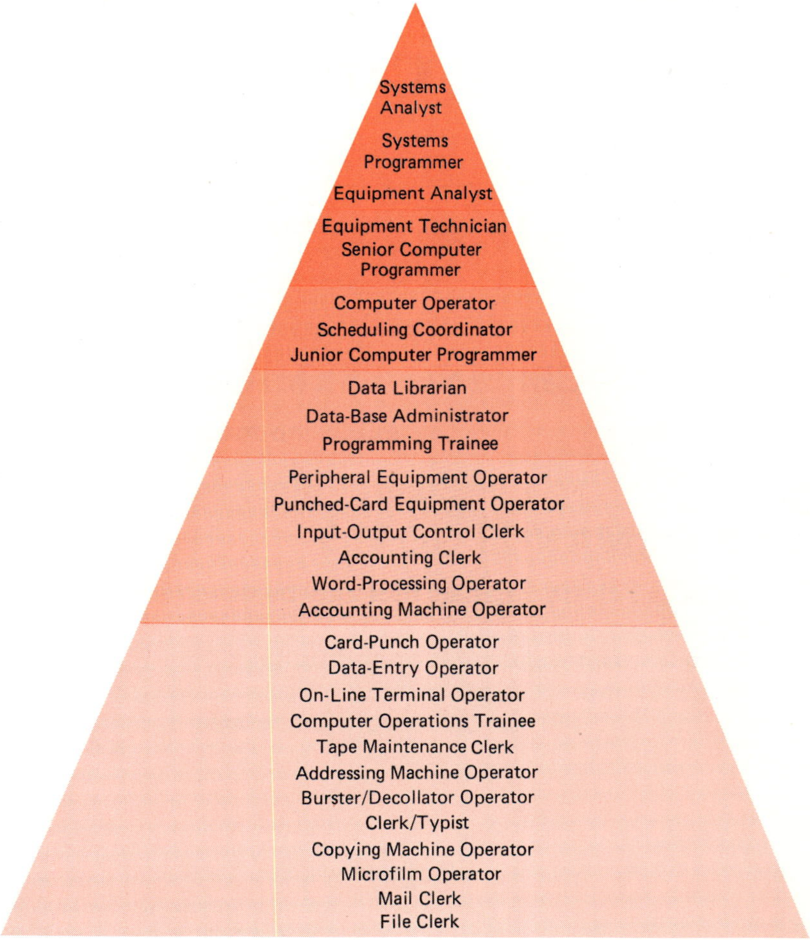

gives you some idea of how many people work at each level. It shows that some employees are beginners. Others are experienced workers with a good deal of responsibility. A computer center, for example, may employ one data processing manager and ten data-entry clerks. As you learn about job requirements, you will see that for some jobs you need work experience or on-the-job training or both. Computer operators may have been successful equipment operators. Data-entry clerks may have been good clerk/typists.

You can also think of a data processing career as a ladder. Each step (rung) on the ladder stands for a different job. The lowest step represents an entry-level job. The higher steps stand for more advanced jobs. The higher the step, the more advanced the job is. Work experience and on-the-job training will start you on your way up the ladder. And the better you do your job, the faster you will climb. Many **career ladders** are possible in data processing. The ladders shown below are only a few of the many

In Chapters 7 through 9 you read about the many kinds of

CAREER LADDERS. These ladders show three different types of data processing careers. Which one interests you the most?

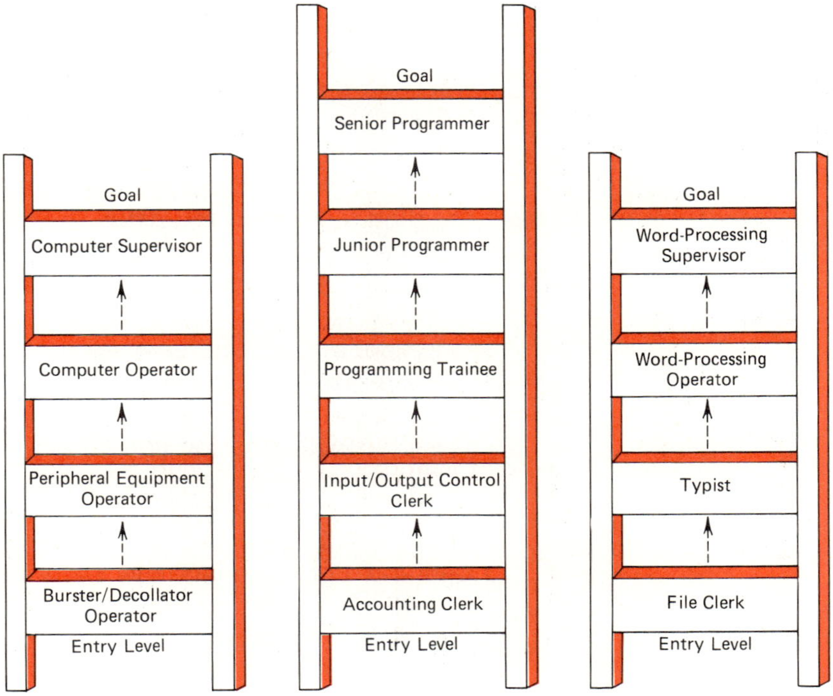

workers needed in data processing systems. In these later chapters you probably came to understand why employees need to work together if a data processing system is to succeed. In Chapter 10 you learned what makes a good data processing professional. Now you are ready to look at some jobs in data processing and to decide where you might fit in. But first you will learn how the characteristics of data processing jobs are compared and ranked by business organizations.

The PEERS Rating System

The U.S. government gives code numbers to jobs, including data processing jobs. These numbers are called DOT code numbers because they are listed in a book called the *Dictionary of Occupational Titles (DOT).* The book describes each of the jobs it lists. Your instructor or your school library may have a copy of this book for you to examine.

Another book about data processing jobs is the *Directory of Data Processing Education.* This book tells you what education and training a person needs for a job in data processing. It also describes the different jobs.

But there are some things you need to know that these books do not fully cover. To tell you about these things, the authors of this book have developed a special job rating system. It is called the **PEERS job rating system.** A PEERS rating is given with each job description in this chapter.

A PEERS rating describes a job in five ways. Each of these ways is called a **job characteristic**. The five characteristics of each job that the PEERS system rates are listed below. Notice that the first letters of the five job characteristics spell out the word PEERS.

Physical activity and environment
Experience
Education
Responsibility and job complexity
Skills

Each PEERS characteristic can be rated on a scale of 1 to 3, depending upon the quantity or quality of the characteristic involved in a particular job. The table presented on the next page shows the meaning of the ratings for each characteristic.

Meaning of the PEERS Ratings

CHARACTERISTIC	RATING OF 1	RATING OF 2	RATING OF 3
Physical activity and environment	Very little effort and comfortable surroundings	Some standing and lifting and/or some noise	Quite a lot of standing and lifting and/or noisy surroundings
Experience	Entry level	One or more years	Two or more years
Education	High school	Vocational/technical training or some college	Four-year college degree
Responsibility and job complexity	Closely supervised; simple tasks	Lightly supervised; more complex tasks (with guidelines given)	Little supervision; many decisions to make in performing job operations
Skills	Few, if any	Some specialized	Many highly specialized

Card-Punch Operator

P	E	E	R	S
2	1	1	2	2

To see how the PEERS rating system works, look at the rating for a card-punch operator shown here. The Physical Activity and Environment rating of 2 means that the job calls for some physical activity and that the card-punch operator works in a somewhat uncomfortable environment, perhaps one that is noisy. A rating of 1 for Experience means that no experience is required; it is an entry-level job. A rating of 1 for Education means that high school graduates work in this job. Most experienced card-punch operators are lightly supervised, and so there is a rating of 2 for Responsibility and Job Complexity. A PEERS rating of 2 for Skills shows that card-punch operators need specialized skills to function in their jobs.

PHYSICAL ACTIVITY AND ENVIRONMENT

The amount of physical effort usually required and the nature of the surrounding environment.

Physical Activity and Environment

Data processing can involve the use of heavy equipment. In some jobs, employees may have to lift heavy supplies such as addressograph plates, punched-card trays, and computer printouts. Other jobs, such as tape librarian or copy machine operator, may require long hours of standing. In addition, some employees may work in a somewhat uncomfortable environment, perhaps one that is noisy. This is often true of a card-punch operator. A PEERS rating of 3 for Physical Activity and Environment would mean that the task calls for quite a lot of activity and that the environment is somewhat uncomfortable. A job in which a worker sits in a quiet room and keyboards data all day would receive a rating of 1.

EXPERIENCE

Previous exposure to a similar job or to several related jobs.

Experience

Experience refers to previous exposure to a similar job or to a variety of related jobs. Entry-level jobs such as file clerk or mail clerk get a PEERS rating of 1 because they require very little, if any, previous experience. Other jobs—such as that of a word-processing operator, which requires one to two years of previous experience as a typist—get a PEERS rating of 2. A PEERS rating of 3 applies to a job that should be given only to an individual who has had two years or more of experience in performing the job functions.

EDUCATION

Intellectual, vocational, and technical training.

Education

The PEERS rating for Education will give you an idea of how much education is needed for each data processing job. Jobs that require a high school diploma have a PEERS rating of 1. Most entry-level jobs in data processing require a high school diploma. A rating of 2 means that vocational/technical training or some college is needed. Jobs that nearly always call for a four-year college degree have a rating of 3.

RESPONSIBILITY

The degree of supervision.

COMPLEXITY

The number of things involved.

Responsibility and Job Complexity

A complex job is one in which an employee must do many different tasks. A person in an entry-level job does not do as many things as a person in a more advanced job. A beginning card-punch operator may only punch one type of input data. This person's job is not complex. Also, the trainee must be closely supervised until he or she knows all the job operations. Such a job would have a rating of 1 for Responsibility and Job Complexity.

An experienced card-punch operator, on the other hand, may handle many kinds of input data in a day. This operator's job is quite complex. Since the operator is experienced, he or she would not be as closely supervised as a beginner. People who are promoted are less closely supervised as they perform their job functions. Their jobs also often become much more complex. A very complex job or a job in which a person has many decisions to make in performing the job would have a Responsibility and Job Complexity rating of 3. (The PEERS ratings given in this chapter for Responsibility and Job Complexity in entry-level jobs are for workers with little experience.)

SKILLS

Special abilities that are learned.

Skills

Skills are special abilities that one learns. The PEERS ratings for Skills give you an idea of how many skills you must have for a particular job. Jobs with a PEERS rating of 1 require few, if any, specialized skills. A rating of 2 indicates that some specialized skills are necessary. For a job with a rating of 3, you must have many highly specialized skills that must be kept up to date. Taking vocational/technical school courses and getting on-the-job training are the best ways to develop and maintain specialized job skills.

CHECK YOURSELF

Supply the missing words.

1. The lowest step on a career ladder represents a(n) __?__ job.
2. You may think of the jobs in a career as a ladder or as a(n) __?__.
3. If a career is thought of in terms of a ladder or pyramid, the jobs requiring the most education, skill, experience, and responsibility are at the __?__.
4. The U.S. government gives code numbers to jobs, and these codes are listed in a book called the __?__ __?__ __?__ __?__.
5. A book that describes data processing jobs and tells what training is required for each job is the __?__ __?__ __?__ __?__ __?__.
6. A job that requires a worker to do many different tasks is said to be __?__.
7. The authors of this book have created a system to describe and compare data processing jobs; this system is identified by the letters __?__.

Careers in Computer Data Processing

As you read in Chapters 7 through 9, the operation of computer data processing systems requires the efforts of many people from data entry, through processing steps, to the handling of data output. In addition, human effort is needed for the planning, development, and maintenance of computer systems and programs on which the operations depend. Thus a number of careers are possible in computer data processing. In this section you will read about careers in data entry, computer operations, computer support activities, and systems and programming.

Computer Data-Entry Careers

A number of jobs in data processing require skill in keyboarding data. A knowledge of typewriting is helpful in learning how to keyboard data on other machines. As you read in earlier chapters, particularly Chapter 5, data can be entered for machine processing on media such as cards, tapes, and disks. The clerks who prepare data in machine-readable form for computer processing are called *data-entry operators* (or clerks). They also have job titles that relate to the media they use, as in the ads shown here. To qualify as a data-entry operator, you need to know how to load, operate, and unload the specific input machine to be used.

Card-Punch
(Keypunch)
Operator

Needed by midtown hospital. Some experience required. Familiarity with medical terminology helpful. Call Mr. Kay, 292-4400.

Data-Entry
Operator

Our client will train a good typist to use key-to-disk devices. Best employee benefits and quick advancement for alert person. Montez Agency, 779-8010.

On-Line Terminal
Operators

We are looking for three high school grads who score high on typing accuracy and who want to get involved in an exciting area of EDP. Call Mr. Davies at Wong Company, 800-5492.

Card-Punch Operator				
P	E	E	R	S
2	1	1	2	2

Card-Punch Operator. A card-punch operator converts source documents into machine-readable punched cards. This involves using the card-punch machines described in Chapter 3. When the operator presses keys on a keyboard, holes are punched in cards.

Punched cards must be carefully handled to prevent damage. Courses in punched-card operations usually show students how to place cards in a machine and how to remove them.

These courses also stress accuracy. Trainees are taught to keyboard data carefully, to check their work, and to correct any errors they find. Obviously, if the data entered is to be useful, it must be accurate. To ensure accuracy, key verification is often required. This means that each character of information is typed a second time (usually by a different operator) to be sure the data has been recorded properly.

Data-Entry Operator				
P	E	E	R	S
1	1	1	2	2

Data-Entry Operator. A data-entry operator uses data-entry machines described in Chapter 5 to enter data for use as input. This task consists of keyboarding data recorded on source documents. As the operator keyboards the data, it is recorded on magnetic disks, diskettes, or tapes.

Machine operation includes selecting various codes and format indicators to allow for machine interpretation of the various data fields. Data-entry operators must work as carefully and accurately as card-punch operators if the data is to be usable for machine processing.

On-Line Terminal Operator. The data-entry clerks described so far have all had to prepare an input medium. But

On-Line Terminal Operator

P	E	E	R	S
1	1	1	2	2

technology now allows operators to enter data into a computer directly, without having to prepare punched cards or record data on magnetic disks, diskettes, or tapes.

Operators who enter data on-line use a variety of terminals, depending on the particular businesses in which they work. When an operator keyboards data on a printing terminal, a printed document is created just as in typing a letter. The keyboarded data is stored in an area called a *buffer*. The operator can check the printed document for errors and then go back and make corrections. The corrected data can be entered right away, or it can be stored in the buffer. When the stored data is needed, it can be moved to the central processing unit.

Very often, a printed record of transactions is not needed. In such cases, a visual display (CRT) terminal can be used instead of a printing terminal. The operator keys in data as on a printing terminal. The CRT screen shows the data that is entered. The operator checks the data displayed on the screen for errors. Corrections can then be made so that only accurate information is entered into the computer.

The major advantage of such on-line data input is that the computer checks and verifies data as it is entered. The computer may immediately request additional input information from the operator. Or the computer may show the operator where an error in format has been made. Reductions in the costs of equipment ensure that on-line applications will continue to increase in the years ahead. Like other data-entry clerks, on-line operators must be very accurate in their work.

Computer Operator

Minimum one-year experience working with large-scale disk-oriented computer systems required. Our computer installation operates three shifts, 24 hr. a day. Apply at State Employment Office, 55 Water Street.

Computer Operations Careers

The people in computer operations include the computer operators, operators of peripheral and punched-card processing machines in a computer installation, burster/decollator operators, and computer operations trainees.

Punched-Card Equipment Operator

A local university is looking for someone to operate its punched-card equipment in its computer installation. They want someone who likes activity and is interested in a career in data processing. Apply at State Employment Office, 55 Water Street.

Peripheral Equipment Operator

Bank needs experienced operator of off-line COM and MICR scanning equipment in its computer installation. Advancement to computer operator likely. Box 9878.

Burster/Decollator Operator

The desire to work in a computer environment and the ability to work hard are the only requirements for this job at one of the city's leading manufacturers. Call for an appointment with Ms. Vincent, 662-9800. Bondini Containers, Inc.

Computer Operations Trainee

Insurance Company is looking for high school grads to enroll in training programs. Interest in computers a plus. Data Basics, Inc., 393-3000, ext. 494.

Computer Operator

P	E	E	R	S
3	2	2	2	2

Computer Operator. As you read in Chapter 4, a computer system is made up of the central processor and the input and output devices needed to perform the jobs of a business. All these parts are under the control of the visual display terminal or computer console. A specially trained computer operator enters processing instructions at the console. This operator may also load magnetic disks or punched cards, mount magnetic tapes, and supply continuous forms for computer output. In a large department, these things will be done by junior computer operators. The computer operator must keep an up-to-date log (record) of all computer data processing activities. He or she must also make sure that all the related computer equipment is kept in working order. The computer operator works with programmers and systems analysts on problems of work flow and in improving throughput. He or she also works with equipment technicians to resolve machine failures. In addition, the computer operator works with data librarians and tape maintenance clerks to be sure that computer programs and data files are available and in good condition. Good teamwork saves computer and other machine time.

The computer operator must have a thorough knowledge of one or more computer systems. He or she needs at least six months' work experience in data processing.

Peripheral Equipment Operator

P	E	E	R	S
3	1	1	2	2

Peripheral Equipment Operator. Special equipment is often used in computer data processing. Some types of equipment, such as card-to-tape converters, document scanners, or data transmission units, were described in earlier parts of this book. The peripheral equipment operator operates this equipment and may also set up and monitor the input and output devices used in computer data processing. In addition, this operator may help the computer operator keep the log up to date.

The peripheral equipment operator usually needs to have a high school education and experience in handling different input media. The skills needed for each task to be done on the machine are usually learned through on-the-job training. In time, a peripheral equipment operator who does the job well may be promoted to computer operator.

Punched-Card Equipment Operator

P	E	E	R	S
3	1	1	1	2

Punched-Card Equipment Operator. Many tasks involving punched-card data can be done without using computer input/output devices. But as computers become smaller and less expensive, punched-card equipment will be used more and more in support of medium- and large-sized computer systems and less and less as a stand-alone system.

As a computer support system, punched-card equipment such

as the reproducer, the interpreter, the sorter, the collator, and the accounting machine is often kept in one room. The punched-card equipment operator is responsible for operating this equipment. For example, rather than take up expensive computer time, businesses often prefer to have their employees use a punched-card accounting machine to prepare lists or computations from decks of punched cards.

Several punched-card machines, including the accounting machine, the reproducer, and the collator, need wired control panels that instruct the machine in the task to be performed. The punched-card equipment operator may be asked to prepare diagram sheets and to document the necessary wiring. From these diagrams, control panels are wired to produce the desired card decks. Once the wiring is tested, however, punched-card machines are used for specific tasks and are seldom rewired. Most punched-card centers have a library of control panels covering standard applications such as payroll and inventory.

Burster/Decollator Operator

P	E	E	R	S
3	1	1	1	1

Burster/Decollator Operator. The burster/decollator operator bursts and separates forms. Computer output is often in the form of multiple-copy continuous forms. Reports can be produced with three or four carbon copies. *Bursting* means removing the unwanted trim (edges of the paper) and separating the perforated forms. *Decollating* means putting the forms into sets and removing the carbon paper from them.

The burster/decollator operator is told how many copies of a form will be needed. Bursting and decollating can be strenuous work, involving thousands of pages of printed output. It is important to do this task well, because if the equipment is operated carelessly, important business reports can be damaged and valuable computer time will have been wasted.

The job of bursting and decollating is an entry-level position requiring no special education or experience. The employee who performs this job well can be considered for training in other areas such as data entry or computer operations.

Computer Operations Trainee

P	E	E	R	S
3	1	1	1	2

Computer Operations Trainee. A large data processing department may hire one or more high school graduates with no training or work experience. These employees are called computer operations trainees. Through on-the-job training, these trainees learn the work that is done by peripheral and punched-card machine operators and by computer operators. Sometimes these beginners are given the chance to be in a training program sponsored by the computer manufacturer whose computer system is used.

Computer Support Activities Careers

A wide variety of functions must be performed to support the computer operations in any business. The larger the computer installation, the more numerous and varied the computer support positions. The data processing careers described in this section perform important functions that are necessary for the success of any computer processing activity. These jobs include the functions of input-output control, scheduling, data library control and tape maintenance, data-base administration, and equipment maintenance.

Input/Output Control

Well-organized, alert worker needed in our data processing department. Will establish input controls, check computer output, and oversee distribution of output to other departments. Call Mr. Barker, 255-6944.

Scheduling Coordinator

To coordinate the activities of a busy data processing department at the downtown headquarters of a major bank. Leadership qualities and the ability to set and enforce deadlines are a must. Any experience in a DP environment will be considered. Send résumés to Box 5660.

Data-Base Adminstrator

Manufacturer has large product data base to maintain. Requires intelligent individual with a minimum of two years data-entry experience and knowledge of computerized data-base input and maintenance procedures. Call our Personnel Dept., 924-7118.

Data Disk and Tape Librarian

Major corporation needs high school grad to take over responsibility for magnetic disk tapes and library. Will catalog, file, and check out disks and tapes. Experience desirable but will consider a trainee. Call Mrs. Perez at 567-8890.

Tape Maintenance Clerk

High school grad needed to keep a library of magnetic tapes in order. Will regularly clean tapes and help librarian catalog them. Come in and fill in an application. Singh Personnel, 1818 Clover Ave.

Equipment Technician

Earn while you learn. Manufacturer of computers is looking for applicants for its training program for computer technicians. Knowledge of electronics required. Contact Anita Smith at 345-1212.

Input/Output Control Clerk

P	E	E	R	S
1	2	1	3	2

Input/Output Control Clerk. As you have probably read in the newspapers, input errors are usually the reason why some people see errors on their bills. A successful data processing department must be very accurate. The last check on input before it is sent to the machines area for processing is often made by the input/output control clerk.

The input/output control clerk keeps track of the work that comes into and goes out of the data processing department. He or she often spot-checks such input as punched cards or tape. Sometimes errors are caught by reviewing job request cards. The totals of input transactions must be correct for balancing output results. All errors must be reported to the clerk's supervisor so that they can be corrected. They must be corrected before machine processing takes place.

Once the machine processing is done, the input/output control clerk prepares the output for distribution, balancing the output results according to the predetermined controls. He or she then sees that the output is delivered to the correct department.

Scheduling Coordinator				
P	E	E	R	S
1	3	1	3	3

Scheduling Coordinator. The data processing department has many jobs to do. It may be asked to prepare customer invoices, produce weekly paychecks for company employees, or list inventory. The scheduling coordinator receives a list of all the data processing jobs to be done and decides on the order in which the jobs are to be done. He or she then gives computer operations a list of jobs to do and tells the supervisor when the jobs must be completed. In this way, important projects will be completed on time. Otherwise, time needed for a project on a tight schedule might be used for a less important job.

When new jobs come in, the scheduling coordinator must try to fit them in. Sometimes he or she may even have to refuse to schedule a job if there is not time to do it.

A person who wants to be a scheduling coordinator must have a background in data processing. He or she should also be familiar with the operations of a data processing department and understand the importance of deadlines.

Data Librarian				
P	E	E	R	S
2	2	1	2	2

Data Librarian (or Data Library Control Clerk or Tape Librarian). A computer installation stores the data it needs in a number of ways. Often data is stored on magnetic disks, diskettes, or tapes. Data recorded on magnetic media must be very carefully maintained, especially if it is used regularly.

Data stored on magnetic disks, diskettes, and tape must be cataloged and filed just like any other business data. Many large businesses and government agencies have a data library. A data librarian keeps an accurate record of the file number and contents of each disk and tape stored in the library. So important is the information on the disks and tapes that many companies have copies made of this data. The copies are kept in a different place. If a fire destroys one data library, the company still has the other one.

A computer operator or computer programmer tells the librarian which disks or tapes are needed. When a disk or tape is borrowed, it must be checked out. When it is returned, it must be checked in. If a disk or tape has been lost or damaged, the librarian immediately takes steps to replace it. Then when it is needed again, it will be available.

Tape Maintenance Clerk. Input and storage media are regularly cared for and maintained. The data library may have

Tape Maintenance Clerk

P	E	E	R	S
2	2	1	1	2

thousands of reels of magnetic tape. With many of these tapes, data is recorded and erased over and over again in business data processing. Special equipment is used to clean and demagnetize magnetic tapes and storage disks. This is the job of the tape maintenance clerk. This clerk also checks all storage media for quality and cleans, catalogs, and stores all usable tapes. Damaged tapes must be removed from use. Otherwise the data stored on them might be lost.

Data-Base Administrator

P	E	E	R	S
1	2	2	2	2

Data-Base Administrator. As described in Chapter 7, a data base is a file of data shared by two or more systems; it is usually maintained in machine-readable form. In modern computer installations the responsibility for ensuring that the information in a data base is current and accurate is often assigned to an experienced office worker called a data-base administrator.

A data-base administrator establishes controls for every type of input transaction that results in a change in a data base. Examples are changes in the data fields of existing file records, the deletion of existing records, and additions to a file. Also, the administrator maintains a running count of the number of records in the data base. This count can then be used to check the file counts made during computer processing operations.

Experience with accounting and clerical control methods, data-entry procedures, and output control techniques is necessary for anyone who wants to be hired as a data-base administrator. Also, a knowledge of the computer processing involved in file maintenance is helpful.

Equipment Technician

P	E	E	R	S
2	3	2	3	3

Equipment Technician. An equipment technician inspects and repairs all of a business's data processing equipment. This is done on a regular basis. Taking good care of equipment prevents costly, unexpected breakdowns. If a breakdown does occur, the technician must quickly repair the damage and return the equipment to service. When breakdowns occur, the delay can be quite costly. For this reason, many companies keep extra equipment just for such emergencies.

Most computer systems are serviced by technicians who are trained and employed by the manufacturers of the systems. However, some large companies train their own equipment technicians.

A good technician can look forward to a career in equipment analysis or sales after several years of experience. A degree in electronics, as well as some business training, will help advance the technician in this career path.

Systems Analysis and Computer Programming Careers

When a new or updated processing system is needed, a systems analyst designs one to suit the needs of the business. Then he or she sets up the procedures for implementing the system.

Systems Analyst

Needed by small manufacturing firm that is converting its manual system to EDP. Will work closely with management in designing and implementing the new system. Minimum three years related experience, knowledge of IBM 4300 model computers required. Call Eddie Jackson at Girard Containers, 336-8900.

Systems Programmer

Will select and maintain operating systems for large IBM computers. Knowledge of on-line processing and data base management systems essential. City Trust Bank, 10 Harris St. See Joan Capel.

Senior Computer Programmer

Major insurance company needs person who knows PL1 and BASIC. Will oversee four junior programmers. Box 828.

Junior Computer Programmer

We need someone with excellent skills in writing COBOL programs. At least 1 yr. exp. with real-time processing systems essential. Call 898-2202.

Programming Trainee

Applicant must have studied computer science. Accounting credits helpful. Chance for fast advancement. 789-1111.

Equipment Analyst

Needed to advise growing company on purchase of computer system to be used primarily for payroll and inventory management. Requires two years of related experience. Reply to Box 7499.

Computer programmers, computer operators, and other data processing employees carry out their work within this system. The education required for the jobs in systems analysis and computer programming ranges from a high school diploma to a graduate degree. Both trainees and people with much work experience are needed.

Systems Analyst				
P	E	E	R	S
1	3	3	3	3

Systems Analyst. The job of the systems analyst is to find ways of setting up and completing data processing work as simply, inexpensively, and quickly as possible. Managers, heads of departments, and salespeople who need vital information (output) from a system go to the systems analyst. This analyst then designs a way of getting that information. For example, a sales manager may ask for a monthly sales report that shows how many of each item were sold. The analyst will then find a way of producing this information every month.

It is the analyst's responsibility to see to it that human effort and machine effort are kept to a minimum while maintaining the highest-quality job performance. Therefore, the analyst must be familiar with each and every task assigned and work very closely with both the data processing department and the department needing the information.

Most systems analysts have a college degree. This degree is usually in business administration or computer science. A systems analyst may also have a graduate degree in business or computer science.

A systems analyst must be a good planner so that employees can use their machines and skills to best advantage. In addition, the analyst must work with a range of people from top managers to clerks. A person who can do this job must be able to get along with people.

Systems Programmer				
P	E	E	R	S
1	3	3	3	3

Systems Programmer. The systems programmer must maintain the computer's operating system programs in a computer data processing department. The systems programmer makes sure that the computer programmers who are coding applications use the computer's operating system properly.

Most systems programmers are college graduates who have had work experience in data processing hardware and software. They must be able to recommend computer operating systems and software packages to management.

Systems programmers are needed in large computer departments and in businesses such as insurance companies, banks, and computer manufacturing companies.

Senior Computer Programmer				
P	E	E	R	S
1	3	2	3	3

Senior Computer Programmer. In large businesses, several programmers can be working on the same project. There may be very experienced senior programmers, less experienced junior programmers, and programming trainees.

The data processing systems developed by the systems analyst are shown in system flowcharts. Often these flowcharts are given to a senior computer programmer. This programmer must then develop program flowcharts and computer programs for all the applications indicated in the system flowcharts.

When the program flowcharts are prepared, the senior computer programmer often supervises the junior computer programmers while they write the step-by-step computer programs. This involves the conversion of each flowcharting instruction into programming language.

In order to supervise other programmers, the senior computer programmer must be able to write instructions for a computer skillfully. Many programmers can write computer instructions in several programming languages. Other programmers specialize in just one programming language.

Junior Computer Programmer				
P	E	E	R	S
1	2	2	3	3

Junior Computer Programmer. A senior programmer will ask a junior programmer to do small tasks or parts of programs. The junior programmer may be given only one program flowchart from a system or subsystem to work on at a time. (Computing hourly earnings might be an example of one part of a system.) The junior programmer converts the program flowchart into programming language. He or she writes step-by-step computer programs. Each set of instructions must be tested through the input, processing, and output operations before the program can be used for processing actual business data.

Programming Trainee				
P	E	E	R	S
1	1	2	3	3

Programming Trainee. To be a programming trainee, a person usually, but not always, needs a college degree. For this job, businesses prefer to hire people who have majored in business or a related area such as data processing or computer science. You could be hired for this job right after college. Or you might be able to move into it from a job in data entry or computer operations.

As a programming trainee, you would perform a number of beginning tasks under supervision. These tasks might include making changes in a program flowchart, or replacing a set of instructions in a computer program, revising the written descriptions that should accompany computer software. In addition, you might also be asked to convert each flowcharting instruction into programming language.

Equipment Analyst				
P	E	E	R	S
1	3	3	3	3

Equipment Analyst. When data processing systems are developed (see Chapters 7 through 9 for examples), equipment decisions often have to be made. If a computer is to be purchased, what type, size, and make will it be? What special peripheral equipment will be needed?

Equipment analysts must know the job to be performed as well as what equipment, new or used, is available to perform it. They must be sure the equipment they buy will do the job efficiently and economically. Since data processing equipment can be bought from many manufacturers, the equipment analyst has to consider each sales presentation carefully before making a purchase recommendation to management.

Most equipment analysts have work experience in both computer programming and systems analysis. They usually have a college degree, and they are able to prepare well-written reports to support equipment recommendations.

CHECK YOURSELF

Supply the missing words.

1. A(n) ___?___ ___?___ searches for the best way to set up a data processing job system.
2. The ___?___ ___?___ works with equipment analysts and technicians to resolve machine failures.
3. A junior ___?___ ___?___ writes step-by-step computer programs.
4. A programming trainee converts each ___?___ ___?___ into a set of detailed instructions in a specified programming language.
5. A(n) ___?___ ___?___ operator runs special data processing equipment such as a card-to-tape converter.
6. The entry-level employee who performs a beginning task such as replacing a set of instructions in a computer program is often called a programming ___?___.
7. A(n) ___?___ computer programmer may supervise junior programmers and programming trainees.
8. A computer ___?___ trainee may be a high school graduate who will learn through on-the-job training.
9. A(n) ___?___ ___?___ typically has experience in both systems analysis and computer programming.
10. The employee who establishes controls for every type of input transaction that results in a change in a data base is known as a(n) ___?___ ___?___ ___?___.

Other Data Processing Careers

There are many opportunities for careers in data processing other than those related specifically to computer activities. All businesses, even those with the largest computer installations, need office workers for clerical activities and for the operation of simpler office equipment. Some of the typical career opportunities open to high school graduates in these areas will be described.

Clerical Processing Activities

The person most likely to be hired for a job in clerical data processing is a high school graduate. Employers are especially interested in graduates who have taken business courses or who have worked part-time in a clerical position. Usually clerical jobs call for collecting data, checking it, and distributing it to the people who need it. Employees, therefore, need to be good at detail. They must also be able to follow instructions and to work well with others.

Businesses are organized in many ways. Large businesses usually have more job titles than small businesses. The jobs you will read about here are found in almost every large business, but many are also found in small companies. In this section, you will read first about entry-level jobs in clerical processing activities.

Mail Clerk

Downtown company seeks alert individual to sort and deliver incoming and inter-office mail. Full benefits package offered. Call Paolo Perrone, 455-9878.

File Clerk

Busy law firm seeks person for alphabetic filing and filing by subject matter. Good benefits and advancement if you are bright and willing. Call Ms. Rivera, 672-9854.

Clerk/Typist

Immediate opening for person with good typing skills. Must be self-starter able to organize own work. Will type letters, file customer records, answer phones in busy order dept. Recruit Agency, 5 Arnold Ave.

Accounting Clerk

Must be high school grad with good figure aptitude and calculator skills. Some college preferred. Knowledge of EDP a plus. Advancement likely for the right candidate. Call Ann Farmer at 933-5121.

Mail Clerk				
P	E	E	R	S
2	1	1	1	1

Mail Clerk. The letters, orders, bills, and other items that come in the mail each day are very important to a business. In addition, there is mail that goes from one department of a business to another. This is called interoffice mail. Both incoming and interoffice mail must be processed quickly and carefully. This is the responsibility of mail clerks. Mail clerks sort the mail that arrives each day from the outside. They also pick up mail from mail stations in each department and sort it. Then they deliver both types of mail. Each business has its own system for mail, which mail clerks must learn. It is important that mail clerks be alert, active, and friendly.

File Clerk				
P	E	E	R	S
2	1	1	1	1

File Clerk. Many documents become part of a business's permanent records. To be useful, these documents must be easy to locate when they are needed. The job of the file clerk is to organize and store documents so they can be found quickly. Storing and finding documents is called storage and retrieval.

The file clerk must be sure to follow the filing methods of the company he or she works for. Several clerks may use the same files in an office. If they use different filing methods, documents may be lost. Then time is wasted looking for them. In some offices, a file clerk must keep a record of who removes material from the files.

The file clerk must be able to read well, follow instructions, and work carefully and quickly.

Clerk/Typist. This entry-level job can lead to a word processing operator job or a data-entry clerk job, or it can lead up the

Clerk/Typist

P	E	E	R	S
1	1	1	2	2

secretarial ladder. The clerk/typist transfers data from source documents to reports, letters, and business forms. He or she must pay attention to detail and be able to work quickly and accurately at a typewriter.

Most clerk/typists have had one or more typing courses. On the job, they are trained to prepare the types of documents they will be responsible for.

Departments such as order and billing, inventory, and payroll need clerk/typists. So do data processing departments, where specification, manuals, and reports must be prepared.

Accounting Clerk

P	E	E	R	S
1	3	1	2	2

Accounting Clerk. "Wanted: Accounting Clerk." This ad is seen very often in the want ad sections of newspapers. Every department that keeps many financial records needs accounting clerks. These clerks must have common sense and good record-keeping skills, and they should like work that calls for a lot of detail and self-checking.

An accounting clerk in a production cost department may be asked to keep track of salary, equipment, and supply expenses. He or she may also be asked to record the costs of a job that has been submitted for manufacturing. After the job is completed, the accounting clerk can find out what should be charged for the job by using the records. Sometimes the cost of a job must be estimated before the job is begun. Some accounting clerks prepare cost accounting reports for the managers of their company.

Careers in Specialized Machines Operations

Word-Processing Operator
Company will train grad with electric typewriter skills to operate a stand-alone word processor. Typing speed is important, but accuracy is essential. Full benefit package and excellent chance for advancement. Ms. Leon, 224-3890.

High school graduates can obtain entry-level jobs that involve operating the office machines you read about in Chapters 2 and 3. These jobs are the easiest to find because there are more of them. Note that the machines discussed in this section are only a few of the many machines that are used to speed up paperwork. The operators of these machines must be able to set up, start, control, and stop the machines.

Copying Machine Operator
The candidate who receives this job will be trained to operate several types of copying machines and will be responsible for deciding which one should be used for different assignments. Harris Employment Agency, 1010 Byer Blvd.

Microfilm Operator
Company will train high school graduate to catalog microfilm and microfiche and to operate microfilm readers. If you've worked part-time as a file clerk, that's a plus. Mrs. Liz Caro, 335-9800.

Addressing Machine Operator
Needed at busy mail order firm. Company will train fast learner to prepare plates and run addressing machine. Two openings. Come in and see us between 8:30 and 5. Quality Personnel, 10 Hudson Ave. West.

Accounting Machine Operator
High school grad with flair for figures needed immediately. Training in NCR accounting machines preferred. Courses in business math and an interest in accounting are pluses. Mr. Sanchez, 981-6700, at Hanson Books.

Word-Processing Operator				
P	E	E	R	S
1	3	1	2	2

Word-Processing Operator. In a large business, specially trained operators may work in a word-processing center. When the same letter is to be sent to many people, a word processor can be used. The operator types the original letter and then supplies the word processor with the address of each person who is to receive a copy of the letter. The word processor can type the letter hundreds of times. On each copy of the letter it inserts a new address.

Some word-processing equipment uses magnetic disks or diskettes to record the typewritten impulses of the original document. Other forms of storage include tape cassettes, magnetic cards, and magnetic stripes.

A word processor can also help keep down the costs of revising reports and other documents. Revising means that old material is taken out and/or new material is added. If a report is stored on magnetic tape or cards, the word-processing operator can erase errors and insert revisions. The word processor can then produce a perfect finished report. This process is called *text editing.*

A word-processing operator must be a skilled typist who understands automatic machine operation. Often an applicant begins as a clerk/typist and is promoted to word-processing operator because he or she showed an ability to plan how printed material will look and to organize large amounts of work.

Copying Machine Operator				
P	E	E	R	S
2	1	1	1	2

Copying Machine Operator. A computer can produce only a certain number of copies. When large numbers of copies of reports or other papers are needed, the copying machine operator is called on to make them. This employee operates duplicating machines, mimeograph machines, and xerography machines.

Another important task of the copying machine operator is to produce copies of charts, tables, and graphs. Sometimes these copies are to be made smaller. Sometimes they must be printed on both sides or in color. The copying machine operator has to keep track of the many different copying jobs that must be done. All the output this operator produces must be both neat and readable.

Microfilm Operator				
P	E	E	R	S
2	1	1	1	2

Microfilm Operator. The number of documents that a business must keep has become very great. Often there is no room to store all the paper documents. Instead, the documents are photographed on tiny film (microfilm). A single roll of microfilm can contain hundreds of business documents. This makes the cost of storage much less. It also makes it easier to retrieve documents.

A special file clerk called a microfilm operator catalogs the filmed documents and then stores the film according to the company's filing system.

The microfilm operator must be trained to use various mechanical devices. This operator should be a very careful person and should have an eye for detail.

Accounting Machine Operator

P	E	E	R	S
1	2	1	2	2

Accounting Machine Operator. Many companies continue to use electronic accounting machines for the processing of small volumes of customer invoices or accounts receivable. Also, modern accounting machines can be used for payroll or general ledger accounting.

As most modern accounting machines have a keyboard similar to the keyboard on an electric typewriter, an accounting machine operator must be skilled at typing. In addition, he or she must be skilled at math to continually check the calculations that the machine performs on the keyboarded data. An accounting machine operator must have knowledge of the control keys on the particular machine to be operated. Usually, the manufacturer of the equipment provides training programs that deal with the features and operation of the equipment.

Addressing Machine Operator

P	E	E	R	S
3	1	1	1	2

Addressing Machine Operator. You have already seen how important incoming mail is to a business. It follows that outgoing mail is very important also. The addressing machine operator is the person who has the task of getting address labels printed for letters, bills, and other outgoing mail. The addressing machine prints the addresses from stencils or plates. The job is finished much more quickly than if it had to be done on a typewriter. Usually, the labels are produced a batch at a time. Each batch is enough for a single mailing.

Data Processing Management

Almost every job in data processing can lead to a career as a supervisor or manager. If you are a data-entry clerk, for example, you can become a supervisor of data-entry operations. If you are a computer operator, you can become a supervisor of computer operations. There are many other such opportunities. The job titles and duties will vary with the employer.

A supervisor or manager must understand business needs and goals. He or she should be good at communicating with others, be good at planning, and be good at following up to see that work is getting done. The supervisor of a data processing operation and the manager of a data processing department plan and direct the work of others. They see to it that the company's standards for quality and quantity are met. These employees make many decisions. Skilled decision makers are an important part of business systems.

Word-Processing Supervisor

Insurance company needs individual to supervise ten word-processing equipment operators. At least three years' experience in a word-processing installation plus experience in a supervisory position are required. Will work closely with supervisors of other data processing units and with company management. Send a résumé to Karl Schlein, Box 7778.

As a supervisor or manager, you would give your own supervisor the most complete reports possible. You would follow up on work being done. You would also offer suggestions for speeding up production and keeping costs down. For example, as the supervisor of a word-processing operation, you might suggest new guidelines for the work flow. Or you might work with an equipment analyst to replace the word-processing equipment with more up-to-date equipment.

Often supervisors and managers must help improve the performance of the employees they supervise. They can do this best if they have once worked in one of the jobs they are now supervising. Managers are team leaders. They must learn to think of every employee as a team member whose work is necessary to complete the assigned tasks.

CHECK YOURSELF

Supply the missing words.

1. A(n) __?__ __?__ delivers business mail.
2. A(n) __?__ __?__ operator runs machines that print addresses from stencils or from plates.
3. A(n) __?__ __?__ stores business documents in an organized way so that they can be quickly found.
4. A(n) __?__ __?__ operator prepares letters and other business documents that must be produced in large numbers or that must be revised often.
5. Some word-processing equipment uses __?__ disks to record the typewritten impulses of the original.
6. When a large number of copies must be made, a(n) __?__ __?__ operator runs the appropriate machine.
7. A supervisor of data-entry operations has probably worked as a(n) __?__ clerk.
8. The __?__ of a data processing department sees to it that the company's standards for quality and quantity are met.

Review Questions

1. Give two examples of career ladders.
2. List five characteristics that may be used to describe and compare data processing jobs.
3. Name three data-entry positions, and describe the work of each.
4. List five types of positions in computer operations.
5. Name four career possibilities in computer support activities, and give one function for each job.
6. List six jobs in the area of systems analysis and computer programming, and name the entry-level position in this area.
7. Give four examples of careers in clerical processing activities.
8. Name five jobs that require the operation of specialized office equipment.
9. Name some of the qualifications for a supervisory position.
10. List the functions of a data processing supervisor.

Comparing Ideas

The questions below are to help you think about what you have learned in this chapter. They are thought questions. There is no one correct answer.

1. Take a field trip to a data processing department. Discuss the data processing pyramid in terms of the company you visit.
2. Find out the salaries in your area for the jobs listed in this chapter. Discuss how these salaries relate to education and responsibilities.
3. Discuss the skill of proofreading (checking the accuracy of a copy against the original). How many of the data processing jobs in this chapter require this skill? Obtain copies of some source documents and try out your proofreading skills.

Data Processing Activities

Activity 1. You will fill in a career planning questionnaire for Sheldon Employment Agency.

Activity 2. Using the questionnaire you filled out in Activity 1, you will complete a career evaluation sheet.

Activity 3. You will use the career evaluation sheet to determine which jobs suit you best. You will then investigate those jobs.

Activity 4. You will go back to the career evaluation sheet to determine which jobs are best for you. You will enter these jobs on a career ladder.

BASIC Project 11
PEERS Ladder

Choosing a career is a very important matter. The PEERS rating system was designed to help you learn more about data processing occupations. In the following exercise, BASIC will be used to decode the PEERS rating for any career you are interested in.

Program Statements
The FOR and NEXT Statements

The following program introduces a new variation of the program loop and two statements that are used together to create such a loop.

The programs in Projects 9 and 10 continued to loop until the user selected the option that caused a branch out of the loop.

A program may also count the number of times a loop has been executed and branch out of the loop when the count has reached a certain number.

In the sample program, the desired number of PEERS codes is INPUT and assigned to the variable NUMBER at line 80.

At line 85 the variable COUNT is assigned the value 1 as the program is about to begin the first loop. This is called *initialization* because the counter is set to its first, or initial, value.

At line 90 a check is made to see if COUNT is greater than the number of codes asked for. If it is, there is a branch to the end of the program. If it is not greater than this number, execution proceeds through the loop.

At line 480, the LET statement increases the value of COUNT by 1. Line 490 causes a branch back to line 90, where the value of COUNT is tested to see if the program should end or go through the loop.

Notice that the value of COUNT keeps increasing by 1 each time the loop is executed. The process of repeating the loop and increasing the value of COUNT is called *iteration*.

FOR/NEXT LOOPS. This flowchart demonstrates the use of FOR and NEXT statements in BASIC.

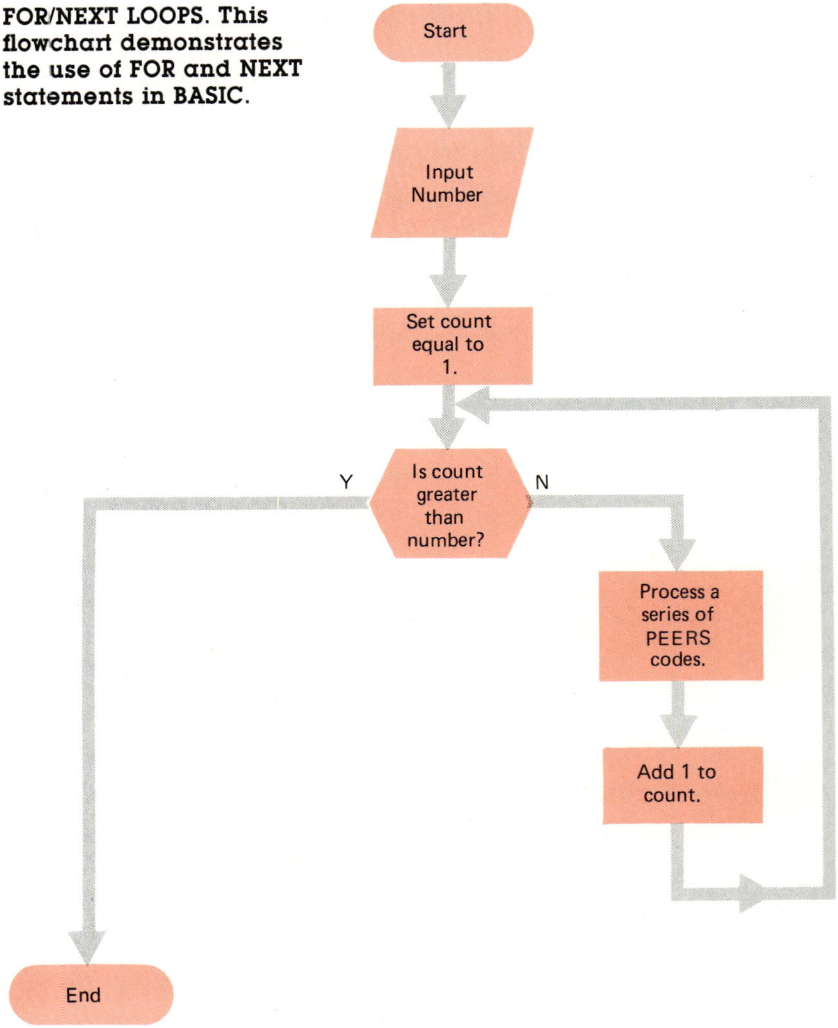

Sample Program

There is a popular shorthand form of this kind of loop called the FOR . . . NEXT loop. This allows us an alternate way to process the PEERS data.

The BASIC statement 90 FOR COUNT = 1 TO NUMBER could take the place of the two statements in lines 85 and 90. It initializes the value of COUNT at 1 and also checks to see if COUNT is greater than NUMBER. The statement 480 NEXT COUNT could replace lines 480 and 490 because it increases the value of COUNT and also causes a branch back to the FOR statement in order to check the new value of COUNT. If COUNT is greater than NUMBER, there is a branch to the line following the NEXT statement. Otherwise, the program continues on the line following the FOR statement.

If this was done, the FOR (90) and the NEXT (480) statements would be separated by many lines of program. A FOR statement, however, must be followed by a NEXT statement somewhere in the program.

As you can see from line 120, multiple input values can be entered on a single line if they are separated by commas. This allows the use of one INPUT statement instead of five. The symbols <> represent the "not equal" conditions.

```
10 REM**************************************************************
20 REM PEERS LADDER DECODER
30 REM TAKES THE FIVE NUMBERS OF THE PEERS CODE
40 REM AND PRINTS QUICK REFERENCE DECODING
50 REM**************************************************************
60 PRINT "HOW MANY PEERS CODES DO YOU WISH"
70 PRINT "DECODED";
80 INPUT N
85 LET COUNT=1
90 IF COUNT>NUMBER THEN 999
100 PRINT "TYPE THE 5 PEERS NUMBERS SEPARATED"
110 PRINT "BY COMMAS";
120 INPUT P,E1,E2,R,S
130 PRINT "PHYSICAL ACTIVITY=";
140 IF P<>1 THEN 160
```

```
150 PRINT "VERY LITTLE"
160 IF P<>2 THEN 180
170 PRINT "SOME"
180 IF P<>3 THEN 200
190 PRINT "QUITE A LOT"
200 PRINT "EXPERIENCE=";
210 IF E1<>1 THEN 230
220 PRINT "ENTRY LEVEL"
230 IF E1<>2 THEN 250
240 PRINT "1 OR MORE YEARS"
250 IF E1<>3 THEN 270
260 PRINT "2 OR MORE YEARS"
270 PRINT "EDUCATION=";
280 IF E2<>1 THEN 300
290 PRINT "HIGH SCHOOL"
300 IF E2<>2 THEN 320
310 PRINT "VOCATIONAL/TECHNICAL"
320 IF E2<>3 THEN 340
330 PRINT "4 YEAR COLLEGE"
340 PRINT "COMPLEXITY=";
350 IF R<>1 THEN 370
360 PRINT "SIMPLE"
370 IF R<>2 THEN 390
380 PRINT "MORE COMPLEX"
390 IF R<>3 THEN 410
400 PRINT "CHALLENGING"
410 PRINT "SKILLS=";
```

```
420 IF S<>1 THEN 440
430 PRINT "FEW"
440 IF S<>2 THEN 460
450 PRINT "SOME"
460 IF S<>3 THEN 480
470 PRINT "MANY"
480 LET COUNT = COUNT + 1
490 GO TO 90
999 END
```

Output

```
HOW MANY PEERS CODES DO YOU WISH
DECODED?2
TYPE THE 5 PEERS NUMBERS SEPARATED
BY COMMAS?2,1,3,2,1
PHYSICAL ACTIVITY=SOME
EXPERIENCE=ENTRY LEVEL
EDUCATION=4 YEAR COLLEGE
COMPLEXITY=MORE COMPLEX
SKILLS=FEW
TYPE THE 5 PEERS NUMBERS SEPARATED
BY COMMAS?2,2,1,1,1
PHYSICAL ACTIVITY=SOME
EXPERIENCE=1 OR MORE YEARS
EDUCATION=HIGH SCHOOL
COMPLEXITY=SIMPLE
SKILLS=FEW
```

Keyboarding Activities

1. Enter and RUN the program given above.
2. Change the sample program so that it uses the FOR and NEXT statements. To do this remove lines 85 and 90 from the program and put in a new line 90.

```
90 FOR COUNT = 1 TO NUMBER
```

Also remove lines 480 and 490. Add this new line.

```
480 NEXT COUNT
```

3. Select five PEERS careers that interest you. Provide the PEERS code for each job title as input for the program.
4. Discuss the output with your supervisor or career counselor.

Enrichment Activities

1. Modify the career selection program so that it will accept the job titles as well as the PEERS codes. The job titles should be displayed with the decoding output data.
2. Modify the program in Project 10 so that it only allows three chances to type the verification line correctly.
3. Modify the programs in Projects 7, 8, and 9 so that a given number of sets of data are processed.

CHAPTER

12

Selecting an Employer

DATA PROCESSING TERMINOLOGY

Service industry | Organization chart | Management information services (MIS)

PERFORMANCE GOALS

- Name the industry fields offering the most rapid growth in data processing in the 1980s.
- State how computer services may be organized in a large company.
- List two differences between data processing work in a small computer installation and data processing work in a large installation.
- Read an organization chart that shows how work functions are divided in a business.
- Name at least five types of data processing applications for which there are employment opportunities in state or local government agencies.

In the last chapter you read about different types of careers in computer work and data processing. And you learned to think about employment in terms of a specific job goal and career ladder. The next step is to focus on a business division or government agency in which you may like to be employed.

If you live near a metropolitan area, it will be easier to pursue the career objectives that you set for yourself. This is because large business organizations and government agencies usually locate their office and administrative operations in or near a city. Their large computer installations are generally located in metropolitan regions as well. However, a small town offers some opportunities for a data processing career in retail, professional, and service businesses. These businesses may use word-processing equipment or minicomputers. Farmers in rural areas now use service bureaus for computer processing of data to monitor crop and dairy production and animal feed quantities.

In this chapter you will learn about selecting a particular employer to whom you may apply for a job. To make this selection properly, you need to be acquainted with data processing opportunities as they differ by type of industry and company size. Also, you should know about the various computer processing activities performed by government agencies that may offer you challenging career opportunities.

Choosing Among Fast-Growing Fields

For the decade between 1980 and 1990, the U.S. Department of Labor estimates a growth of 16 million jobs in the United States, bringing total nationwide employment to the figure of 114 million people. During this period, the number of office (or white-collar) jobs will increase more than the number of factory (or blue-collar) and agricultural jobs.

The increase in the total number of office workers includes a rapid growth in the number of data processing job opportunities in certain industries. The fastest-growing area for office workers—specifically, data processing workers—is called the **service industry.** This employment area includes a variety of business activities. One example is medical services (offices of hospitals, doctors, dentists, medical laboratories, blood banks, and nursing homes). Another is professional services for accounting, legal, and tax matters. Yet another includes workers in hotels, motels, and inns. Then there are opportunities in radio and TV broadcasting stations and in miscellaneous business services such as personnel agencies and typing, photocopying, and cleaning services.

The second industry field that will offer rapid growth in data processing employment in the eighties encompasses banking, financial, insurance, and real estate activities. Third and fourth in projected future growth, respectively, are the fields of retailing (food stores, restaurants, fast-food businesses, and shops selling general merchandise) and computer services (software and service bureau operations).

It has been estimated that by 1985 the percentage breakdown of the total number of data processing workers by industry will be as shown in the table. It is wise to plan for careers in growing industries that will need computer and data processing workers. Once you have broadly focused on a type of industry, you can later narrow your focus to specific companies within the industry when you seek a job.

PERCENT OF TOTAL NUMBER OF DATA PROCESSING WORKERS	INDUSTRY FIELD OF EMPLOYMENT
22.5%	Service industry, excluding computer services
18.7	Manufacturing plants, excluding computer manufacturers
13.7	Banking, finance, insurance, and real estate services
12.3	Computer service companies
10.4	Retailing and wholesaling establishments
9.9	Government agencies
6.3	Computer manufacturers
4.4	Transportation and communication companies
1.8	All other
100.0%	

Choosing Between Large and Small Businesses

All businesses have data that must be processed.

You know from examples given in this book that all businesses, even small ones, have data that must be processed. Even if you work on your own, you probably process data. A person who delivers newspapers, for example, must keep track of such data as the number of papers delivered, the amounts collected from customers, and the balances due from the customers.

Suppose a group of people decide to set up a cooperative for buying vegetables, fruit, and dairy products. They buy large quantities of food at special rates, and then they divide what they buy among themselves. These people are not trying to earn money; they are just trying to save money. Still, they must keep data about how much they pay for the food to make sure they are saving as much money as possible. They also need data to decide how to divide the costs of the food among themselves.

A larger nonprofit organization would have greater data processing needs. For example, all hospitals maintain a variety of information about patients. The accounting office needs to know the charges to be billed to patients for stays in the hospital and for laboratory tests. Doctors and nurses must have data about the treatment and medicines given to patients. To satisfy its data processing needs, a modern hospital maintains a computer record for each patient. The computer record is begun when the patient enters the hospital. A member of the admissions staff enters the patient's name, address, and other relevant information on a terminal. Every time a test or treatment is given to the patient, this additional information is inputted. Such an on-line system gives an accurate and up-to-date record about each patient.

In a small business, like the neighborhood cooperative that was described, one person may be responsible for all data processing activities. In a large business, however, a much larger amount of data must be processed, and employees and data processing activities must be organized into manageable working units.

SMALL BUSINESS DATA PROCESSING. Nonprofit organizations, like a local neighborhood food cooperative, could use a small business computer for their data processing needs. Hazel Hankin

Computer Services in a Large Business

In all of a company's divisions and departments, data must be processed. At the Good Times Paper Company, as we have already seen in previous chapters, data processing is important in such departments as order and billing, inventory management, and payroll. In the production division, workers record customer orders. In the research and development department, workers estimate costs for new products. In the personnel department, workers keep records about new employees and about employees who are leaving or who are sick. All these departments have activities that involve data processing, and all are possible work sites for students of computers and data processing.

In a large business, the data processing department is usually located in one place. This allows for the efficient and economical use of equipment.

In order for computer equipment to be used as efficiently and economically as possible, it is frequently located in one place (centralized) in a large business. In this way it can be used by all departments that have data to process. The responsibility for overseeing the computer activities of the whole business is assigned to a director (or even a vice president) of the organization. In recent years the job title for this individual often has been director (or vice president) of **management information services (MIS).** Management information services is another name for the computer services function. Decision support services (DSS) is another term used to describe this function.

The division in which computer processing or MIS activities occur depends on the business. For example, at the Good Times Paper Company, the computer services are part of the administrative services division. In other businesses, the MIS activities may be part of the financial services division, or they may be organized into a separate division.

How are responsibilities organized within computer processing (or MIS) activities? One way is shown in the chart on page 284. This organization chart shows the organization of the computer services department of the Good Times Paper Company. It is typical of organizations found in other businesses. At the Good Times Paper Company, the MIS activities are divided into two general areas: (1) systems and programming, and (2) computer center. Each group, in turn, is subdivided into smaller units as shown in the chart. All together, there are five functional groups. For a large staff, there may be more than one supervisor. For example, if there are many employees on the computer operations staff, they may report to supervisors in smaller groups of three to ten workers. The chart shows how each supervisor reports to a manager.

Careers in data processing management are discussed in Chapter 11. The responsibilities of management include setting

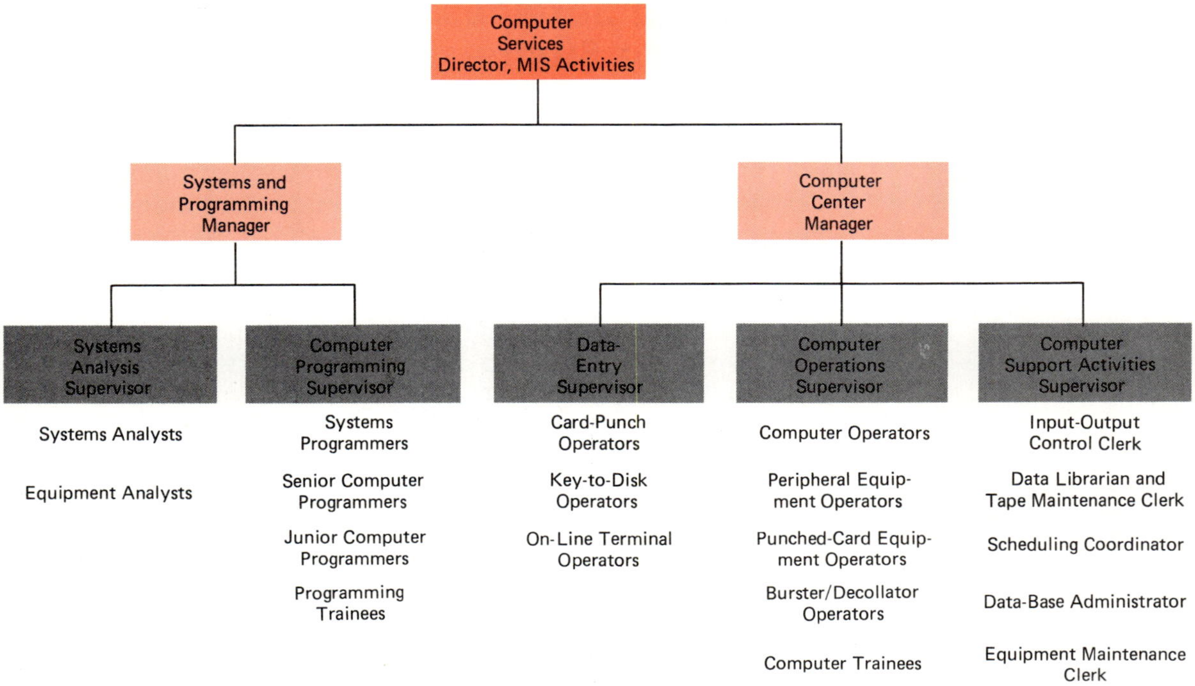

MIS ORGANIZATION CHART. This organization chart shows the reporting lines for the major functional groups in a computer services department. Think about career opportunities, industry projections, and job requirements for the positions in each group. How would you present your qualifications for one of these positions?

Supervisors and managers set priorities, establish schedules, and make sure that projects are completed properly and on time.

priorities, establishing schedules, and following up to see that projects are completed properly and on time. Management generally sets production standards and evaluates the employees against these standards. The evaluation form used by the Good Times Paper Company is shown on the next page. Note that the evaluator must comment on the employee's current performance and career goals. He or she must also make suggestions about what steps should be taken to improve the employee's performance. The form shown is for purposes of formal evaluation. A good supervisor or manager keeps employees informed throughout the year on how well they are doing their jobs.

Before seeking a job in a large business, you should try to find out how the business is organized. You may ask friends about the company, request an annual report from the company, or ask a local librarian for information. (The annual reports issued yearly by publicly held companies will often describe the company's structure and its future plans, as well as its financial performance in the past.)

Confidential Office Employee Performance Appraisal Record

Soc. Security No.	Employee Name	Div.	Department	Wk. Loc.	Date of Hire
062 36 9745	Sara Luna Paco	80	Data Processing	Denver	01/15/—

Position Title: Data-Entry Clerk How Long Under Your Supervision? 6 months Postpone this Appraisal Until (Date): not applicable

Performance Comments

What aspects of the employee's duties are handled in an outstanding manner? This employee's very pleasant "will do" manner helps her to work effectively with other employees.

What aspects of the employee's duties are not handled as well as should be expected? This employee must learn to check her work more carefully, to find her own errors, and to correct them before submitting the work to her supervisor.

Performance Rating

Considering all performance factors, please check the statement that most nearly fits this employee's overall performance on the current job in the last twelve months:

- ☐ A. Superior performance. Consistently exceeds job standards
- ☐ B. High standard of performance. Consistently meets, and occasionally exceeds, job standards.
- ☐ C. Performance normally expected of qualified employee.
- ☒ D. Performance not up to desired standard; should show improvement.
- ☐ E. Poor performance. Cannot be retained on job without immediate improvement.

Development Plans

State your plans and objectives for improving the employee's performance (consider increased responsibility, coaching, on-the-job training, etc.)

We are keeping track of her productivity scores, which include reductions for errors. This practice is giving her more incentive to correct her mistakes. She has begun to improve.

If formal training programs will help the employee, please code (using the course list in the instructions) those programs that the employee needs:

1. 03* 2. ______ 3. ______ 4. ______ *03: Proofreading

Promotion Readiness (Please check the most appropriate statement)

- ☐ A. Has demonstrated capacity for continued growth; can move now or within six months to a higher level of responsibility.
- ☐ B. Has demonstrated capacity for continued growth, but needs six to twelve more months at present level before significant move can be made.
- ☐ C. Has demonstrated capacity for growth, but probably will not be ready for movement to levels of higher responsibility within the next twelve month period.
- ☒ D. Appears, at this time, to be limited to present position or to a comparable level of responsibility.

Please explain any factors limiting transfer or promotion possibilities: See above. This employee will be reevaluated in three months.

Employee Potential

Indicate next position, if any, you believe employee could perform: See above.

Appraisal Discussion (REQUIRED)

What comments were made by the employee when performance and future were discussed? The employee admits that she has pushed for quantity over quality. She knows she must improve her accuracy and does respond well to constructive criticism.

If this appraisal will not be discussed with the employee, explain why: not applicable

Appraised By: Martin Hoffman Date 7/16/—

Appraisal Approved By: Florence Ling Date 7/17/—

EMPLOYEE PERFORMANCE APPRAISAL. More and more employers involve their employees in performance discussions. Together the manager and the employee address achievements and performance gaps, agree on necessary next steps, and plan for training and on-the-job coaching to make the employee more effective.

Data Processing in a Small Business

The chart of the computer activity at the Good Times Paper Company illustrates well the specialization (or division) of job functions in a large company. The reasons for job specialization were discussed in Chapter 10. Usually, the smaller the work group, the less the job specialization. In a small business an employee may become a jack-of-all-trades, meaning that he or she has the training and skills for doing a variety of the functions involved in running the business. This position may appeal to beginning data processing employees, because it allows them to get an overview of a business.

Usually, the processing operations to be performed in a small business are much less complex than those in a larger organization. Take, for example, the data processing work done in the office of a small retail store. A minicomputer, such as the IBM System 32, often is used for the processing of customer invoices, accounts receivable, and inventory and for general ledger accounting and payroll processing. Depending upon the input volume of transactions, only two full-time employees may be required to handle all the data processing operations from input through output. Both employees would be trained to enter input through on-line terminals of the computer. Also, both would be trained to operate the computer, to produce the required output reports, and to check and balance the output reports against controls. Even microcomputer systems with preprogrammed software will require staffing and some job specialization.

Many data processing workers have a preference for large versus small computer departments. Some like the specialization and complexity of tasks involved in working with large computer departments and MIS activities. Other individuals prefer a working environment with fewer employees and a job involving many different operations. Which job environment would you like best?

CHECK YOURSELF

Supply the missing words.

1. Large businesses and government agencies generally locate their office and administrative operations in or near a(n) ___?___.
2. Farmers may use ___?___ ___?___ for computer processing of data.
3. Between 1980 and 1990, the number of ___?___ jobs will increase more rapidly than the number of factory and agricultural jobs.

4. The fastest-growing industry field for data processing personnel is called the __?__ __?__.
5. Computer equipment can often be used more efficiently and economically in a large business if it is __?__.
6. The director of __?__ __?__ __?__ oversees the computer activities of a large business.
7. Computer services in a large business may be divided into two general areas: systems and programming and __?__ __?__.
8. A(n) __?__ __?__ form may be filled in once a year, twice a year, or four times a year to keep an employee informed about how he or she is doing on the job.
9. In a(n) __?__ business, jobs are generally less specialized, and employees are trained in a variety of functions.
10. Large businesses generally have __?__ complex data processing operations than small businesses.

Choosing a Division in a Company

Businesses are usually organized into divisions, which are subdivided into departments.

Most businesses are organized into divisions, and each division is responsible for different areas of the business's activities. Each one of the divisions is usually further divided into two or more departments. The names and responsibilities of the various divisions and departments depend upon the particular business. In this chapter, we will look at how a manufacturing business might be organized. As our example, we will use the Good Times Paper Company.

An organization chart shows the structure of a company.

Look at the chart on page 288 for the Good Times Paper Company. This chart is called an **organization chart** because it shows the organization of a business (how responsibilities are divided up within a business). The organization chart shows how the activities of the Good Times Paper Company are structured. As you can see, Good Times Paper has five divisions. These divisions are typical of manufacturing companies. The person in charge of each of these divisions at this company reports to the president. The chart also shows that each of the five divisions is further divided into departments.

We will now take a closer look at the kind of work the Good Times Paper Company's five divisions and their departments do.

Research and Development Division

The research and development division of Good Times Paper develops new products and improves old ones. It also does research to find out whether customers will buy the new and improved products.

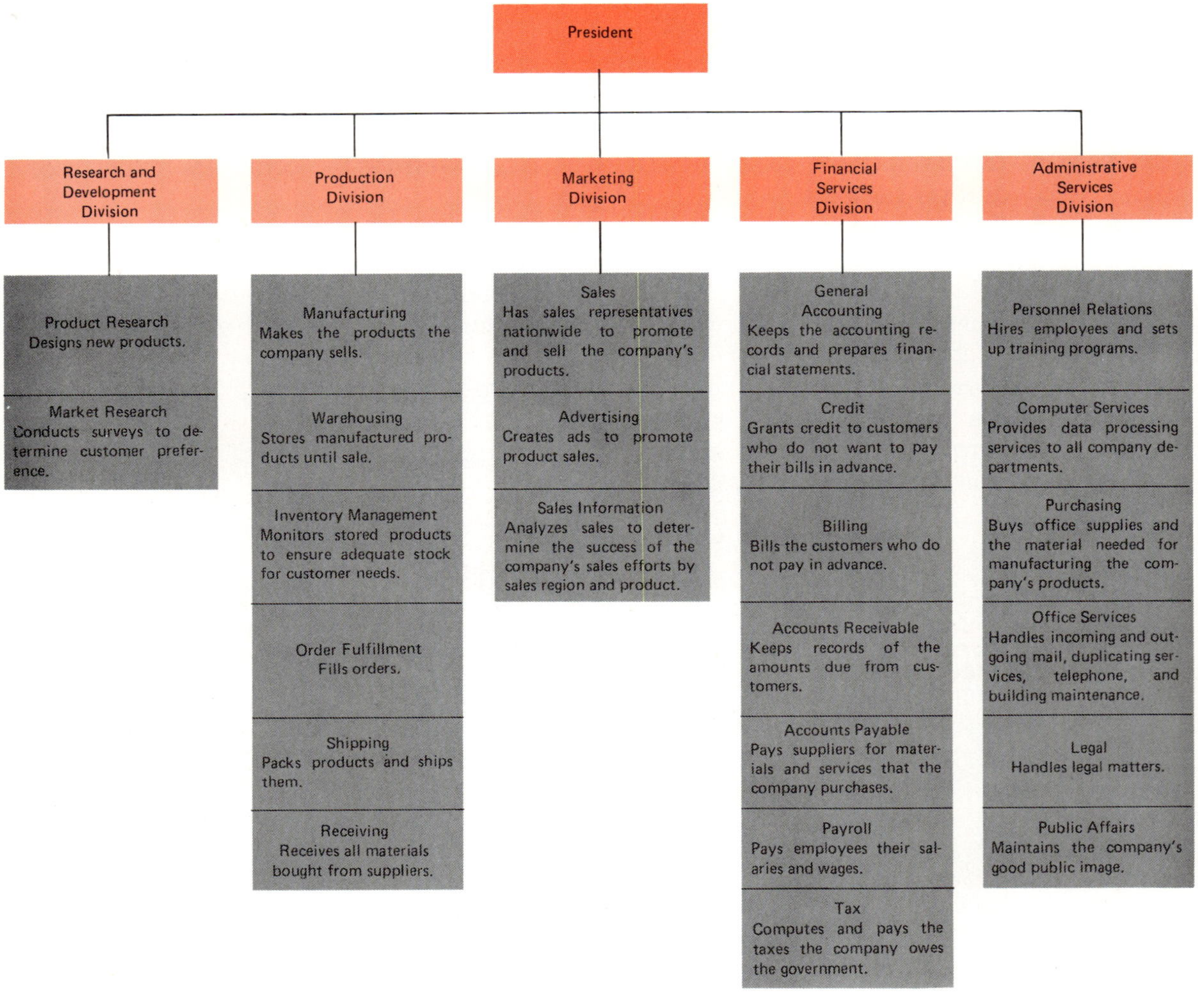

ORGANIZATION CHART FOR THE GOOD TIMES PAPER COMPANY

Production Division

The production division of the Good Times Paper Company manufactures the company's products and sees that they are sent tc customers.

Marketing Division

The marketing division of Good Times Paper promotes and sells the company's products. This company's customers are mostly department stores, gift shops, and bookstores.

"I hear they're doing some amazing things with computers these days." Cartoon by Steve Attoe, *Datamation*, January 1981, page 125

Financial Services Division

The financial services division prepares invoices (bills) to send to Good Times Paper Company's customers and keeps track of the amounts customers owe. It also keeps records of the income received from sales and records of all the costs of operating the business. In addition, this division develops long-range plans for increasing the business's profits.

Administrative Services Division

The administrative services division performs a variety of functions essential to the day-to-day operation of the company. Included are the functions of personnel relations, computer services, purchasing, office services, legal work, and public affairs.

Choosing a Government Agency

Just as the use of computers has grown in business, more and more computers are being used at all levels of government. The country's growth in population, together with a greater number of government-sponsored programs, has increased the need for data processing. This is true for federal, state, county, and local government agencies.

As mentioned earlier, by 1985 it is likely that 9.9 percent of all data processing workers in the country will be employed by a government agency. Of these workers, 5.7 percent will work for the federal government. The remaining 4.2 percent will be employed by state, county, or local public agencies.

Data processing activities of the federal government are concentrated in the Washington, D.C. area, although many federal agencies have regional computer processing centers located throughout the country. Among the largest computer centers in the federal government are those that are devoted to processing census data, payments for social security benefits, and retirement benefits for military veterans and federal civilian employees. Military and defense installations scattered throughout the country usually have a computer to handle payrolls and inventories of supplies.

State, county, and local government agencies also may offer opportunities for data processing employment. A few examples of the kinds of computerized systems now commonly used in these agencies will illustrate the variety of processing jobs that may be available. Like the federal government, state agencies need computers for processing tax receipts and unemployment insurance payments, preparing budgets and payrolls, and analyzing economic and environmental data. In addition, each state has a major recordkeeping task in handling the registration of automobiles and other motor vehicles and in issuing and maintaining current and accurate driver licenses.

County and/or local (city or town) governments may use computers in still different ways. Records of property ownership must be updated every time a house is sold. Some towns and cities use computer processing to speed up the counts of votes in elections. To eliminate the task of hand-counting each ballot, optical scanners are used to read the marks on the ballots. With this system votes are counted more quickly and accurately than by hand. Computer centers are becoming more common in schools. Computers are used for student registration, recordkeeping, class

Familiarity with computers is a plus if you choose a career as a police officer. On-line computer terminals have been installed in some patrol cars. Courtesy Motorola, Inc.

scheduling, and teaching through computer-assisted instruction. Local hospitals may use computers for keeping patients' records, maintaining inventory supply records, and making medical diagnoses. Often even small public libraries have computer service bureaus handle their book circulation records.

Very effective use of computers is made in law enforcement. Computerized data banks containing information about criminals are now maintained in state agencies as well as in the National Crime Information Center. This makes it possible for a police

Car telephones use microprocessors to provide convenient features like storing frequently-used phone numbers, placing calls to such numbers at a touch, and redialing busy numbers. Courtesy Harris Corporation

officer in a patrol car to run a check on a suspicious-looking driver or car within seconds. In some locations patrol cars are equipped with an on-line computer terminal. By keying in the name and address of an individual or the license number of a car, a police officer will know whether the driver of the car should be questioned. If a patrol car does not have an on-line terminal, the police officer can contact the police headquarters through a radio system. Headquarters, in turn, uses an on-line terminal to check the driver's information and then notifies the police officer by radio of the result of the check.

As you can see, government agencies offer many different types of work to a job seeker. Computer and data processing skills can be a primary focus of a career, or they can be an aid in performing another kind of job. It is wise to consider all the alternatives when selecting an employer.

CHECK YOURSELF

Supply the missing words.

1. A business shows the relationships of its departments on paper with a(n) __?__ __?__.
2. The manufacturing __?__ of the production division at Good Times Paper actually makes the company's products.
3. The three departments of the Good Times Paper Company's marketing division are sales, advertising and promotion, and __?__ __?__.
4. Sales representatives are members of the sales department of the marketing __?__ at this company.
5. The payroll __?__ of the financial services division pays employees and keeps payroll records at the Good Times Paper Company.
6. Accounts payable is a(n) __?__ of the financial services division at Good Times Paper.
7. At Good Times Paper, the data processing department is part of the __?__ __?__ division.
8. Growth in our population and in social service programs has resulted in a significant __?__ in the volume and complexity of government's data handling.
9. By 1985, __?__ percent of all data processing workers in our country will be employed by a government agency.
10. To eliminate the task of counting voters' ballots by hand, __?__ __?__ may be used to read the marks on the ballots.

Review Questions

1. List the four industry fields that will have the most rapid growth in data processing jobs in the 1980s.
2. Describe the types of businesses that make up the service industry.
3. List two differences between data processing work in a small installation and data processing work in a large computer center.
4. Give another name for the computer services function.
5. Describe the two general areas of responsibility for MIS activities.
6. Name five functions of data processing that require supervision.
7. List five divisions that may be found in a typical manufacturing company, and define the functions of each.
8. List five types of activities that may be classified as administrative services.
9. Name four types of computer processing done by the federal government.
10. Give six examples of computer processing that may be performed by state, county, or local government agencies.

Comparing Ideas

The questions below are to help you think about what you have learned in this chapter. They are thought questions. There is no one correct answer.

1. Why do you think many companies originally made the data processing department a part of the financial services division? (*HINT:* For what types of business activities were computers first used?)
2. What is a computer service bureau? How does it differ from a data processing department in a large business?

Data Processing Activities

Now you can begin to think seriously about a career in data processing. Below is a summary of how you will go about it. You will find the actual information and the forms you need in your *Data Processing Work Kit.*

Activity 1. You will review and update batch reports for management information and decision making.

Activity 2. You will develop an organization chart for a regional data processing center.

BASIC Project 12
Questionnaire

By now you realize that a business organization is like any other organization. It has departments and people with responsibilities. One thing common to all organizations is the need for the evaluation of performance. The following exercise will show you how BASIC can be used to evaluate an employee's performance on a question and answer test.

Program Statements
READ and DATA Statements

Computer programs can be used to store and retrieve business data. The READ statement acts as an INPUT statement. In addition, the value or list of values in the READ statement is stored in a DATA statement within the program itself. The list of values stored in the DATA statement may then be accessed by one or more READ statements.

DATA statements may appear anywhere in the program as long as they come before the END statement.

READ The READ statement starts with the word READ, which is followed by numeric or string variables.

DATA The DATA statement begins with the word DATA, which is followed by a value or list of values.

Sample Program

Study the flowchart on the next page before you review the sample program on pages 296 and 297. The DATA statement section of the program contains the questions (even-numbered) and the correct answers (odd-numbered). This program can be quickly modified to accommodate new or additional questions.

Businesses use computers to process large amounts of data. This data, such as employee records, is stored outside the program,

READ/DATA STATEMENTS. This program flowchart illustrates the use of READ and DATA statements in BASIC

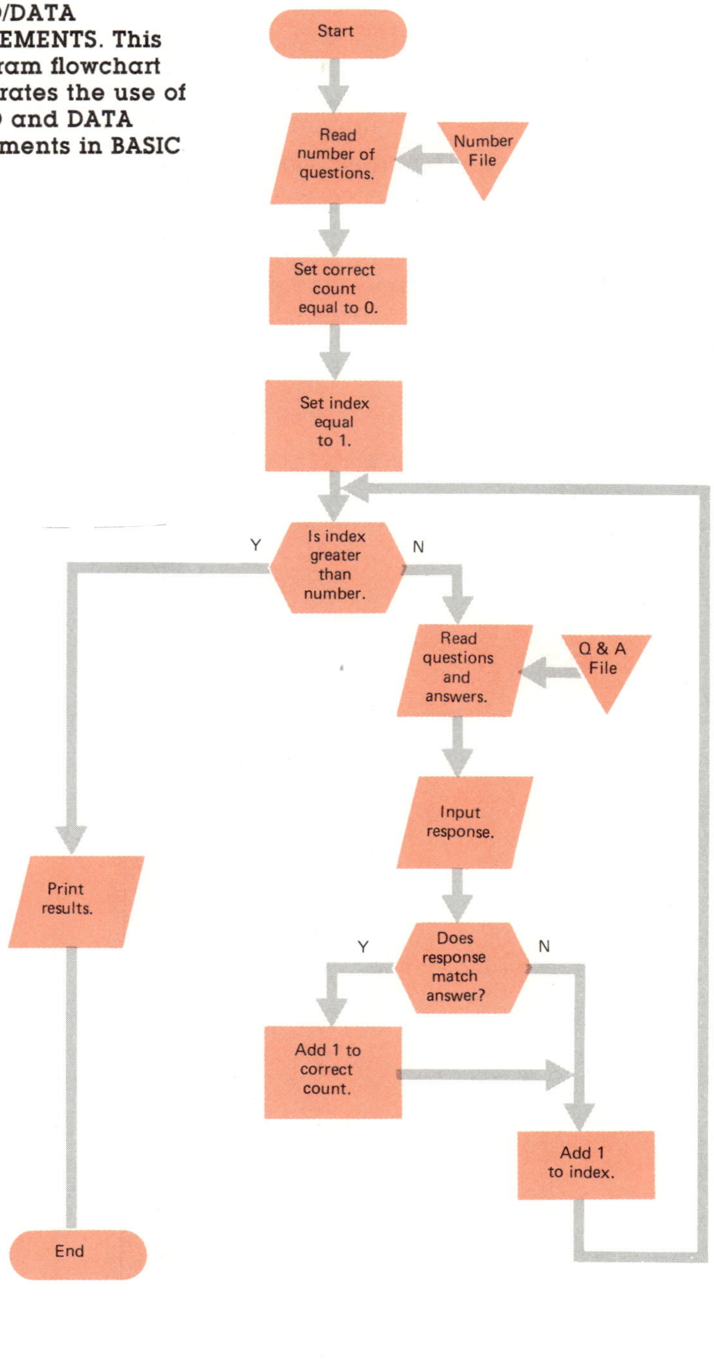

generally on magnetic tape or disks, in *files*. The program can INPUT data from or PRINT data to a file just as it can from and to a terminal.

BASIC DATA statements allow the programmer to set up the equivalent of a file inside the program. This is useful when one is working with a computer that does not have the capability of working with files.

```
110 REM*************************************************************
120 REM READS QUESTIONS FROM DATA STATEMENTS AND
130 REM CHECKS ANSWER FROM USER
140 REM*************************************************************
145 PRINT "RESPOND TO EACH STATEMENT BY TYPING TRUE OR FALSE"
150 REM READ IN NUMBER OF QUESTIONS
160 READ N
170 LET C=0
175 LET I=1
180 IF I>N THEN 280
190 READ Q$,A$
200 PRINT I;Q$;
210 INPUT I$
220 IF I$=A$ THEN 250
230 PRINT " SORRY, WRONG ANSWER"
240 GOTO 265
250 PRINT " GOOD"
260 LET C=C+1
265 LET I=I+1
270 GOTO 180
280 PRINT
290 PRINT "QUIZ IS OVER. YOU GOT";C;"OUT OF";N;"CORRECT"
300 PRINT
```

```
310 REM TYPE DATA STATEMENTS BELOW THIS LINE
320 REM FIRST DATA LINE IS NUMBER OF QUESTIONS
325 REM ANSWERS ON ODD LINES
330 DATA 5
340 DATA "A LINE PRINTER IS A DEVICE USED FOR INPUT"
355 DATA "FALSE"
360 DATA "TESTING IS OFTEN USED TO SCREEN EMPLOYEES FOR PROMOTION"
375 DATA "TRUE"
380 DATA "ENLISTMENT IN MILITARY MAY PROVIDE COMPUTER TRAINING."
395 DATA "TRUE"
400 DATA "COMPUTING IS LESS EXPENSIVE NOW THAN 5 YEARS AGO"
415 DATA "TRUE"
420 DATA "OUTPUT FORMS ARE USED FOR DATA ENTRY"
435 DATA "FALSE"
999 END
```

Output

```
RESPOND TO EACH STATEMENT BY TYPING TRUE OR FALSE
1     A LINE PRINTER IS A DEVICE USED FOR INPUT?  FALSE
 GOOD
2     TESTING IS OFTEN USED TO SCREEN EMPLOYEES FOR PROMOTION?  TRUE
 GOOD
3     ENLISTMENT IN MILITARY MAY PROVIDE COMPUTER TRAINING?  TRUE
 GOOD
4     COMPUTING IS LESS EXPENSIVE NOW THAN 5 YEARS AGO?  FALSE
 SORRY, WRONG ANSWER
```

```
5     OUTPUT FORMS ARE USED FOR DATA ENTRY?  FALSE
 GOOD
QUIZ IS OVER. YOU GOT 4 OUT OF 5 CORRECT
```

Keyboarding Activities

1. Enter and RUN the program listed above.
2. Respond to each statement by typing TRUE or FALSE.
3. Modify the program so that either T or F will be accepted as a correct answer.
4. Modify the program so that it uses a FOR . . . NEXT loop. Substitute a FOR statement for lines 175 and 180 and a NEXT statement for lines 265 and 270.

Enrichment Activities

1. Create a testing program that will score a 15-question quiz.

   5 true and false items
   5 fill-in questions
   5 multiple-choice questions

2. Find out if your computer system is capable of using files. If it is, rewrite the sample program to INPUT the questions and answers from a file instead of from DATA statements. Consult the reference manual or your instructor for details on how to do this.

CHAPTER

13

Personal Computing

DATA PROCESSING TERMINOLOGY

Personal computing
Personal computer
Microcomputer
Microprocessor
Read-only memory (ROM)
Random-access memory (RAM)
User-programmable memory
Packaged software
Software houses
Pascal
BASIC

PERFORMANCE GOALS

- Define *personal computing*, and compare it with business data processing.
- Name three ways to create a microcomputer system.
- Select computer hardware and software for personal computing.
- List several types of programs useful to the home user, whether for business or consumer needs.

In Chapter 5 you read about computer systems ranging from the smallest computers to the really large computers. In chapters that followed you learned about the different ways in which all sizes of computers are used to process business data. In this chapter you will learn about personal computing as distinguished from business data processing.

Personal computing is using a computer to meet the needs of an individual or family.

Personal computing is the use of a computer to meet the data processing needs of one particular person or family. Usually personal computing is done in the home. The equipment used by an individual or family members for computing at home is called a **personal computer.**

The data processing needs of an individual or family that can be met with a personal computer include accounting for income and expenses, budgeting, computing taxes that are owed to the government, maintaining mailing lists, and analyzing the income from and worth of stocks, bonds, and other investments. In addition, the same personal computer can be used by family members for games or for computer-instructed educational programs. The term *personal computing* also is used to describe computer processing done by a self-employed or professional business person. Such an individual (for example, a lawyer) may use a computer in the home or in a small office to keep track of the costs that are to be billed to clients.

Personal computing can be done either by using a small computer installed in the home or by using a home computer terminal that is connected to a computer service bureau equipped with a computer large enough to handle many personal computing customers. When a computer is installed in the home for personal computing, it usually is a very small machine. Often the personal computer is a microcomputer, although a larger system can be accessed by telephone hookup. Machines appropriate for personal computing generally are of low cost and do not require any special installation. You can buy a home computer in a store, plug it in, and start using it.

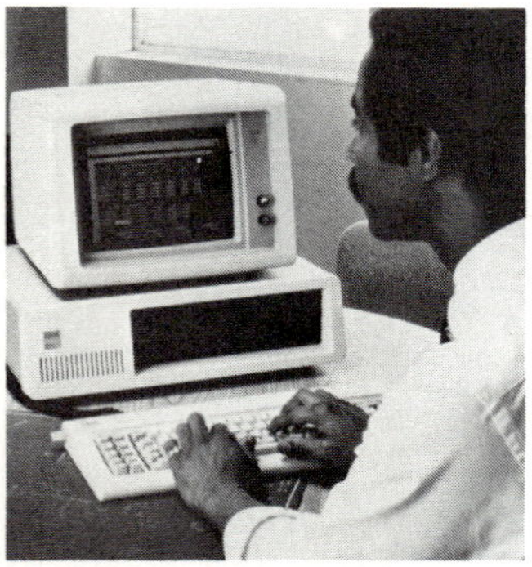

PERSONAL COMPUTERS. Personal computers can be used by self-employed or professional business persons for a variety of data processing tasks.
Courtesy IBM Corporation

Selecting a Personal Computer

The demand for personal computers is growing enormously. Equipment forecasters have estimated that the number of personal computers will quadruple between 1980 and 1985. Industry experts believe that a total of 1.8 million personal computers will be installed by 1985. There are now computer stores where potential users can learn firsthand what equipment is available, what software can be used with it, and what the costs are.

COMMON PERSONAL COMPUTERS

Apple
TRS-80
IBM
Commodore
Atari
Texas Instruments

At the time of this writing, the personal computers sold in the greatest numbers were those known as Apple, TRS-80 (Radio Shack), and IBM. Others that had programming languages and software likely to appeal to the personal computer user included Commodore, Atari, and Texas Instruments. These computers are widely available and relatively inexpensive, depending on the number of options selected.

Advantages of Microcomputers

Microcomputers are popular for personal computing because you can start out with just a CPU and a keyboard. As you become more skilled at using the equipment, you can add input, output, and storage units. One reason for the popularity of a microcomputer is that even as a beginner, you can unpack a microcomputer, plug it in, and start using it immediately with the software provided by the manufacturer. Often the user hooks up with a TV set to generate business news or a popular space game. In the next decade, personal computers will provide access to many more personal and business services.

Types of Microcomputer Systems

The central unit for processing and control in a microcomputer is a microprocessor.

Microcomputer systems, the smallest of the computer systems developed by the early 1980s, use a microprocessor as the central unit for processing and control. The **microprocessor** works with

COMPUTER STORE. Computer stores are places where you can buy microcomputers and software packages for personal or business use. Hazel Hankin

MICROCOMPUTERS. Microcomputers can be used by every member of a family. Children can use a microcomputer to learn basic skills, adults can use a microcomputer to manage household finances, and all members of the family can enjoy entertaining computer games. Courtesy Apple Computer

input and output units in the same way as the central processing unit you read about in Chapter 5. A microcomputer is a complete digital computer. It is called a **microcomputer** because of its small size (*micro* means small). The input unit is like a typewriter keyboard. The output devices most commonly used are visual display terminals and printers. The printer, like printers for larger computers, provides a hard copy of the work done by the computer. Some home users use standard television sets as output devices.

With the availability of microcomputers, a home user and a professional business person can have cost-effective computer processing. They can apply computer systems to a variety of data processing tasks. Microcomputer elements, starting with a microprocessor, can be purchased and hooked up to create a computer system capable of as many of the data processing functions as the user is willing to pay for. Like the central processing unit you read about earlier, the microprocessor tells the input, output, and storage units what to do and when to do it. Because the microprocessor controls the microcomputer system, it is often called a *controller*.

The computer memory stores (1) programs and (2) data for programs to work on.

The computer memory meets two storage needs: it stores the program being used, and it stores data the program is working on. The most widely used programming language for personal computing is BASIC. The specific instructions for BASIC vary somewhat with the manufacturer of the microcomputer.

The input, output, and storage units that can be purchased for a microcomputer system perform the same functions as the units for minicomputer systems or larger computer systems. The difference is in scale. As is the case with larger computer systems, mi-

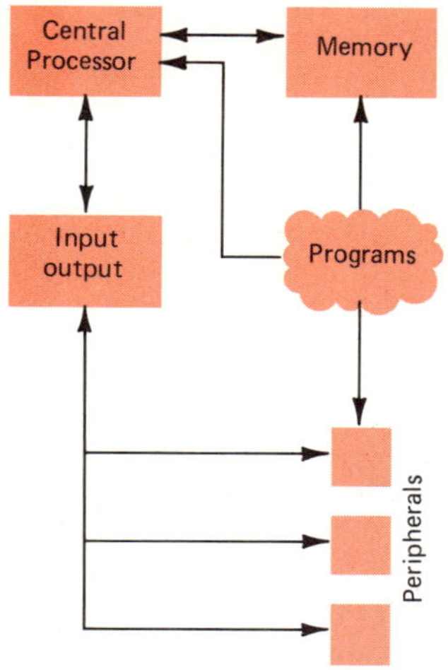

COMPUTER STRUCTURE. The units shown in this diagram are common to all computers, including microcomputers.

crocomputers store information in binary form. Each signal has either one of two values, for example, one or two, on or off, and true or false. The symbols 1 and 0 are combined in such a way that each instruction for the computer has a unique, or single, code. The instruction codes are stored in the order in which they are to be used to process data.

Like minicomputer systems and larger computer systems, microcomputers are manufactured with different capabilities. Some are known as *bare bones* and are usable only by an expert. Others, called *all-in-one machines,* can be compared with a stereo system in that input and output devices and storage media can be purchased together. Just as music lovers once had to develop their own high-fidelity sound systems, computer hobbyists in the early 1970s had to assemble their own microcomputers. Now computer stores and department stores sell both basic units and fully assembled microcomputer systems complete with cassette units and printers. Each approach is described more fully below.

Read-only memory (ROM) is used to store programs that the user cannot change.

Random-access memory (RAM) is used to store data and programs that the user can change.

- The *microprocessor approach* permits custom design of the memory and input/output structure. The system designer must design a system for connecting the parts, assemble them, and then test the system to be sure it works. Computer hobbyists often use this approach.
- A microcomputer houses both the memory and the microprocessor. Such a system needs to be carefully assessed in terms of both near-term and long-term needs because there is limited memory and input/output capability.
- A *microcomputer module* allows for expansion as needed because the basic hardware contains just a microprocessor and read-only memory (ROM). **Read-only memory** means that no changes can be made in the programs. Memory that can be changed is known as **random-access memory** (RAM). Since RAM can be programmed again and again, it is sometimes called **user-programmable memory.** Only a limited amount of random-access memory (RAM) is available for the user's data and programming instructions.

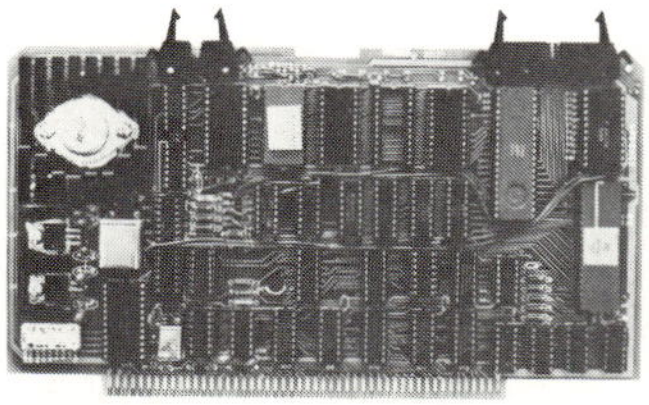

PERSONAL COMPUTER BOARD. This single-board computer is typical of the microprocessor approach. It must be combined with other units to create a complete personal computer system. Courtesy Ackerman

A book published by Texas Instruments for Radio Shack provides the table shown on page 304 comparing three approaches to assembling a personal computer.

Microcomputer modules are most popular with individuals who want a personal computer for home use. Like the memory of larger computers, microcomputer memory is usually not enough for all the records you would need. Either floppy disks, hard disks, or audio-cassettes are used to provide additional storage space

A Commodore PET microcomputer is pictured here. This unit is a complete personal computer. It is typical of a unit an individual might buy for home use. Courtesy Commodore

Comparison of Microcomputer Alternatives*

APPROACH	ADVANTAGES	DISADVANTAGES
Microprocessor	Can be configured to meet any system requirements.	Must be assembled into final system form.
Microcomputer	Single-chip systems with low assembly costs possible.	Fixed input/output configurations. Memory is not easily expandable.
Microcomputer Modules	Pre-wired as a microcomputer module with provisions for memory and input/output expansion. Ideal for initial low cost start on small system.	Relatively expensive if large numbers of identical systems are required.

**Source:* Radio Shack, *Understanding Microprocessors* (Texas Instruments Learning Center, 1979), p. 8-3. Reprinted by permission.

that is permanent. You read about floppy disks in Chapter 3. An audio-cassette drive that is part of a home tape recorder serves as a storage unit once you plug the computer into its microphone jack. To send the data back into memory, you plug the earphone output jack into the computer.

CHECK YOURSELF

Supply the missing words.

1. __?__ __?__ is the use of a computer to meet the data processing needs of an individual or a family.
2. Experts believe that nearly two million __?__ __?__ will be installed by 1985.
3. Two personal computers now sold include __?__ and __?__.
4. Microcomputers are popular for personal computing because you can start out with just a(n) __?__ and a(n) __?__.
5. The central unit for processing and control in a microcomputer is called a(n) __?__.
6. The most widely used microcomputer language is __?__.
7. __?__ __?__ memory means that no changes can be made in the programs.
8. __?__ __?__ memory refers to memory that can be changed.

How to Use a Personal Computer

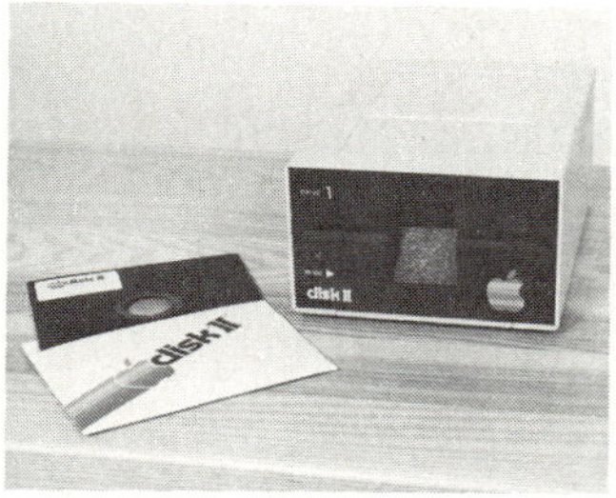

DISK DRIVE. A floppy disk drive for the APPLE II computer is shown here. The controller, which contains the programming for running the computer, plugs into the CPU. Courtesy Apple Computer

More and more programs designed for specific personal computing applications are available from the microcomputer manufacturers and from software houses. The range of software includes games, personal finance programs, scientific applications, educational programs, and applications for small businesses. Some of the software is general-purpose software that is designed to meet the needs of a large number of users. Other software is designed to meet the needs of members of a particular profession, such as doctors, lawyers, accountants, and real estate agents. For example, real estate professionals now have on-line access to real estate listings and other services. Such services, in combination with accounting and tax packages, mean that virtually every business need can be met with a very small, inexpensive computer in the home. Home professionals who want to advertise their services or collect overdue payments find the word-processing capabilities of computers useful. Usually, just some inexpensive software and a printer are needed for such an application.

Using Packaged Programs

Packaged programs are programs already written that you can buy.

As with minicomputers and the larger computers, you can either write your own programs or use programs created by someone else. Computer software available from the manufacturers or from software houses is sometimes called **packaged software.** A large number of packaged programs are available. Your instructor can provide you with references dealing with software houses and the specific packaged programs available for use with microcomputers. These references provide information on one or more software media (such as tapes or floppy disks) that contain the programs, and they give the range of purchase prices for particular applications.

Like the microcomputer manufacturers, a number of **software houses** make available both personal and business software. Thus if you wanted to set up an accounts receivable system and a payroll system for a small business, you would find programs available. You would also find programs for analyzing personal investments and for assessing the benefits of home ownership. At the time of this writing, prices ranged anywhere from $15 to $25 for a simple inventory or payroll program to $1,750 and up for the programs needed to manage a small business.

If you are interested in purchasing computer software, you need to be sure it can be used as is on the personal computers avail-

PERSONAL COMPUTER PROGRAM. This computer printout shows a partial checkbook balancing program written in BASIC. See if you can find the input data, the programming statements, and the documentation. Stefen Sunderland, "On Computing," Summer 1979

```
10 DIM NUM(101),DATE$(101),ESTAB$(101),AMNT(101)
11 PRINT
12 PRINT "*CHECKBOOK*"
13 PRINT "CAUTION ******* ENTER ALL DATES AS XXXXX"
14 PRINT
15 INPUT "DO YOU WISH A LIST OF CURRENT CHECK DATA (Y OR N)";B$
20 IF B$ "Y" THEN GOSUB 1000 ELSE 30
30 INPUT "DO YOU WISH TO DELETE CURRENT CHECK DATA (Y OR N)";B$
40 IF B$ "N" GOTO 103
50 IBAL 0
60 NCHKS=0
61 NUM(1)=9999
62 DATE$(1)="99/99"
70 PRINT "ALL CHECKS DELETED AND CURRENT BALANCE SET TO 0.00"
80 INPUT "NEW STARTING BALANCE";IBAL
90 INPUT "IS NEW BALANCE CORRECT (Y OR N)";B$
100 IF B$ "N" GOTO 80
102 GOTO 110
103 PRINT
104 PRINT "INITIAL BALANCE =";IBAL
105 PRINT
110 PRINT
120 PRINT
130 PRINT "TO ENTER CHECK DATA ENTER THE NUMBER OF THE CHECK,"
140 PRINT "THE DATE OF THE CHECK,THE ESTABLISHMENT TO WHICH"
150 PRINT "THE CHECK WAS ISSUED,AND THE AMOUNT OF THE CHECK"
160 PRINT
170 PRINT
180 PRINT "TO ENTER A DEPOSIT ENTER A ZERO FOR THE CHECK"
190 PRINT "NUMBER,THE DATE ON WHICH THE DEPOSIT WAS MADE,"
```

```
200 PRINT "DEPOSIT FOR THE ESTABLISHMENT,AND THE AMOUNT"
210 PRINT "OF THE DEPOSIT"
220 PRINT
230 INPUT "ENTER CHECK OR DEPOSIT DATA";N,D$,E$,A
231 PRINT

1070 NEXT 7
1080 PRINT
1090 RETURN
2000 REM ENTER DEPOSIT INTO TABLE

4090 IF E$="DEPOSIT" THEN ESTAB$(Z)="**DEPOSIT**" ELSE
ESTAB$(Z)=E$
4100 AMNT(Z)=A
4102 REM CALCULATE BALANCE
4104 CBAL=IBAL
4106 FOR ZZ=1 TO Z
4108 IF ESTAB$(ZZ)="**DEPOSIT**" THEN CBAL=CBAL+AMNT(ZZ) ELSE
CBAL=CBAL-AMNT(ZZ)
4110 NEXT ZZ
4112 PRINT
4113 PRINT "NO. DATE ESTABLISHMENT AMOUNT BALANCE"
4114 PRINTNUM(Z);TAB(5);DATE$(Z);TAB(14);ESTAB$(Z);TAB(36);AMNT(Z);
TAB(48);CBAL
4115 PRINT
4120 IF NCHKS 101 GOTO 4130 ELSE RETURN
4125 IF ESTAB$(1) "**DEPOSIT**" THEN IBAL=IBAL+AMNT(1) ELSE
IBAL=IBAL-AMNT(1)
4130 FOR Z-1 TO NCHKS-1
4140 Z1=Z+1
4150 NUM(Z)=NUM(Z1)
4160 DATE$(Z)=DATE$(Z1)
```

PACKAGED SOFTWARE

able to you. You should also be sure that you have the necessary input and output devices. Your instructor can provide you with a list of addresses to write to for additional information.

Adapting a Packaged Program

Computer hobbyists have been creating their own programs and adapting packaged programs for a long time. So have experienced programmers employed by the computer manufacturers and other major employers in business, industry, and government. For the uninitiated, however, the task of reworking a packaged program to meet personal needs can be overwhelming. This task calls for both a high level of programming skill and ease in using the language in which the program has been written. Since some packaged programs are written in BASIC and Pascal and the details of these languages can vary somewhat with the manufacturers, the difficulties multiply. The following approach is suggested for most personal computer users.

- Start out with programs provided by the computer manufacturer. Adapt your needs to the programs.
- When you are comfortable with these programs, try other packaged programs that are compatible with your personal computer.
- Try writing your own programs for simple tasks such as computing interest earned in your savings account, verifying your checking account balance, and verifying deductions from your gross pay.

Once you are comfortable with the above, you may want to experiment with modifying steps in a packaged program to meet your needs. Check yourself carefully on the details, though. Remember that these details can vary from manufacturer to manufacturer and that any mistakes in logic or syntax will cause you to miss getting the desired results. CHECKBOOK, a sample program is reprinted on the next page with the permission of Radio Shack.* A partial program listing of CHECKBOOK is given on pages 310 and 311. In their book, the authors summarize the several functions of the program and provide guidance for making easy changes. This program would help a family handle its personal finances, and it would be useful to the self-employed business person. Other programs are available for Radio Shack com-

*_Source:_ Tom Rugg and Phil Feldman, _32 BASIC Programs for the TRS-80 (Level II) Computer_ (Dilithium Press, 1980), pp. 3–18.

puters. One called LOAN is used for evaluating alternatives for borrowing money. Another program, MILEAGE, can help an individual keep track of gasoline consumption, miles driven, and gasoline mileage.

PROGRAM SAMPLE. This program enables the user to compare deposits and checks actually written with the statement prepared by the bank. This is the procedure individuals and businesses normally follow each month. The difference is that this procedure is computerized.

SAMPLE RUN

```
                         CHECKBOOK BALANCER
FIRST, COMPARE THE BANK STATEMENT WITH YOUR CHECKBOOK.
MAKE SURE THE STATEMENT AND THE CHECKBOOK SHOW THE SAME FIGURES
FOR EACH CHECK AND DEPOSIT.
MAKE A MARK IN THE CHECKBOOK NEXT TO EACH CHECK AND DEPOSIT LISTED
ON THE STATEMENT.
WHAT'S THE ENDING BALANCE SHOWN ON THE STATEMENT?
? 520.16
NOW FIND THE MOST RECENT CHECK THAT IS SHOWN ON THE BANK STATEMENT.
WHAT IS THE CHECK NUMBER OF THIS CHECK?
? 1652
WHAT BALANCE DOES YOUR CHECKBOOK SHOW AFTER CHECK NO. 1652?
? 480.12
ENTER THE AMOUNT OF EACH DEPOSIT THAT IS SHOWN IN YOUR CHECKBOOK
PRIOR TO CHECK NO. 1652 BUT IS NOT ON THE STATEMENT.
WHEN NO MORE, SAY 'END'
? END
TOTAL = 0
NOW ENTER THE AMOUNTS OF ANY CHECKS THAT ARE IN YOUR CHECKBOOK
PRIOR TO CHECK 1652 BUT THAT HAVE NOT BEEN SHOWN ON A BANK
STATEMENT YET. WHEN NO MORE, SAY 'END'
? 35.04
? 10
? END
```

PARTIAL PROGRAM LISTING

```
100 REM: CHECKBOOK
110 REM: COPYRIGHT 1979 BY TOM RUGG AND PHIL FELDMAN
120 CLEAR 50:DEFDBL C,D,S,R,T,W:CLS
130 PRINT TAB(9);"CHECKBOOK BALANCER"
140 PRINT
150 MC=50:MD=50:MS=50:MR=50
160 DIM C(MC),D(MD),S(MS),R(MR)
170 TC=0:TD=0:TS=0:TR=0:NC=0:ND=0:NS=0:NR=0
180 E$="ERROR, RE-ENTER, PLEASE."
190 PRINT"FIRST, COMPARE YOUR BANK STATEMENT"
200 PRINT"WITH YOUR CHECKBOOK."
220 PRINT"MAKE SURE THE STATEMENT AND THE"
230 PRINT"CHECKBOOK SHOW THE SAME FIGURES"
240 PRINT"FOR EACH CHECK AND DEPOSIT."
250 PRINT:PRINT"MAKE A MARK IN THE CHECKBOOK NEXT TO"
260 PRINT"EACH CHECK AND DEPOSIT LISTED"
270 PRINT"ON THE STATEMENT.":PRINT
280 PRINT"WHAT'S THE ENDING BALANCE SHOWN"
290 PRINT"ON THE STATEMENT?":INPUT SB
300 PRINT:PRINT"NOW FIND THE MOST RECENT CHECK THAT"
310 PRINT"IS SHOWN ON THE BANK STATEMENT."
330 PRINT"WHAT IS THE CHECK NUMBER OF THIS CHECK?"
340 INPUT LC
350 IF LC=INT(LC) THEN 380
360 PRINT"NO, NOT THE AMOUNT OF THE CHECK."
370 GOTO 300
380 PRINT
390 PRINT"WHAT BALANCE DOES YOUR CHECKBOOK"
400 PRINT"SHOW AFTER CHECK NO.":LC
410 INPUT CB
420 PRINT
430 PRINT"ENTER THE AMOUNT OF EACH DEPOSIT"
```

```
440 PRINT"THAT IS SHOWN IN YOUR CHECKBOOK"
450 PRINT"PRIOR TO CHECK NO.";LC
460 PRINT"BUT IS NOT ON THE STATEMENT."
470 A$="WHEN NO MORE, SAY 'END'":PRINT A$
480 INPUT R$
490 IF R$="END" THEN 545
500 IF VAL(R$)>0 THEN 520
510 PRINT E$:GOTO 470
520 ND=ND+1:D(ND)=VAL(R$):TD=TD+D(ND)
530 IF ND<MD THEN 480
540 L$="NO MORE ROOM.":PRINT:PRINT L$
545 PRINT:PRINT"TOTAL =":TD:PRINT
550 PRINT"NOW ENTER THE AMOUNTS OF ANY CHECKS"
560 PRINT"THAT ARE IN THE CHECKBOOK PRIOR"
570 PRINT"TO CHECK":LC:"BUT THAT"
580 PRINT"HAVE NOT BEEN SHOWN ON A BANK"
590 PRINT"STATEMENT YET."
600 PRINT:PRINT A$
610 INPUT R$
```

Writing Your Own Programs

COMMON PROGRAMMING LANGUAGES

BASIC
FORTRAN
COBOL
APL
Pascal
Assembler

Earlier in this textbook you read about programming and operating a computer. The programming languages used on personal computers include BASIC, assembler, FORTRAN, COBOL, APL (which stands for "a programming language"), and Pascal. In Chapter 6 you saw examples of several programming languages, including BASIC and Pascal. BASIC is used on almost every personal computer. The several personal computers mentioned earlier in this chapter have BASIC; some also offer one or more of the other programming languages. By the early 1980s more and more microcomputer manufacturers were developing computers for Pascal. Because microcomputers are generally sold with self-study guides, the beginner can learn programming at home. In the early 1980s most of these guides were written for programming in BASIC, but it is expected that guides for programming in other languages will follow.

Pascal is the only programming language to win widespread

```
{COMPOUND INTEREST PROGRAM}
PROGRAM COMPOUND (INPUT,OUTPUT);
CONST
   FOREVER=FALSE;
VAR
   PRINCIPAL,INTEREST,INTERESTRATE:REAL;
   YEARS,YEAR:INTEGER;
BEGIN {BEGIN MAIN PROGRAM}
REPEAT
   WRITELN;
   WRITE ('INITIAL PRINCIPAL?');
   READLN (PRINCIPAL);
   WRITE ('INTEREST RATE (%)?');
   READLN (INTERESTRATE);
   INTEREST:=INTERESTRATE/100.0+1.0;
   WRITE ('NUMBER OF YEARS?');
   READLN (YEARS);
   WRITELN ('     YEAR     PRINCIPAL');
   WRITELN ('     START$',PRINCIPAL);
   FOR YEAR:=1 TO YEARS DO
       BEGIN
       PRINCIPAL:=PRINCIPAL*INTEREST;
       WRITELN (YEAR,'      $',PRINCIPAL);
       END
UNTIL FOREVER
END.
```

COMPOUND INTEREST PROGRAM IN PASCAL. This program enables the user to compute compound interest with the aid of a personal computer. What differences do you see between Pascal and BASIC so far? Courtesy of Paul Friedman and "On Computing," Spring 1981

acceptance since the development of BASIC, COBOL, and FORTRAN in the 1960s. Because it is comparatively simple and is structured, it may be better for beginners than some of the programming languages developed earlier, Pascal has become popular enough that several manufacturers have added it to the programming languages available with their hardware. Some experts go so far as to predict that Pascal will replace BASIC as the main language for microcomputers. They claim that the structure of Pascal helps individuals avoid some of the errors that are typically made when some of the longer-standing programming languages are used.

PROGRAMMING FLOWCHART. Here you see the major steps in planning and creating a program for a personal computer. What differences do you see between this sequence and the logic you studied in Chapter 6?

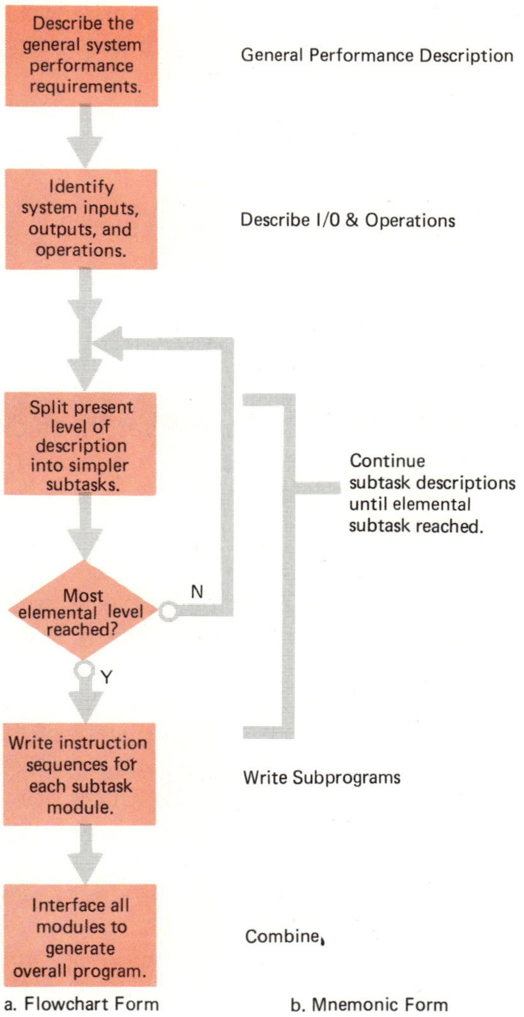

They also claim that Pascal is more portable—easier to convert—than the other programming languages.

As you learned in Chapter 6, a flowchart is used to show graphically the relationships in a program. This is true in personal computing as well as in business data processing. The flowchart shown on page 313 illustrates the steps required in creating programs for a microcomputer.

Numerous articles in the magazines *Byte* and *Popular Computing* lead the experienced microcomputer user, as well as the beginner, through applications of interest to consumers and professionals. One example is this program for summarizing monthly banking transactions made by telephone. In an electronic funds transfer system (EFTS), an individual enjoys two benefits from his or her savings account. Interest is earned every day, and the individual can use the account to pay bills by telephoning a banking operator.

Who Should Use a Personal Computer?

Selecting the right computer, like selecting the right school or car, is all-important. Only if you have thought through your needs and wants and planned accordingly will you be satisfied with your microcomputer. In deciding whether or not to use a personal computer, think about the following.

- List the jobs you want the computer to do. Examples of jobs are balancing your checkbook, developing a budget, and storing the addresses of schools or potential employers.
- Match up your list with the capabilities of the microcomputers available. For example, consider your storage needs. Many perts suggest a minimum of 16K bytes of programming memory.
- Be sure that software for performing your jobs is available for the model you select, either through the manufacturer or through a local computer store.
- Consider the languages available on the system. Be sure the software includes BASIC or Pascal, or other programming languages of interest to you, such as COBAL, FORTRAN, assembler, and so on.
- Check on the reputation of the computer manufacturer. Be sure that you will get the support you need. Computer clubs, vendor references, and the Better Business Bureau can all be useful sources of information.

- Be sure the necessary input and output devices are available. For example, if you want to use a personal computer for job applications, you need to be sure that the typefaces, paging mechanism, and formatting capability meet such word-processing needs as well as your computing needs.

A Dry Run

Once you think you know what you want, visit computer stores, computer companies, large department stores, and office equipment dealers. Ask for a hands-on demonstration tailored to your needs. You may want to have several such demonstrations. Before you make a commitment to a particular model, check with personal computer users.

CHECK YOURSELF

Supply the missing words.

1. __?__ software is available from the computer manufacturers or from software houses.
2. The software available for microcomputers includes an inventory program, a(n) __?__ program, and a personal investment program.
3. Two of the languages in which programs for microcomputers are written are BASIC and __?__.
4. With the appropriate input/output devices, a microcomputer can be used for both computing and __?__ __?__.
5. Most of the popular programming __?__ are available on microcomputers.
6. Several manufacturers have added Pascal to the programming languages available with their hardware because it is both portable and __?__ to use.
7. Many experts suggest __?__ of programmable memory for a microcomputer.
8. Computer clubs, vendor references, and the Better Business Bureau can help you check on the __?__ of a computer manufacturer.

Review Questions

1. Define the term *microcomputer system.*
2. Compare a microcomputer system with a minicomputer system or a larger computer system. What do these systems have in common?
3. Name three or more manufacturers of microcomputer systems.
4. Explain the difference between a microprocessor and a microcomputer.
5. Describe the role of the user of a microcomputer system.
6. Name three ways of obtaining software for a microcomputer. Which one would you choose? Why?
7. Name four programming languages that can be used with microcomputers.
8. List two reasons for the popularity of Pascal.
9. List the steps you would take to decide which microcomputer you would choose for your personal data processing needs.
10. Name three functions for which a microcomputer can be used by a small business.

Comparing Ideas

The questions below are to help you think about what you have learned in this chapter. They are thought questions. There is no one correct answer.

1. Why do you think many companies originally made the data processing department a part of the financial services division? (*Hint:* What types of business activities were computers first used for?)
2. What is a computer service bureau? How does it differ from a data processing department in a large business?

Data Processing Activities

Now you can try out the kinds of data processing activities business workers perform. Below is a summary of the work you will do. You will find the actual information and business forms you need in your *Data Processing Work Kit.*

Activity 1. You will gather cost information on a minimum of two microcomputer systems. Each microcomputer system must be capable of meeting the requirements specified.

Activity 2. You will distinguish between one-time costs associated with the purchase of microcomputer hardware and ongoing usage expenses.

BASIC Project 13
Computer Club Accounting Project

Microcomputers and application software packages can help managers to operate many small businesses. The following exercise will show you how BASIC can be used to produce simple accounting reports such as an income statement.

Program Statements

A *subroutine* or *subprogram* is a set of instructions that are generally used more than once. The instructions are written once, and the *main program* has statements that call the subprogram when needed. This way, the instructions do not have to be repeated each time they are needed.

In BASIC the GOSUB statement causes a branch to the line number where the subroutine begins. Execution proceeds through the subroutine until its last statement, RETURN, is reached. This causes a branch back to the line after the GOSUB statement. The usefulness of the subroutine comes from the fact that it may be branched to from several places in the main program.

In the sample program the subroutine that begins on line 1000 is used twice. Line 250 causes a branch to line 1000. Execution then continues through lines 1010, 1020, and 1030. At line 1030 the RETURN statement causes a branch to line 260, the line after the GOSUB statement.

Line 290 also causes a branch to the subroutine at line 1000, but this time the RETURN is to line 300, the next line after the GOSUB statement that made the subroutine call this second time.

The RETURN statement contains no line number because the point of return from the subroutine depends upon the line number of the particular GOSUB statement that caused entry into it.

GOSUB The GOSUB statement begins with the word GOSUB; this word is followed by a line number.

RETURN The RETURN statement consists of the word RETURN. It causes a branch to the line after the GOSUB statement.

SUBROUTINES. This program flowchart illustrates the use of a BASIC subroutine.

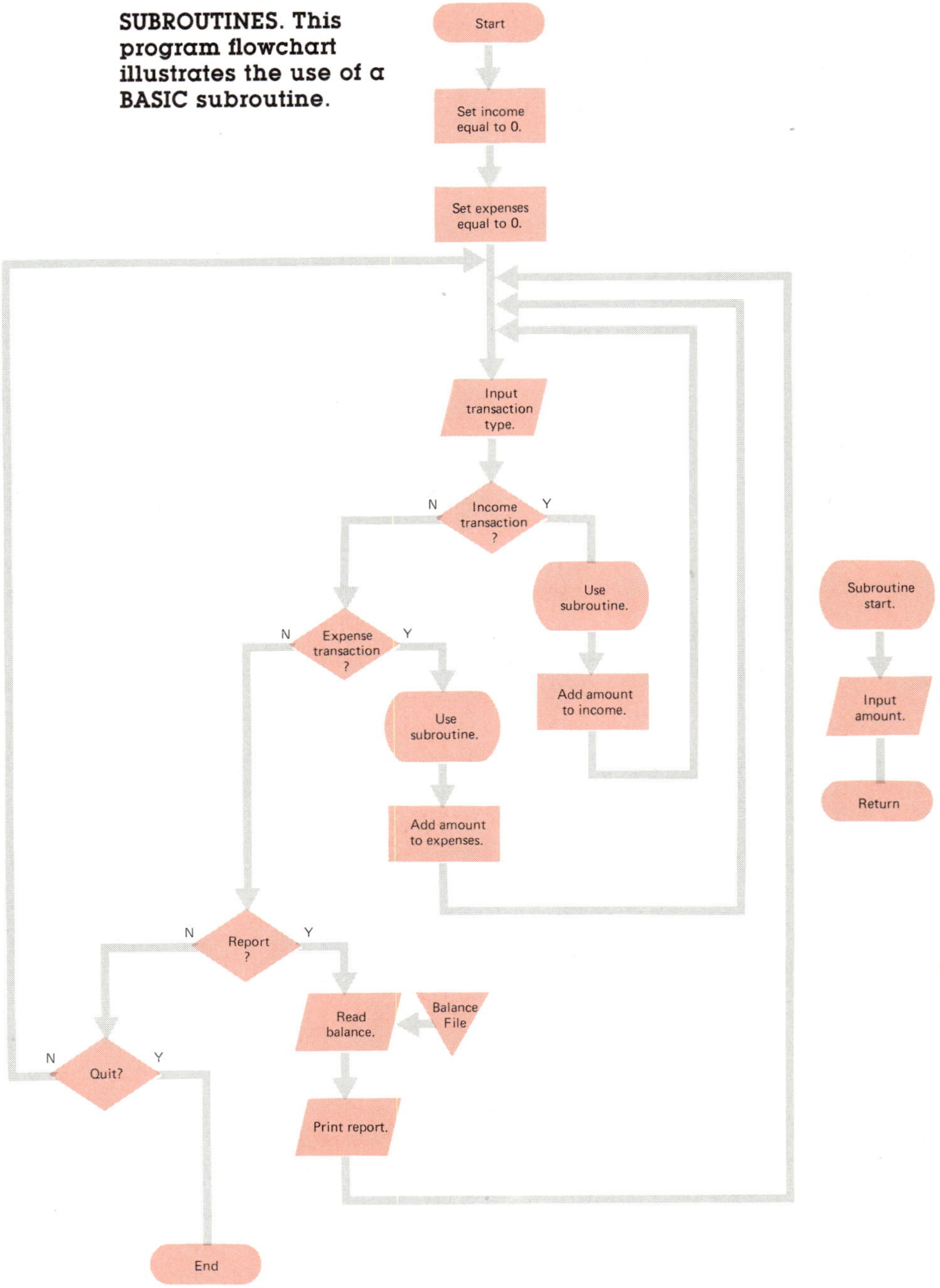

Just as a READ statement must have a matching DATA statement, the GOSUB statement must have a matching RETURN statement.

Sample Program

In this program the subroutine is very short and is used only twice by the main program. It would be just as easy to write out the needed instructions twice. However, subroutines may be complex and could be called frequently.

Modern data processing relies heavily on the use of subprograms. Many large computer systems have libraries of frequently needed subprograms. They are stored on tape or disks and can be called by a variety of programs. This is discussed further in Project 14.

NOTE: This program is designed to compute the income and expenses once for the entire session. The data in line 430 can be read only once.

```
110 REM ***********************************************************
120 REM INCOME AND EXPENSES FOR COMPUTER CLUB
130 REM ***********************************************************
142 LET E=0
144 LET I=0
150 PRINT "TRANSACTION TYPE PLEASE? (ENTER ? FOR HELP)"
160 INPUT T$
170 IF T$="I" THEN 240
180 IF T$="E" THEN 280
190 IF T$="R" THEN 320
200 IF T$="Q" THEN 9999
210 PRINT "TYPE 'I' FOR INCOME, 'E' FOR EXPENSE,"
220 PRINT "      'Q' TO QUIT OR 'R' FOR REPORT"
230 GOTO 150
```

```
240 REM INCOME ITEM
250 GOSUB 1000
260 LET I=I+A
270 GOTO 150
280 REM EXPENSE ITEM
290 GOSUB 1000
300 LET E=E+A
310 GOTO 150
320 REM REPORT
330 READ B
340 PRINT "REPORT FOR THIS SESSION"
350 PRINT "TOTAL OF INCOME ITEMS = ";I
360 PRINT "TOTAL OF EXPENSE ITEMS = ";E
370 PRINT "DIFFERENCE (INCOME - EXPENSE) = ";I-E
380 PRINT "OLD BALANCE ";B;" NEW BALANCE ";B+(I-E)
390 GOTO 150
425 REM PUT BEGINNING BALANCE IN DATA STATEMENT ON LINE 430
430 DATA 176.25
1000 REM SUBROUTINE
1010 PRINT "AMOUNT";
1020 INPUT A
1030 RETURN
9999 END
```

Output

```
TRANSACTION TYPE PLEASE? (ENTER ? FOR HELP)
? ?
```

```
TYPE 'I' FOR INCOME, 'E' FOR EXPENSE,
     'Q' TO QUIT OR 'R' FOR REPORT
TRANSACTION TYPE PLEASE? (ENTER ? FOR HELP)
? I
AMOUNT?78
TRANSACTION TYPE PLEASE? (ENTER ? FOR HELP)
? E
AMOUNT?13
TRANSACTION TYPE PLEASE? (ENTER ? FOR HELP)
? R
REPORT FOR THIS SESSION
TOTAL OF INCOME ITEMS = 78
TOTAL OF EXPENSE ITEMS = 13
DIFFERENCE (INCOME - EXPENSE) = 65
OLD BALANCE 176.25    NEW BALANCE 241.25
TRANSACTION TYPE PLEASE? (ENTER ? FOR HELP)
? Q
```

Keyboarding Activities

1. Enter and RUN the program listed above.
2. The total income and total expenses for the Computer Club for this month were as follows.

Monthly income	145
Monthly expenses	31

   Enter these amounts to compute the new balance.
3. Replace the data in line 430 with a new beginning balance, and repeat step 2.

Enrichment Activities

1. Modify the report section of the income and expense program so that it conforms to accounting standards: income on the left and expenses on the right of your output report.

2. Research the use of the RESTORE statement on your computer system. RESTORE allows you to enter multiple income and expense items. Create a program that will allow multiple entries for income or expenses.

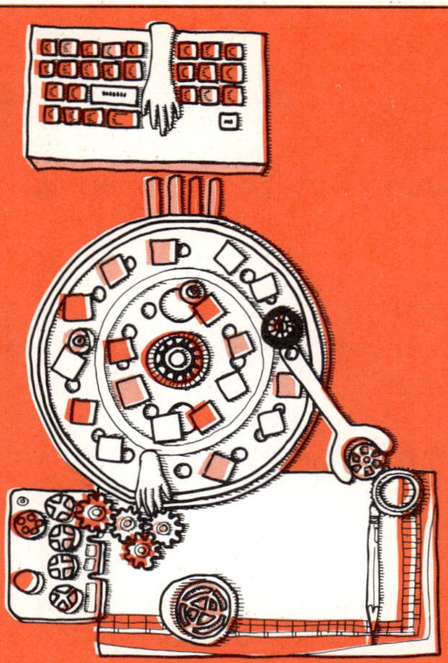

CHAPTER

14

The Future: Data Processing and You

DATA PROCESSING TERMINOLOGY

Technology
Data processing technology
Nanosecond
Picosecond
Josephson junction
Optical disk memory
Voice (or speech) recognition equipment
Optical systems
Home information networks
Privacy Act of 1974
Interest test
Achievement test
Aptitude test

PERFORMANCE GOALS

- Name four areas of change in data processing technology.
- List six ways in which computers are being improved.
- List three characteristics of office work in the future.
- State four ways in which a home information network may benefit society.

- **Name two risks of computer intrusion into personal privacy.**
- **Give two examples of the past growth in office jobs, and predict the future impact of technology changes on data processing careers.**
- **List sources of information on data processing careers.**

You have read about the various pieces of equipment used to produce data and about some common types of business data processing systems. You have also read about ways in which businesses divide up responsibilities and about the many different jobs now available in business offices.

The number of office jobs has increased rapidly during past years. The type of work done in the office has also changed a great deal. But what will happen in the future? You have learned that the use of computers to process data is growing. Will there thus be fewer office jobs as the capabilities of computers are expanded?

Changes in Data Processing Technology

Since this country was first settled, its population has increased each year. Fortunately, the production of agricultural crops and industrial goods has also increased each year. This has permitted the people of the United States to have a higher standard of living than those in many other countries. Growth in agricultural and industrial production in any country, and the associated improvement in the standard of living, is made possible by advances in technology. Simply defined, **technology** is the science that deals with methods and equipment for performing work. **Data processing technology** is the science that deals specifically with methods and equipment for data or information handling.

FOUR AREAS OF CHANGE IN DATA PROCESSING TECHNOLOGY

1. **Computers**
2. **Data storage**
3. **Voice input**
4. **Data communications**

In the next 20 years we probably will not see any events as revolutionary or as important to data processing as the introduction of the computer. We will see, however, tremendous improvements in today's technology, particularly in four areas: (1) computers, (2) data storage, (3) voice input, and (4) data communications.

Improvements in Computers

Since the use of computers in business data processing began in the early 1950s, enormous improvements have been made in computer hardware and software. The trend has been toward smaller, faster, and cheaper computers. Three other advantages

ONGOING COMPUTER IMPROVEMENTS

1. **Price**
2. **Reliability**
3. **Speed**
4. **Size**
5. **Convenience of installation**
6. **Storage capacity**

have come with improved equipment. Newer computers are more reliable, and costly breakdowns of the machines are less likely to occur. Also, today's equipment is easier to install and to put in operation than older models of computers. Modern small computers can be installed in any office and do not require a special, cool, dust-free environment as did all early machines. Still another advantage of advances in computer technology has been the simplification of the task of computer programming.

As described in Chapter 4, the development of large-scale integrated (LSI) circuitry and then very large scale integrated (VLSI) circuits resulted in significant improvements in the last generation of computers. It has made possible the miniaturization of computer components to the point that a powerful minicomputer now requires no more space than a standard office desk. Smaller office computers that fit on desk tops are also available.

The speed of computers has increased a hundredfold in recent years and continues to amaze us. With VLSI circuitry it is not uncommon to hear of machine calculations performed in nanoseconds. (A **nanosecond** is one billionth of a second.) Machine switching operations in the fastest machines occur in picoseconds. (A **picosecond** is one trillionth of a second.)

One reason why newer computers are cheaper is that production costs are going down. Integrated circuits can be mass-produced. Mass production is a cost-saving method of manufacture.

In spite of the enormous progress that has already been made in producing smaller, faster, and cheaper computers, thousands of computer designers are working in laboratories to develop even better computers. It is now believed that the next generation of computers will be at least 20 times faster than the computers available today. Scientists say that improved performance will come from a new type of switching device that will replace the present semiconductor switches used in computers. The new switch is known as a **Josephson junction**; it is named after Brian Josephson, a British scientist credited with the technology development. The Josephson switch permits information to be transferred within a computer at much faster speeds than can be achieved in computers made with semiconductor switches. Use of the superfast switch should result in a future generation of smaller, faster, and cheaper computers that will be more reliable and easier to install and to program than the computers presently available.

Advances in Data Storage Capacities

The first computers used for business data processing had very limited capacities for the storage of data. Now a much greater

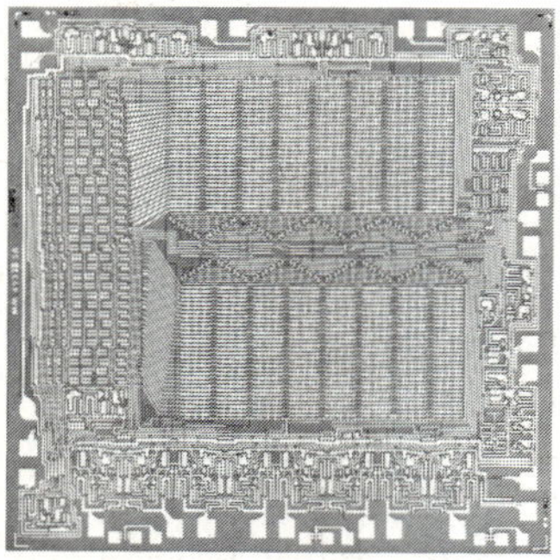

MEMORY CHIPS. This tiny semiconductor memory chip contains 4,096 bits of data. The actual chip is about as large as this box: □. Courtesy Electronic Magazine

amount of data can be stored in computer memory devices. A typical floppy disk holds 2.5 million characters, and over 300 million characters can be stored on a rigid magnetic disk. Each year there have been significant increases in main memory storage densities and in secondary storage capacities. Nevertheless, significant future advances in data storage are expected.

It is predicted that by 1990 magnetic-tape and magnetic-disk storage units will be replaced by new technology. The use of semiconductors and the new magnetic bubbles for main memory storage may also be out of date by that time. Scientists believe that **optical disk memories** will offer improvement over present data storage methods in terms of capacity, cost, and speed of access time. Optical disk memories based on the use of laser beams for the recording and reading of data have already been built in laboratories. Data is recorded on a metal-coated disk by a laser beam. The laser beam makes tiny pits, each 1/100 the diameter of a human hair. In each pit a bit of information can be stored. Data is read from the disk by reflecting laser light from the pits. In optical disk memory units already built, as many as 10 billion bits of information can be stored on each side of a disk. A second new type of data storage unit that may be practical for storing huge files of data at a low cost is the video disk. Video disks are now being developed for home entertainment use with televisions.

Data Entry by Voice Input

The different types of equipment typically used for entering data into today's computers are described in Chapter 5. Their use in computer systems is illustrated in Chapters 8 and 9. In addition, since 1972 there has been limited use of more expensive data-entry equipment that permits data entry by voice (or speech) recognition. **Voice (or speech) recognition equipment** translates what is said by a person into machine-readable data.

At the present time, voice recognition equipment is used only in highly specialized situations where the individual is engaged in some activity requiring use of the hands, making the keying of input data impractical. For example, an individual sorting and inventorying items may need to input data but cannot do so while physically handling the items.

LIMITATIONS OF VOICE INPUT

1. **Small vocabulary capacity**
2. **Slow**
3. **Expensive**

The capacity of the voice recognition equipment that is now available is limited to numbers and specialized words related to the task being recorded. Thus a voice recognition unit has a vocabulary of words specially designed for a particular application. A typical system recognizes fewer than 50 words. Each digit of a number and each letter of a word must be individually spoken. For example, the number 13,506 is spoken as one, three, five, zero, six. This method of input is currently slower than the method whereby an experienced data-entry operator keyboards the same data. The voice recognition unit is considerably more costly than a card-punch or key-to-disk device. The recognition unit must be trained (or adjusted) to recognize the speech of a particular operator. The operator wears a headset-type microphone and speaks the numbers or words into it. Normally, the headset is wired to the voice recognition unit, but wireless microphones can be used where operator mobility is important. It is expected that there will be technology improvements that overcome these disadvantages of voice recognition equipment. When improved equipment is available, voice recognition by machine will be a practical and inexpensive way to enter data into a computer.

Advances in Data Communications

FAST MEANS OF DATA TRANSMISSION

1. **Telephone**
2. **Satellite**
3. **Microwaves**
4. **Optical systems**

Improvements in techniques for communicating data will become increasingly important to the growth of computer data processing. Data entered at a terminal keyboard located in one city must be transmitted quickly and cheaply to a computer located in another city or even in another country. For example, to confirm a customer order, a sales representative in San Francisco may need to request up-to-the-minute inventory information from a computer located in a New Jersey warehouse. If a company has a distributed computer system, such as the type described in Chapter 5, data may be transmitted daily from ten or more minicomputers located in different cities in the country to a large computer located at the corporation headquarters.

At the present time, data that must be communicated quickly is often transmitted by telephone lines, although satellite and microwave communication facilities are also used to transmit data from city to city and from country to country. For example, data can be transmitted via satellite from Los Angeles to Tokyo or from Los Angeles to New York. Further improvements are expected in the speed and cost of data transmission by satellite and microwave.

FACSIMILE TRANSMISSION. In the future we will see more facsimile transmission between word processing centers across the United States. Courtesy Burroughs Corporation

New communications technology, called **optical systems,** offers an opportunity for significant improvement in data transmission. Optical systems use glass fibers carrying laser signals for the transmission of data. A single glass fiber, which has the same diameter as a human hair, can carry 50 million bits of information each second. This is enough capacity to transmit in one hour the contents of 40,000 typical books in the Library of Congress in

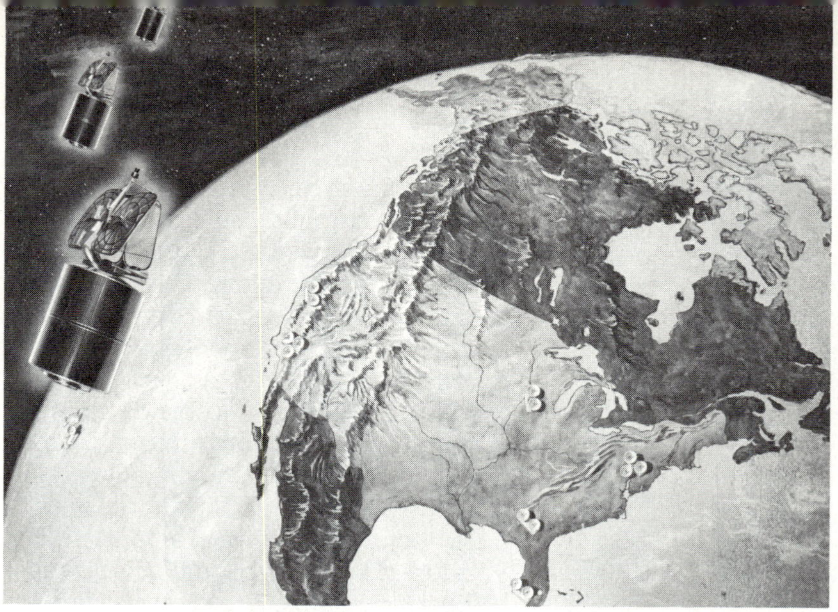

SATELLITE TRANSMISSION. Satellites make it possible to transmit data from one location to another many thousands of miles away.
Courtesy ATT/GTE

Washington, D.C., to Los Angeles. When optical systems are available for commercial use, the speed of transmission will be faster, and the cost will be less than it is today. Some scientists even predict that future development of optical system technology will make space satellites obsolete for data transmission.

CHECK YOURSELF

Supply the missing words.

1. ___?___ ___?___ technology is the science that deals with methods and equipment for data or information handling.
2. The development of ___?___ ___?___ ___?___ resulted in significant improvements in the last generation of computers.
3. One trillionth of a second is called a(n) ___?___.
4. A new switch that permits information to be transferred faster than with semiconductor switches is called a(n) ___?___ ___?___.
5. Laser beams record and read data on ___?___ ___?___ memories.
6. ___?___ disks are being developed for home entertainment use.
7. ___?___ ___?___ equipment translates human speech into machine-readable data.
8. Data to be communicated quickly may be transmitted by telephone, satellite, and ___?___.
9. Glass fibers carrying laser signals for data transmission are used in ___?___ ___?___.

Impact of Technological Changes on Business Data Processing

How will the future changes in data processing technology we have described affect office work in the future? There are three commonly accepted predictions.

1. More and more individuals doing office work will be interacting with computer systems.
2. The number of paper documents will decrease.
3. The number of workers using terminals will increase.

Increased Use of Computers in Business

In the past, forecasts of future uses of computers have always been too low. Many more computers have been sold than even the manufacturers of the equipment predicted would be sold. Now it is said by some that by 1990 there will be yearly sales of almost one million business and personal computers and that in business alone several million computers will have been installed. Only time will tell whether this forecast is overly optimistic.

Regardless of the appropriateness of the numbers forecast, experts in the computer field believe that by 1990 almost every business will be using computers. This prediction includes both customer-purchased equipment and the use of service bureaus. As technology results in the production of smaller, faster, and cheaper machines, more and more businesses can acquire their own computers. In addition, by the end of the 1980s it is expected that many individuals in managerial, professional, and administrative positions will have their own desk-top computers. These computers are likely to perform basic calculations and other functions handled by the low end of today's word processing equipment, which in the future will be hard to distinguish from computers. The computer will also serve as a terminal input device for storing information electronically and for copying selected text and numeric data. Through electronic communication systems, computers at individual work stations will be linked together to form an electronic mail system within the business organization. By 1981, at least one computer manufacturer, Wang, had already manufactured such a system, called Mailway.

ELECTRONIC MAIL. Electronic mail service such as the Electronic Computer Originated Mail system (E-COM) of the U.S. Postal Service, allows businesses and individuals to transmit messages electronically around the country using telecommunications networks. Several private companies also offer electronic mail service.
Courtesy U.S. Postal Service

Disappearance of Paper Documents

In tomorrow's office, fewer paper documents will be stored. Instead, data will be kept in computer (or word-processing) mass

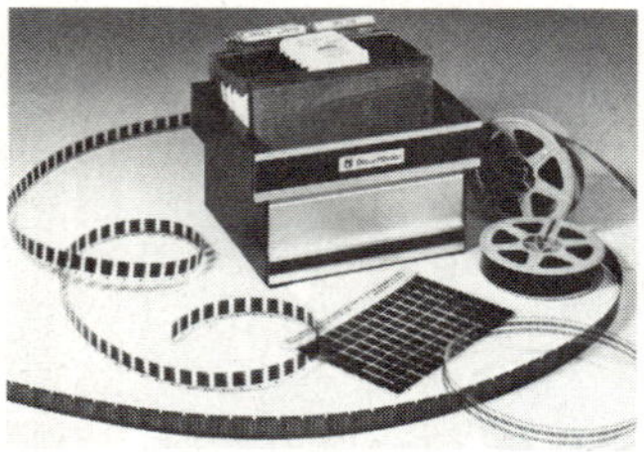

MICROFORMS. The use of microfilm, microfiche, and aperture cards has greatly reduced the need for paper documents. Such use has also enhanced data retrieval.
Courtesy Bell & Howell

storage units or in automated microform storage devices. This change has already begun. However, making it even more widespread is not easy. One reason is that people have always been very fond of paper documents. To a large extent they still are today. People like being able to see and hold their correspondence, invoices, paychecks, inventory cards, and other transaction records.

It is this feeling that is resulting in slow progress toward the *checkless society*. This is the name given to a time in the future when it is predicted we will not have to deposit paychecks in the bank or write checks to pay bills. Progress in this direction is evident in that, for example, some companies no longer issue paychecks. Each employee receives an earnings statement, and the employer delivers a magnetic tape to the bank. The bank puts the tape on a computer. Then the computer credits each employee's account and debits the employer's account. If an employee has a bank credit card, he or she can use the card to purchase gasoline, food, and clothes and to authorize the bank to pay household bills. In this way, the income for a pay period can be spent without writing a single check or paying out any cash. With the exception of the earnings statement and the credit card receipts, no paper documents have been created.

Of course, although the paper document has been eliminated, the information that would be on that document still exists. People who store and retrieve information will be needed even in a checkless society. The difference will be in the way in which the information is processed. We can expect to see fewer paper documents and more automated storage and retrieval equipment.

Wider Use of Terminals

As you have already read, in the office of tomorrow many more workers will use computers. Employees ranging from entry-level office workers to managers will use terminals to enter data for processing or automated storage. The same terminals will be used to retrieve data from computer memories, from microform files, and even from word-processing storage units. There will also be an increase in the use of on-line terminals for applications that require immediate feedback.

On-line terminal operation is expected to be the fastest-growing area of data entry.

Forecasts indicate a greater increase in the number of terminals than in the number of computers themselves. It has been estimated that by 1990 there will be one computer terminal for every six white-collar workers in the United States. More than 15 million terminals linked to computers via communications channels will be in operation, a more than sixfold increase from the 2.5 million plus units in use by the 1980s. Producers of computer

ELECTRONIC BANKING. An automated teller machine (ATM) is activated by a plastic card with magnetic strip. Such terminals are part of the trend toward a "cashless" society. Courtesy Citibank

equipment are concentrating on producing more flexible and less expensive terminal devices. These will be used to improve existing data processing applications and to make new computer applications possible.

It has been forecast that in the future many more salesclerks will use point-of-sale terminals. We will see these terminals in the form of simple keyboards, data-entry cash registers, and visual display sales terminals. All will record information at the point of sale for entry into a computer. This data will be available immediately for updating inventories, scheduling shipments, and preparing bills.

The increased use of terminals for on-line data entry probably will mean that fewer card-punch operators will handle computer input. But it will also mean that many more people in jobs other than card-punch jobs will use on-line computer terminals. They will be used by salesclerks, cashiers, bank tellers, supermarket checkout clerks, librarians, and newspaper editors, for example.

CHECK YOURSELF

Supply the missing words.

1. We can expect to see more ___?___ used for data processing in business.
2. Computers are becoming smaller, ___?___, ___?___, more reliable, and easier to maintain and program.
3. The number of paper documents filed in the office will ___?___ in the future.

4. In the future many more employees will be using __?__ to enter data into computer storage units.
5. __?__ is an example of an electronic mail system within a business organization.
6. The term __?__ __?__ is used to describe a time in the future when we will pay bills without paper transactions.
7. It is estimated that by 1990 there will be one computer terminal for every __?__ white-collar workers in the nation.

Impact of Computers on You and Society

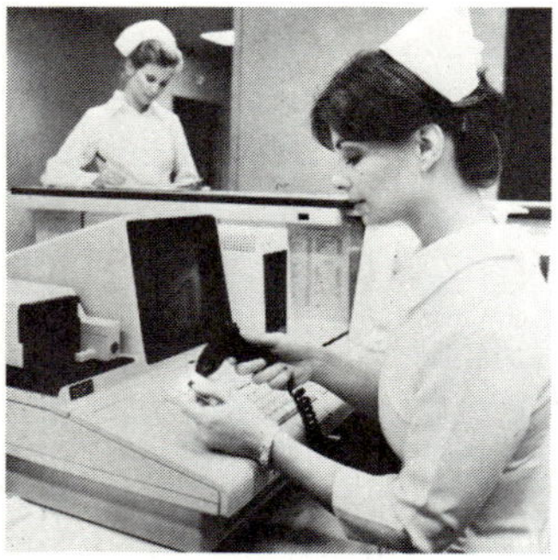

ON-LINE SYSTEMS. Processing patient records using an on-line system is a common procedure in many hospitals. Computers also provide diagnostic aid to medical personnel. Courtesy NCR Corporation

Throughout this book you have read about the impact computer technology has already had on information handling in business. Many people believe that in the decades to come computer technology will greatly influence life styles. If the computer is used appropriately, it can create many benefits. For example, medical diagnostic aid and educational opportunities can be extended to individuals in remote areas who do not now have such services available. Also, computers will provide information in the home through home information networks. On the other hand, computer technology can be misused. We read often about some malfunction in an important computer operation. The problem is usually caused by an error in computer programming. For example, it was because of a programming error that the Skylab space station fell to earth in 1979, endangering the lives of many. If programmed properly, Skylab would have been directed outward in space for a harmless disintegration there.

Examples of both the good and bad impacts that computer technology may have on society will now be discussed. The first example, a home information network, is a potential benefit. The second, intrusion on personal privacy, is potentially harmful to society.

THREE NONBUSINESS AREAS IN WHICH THE USE OF DATA PROCESSING IS EXPECTED TO GROW RAPIDLY

1. **Medicine**
2. **Education**
3. **Home information networks**

Home Information Networks

Home information networks make it possible to receive selected items of news or reference information at home when you want them. The information is stored in a central computerized data bank. When an individual requests information at a home terminal, the information is displayed on a TV-like screen or a printer at home.

The Touch-Tone telephone that is now used in homes can, with a minor change, also be used as a computer input terminal. The telephone buttons become the keys of a terminal input device. By keying in a code number, an individual will be able to request information from an outside computer storage unit. News about international events, sports results, business news, and consumer news will all be available. The computer will respond in seconds with the requested information. With a home information network, there are endless opportunities for other uses too. For example, computer-assisted instruction can be done at home instead of in a classroom. The Touch-Tone telephone terminal unit can also be used to obtain on-line banking services, assistance in computing monthly bills or income taxes, or merchandise from local stores.

Many different home information network systems are now being tested in this country and in other countries. In some of these systems, the homes participating in the network are connected by telephone lines or TV cables to the central information office. In other systems, the user-requested information is broadcast from a central source. Then it is picked up by a special decoding unit attached to the home TV set.

It is agreed that two types of home information systems will be widely used. *Teletext* is the name given to a system that provides one-way transmission of electronic data (whether in the form of words, numbers, or graphics) from a central data base to the screen of a home TV set. The transmission may be via air waves, cable, or phone lines. The information displayed on the home TV screen may include a variety of subjects such as news items, airline schedules, recipes, catalog pages from local shops, health guides, and schedules of sports or community events.

In another type of home information network service, called *Videotext*, a person at home uses a small computer keyboard to respond to the information displayed on the TV screen and request additional information. Videotext is the two-way version of Teletext.

Computer Intrusion Into Personal Privacy

The advantages of files of data in machine-readable form called data banks are described in Chapter 7. Without computerized files of information, businesses and government agencies would be handicapped in dealing with the modern world. Banks, finance and credit agencies, insurance companies, and retail stores are only some of the business organizations that maintain files of data (or data banks) about their customers. Government agencies have even larger data banks for recording information about individuals. The U.S. Census Bureau, the Internal Revenue Service, the Social Security and Veterans administrations, the FBI, and the Department of Justice are just some of the federal agencies that maintain data banks on individuals in the country. State and local governments also maintain data banks.

Two risks are associated with the maintenance of data banks, either in private business or in government. First there is the danger of human or machine error. An error can lead to the recording of incorrect information about an individual. For example, a credit agency might record in its file that you have not paid a particular bill that in fact you have paid. Such a record could affect the willingness of another store to let you open a charge account. The second risk associated with data banks is that the information in them might be misused. For example, medical history information about an individual might be wrongly interpreted by an insurance company. This could mean that the individual might have difficulty getting the insurance he or she wants.

The Privacy Act of 1974 grants people the right to become aware of information on file about them in federal government agencies.

Concern about the possible risks just described has led to actions to protect the personal privacy of each individual with respect to information in data banks. Federal legislation, the **Privacy Act of 1974,** grants each individual the right to become aware of all the information kept about him or her in the files of federal government agencies. This law also provides each individual with the opportunity to correct any false data. In addition, each federal agency is responsible for ensuring that the information it has stored is not misused. Some states have passed similar laws to protect the privacy of information maintained by state agencies. In 1979, the President of the United States asked Congress to pass legislation extending the provisions of the Privacy Act of 1974 to cover all data banks, including those maintained by business and nonprofit organizations.

CHECK YOURSELF

Supply the missing words.

1. The Skylab space station fell to earth in 1979 because of a(n) __?__ error.
2. __?__ __?__ __?__ will make it possible to use home terminals to get information on airline schedules, tax matters, community events, and many other items of interest.
3. Teletext is one type of __?__ __?__ __?__.

4. One risk associated with data banks is that __?__ information might be recorded in a bank.
5. A second risk associated with data banks is that the information in a bank might be __?__.
6. The Privacy Act of 1974 protects the privacy of individuals about whom information is stored in the files of __?__ government agencies.

Outlook for Data Processing Careers

Despite the availability of more and faster computers, the demand for office workers will continue to increase in the future. But before making predictions about the future in office jobs, let us look at the past growth in these jobs.

Growth in Office Jobs

In 1900 more people were working on farms than in factories or in offices. The economy of the United States was then based primarily on agriculture. By 1930, however, the United States had changed to an industrial economy. There were more people employed in factories than on farms. Office workers also outnumbered farm workers by this time. Office jobs, however, were fewer in number than factory jobs. But after 1930, the need for office workers in the United States grew tremendously. By 1960 the number of people employed in offices exceeded the number employed in factories. During the same period the number of farm workers continued to decline.

It is estimated that today, 50 percent of U.S. workers will be office workers. Many of them will operate on-line terminals and other data processing equipment.

What will happen in the future? The U.S. Census Bureau predicts that office employment will continue to grow. It further predicts that by 1990, 50 percent of all the people employed in this country will be doing some kind of office job. That would mean 58 million people. The opportunities for a wide variety of data processing careers are obviously encouraging.

Expansion of Data Processing Careers

As additional uses are made of computers, more people will be required to work with a computer. People will be needed to design computer systems, write computer programs, operate the equipment, and repair the hardware. It has been estimated that by 1990 as many as one in every five people in the U.S. labor force will need some knowledge of data processing. In addition,

CAREER OPTIONS. This computer's software includes stored programs capable of performing tests on the operating system. The need for field maintenance creates many career opportunities for new employees. Courtesy Burroughs Corporation

by that time the job of six out of every ten in the labor force will depend in some way on data processing.

Thus, although computers are getting faster and faster and card-punch data entry is being replaced by newer methods of data input, the total number of people involved in data processing work is increasing enormously. Even if you do not choose a career in computer operations or in systems and programming, it is likely that you will need to be familiar with computer processing in your work.

Regardless of the career you choose, computers will increasingly be your helpmates. You owe it to yourself to consider carefully your interests, skills, and special abilities. Develop a career ladder that will lead to a successful future in data processing. Remember always that every technological breakthrough will create a greater demand for skilled workers.

Learning about computer terminology, the uses of computers, and employment opportunities in computer data processing should not stop with this textbook. Look into other instructional opportunities available to you. The so-called computer revolution is upon us. Just as the automobile introduced a new era of mobility, the computer will bring us to new heights of productivity. Education, training, and diligence can make you a partner in the progress of business data processing.

Sources of Career Information

QUESTIONS FOR YOUR INSTRUCTOR OR COUNSELOR

1. **Available jobs**
2. **Appropriate courses**
3. **Employment statistics**
4. **Regional employment**

You now have some understanding of the technology of data processing, the various data processing jobs, and the kinds of jobs that are most likely to be in demand in the future. You may have a number of questions: Where can I go to ask about the jobs available in my part of the country? How do I learn about the courses that are best suited to the type of career I am most interested in? How can I find out how many persons are employed in a particular job? Where is the kind of work I am interested in most likely to be in demand? An instructor or counselor may provide answers, and there are also other sources of information.

Government Agencies and Community Associations. Several government and community agencies can help job seekers obtain useful information and make a realistic career choice. There are a number of such agencies. Probably those that would be most helpful to you are the U.S. Department of Labor, the U.S. Office of Education, and the chamber of commerce for the city or town in which you plan to seek employment.

U.S. Department of Labor
Employment and Training Administration
U.S. Employment Service
Patrick Henry Building
601 D Street, N.W.
Washington, DC 20004

Every state has a department of vocational education. The agency in your state can provide you with information on data processing training programs where you live.

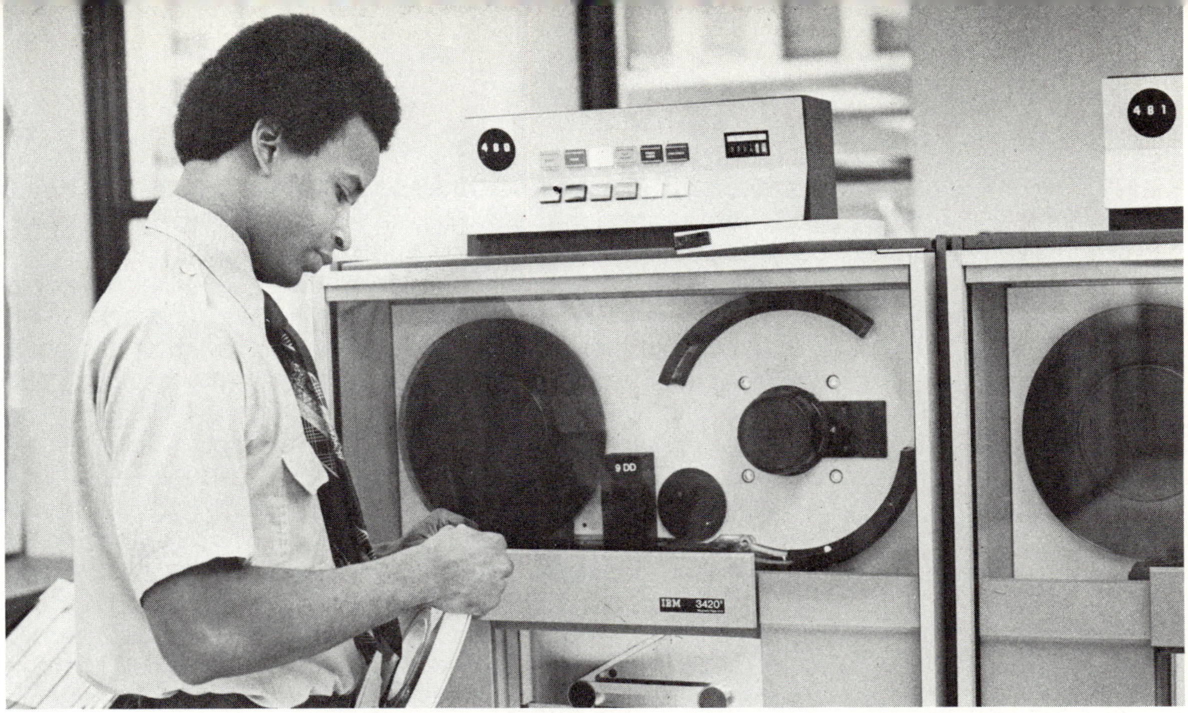

CAREER OPPORTUNITIES. The demand for computer professionals will escalate rapidly in the 1980s. Experts predict a shortage of at least 100,000 employees for field services by 1990. Courtesy IBM Corporation

The Employment and Training Administration makes information about typical jobs available to the public. Information about the availability of various jobs and about the skills, education, and training required for them is included.

U.S. Office of Education
400 Maryland Avenue, S.W.
Washington, DC 20202

The U.S. Office of Education publishes materials relating to education. Some of these publications deal with career education in general. Others deal with specific careers and with opportunities for further education. The U.S. Office of Education also publishes directories of educational institutions and compiles educational statistics and projections.

World Wide Chamber of Commerce Directory
Johnson Publishing Co.
Box 455
Loveland, CO 80537

There are chambers of commerce in cities and towns throughout the country. They provide information on the availability of particular types of jobs in their area. These agencies can also refer you to major employers that offer a wide range of career opportunities.

ACM
1133 Sixth Avenue
New York, NY 10036

The Association for Computing Machinery sponsors high school and college computer clubs. It also holds lecture series for people employed in data processing. ACM issues several journals and special-interest publications.

AEDS
1201 16th Street, N.W.
Washington, DC 20036

The Association for Educational Data Systems holds meetings for educators, administrators, and industry personnel. These people exchange ideas about the latest methods of processing data for education. The use of the computer as an educational tool is one of the major concerns of AEDS.

ASIS
1010 16th Street, N.W.
Washington, DC 20036

AFIPS
210 Summit Avenue
Montvale, NJ 07645

ASM
24587 Bagley Road
Cleveland, OH 44138

DPMA
505 Busse Highway
Park Ridge, IL 60068

IWPA
Maryland Road
Willow Grove, PA 19090

SDE
247 Edythe Street
Livermore, CA 94550

Trade and Professional Associations. There are many trade and professional associations that can provide information on data processing technology and careers.

The American Federation of Information Processing Societies represents the United States in international organizations interested in information processing. AFIPS sponsors research and holds conventions. There are lectures, manufacturers' exhibits, and publishers' exhibits at the conventions.

The Association for Systems Management helps business develop better management systems and procedures. ASM promotes higher standards for professional education and seeks ways to improve employee competence.

The Data Processing Management Association sponsors meetings for exchanging ideas about data processing management. It also holds lectures designed to improve industry-related knowledge and professional competence. DPMA issues a certificate in data processing (CDP) to persons who meet certain requirements, including passing a written examination in data processing.

The International Word Processing Association encourages the exchange of information on the progress of word-processing methods and systems. It sponsors conferences and issues monthly and bimonthly publications.

The Society of Data Educators holds meetings at which invited speakers lecture and then has question-and-answer sessions on matters relating to data processing education. SDE publishes a journal and other materials for data processing educators. It issues a certificate in data education (CDE) to those educators who qualify.

CAREER INFORMATION. ***Discover*, IBM's Computerized Vocational Information System (CVIS), provides information on hundreds of careers. Students key in their interests, backgrounds, and skills, and retrieve data on their best opportunities.** Courtesy IBM Corporation

Career Counseling

Psychologists and educators, working together, have developed a number of tests that are useful in career counseling. These tests include interest tests, aptitude tests, and achievement tests. They are published by businesses that specialize in constructing tests. These tests are usually administered by schools and employers, under the direction of qualified test administrators. The results of the test an individual takes are interpreted by a specialist. In interpreting the test results, the specialist takes into account age, educational background, job experience, and other relevant factors. Your guidance counselor or a career specialist can help you decide whether such tests could be helpful to you in choosing and preparing for a career.

Interest Tests. Interest tests allow you to compare your likes and dislikes with those of persons who have done well in the careers you feel might suit you. A trained career counselor can suggest careers that are appropriate for you by looking at your interests along with your specific skills and areas of knowledge.

Once you have chosen a career and are ready to apply for a job, you may be asked to take an aptitude test, an achievement test, or one or more of both of these types of tests.

Aptitude tests assess your capacity for learning in a particular subject or occupational area.

Aptitude Tests. **Aptitude tests** are designed to measure how well you are suited for training in a particular skill. The most common aptitude tests center around clerical, numeric, and logical aptitudes. For a data processing career, you might take a test measuring your aptitude for systems and programming. Such a test often includes sections on completing alphabetic, numeric, and geometric patterns, as well as a variety of computations. Try out these sample questions.

An Alphabetic Pattern
Select the next letter in the series, assuming that the series will follow the same pattern: abd, cdf, efh, ghj, ij ____

(A) k (B) m (C) l (D) n

A Numeric Pattern
Select the next number in the series, assuming that the series will follow the same pattern: 2, 4, 8, 16, 32 ____

(A) 128 (B) 64 (C) 68 (D) 48

A Geometric Pattern
Select the next figure in the series below, assuming that the series will follow the same pattern.

APTITUDE TESTS. Many tests assess the test-taker's aptitude for abstract reasoning. This example requires the reader to notice the movement of a dot clockwise, from quarter to quarter.

Achievement Tests. **Achievement tests** are used to assess your skills in a certain area or gauge your level of performance. They may be used to measure your ability to use computer equipment or other office machines, for example. Try this sample question.

Clerical Speed and Accuracy
Select the one that matches this name: J. Martin Smithers

(A) J. Martin Smithers (B) J. Martin Smither
(C) J Martin Smithers (D) J. Martin Smitheers

It is important to remember that you may feel uncertain when you take commercially available achievement tests or other tests that measure your performance. You cannot expect to be familiar with every variation of equipment or with a particular employer's standards for performance. Feel free to ask questions about the type of task, the particular equipment used, and the employer's expectations. Applying for a job can tell you a great deal about what to expect once you are on the job. Try your best on all tests, and always ask for a review of your performance.

Sample aptitude and achievement tests are sold at most large bookstores and can also be ordered by mail. They are designed to be similar to the tests that are administered to applicants for employment, higher education, and scholarships. These sample tests often include instructional material. The reader is referred to appropriate self-help sections if he or she shows weaknesses after having taken one or more sample tests. Simulating the test conditions and assessing your strengths and weaknesses and then working for improvement in those areas in which you need help can be valuable to you later on. Some day you may need to do well on tests in order to be considered for the next step in your career ladder. Preparation will help your climb.

CHECK YOURSELF

Supply the missing words.

1. By 1930 the United States had changed from an agricultural economy to an industrial economy, and there were more people employed in ___?___ than in ___?___.
2. It is predicted that by 1990 as many as ___?___ percent of the people employed in this country will be doing work in an office.
3. In 1990 one out of every ___?___ people employed will need some data processing knowledge.
4. In the future more people will be needed to operate and repair computers, design systems, and write ___?___.
5. A(n) ___?___ test measures skills in a particular area.
6. A(n) ___?___ test can help you to assess your capacity for learning in a particular subject area or occupational area.
7. Schools and employers sometimes administer ___?___ that can be useful in career counseling.
8. A(n) ___?___ test allows you to compare your own likes and dislikes with those of persons who are successful in an area attractive to you.

name 3 devices that will increase data storage capacity of computers

Review Questions

1. Define the term *data processing technology,* and describe four areas of technological improvements.
2. List six ways in which computers are being improved.
3. Name the type of circuit that is expected to increase the speed of computers in the future.
4. Describe an optical disk memory.
5. Name three disadvantages of present voice recognition equipment.
6. Describe an optical system for communications.
7. List three ways in which changes in data processing technology will affect office work in the future.
8. Describe the benefits of a home information network, and explain how such a network operates.
9. Name two risks associated with the maintenance of data banks.
10. Describe the growth in office jobs to date, and state the expectations for future.

Comparing Ideas

The questions below are to help you think about what you have learned in this chapter. They are thought questions. There is no one correct answer.

1. Contact a local computer manufacturer or supplier, and obtain a current equipment price list and a copy of a previous (outdated) price list. Compare the two. Discuss the reasons why prices may have increased or decreased.
2. A medium-sized printing company is purchasing a computer. The systems analyst responsible for choosing a system says that speed is not a major factor in selecting the computer. Why do you think the systems analyst believes that?
3. Try to locate and visit a business in your area that uses terminals or point-of-sale equipment. Discuss how this equipment affects office work and customers.
4. Discuss with your vocational counselor or teacher some pointers on how to get a job and your questions about specific data processing jobs. Which jobs interest you the most? the least? Why? Would you pursue a data processing career?

Data Processing Activities

Now you can try out the kinds of data processing activities business workers perform. Below is a summary of the work you will do. You will find the actual information and business forms you need in your *Data Processing Work Kit.*

Activity 1. You will be given an interest test.
Activity 2. You will take an achievement test in clerical speed and accuracy.
Activity 3. You will be given a test to measure your programming aptitude.

BASIC Project 14

A Menu Program

You have learned that the use of computer terminals in the office and home will continue to grow. Not everyone who uses computers has to know how to program, for there are programs that are written for use by nontechnical people. These programs (often called *packaged programs*) are menu driven. This means that an individual can use a program by answering the questions presented by the computer program.

In the BASIC projects you have completed, all the programs are menu driven. Once they are entered into a computer, a nontechnical user can input data, and the computer will produce output. The user-friendly programs will make it possible for millions of users to take advantage of computer hardware in their offices and homes.

Program Statements

Chaining Programs

Most computer systems can be programmed to connect or access multiple programs. This is referred to as *linking or chaining programs.* You should discuss this capability with your supervisor so that you can understand the way that this is done on your computer system.

The objective of this exercise is to produce a master menu. Such a menu will allow a user to select a particular program from a library of computer programs. Reducing the amount of knowledge that a user must have increases the number of users who can benefit from computer software. Remember that professional computer programmers usually write programs for other people to use.

Input

Since each system handles chaining in a different way, you will have to consult the manual for your system or your supervisor to get the correct BASIC command.

The ability to connect programs in a user library is an important asset to any computer system. Each individual program may need to be modified so that the user will return to the master menu after the program execution is completed.

Take special notice of the REMARK statement in line 50. It is good practice to keep track of changes or revisions that you make in programs. You should include in each program you write your name, the date, and a revision number. The first attempt would be version 1. Each time you improve the program, you should change the version number. It is not uncommon to have a program that has gone through dozens of revisions.

```
10 REM MASTER MENU PROGRAM
20 REM CHAINS TO INTRO, LABEL, LETTER
30 REM BATCH, INVEN, ONLINE, SAVE,
40 REM SALARY, KEY, PEERS, QUIZ, CLUB
50 REM VERSION 1 BY A. PROGRAMMER
70 PRINT "WHAT IS YOUR FIRST NAME";
80 INPUT A$
90 PRINT "WELCOME TO OUR COMPUTER CENTER";A$
100 PRINT
110 PRINT "WHICH PROGRAM WOULD YOU LIKE?"
120 PRINT
130 PRINT "#1"TAB(10)"INTRO"
140 PRINT "#2"TAB(10)"LABEL"
150 PRINT "#3"TAB(10)"LETTER"
160 PRINT "#4"TAB(10)"BATCH"
170 PRINT "#5"TAB(10)"INVEN"
180 PRINT "#6"TAB(10)"ON-LINE"
190 PRINT "#7"TAB(10)"SAVE"
200 PRINT "#8"TAB(10)"LOAN"
210 PRINT "#9"TAB(10)"SALARY"
```

```
220 PRINT "#10"TAB(10)"KEY"
230 PRINT "#11"TAB(10)"PEERS"
240 PRINT "#12"TAB(10)"QUIZ"
250 PRINT "#13"TAB(10)"CLUB"
260 PRINT "#99"TAB(10)"EXIT MASTER MENU"
270 PRINT "ENTER THE NUMBER OF THE PROGRAM YOU WOULD LIKE";
280 REM ENTER CHAINING STATEMENTS HERE
999 END
```

Output

```
WHAT IS YOUR FIRST NAME? GENE
WELCOME TO OUR COMPUTER CENTER GENE
WHICH PROGRAM WOULD YOU LIKE?
#1      INTRO
#2      LABEL
#3      LETTER
#4      BATCH
#5      INVEN
#6      ON-LINE
#7      SAVE
#8      LOAN
#9      SALARY
#10     KEY
#11     PEERS
#12     QUIZ
#13     CLUB
#99     EXIT MASTER MENU
ENTER THE NUMBER OF THE PROGRAM YOU WOULD LIKE? 7
```

```
SAVE
TYPE BEGINNING BALANCE? 125
TYPE DEPOSIT AMOUNT? 33
TOTAL NOW IN ACCOUNT IS 158
INTEREST (6.5%) IN 1 YEAR WILL BE 10.27
WHICH PROGRAM WOULD YOU LIKE? 99
DONE
```

Keyboarding Activities

1. Enter the program statements listed above.
2. Ask your supervisor to explain the method of chaining programs.
3. Complete the program, and test the branching capability.

Enrichment Activity

Create your own user library. Use any programs you have written in this course or other personal programs. Keep track of how many programs a user has accessed, and print the number of programs when the user exits the master menu.

GLOSSARY

abacus The earliest calculator, invented over 2,000 years ago and still used today.

accounting machine A device that can record, sort, compute, and report data. Such a machine can be programmed to perform certain operations automatically.

administrative support system A system that electronically links together office typing, filing, copying, and mailing functions.

alphanumeric A coding system made up of both numeric and alphabetic characters.

American National Standards Institute (ANSI) A nonprofit organization made up of more than 140 trade associations and professional societies and 750 companies. ANSI coordinates the standardization of methods, terms, procedures, and symbols.

analog computer A computer that solves problems by measuring; that is, by determining the amounts or changes in amounts of physical units such as heat or speed.

applications packages Often called *canned programs,* these programs are purchased or leased from software houses or supplied by the hardware manufacturer. Such programs are available for a wide variety of business data processing systems such as payroll, inventory, and accounts receivable and payable.

arithmetic/logic mechanism or unit (ALU) A part of the central processing unit that performs computations and makes comparisons as instructed.

automated data processing (ADP) Work that requires only limited effort by people. Computer data processing is the most advanced stage of data processing to date.

BASIC (Beginner's All-Purpose Symbolic Information Code) An English-like programming language that is easy to learn, can be used for business or mathematical work, is available on many microcomputers and minicomputers, and is used interactively.

batch processing The term applied to the collection of data for a specified period and subsequent processing of the data as a unit. The data can also be prepared at a different site and sent by mail or transmitted by remote terminal to a central location for processing.

binary system A computer numbering system based only on 0 and 1. Because this system contains only two digits, it is often called the *base-two system.*

bits (binary digits) The two values that result from current passing through magnetic cores. Each core is given a value of either "0" or "1," depending on the direction in which it is magnetized.

branch An instruction in a computer program that chooses one or two or more alternatives defined by the computer programmer.

buffer A temporary storage area for data. Buffers are needed when data must be transmitted from a slower to faster device or the reverse.

calculator A machine that can be used for addition, subtraction, multiplication, and division. The most widely used calculator is the electronic calculator, with either a display screen, a printed tape, or both.

card punch The output device for producing punched cards from the results of computer data processing. It can either be combined with a punched-card reader or used as a separate device.

card-punch machine A keyboard-operated machine that records data in punched cards. It changes information from human-readable form to machine-readable form.

cathode ray tube (CRT) The name applied to a terminal equipped with a keyboard and a TV-like screen. A cathode ray tube is actually an electron beam device on which images are produced at a visual display terminal. The device makes possible the complete display of blocks of stored information on the screen without producing hard copy, although hard copy can also be produced by a printer hooked up to the computer.

central processing unit (CPU) or central processor The computer mechanism that houses the arithmetic/logic mechanism, the main storage unit, and the control unit.

classifying Identifying data and distinguishing one kind of data from another. This step usually calls for assigning code numbers or code letters.

coding A computer programmer's translation of instructions in a program flowchart into a programming language for the computer.

communicating Sending data from one place to another. Data can be transmitted manually or by machine.

compiler A language translator for converting into machine language each instruction written by the computer programmer. For example, a COBOL compiler would translate each COBOL programming instruction into several very detailed machine-language instructions.

computer The most advanced stage of data processing known to date. A computer is an electronic machine that performs high-speed calculating and other processing operations on input data.

computer hardware The physical equipment used for computer data processing, such as input devices, the central processing unit, storage devices, and output devices.

computer operator The person responsible for both loading and unloading the input and output devices and for monitoring the computer through processing.

computer-output-microfilm (COM) device Converts data on magnetic tape to data on microfilm cassette or microfiche. COM is particularly useful for storing and retrieving a large number of sequential records such as a company's financial statements for a particular year.

computer program A complete list of instructions telling the computer what work to perform and how to perform it. A computer program is written in a programming language.

computer programmer The person who writes a computer program, or series of instructions for the computer.

computer software The set of programs needed to instruct the computer.

computer system A specific group of physically attached devices that perform processing operations. Input, central processing, storage, and output devices are generally included.

computing Performing one or more of the arithmetic operations of addition, subtraction, multiplication, and division.

console A part of the control unit that enables the computer operator to communicate with the central processing unit.

continuous work flow A step-by-step flow from one operation to the next.

control unit The part of the central processing unit that interprets the instructions in a computer program. The control unit calls on the input mechanisms, the storage unit, the arithmetic/logic mechanism, and the output mechanism as needed to have the instructions carried out.

data Facts that appear as a collection of numeric and alphabetic characters.

data base An organized set of files that can be used for more than one application.

data-base management software A program package that can be purchased from computer manufacturers or software service companies. It is a set of standard machine instructions that make it easier for a programmer to write a program for handling the storage, updating, and retrieving of data in a file such as a customer file used for billing.

data-base management systems (DBMS) Computer software designed to organize and maintain the information in data bases.

data entry The function of recording data in machine-readable form.

data field The columns assigned to each type of data. A data field is made up of one or more columns as determined by the largest data item to be recorded in that field.

data processing All the processing operations that occur in converting input data to useful output data.

data processing system The organization of people, machines, and procedures required to produce information about a particular activity.

An effective data processing system is one that provides the data needed, in the form desired, at minimum cost.

data processing technology The science of information handling.

desk-debugging The programmer's self-check on the accuracy and clarity of each phase of the work assignment. This manual check enables the programmer to find a number of errors before the program is tested on the computer.

diagnostics Computer-generated error messages that identify mistakes in coding. The computer programmer must correct these mistakes before rerunning the program.

digital computer A computer that solves problems by counting; that is, by adding, subtracting, multiplying, or dividing numbers. It performs data processing operations sequentially.

division of labor The assignment of work to teams of workers, each with a limited number of specialized tasks.

documentation The illustrations and explanations that should accompany the computer printout of a *working* program. Documentation includes both the general information needed by the user of the program and the specific information needed by the computer operator or by the computer programmer if the program needs updating later.

electronic distribution **(or electronic mail)** The communication of information automatically from machine to machine.

field The columns assigned to each data item. The number of columns in a field is determined by the longest piece of data to be recorded in the field.

file A collection of records about a particular business activity. Data is stored in a file and retrieved from a file regardless of the type of storage device used.

file maintenance The task of updating records in a file so that the file contains the latest information. New records are inserted in the master file, data in existing records changed, and inactive records removed from the file.

flowchart A diagram showing the step-by-step instructions in a computer program. Such a diagram is prepared before the instructions to the computer are written in a language that can be understood by the computer.

flowcharting symbols A set of rectangular, diamond, and other geometric shapes used to represent operations, data flow, or equipment in a flowchart. American National Standard flowcharting symbols are commonly used.

forms design The planning of forms intended to communicate the data needed for particular transactions.

hard copy Data recorded in a form readable by human beings. Hard copy can be prepared manually or by machine.

hardware The physical equipment making up a computer system. It includes input devices, storage devices, a central processing unit, output devices, and a control unit.

hexadecimal system A computer numbering system based on 16 digits.

home information networks Communications systems where information is stored in a central computerized data bank and displayed on a TV-like screen or printer on request.

input data A collection of data to be entered into the computer and processed. This data can be entered by on-line terminal, as well as with punched cards, disks, and tapes. The physical equipment used is called *input devices.*

input/output (I/O) devices Mechanisms for reading in data to be processed and for reporting the results of processing.

inputting The recording operation, referring to the transfer of data entered at a keyboard or other device into the computer.

integrated circuits Electronic components organized in microcircuits. As these circuits became more compact, they were called *large-scale integrated* (LSI) and *very large-scale integrated* (VLSI) circuits.

intelligent terminal A special type of terminal having a small memory and a processing unit in addition to the keyboard and the display unit typical of other terminals. The term *intelligent* is applied because such a terminal can perform certain processing functions independently of the computer's central processing unit.

interactive processing The ability of the user of a remote terminal to request information at the keyboard and to obtain results speedily. This is also called *real-time processing* because the data for a particular event is entered and processed as the event occurs.

job control statement A link between the computer and the job to be processed. Each statement either identifies the job to be processed or describes its requirements to the system.

job request card The form on which a department records the instructions for work submitted to the data processing department. These instructions specify the computer model to be used, the estimated running time, the output device to be used, the output medium, and the dates by which the output is needed.

key-to-storage devices Keyboard devices that are similar to the keyboard of a card punch. However, instead of recording data in the form of punched holes in individual cards, the data-entry clerk records data in the form of magnetized spots on tape.

magnetic memory A device on which data is stored in the form of magnetized spots that can be read only by machine. Storage media such as magnetic chips, cores, disks, diskettes, and tape are all typical examples of magnetic memory.

mainframe Another name for the central processing unit of a computer system. This unit includes a control unit and an arithmetic/logic unit.

management information services A centralized responsibility for a company's computer activities and services.

management information system (MIS) A data processing system that provides information to management. The objectives differ for each management information system because each system provides information on a separate business data processing activity.

master file The main file of records in a data processing system.

menu The list of user choices or possible actions shown at the screen of a visual display terminal or the hard copy generated by a printer. Choices are usually expressed in English-language statements for ease of use.

microcomputer A small but complete digital computer having an input unit like a typewriter keyboard. The most commonly used output devices are visual display units and printers.

microfilming A mechanical method of storing data by photographing it in miniature.

microforms (or microimages) Images too small to read without magnification. They can be stored in several ways for retrieval on a microfilm reader.

microprocessor The central unit for processing and control in a minicomputer. A microprocessor is to a personal computer what a CPU is to a larger computer. Because the microprocessor tells the input, output, and storage units what to do and when to do it, a microprocessor is often called a *controller.*

minicomputer A computer having a smaller capacity for both primary and secondary storage than medium-size and large-size computers.

nanosecond One billionth of a second.

on-line terminal An input device with which it is possible to enter data directly into the storage or processing unit of a computer system. This type of input device is often located apart from other machine units.

one-time costs The costs of putting a data processing system into operation. A cost analysis for the system must include a comparison of the estimated costs with the costs of the work already being done.

operating system A set of manufacturer-developed programs that perform three functions. They provide coded instructions for certain repetitive operations, they keep track of the running time for each job, and they schedule the sequence of jobs so as to perform the work in the shortest possible time.

optical character reader (OCR) or optical scanner A machine that accepts data recorded by hand, by typewriter, or by printer, reads the typed data, and converts it into machine-readable form for input to a computer or word processor.

organization chart A diagram that shows the organization of a business; that is, how responsibilities are divided up within a business.

output data Useful information produced at the end of a business cycle.

packaged software Computer software available from the manufacturers or from software houses. Both personal and business programs are available.

parallel systems Two or more systems used at the same time for the same purpose. Using both for a predetermined time allows the company to test the accuracy and effectiveness of the new system by comparing its results with those of the old system.

Pascal A general-purpose programming language structured so that large programs can be distributed for team programming.

peripheral operations The tasks relating to using other equipment needed for computer data processing. These operations can include the input and output devices used with a computer. They can also include work with special equipment such as an electronic label printer or an electronic optical scanner.

personal computing The use of a computer to meet the data processing needs of a particular person or family. The computer itself is usually called a *personal computer.*

primary storage Data stored inside the central processor.

printer A widely used output device used with a computer to print hard copy on business reports or documents. An *impact printer* produces printed results by striking a metal character against an inked ribbon. A *nonimpact printer,* newer and ribbonless, can produce business forms and reports in a variety of typefaces.

procedure The step-by-step operations that must be performed to accomplish a particular task.

program A series of instructions written by a computer programmer for the computer.

program flowchart A diagram that shows graphically each action to be taken by the computer. Such a diagram is made up of geometric shapes used as symbols for particular operations in the data processing cycle.

programming Preparation of a comprehensive list of instructions for computer processing.

programming language The special language used in writing a computer program. The translation of each flowchart instruction into a programming language instruction is known as *coding.*

punched card A rectangular form with numbered rows and columns in which data is recorded by punching holes. Punched cards are still used for input data at many computer processing centers even though direct data entry is becoming increasingly widespread.

random-access memory (RAM) Storage that allows for changes to be made in the computer programs. Since such storage can be used over and over, it is sometimes called *user-programmable memory.*

read-only memory (ROM) Limited storage that allows for changes to be made in the computer programs.

real-time processing The immediate processing of data as it occurs and is keyed.

record All the data in a file for a particular product, customer, supplier, or employee.

recording The writing of data by hand or the keying of data by machine. Recording is the starting point of business data processing.

reporting Making the results of data processing available. This is usually the last step in the data processing cycle.

reproducing Duplicating selected data items. Data can be reproduced either in human-readable form or in machine-readable form.

retrieving Searching for, locating, and removing data.

scanner An input device that can accept data from source documents in typed, hand-printed, or machine-printed form. This device, also called a character reader, can be either a magnetic ink character reader (MICR) or an optical-character-recognition (OCR) scanner.

secondary storage A storage unit located outside the computer that may or may not be permanently connected to the computer. This type of storage is used for data that is used less frequently and that does not need to be retrieved immediately.

semiconductor A primary storage device consisting of small chips of silicon on which memory circuits and support circuits are etched. It is used for primary storage in the most recent computer models.

service bureaus Companies that provide data processing services for a fee based on equipment, software, and personnel usage.

shared logic system Individual input units with

keyboards and visual display units connected to one central processing unit (CPU). These units usually share a separate daisy wheel or faster printer.

shared-processor input device An on-line terminal that competes with other on-line terminals for the use of the central processor.

software The list of instructions (programs) and other procedures the computer system uses in processing data. Such materials contrast with the physical equipment that makes up a computer system, which is known as *computer hardware.*

sorting Arranging related information in a desired sequence (order). Data can be stored either numerically or alphabetically.

source document A business form on which data is recorded as the starting operation in a data processing cycle.

stand-alone machine A machine that operates independently of other machines. A stand-alone system has at least four units: a data-entry keyboard, a memory unit, a logic unit, and a printing device.

standardization The process of making procedures and job responsibilities uniform within a single business and similar from business to business.

storage device A device for holding or sharing a computer program, input data, and file data needed for computer processing.

stored program A series of instructions stored in the computer and then processed.

storing Saving data for future use. The period of time the data remains in storage can vary from seconds to years.

string A series of letters, numbers, punctuation marks, or other symbols. Examples include names, addresses, and telephone numbers.

subroutine (or subprogram) A set of instructions generally used more than once. The instructions are written only once, but the main program has statements that call the subprogram when needed.

symbolic form A technique that enables programmers to write instructions in a combination of alphabetic and numeric codes instead of only in numeric codes. An example of a programming language in symbolic form is assembler.

systems analyst The person responsible for determining the most effective way of doing work. Part of this responsibility is determining the most efficient equipment for processing data.

systems flowchart A diagram made up of standard flowcharting symbols used to identify the steps in a particular system being designed.

telecommunications The transmission of data electronically by telephone circuits, microwave networks, or satellite transmission.

terminal A keyboard device connected to a computer system for the input or output of data. On-line terminals are connected directly to the computer either by calls or by ordinary telephone lines or a special data communications network.

time sharing The use of a particular central processor by a number of interactive users at terminals. The user generally communicates with the computer by way of an English-like language.

turnkey package The combination of hardware and software to perform a specific business task. Use of such applications packages is common in small businesses making their first computer purchase.

unconditional branch One or more instructions to be executed in a particular sequence without exception.

visual display terminal A data-entry unit equipped with a keyboard and a TV-like screen for displaying input data, programming instructions, or output data. Such equipment is sometimes called a CRT, for cathode ray tube terminal.

voice (or speech) recognition equipment Data-entry equipment that accepts human speech as input data and translates what is said into machine-readable data. The limited capacity of the first such equipment allowed only for the recognition of numbers and specialized words directly related to the immediate task.

word processing The transformation of information into readable form through the management of procedures, equipment, and personnel. Because the newer word processing equipment can perform many of the ten data processing operations, such equipment is sometimes called information processors.

INDEX